AF334705

Leiko Ikemura

Nach neuen Meeren
Toward New Seas

Herausgegeben von | Edited by
Anita Haldemann

Mit Texten von | With essays by
Anita Haldemann, Stefan Kraus, Mitsue Nagaya

KUNSTMUSEUM BASEL

PRESTEL
Munich · London · New York

Die Ausstellung wird unterstützt durch |
The exhibition is supported by
Stiftung für das Kunstmuseum Basel
Claire Sturzenegger-Jeanfavre Stiftung

Foreword

During her artistic career, which has already lasted over forty years, Leiko Ikemura has created a unique synthesis of Japanese and Western culture. Her art has developed out of the confrontation with otherness and the appropriation of new languages, her path marked by repeated embarkation *Toward New Seas*. Thus, for instance, after completing her studies in Spain in 1972 she decided to remain in Europe, where she still lives today. The years she spent in Switzerland from 1979 to 1983 were formative, for it was here that her career as a professional artist began, with her first gallery exhibitions in Zurich and Bern.

In the early 1980s, Ikemura made a splash in the lively Swiss art scene with her powerful drawings and figurative painting. She belonged to a new generation of artists—including Martin Disler, Josef Felix Müller, Klaudia Schifferle, and Anselm Stalder—who had returned to celebrating embodiment and confrontation after the heyday of conceptual art had passed. Official recognition soon followed when in 1981 she received prizes from the Stiftung für die Graphische Kunst der Schweiz (Foundation for the Graphic Arts in Switzerland) and the renowned Kiefer Hablitzel Foundation.

A turning point came in 1983, when Ikemura was named *Stadtzeichnerin* (graphic artist in residence) of Nuremberg and was able, for many months, to devote herself full-time to drawing and painting. This was followed by exhibitions at the Kunstverein Bonn in 1983 and the Kunsthalle Nürnberg in 1984, which attracted a great deal of attention. However, unable to identify with the male-dominated scene of the Neuen Wilden, she became aware of a desire to develop her own approach, one that would eventually more strongly integrate her Japanese roots. In 1985 she began again to make regular visits to Japan, and in 1989 another sojourn in Switzerland, in the mountains of

Canton Grisons, proved to be pathbreaking. In 1991, while already living in Cologne, Ikemura was appointed a professor at the Universität der Künste Berlin (then called the Hochschule der Künste). Since then, her work has been exhibited and acknowledged around the world.

Ikemura's work unfolds in many media, from drawing, printmaking, painting, and sculpture—particularly ceramics—to photography and even poetry. Her earlier work of the 1980s, with its expressive but enigmatic charcoal drawings and large-format paintings, is less known today. Its central themes are aggression, violence, and conflict between men and women. Inspired by her stay in the Swiss mountains in 1989, she developed, in the group of works titled *Alpenindianer* (Alps Indians), a new visual language that led to the melding of body and landscape. These were followed by somewhat archaic-looking hybrid beings that increasingly found form in sculpture as well.

In the 1990s she became known for her female figures that appeared to be poised at a juncture between two worlds. The "girls" became an official hallmark. They elude more precise characterization, for their facial features and ages remain unspecific. Yet these representations are by no means harmless. Hands digging into eye sockets suggest violent and (self-)destructive impulses.

The idea that a person is not hierarchically removed from their environment but rather is continually transformed by it has also played an increasingly greater role in Ikemura's work since 2000, albeit in a stylistically different form than during the 1980s. In her most recent paintings, Ikemura creates cosmic landscapes out of amorphous forms. The holistic understanding of nature characteristic of Japanese Shintoism, with its notion of spirits and the sacral animation of mountains, cliffs, and plants, manifests itself in Ikemura's work not only in its

Vorwort

Leiko Ikemura hat in ihrer bereits über vierzig Jahre umfassenden künstlerischen Tätigkeit eine einzigartige Synthese zwischen der japanischen und der westlichen Kultur geschaffen. Ihre Kunst entwickelte sich in der Auseinandersetzung mit dem Fremdsein und der Aneignung neuer Sprachen, ihr Weg ist geprägt vom wiederholten Aufbruch *Nach neuen Meeren*. So entschied sie sich nach einem Studienaufenthalt in Spanien 1972, in Europa zu bleiben, wo sie noch heute lebt. Prägend wurden die Jahre, die sie von 1979 bis 1983 in der Schweiz verbrachte, denn hier begann ihre Laufbahn als Künstlerin mit ersten Galerie-Ausstellungen in Zürich und Bern.

In den frühen 1980er-Jahren machte Ikemura Furore mit ausdrucksstarken Zeichnungen und figurativer Malerei im Kontext einer bewegten Schweizer Kunstszene. Sie gehörte zu einer neuen Generation von Künstlern – etwa Martin Disler, Josef Felix Müller, Klaudia Schifferle und Anselm Stalder –, die nach der Konzeptkunst wieder Körperlichkeit und Konfrontation zelebrierten. Schon 1981 erlangte Ikemura mit der Verleihung der Preise der Stiftung für die Graphische Kunst der Schweiz und der renommierten Kiefer Hablitzel Stiftung offizielle Anerkennung.

Ein Wendepunkt kam 1983, denn als Stadtzeichnerin von Nürnberg konnte Ikemura sich erstmals über viele Monate ausschliesslich dem Zeichnen und Malen widmen. Die ersten Ausstellungen im Kunstverein Bonn 1983 und in Nürnberg 1984 erregten Aufsehen. Gleichzeitig entwickelte die Künstlerin in der Folge ein Bewusstsein dafür, dass sie einen eigenen, ihre japanischen Wurzeln stärker integrierenden Ansatz entwickeln wollte, zudem konnte sie sich mit der männlich dominierten Szene der Neuen Wilden nicht identifizieren. Regelmässig besuchte Ikemura nun Japan; 1989 wurde ein weiterer Aufenthalt in der Schweiz, in den Bergen des Kantons Graubünden,

zu einer wegweisenden Erfahrung. Als sie bereits in Köln lebte, erhielt Ikemura 1991 eine Professur an der Universität der Künste Berlin (damals Hochschule der Künste). Seither wird ihr Werk weltweit ausgestellt und rezipiert.

Ikemuras Kunst entfaltet sich in vielen Medien, von der Zeichnung, Druckgrafik, Malerei und Skulptur – insbesondere Keramik – über die Fotografie bis zur Poesie. Heute weniger bekannt ist das frühe Werk aus den 1980er-Jahren mit kraftvollen, aber auch rätselhaften Kohlezeichnungen und grossformatiger Malerei. Aggression, Gewalt, der Kampf der Geschlechter waren zentrale Themen. Infolge ihrer Eindrücke in den Schweizer Bergen 1989 entwickelte sie eine neue visuelle Sprache, die zu einer Verschmelzung von Körper und Landschaft in der Werkgruppe der *Alpenindianer* führte. Darauf entwickelte sie archaisch anmutende Hybridwesen, die vermehrt auch in der Skulptur zur Form fanden.

In den 1990er-Jahren wurde Ikemura bekannt für weibliche Figuren, die in Zwischenwelten zu verharren scheinen. Die «Girls» wurden förmlich zu ihrem Markenzeichen. Sie entziehen sich genauerer Charakterisierung, denn Gesichtszüge und Alter bleiben unspezifisch. Doch harmlos sind die Darstellungen mitnichten, denn etwa in den Händen, die in die Augenhöhlen gebohrt sind, schwingen auch (Selbst-)Zerstörung und Gewalt mit.

Die Auffassung, dass sich der Mensch nicht hierarchisch von seiner Umgebung abgrenzt, sondern sich wie diese unablässig transformiert, spielt seit 2000 eine zunehmend wichtige Rolle in Ikemuras Werken, ausserdem hat sie zu anderen stilistischen Ausdrucksformen gefunden als in den 1980er-Jahren. In ihren jüngsten Gemälden lässt sie kosmische Landschaften aus amorphen Gebilden entstehen. Inhaltlich manifestiert sich der japanische Shintoismus, der ein holistisches Naturverständnis, Geister und spirituelle Belebung von Bergen, Felsen

content. Today more than ever, her manner of painting harkens back to East Asian ink painting. Not least, these works express concern for the future of our planet in the face of the increasing threat to our living environment.

The exhibition *Leiko Ikemura—Toward New Seas* is the product of a long relationship between the artist and the Kunstmuseum Basel. The former director of the Kupferstichkabinett (Department of Prints and Drawings), Dieter Koepplin, began to collect drawings by the young artist for the Kupferstichkabinett in 1982 with the help of the Karl August Burckhardt-Koechlin-Fonds. This gave rise to an intensive dialogue that culminated in an extensive exhibition in 1987 at the Kunstmuseum Basel, Gegenwart.

Today the museum possesses not only the largest collection of drawings by Ikemura (with 144 sheets), but also, since 2018/19, paintings and sculptures thanks to gifts from Koepplin as well as Catherine and Bernard Soguel-Dreyfus. This collection provides the ideal basis to present the development of Ikemura's work from its inception to the present in a concentrated exhibition. As befitting her multifaceted artistic activity, drawing, painting, and sculpture will be presented in dialogue with one another.

From January 18 to April 1, 2019, the exhibition appeared under the title *Leiko Ikemura: Our Planet—Earth & Stars* at the National Art Center Tokyo with a substantially more extensive selection of works. We are grateful to director Tamotsu Aoki for the collaboration. This is the first time that institutions in Japan and Switzerland have worked with each other to realize an exhibition of Ikemura's work. Great thanks are due, above all, to chief curator Mitsue Nagaya for the enjoyable and highly productive collaboration and for her exceptional work in mounting the exhibition in Tokyo, as well as for facilitating the works on loan from Japan.

Many lenders, private collectors, and public institutions have generously supported our exhibition. We thank everyone for their great trust. The exhibition would not have been possible without the generous financial support of private parties who wish to remain anonymous and the Foundation for the Kunstmuseum Basel. The catalog was conceived and designed by Sibylle Ryser, Basel, and has been produced with great care by Prestel Verlag under the direction of Anja Besserer.

We are particularly grateful to Leiko Ikemura, for without her multifaceted and ambitious work, as well as her constructive collaboration and many loans, the exhibition would not have been possible in this form. She has not only supported the project, together with Philip von Matt and her studio team, but has developed the exhibition concept from the beginning along with lead curator Anita Haldemann and assistant curator Karoline Schliemann.

Josef Helfenstein
Director, Kunstmuseum Basel

und Pflanzen kennt, und in der Malweise greift Ikemura heute stärker als je auf ostasiatische Tuschemalerei zurück. Nicht zuletzt sprechen diese Werke von einer Sorge um die Zukunft unseres Planeten angesichts der zunehmenden Bedrohung unseres Lebensraumes.

Die Ausstellung *Leiko Ikemura – Nach neuen Meeren* ist Frucht einer langjährigen Beziehung des Kunstmuseums Basel mit der Künstlerin. Der ehemalige Leiter des Kupferstichkabinetts, Dieter Koepplin, begann 1982, mithilfe des Karl August Burckhardt-Koechlin-Fonds Zeichnungen der jungen Künstlerin für das Kupferstichkabinett zu sammeln. Daraus ist ein intensiver Dialog entstanden, der 1987 in einer umfangreichen Ausstellung im Kunstmuseum Basel, Gegenwart, mündete.

Heute besitzen wir mit 144 Blättern nicht nur die weltweit grösste Sammlung von Zeichnungen Ikemuras, sondern seit 2018/19 dank Schenkungen von Dieter Koepplin sowie Catherine und Bernard Soguel-Dreyfus auch Gemälde und Skulpturen. Dieser Bestand bildet die ideale Grundlage, um die Entwicklung von Ikemuras Werk bis in die jüngste Gegenwart in einer konzentrierten Ausstellung vorzustellen. Wie es ihrer vielseitigen Tätigkeit entspricht, werden Zeichnung, Malerei und Skulptur im Dialog präsentiert.

Die Ausstellung wurde vom 18. Januar bis 1. April 2019 unter dem Titel *Leiko Ikemura. Our Planet – Earth & Stars* im National Art Center Tokyo in einer deutlich umfangreicheren Werkauswahl gezeigt. Wir danken dem Direktor Tamotsu Aoki für die angenehme Zusammenarbeit. Zum ersten Mal haben zwei Institutionen in Japan und der Schweiz kooperiert, um gemeinsam eine Ausstellung mit Leiko Ikemura zu verwirklichen. Grosser Dank gebührt vor allem der Chefkuratorin Mitsue Nagaya für die erfreuliche und sehr produktive Zusammenarbeit sowie die souveräne Umsetzung der Ausstellung in Tokio und die Vermittlung der Leihgaben aus Japan.

Viele Leihgeber – private Sammler und öffentliche Institutionen – unterstützen die Ausstellung grosszügig. Wir danken allen für das grosse Vertrauen. Ohne die generöse finanzielle Unterstützung von Privatpersonen, die ungenannt bleiben möchten, und der Stiftung für das Kunstmuseum Basel hätten wir die Ausstellung nicht realisieren können. Der Katalog wurde von der Buchgestalterin Sibylle Ryser, Basel, konzipiert und umgesetzt und mit Sorgfalt vom Prestel Verlag unter der Leitung von Anja Besserer produziert.

Unser ganz besonderer Dank gebührt Leiko Ikemura, denn ohne ihr vielseitiges und anspruchsvolles Werk, die konstruktive Zusammenarbeit und die Bereitstellung von Leihgaben wäre die Ausstellung in dieser Form nicht möglich gewesen. Sie und Philipp von Matt sowie das Studioteam haben das Projekt von Anfang unterstützt und auch das Ausstellungskonzept zusammen mit der verantwortlichen Kuratorin Anita Haldemann und der Assistenzkuratorin Karoline Schliemann entwickelt.

Josef Helfenstein
Direktor, Kunstmuseum Basel

Leiko Ikemura— Drawings and Watercolors

Anita Haldemann

Drawing in Context

Leiko Ikemura first became known in the early 1980s as a graphic artist, and the focus of her first three solo exhibitions (Bonner Kunstverein, 1983; Kunsthalle Nürnberg, 1984; Kunstmuseum Basel, Gegenwart, 1987) was her works on paper, as also evidenced by the drawings depicted on the covers of the catalogs. Around 120 drawings and twelve paintings were shown in Basel in 1987.[1] Not until later did Ikemura's painting begin to receive greater attention.

In Ikemura's work, drawings and watercolors are not sketches or preliminary studies in the service of another medium but have predominantly been an autonomous form of expression from the start. Because they continue to play an important role in her artistic activity to this day, they are presented in this exhibition in consistent dialogue with her paintings and sculptures. In this way, the drawings and watercolors can be situated in the context of the artist's oeuvre as a whole. Through some trenchant curatorial juxtapositions, works in a variety of media from various phases of her artistic production are brought into conversation so that they expand upon and complement one another. For instance, the patinated bronze sculpture *Memento Mori* from 2013 is placed in front of the monumental black-and-white drawing titled *Garten der Lüste* (Garden of Desire, 1983) **(cat. 92, pp. 132/33, cat. 93, p. 140)**, which was produced thirty years earlier. Such conjunctions provide a fresh perspective on earlier work and engender resonances that cut across a variety of media.

At first glance, Ikemura's work appears to be subject to a great deal of stylistic change. The drawings in particular explore a variety of expressive possibilities that are at first rather linear but later involve more overall surface design **(e.g., cat. 3, p. 52, cat. 106, p. 138)**. Friedemann Malsch, in 1998, defined the internal coherence of Ikemura's art as an expression of an inherent attitude and strength.[2] This inherent attitude is a searching that is not only active but leaves itself open to external influences and demonstrates itself as a commitment. Friedrich Nietzsche's poem "Toward New Seas" ("Nach neuen Meeren") expresses precisely this spirit of a continual setting out: the artist as adventurer whose goal is not really discovery or conquest. What is essential, rather, is the courage to venture into uncharted territory and endure the uncertainty of the voyage into the unknown. Ikemura's thematic and stylistic arcs can be traced through the decades if we follow certain subjects—such as the interwovenness of woman and tree—in drawings, paintings, and sculptures from different work periods. Doing so makes evident that the rich foundation of the earlier drawings continues to resonate in the current work, stimulating and supporting it.

The Drawing as "Now"

Ikemura's brilliant beginning as a graphic artist in the 1980s was due to the ease with which she moved in the medium of drawing from the start **(cat. 2–25, pp. 48–63)**. Young artists commonly first develop their themes and find a path toward their own forms of expression in drawing—Joseph Beuys, Bruce Nauman, and Rosemarie Trockel, to name just a few. Drawing is not only easy to manage in practice—it needs nothing more than paper and pencil—but is also spared the pressure of finality: traditionally, it is the medium of investigation and experiment that offers an open space. Ikemura confirmed this

---

1   *Leiko Ikemura*, exh. cat. (Bonn: Bonner Kunstverein, 1983); *Leiko Ikemura: Stadtzeichnerin von Nürnberg 1983*, exh. cat. (Nuremberg: Kunsthalle Nürnberg, 1984); *Leiko Ikemura: Gemälde, Zeichnungen 1980–1987*, exh. cat., ed. Museum für Gegenwartskunst Basel (Basel: Kunstmuseum, 1987). See also Dieter Koepplin et al., "Vorwort," in *Leiko Ikemura: Gemälde, Zeichnung 1980–1987*, 3–4.

2   *Leiko Ikemura im Gespräch mit Friedemann Malsch* (Kunst heute Nr. 20), ed. Gisela Neven Du Mont and Wilfried Dickhoff (Cologne: Kiepenheuer & Witsch, 1998), 10.

Leiko Ikemura –
Zeichnungen und Aquarelle

Anita Haldemann

Zeichnung im Kontext

Leiko Ikemura wurde Anfang der 1980er-Jahre zunächst als Zeichnerin bekannt, und so lag der Fokus der ersten drei Einzelausstellungen (1983 Bonner Kunstverein; 1984 Kunsthalle Nürnberg; 1987 Kunstmuseum Basel, Gegenwart) auf den Papierarbeiten, was sich auch in den abgebildeten Zeichnungen auf den Katalogumschlägen widerspiegelt. In Basel waren rund 120 Zeichnungen und zwölf Bilder zu sehen.[1] Erst mit der Zeit wurde Ikemuras Malerei stärker wahrgenommen.

Zeichnungen und Aquarelle sind in Ikemuras Werk nicht Skizzen oder Vorstudien im Dienste eines anderen Mediums, sondern äussern sich von Anfang an mehrheitlich autonom. Da sie bis heute eine wichtige Rolle in ihrer künstlerischen Tätigkeit spielen, werden sie in der gegenwärtigen Ausstellung konsequent im Dialog mit Gemälden und Plastiken gezeigt und so auch im Gesamtœuvre kontextualisiert. Mithilfe weniger pointierter kuratorischer Setzungen werden Werke unterschiedlicher Medien und Werkphasen zum Zwiegespräch eingeladen, sodass sie einander ergänzen und erweitern. Beispielsweise wird die Plastik *Memento mori* von 2013 aus patinierter Bronze vor der monumentalen Schwarz-Weiss-Zeichnung mit dem Titel *Garten der Lüste* (1983), die dreissig Jahre zuvor entstanden ist, platziert **(Kat. 92, S. 132/33, Kat. 93, S. 140)**. Frühere Arbeiten erfahren durch solche Gegenüberstellungen eine Aktualisierung und es entstehen Resonanzen quer durch die unterschiedlichen Medien.

Auf den ersten Blick scheint Ikemuras Werk vielen Stiländerungen zu unterliegen. Gerade die Zeichnungen entfalten eine Fülle von Ausdrucksmöglichkeiten, die zunächst eher die Linie betonen, später die Flächengestaltung stärker einbeziehen **(Kat. 3, S. 52, Kat. 106, S. 138)**. Friedemann Malsch hat 1998 die innere Kohärenz von Ikemuras Kunst als Ausdruck einer inneren Haltung und Stärke beschrieben.[2] Diese innere Haltung ist ein Suchen, das nicht nur aktiv ist, sondern sich auch äusseren Einwirkungen aussetzt und sich als Hingabe erweist. Das Gedicht «Nach neuen Meeren» von Friedrich Nietzsche bringt genau diese stetige Aufbruchstimmung zum Ausdruck: Die Künstlerin als Abenteurerin, deren Ziel weniger die Entdeckung oder Eroberung ist als vielmehr der Mut, den Aufbruch ins Unbekannte zu wagen, die Ungewissheit vor der Reise «ins Blaue» auszuhalten. Konkret lassen sich motivische und stilistische Bögen über die Jahrzehnte ziehen, wenn man etwa das Sujet der Verschränkung von Frau und Baum in Zeichnungen, Gemälden und Skulpturen aus verschiedenen Werkphasen verfolgt. Dabei zeigt sich, dass der reiche Fundus der frühen Zeichnungen bis ins aktuelle Werk nachklingt, dieses trägt und befruchtet.

Die Zeichnung als «Jetzt»

Der fulminante Start als Zeichnerin in den 1980er-Jahren ist der Leichtigkeit zu verdanken, mit der sich die Künstlerin von Anfang an in diesem Medium bewegte **(Kat. 2–25, S. 48–63)**. Es ist durchaus üblich, dass junge Künstler zunächst mit Zeichnen ihre Themen entwickeln und den Weg zu einer eigenen Ausdrucksweise finden, so gingen beispielsweise auch Joseph Beuys, Bruce Nauman oder Rosemarie Trockel vor. Nicht nur in der Ausübung ist das Zeichnen einfach zu bewerkstelligen – es genügen Stift und Papier –, es bleibt auch vom Druck der Endgültigkeit verschont, ist es doch traditionell das

1 *Leiko Ikemura*, Ausst.-Kat. Bonner Kunstverein, Bonn 1983; *Leiko Ikemura. Stadtzeichnerin von Nürnberg 1983*, Ausst.-Kat. Kunsthalle Nürnberg, Nürnberg 1984; *Leiko Ikemura. Gemälde, Zeichnungen 1980–1987*, Ausst.-Kat. Museum für Gegenwartskunst Basel, Musée cantonal des Beaux-Arts, Lausanne, Neue Galerie der Stadt Linz, Wolfgang-Gurlitt-Museum, Ulm, Stadtgalerie Saarbrücken, hrsg. vom Museum für Gegenwartskunst Basel, Basel: 1987. – Siehe auch: Dieter Koepplin, Erika Billeter, Peter Baum und Bernd Schulz, «Vorwort», in: Ebd., S. 3–4.

2 Vgl. *Leiko Ikemura im Gespräch mit Friedemann Malsch* (Kunst heute Nr. 20), hrsg. von Gisela Neven Du Mont und Wilfried Dickhoff, Köln 1998, S. 10.

in a talk with Gerlinde Gabriel in 1983: "Drawings are for me *now,* while painting on the other hand, because of its resistance, signifies *pathways.*"[3] In contrast to painting, drawing is immediacy: "Because painting is built up of various components, it is much more cumbersome than drawing. I'm not saying that drawing is easier, but it is more direct and basic."[4]

Dieter Koepplin, who began collecting Ikemura's drawings for the Basel Kupferstichkabinett (Department of Prints and Drawings at the Kunstmuseum Basel) in 1982, locates this "originary primacy of the drawing" within her work in, on the one hand, its origins in haiku, the succinct traditional form of poetry with a consciousness of the past far from any "gigantomania and pretention."[5] On the other hand, it is also important to consider that when Ikemura arrived in Switzerland in 1979 with academic training from Seville, she encountered an artistic climate that was particularly attentive to drawing and, to a certain extent, printmaking.

The growing interest for drawing had been encouraged by three influential exhibitions. At the Kunstmuseum Basel, in *Zeichnen / Bezeichnen,* Koepplin had shown various positions from Beuys to A. R. Penck around 1970.[6] The Kunsthaus Zürich presented *Drawing Now—Zeichnung heute,* a traveling exhibit from the Museum of Modern Art in New York curated by Bernice Rose that aimed to establish drawings as key works of the avant-garde of the previous twenty years.[7] Finally, in the Lucerne exhibition *Mentalität: Zeichnung* (Drawing: A Mindset), Jean-Christophe Amman situated drawing as a characteristic expression of a Swiss sensibility.[8] Artists such as Dieter Roth, André Thomkins, and Markus Raetz had already consciously sought the public eye as draftsmen, and in 1971 and 1972 Koepplin devoted a solo exhibition each to Thomkins and Raetz. In 1983, there was a solo exhibition of the young artist Martin Disler, to whose generation Ikemura belongs.

Drawing "in the Forefield of Reflection"

In this environment, Ikemura's works on paper quickly attained recognition—for instance, she was awarded prizes from the Stiftung für die Graphische Kunst in der Schweiz (Foundation for the Graphic Arts in Switzerland) and the Kiefer Hablitzel Foundation in 1981, as well as a fellowship as the *Stadtzeichnerin* (graphic artist in residence) of Nuremberg in 1983. The 120 drawings from 1980 to 1987 that are in the collection of the Basel Kupferstichkabinett today represent only a small portion of Ikemura's production from that time.[9] Until 1983, the sheets remained rather small, mostly in A5 or A4 format. They are executed in charcoal in a linear manner, occasionally with a few shadows or thinner lines drawn with pen, chalk, or colored pencil **(cat. 9, p. 51, cat. 16, p. 60, cat. 17, p. 60)**. They were produced for their own sake rather than for any specific purpose. Only a few sheets are sketches made for later paintings.[10]

The sheets were produced in quick succession. This process can be described as a kind of flow, for there is no going back, no correcting, only the next sheet, on which Ikemura begins entirely anew. The artist describes each drawing as a "seismograph of the soul," as a reflection on paper of psychological and spiritual states.[11] The drawing process entails capturing inner images: "In the forefield of reflection, that is where I draw; for drawing is the vehicle of the images that are rolling past in my mind."[12] The drawings do not reflect a preexisting idea but arise in the very moment where a thought or image is first grasped. Hans-Jürgen Schwalm describes this as the thin line between discovery and invention, where a thought becomes visible.[13]

The drawing hand is not simply an instrument of implementation but plays its own palpable part in the process. At times it exercises such great pressure with the charcoal that the thin paper is almost torn **(cat. 21, p. 63)**. It intensifies lines and emphasizes a form or the flow of energy through the concentration of strokes **(cat. 9, p. 51, cat. 22, p. 62)**. Thick, deep, black lines alternate with thinner ones and are occasionally supplemented with flat shading that is more than just descriptive **(cat. 19, p. 62)**. These lines convey no hesitation, nothing provisional. These are not fleeting sketches but self-confident, concentrated drawings.

3   Ikemura in "'Erotik in ihrer Ausstrahlung hat eine unaussprechbare Trauer': Ein Gespräch mit Leiko Ikemura von Gerlinde Gabriel," in *Leiko Ikemura: Stadtzeichnerin von Nürnberg 1983,* 12; emphasis in original.

4   Ikemura in "'Wir Menschen leben auch vom Ahnen': Leiko Ikemura im Gespräch mit Alexander Pühringer," *Noëma Art Journal* 39 (1995): 54.

5   See Ikemura's statement in Dieter Koepplin, *Leiko Ikemura: Gemälde, Zeichnungen 1980–1987,* exh. leaflet (Basel: Kunstmuseum, 1987): "The art of the haiku is for me universally valid, all my drawings are related to it. The essence of haiku is poetry in its most concise form, conscious of the past, far from gigantomania and pretention."

6   *Zeichnen / Bezeichnen: Zeichnungen aus der Sammlung Mia und Martin Visser, Bergeyk,* exh. cat. (Basel: Kunstmuseum, 1976).

7   The exhibition was also shown in 1976/77 at Staatliche Kunsthalle Baden-Baden, Graphische Sammlung der Albertina in Vienna, Henie Onstad Kunstsenter in Oslo, and the Tel Aviv Museum of Art.

8   *Mentalität: Zeichnung: Christian Ludwig Attersee, Anton Bruhin, Martin Disler, Markus Dulk, Helmut Federle, Heiner Kielholz, Claude Sandoz, Hugo Suter, David Weiss,* exh. cat. (Lucerne: Kunstmuseum, 1976). See also Beat Wismer, "Über die Peripherie um Zentrum (und mitten ins Herz): Ein Versuch über die Arbeit auf dem Papier in der Schweizer Kunst des 20. Jahrhunderts," in *Im Reich der Zeichnung: Zeichnungen und Arbeiten auf Papier: Werke des 20. Jahrhunderts aus dem Aargauer Kunsthaus Aarau,* exh. cat., ed. Stephan Kunz and Beat Wismer (Aarau: Aargauer Kunsthaus, 1998), 8–15.

9   The drawings were acquired through purchase or gift from 1982 to 1989. Another group was acquired in 1998/99.

10   See Dieter Koepplin, "Leiko Ikemura," in *Räume heutiger Zeichnung: Werke aus dem Basler Kupferstichkabinett,* exh. cat. (Basel: Kunstmuseum, 1985), 102.

11   *Leiko Ikemura im Gespräch mit Friedemann Malsch,* 79.

12   Ikemura in Margarethe Jochimsen, "Sprung über die Zeit, aus einem Gespräch während einer langen Nacht," in *Leiko Ikemura* (1983), 68.

13   Hans-Jürgen Schwalm, "Dazwischen," in *Leiko Ikemura: Skulptur, Malerei, Zeichnung,* exh. cat. (Bielefeld: Kerber Verlag, 2004), 9.

Medium des Suchens und Experimentierens, das Freiraum gewährt. Dies bestätigt die Künstlerin 1983 in einem Gespräch mit Gerlinde Gabriel: «Die Zeichnungen sind für mich *Jetzt,* und das Malen hingegen, wegen des Widerstands, bedeutet Wege.»[3] Im Gegensatz zum Malen sei das Zeichnen das Unmittelbare: «Weil Malen aus verschiedenen Komponenten herausgebildet wird, ist es viel schwieriger als die Zeichnung. Ich sage nicht, dass Zeichnen leichter ist, aber es ist direkter und wesentlicher.»[4]

Dieter Koepplin, der Ikemuras Zeichnungen ab 1982 im Basler Kupferstichkabinett sammelte, verortet das «ursprüngliche Primat der Zeichnung» innerhalb ihres Werks in der japanischen Herkunft der Künstlerin: einerseits im Haiku, dieser knappen und traditionellen Form der Poesie, dem Bewusstsein der Vergänglichkeit, fern von «Gigantomanie und Prätention».[5] Als weiterer Aspekt ist jedoch zu berücksichtigen, dass Leiko Ikemura, als sie 1979 mit einer akademischen Ausbildung aus Sevilla in die Schweiz kam, in ein künstlerisches Klima eintrat, in dem der Zeichnung und in gewissem Masse auch der Druckgraphik besondere Aufmerksamkeit geschenkt wurde. Das wachsende Interesse an Zeichnung war 1976 durch drei einflussreiche Ausstellungen gefördert worden: Im Kunstmuseum Basel hatte Dieter Koepplin in *Zeichnen/Bezeichnen* unterschiedliche Positionen um 1970 von Beuys bis A. R. Penck gezeigt.[6] Im Kunsthaus Zürich folgte mit *Drawing Now – Zeichnung heute* (1976) eine von Bernice Rose kuratierte Wanderausstellung des Museum of Modern Art in New York, die Zeich-

nungen als Schlüsselwerke der Avantgarde der vorausgegangenen 20 Jahre zu etablieren beabsichtigte.[7] In der Luzerner Ausstellung *Mentalität Zeichnung* hatte Jean-Christophe Ammann schliesslich die Zeichnung als typischen Ausdruck einer schweizerischen Sensibilität neu positioniert.[8] Künstler wie Dieter Roth, André Thomkins und Markus Raetz waren bereits seit den 1960er-Jahren bewusst als Zeichner in den Fokus der Öffentlichkeit getreten, und Dieter Koepplin widmete denn auch Thomkins und Raetz 1971 bzw. 1972 je eine Einzelausstellung. 1983 folgte eine Soloausstellung des jüngeren Martin Disler, dessen Generation auch Ikemura angehört.

Zeichnen «im Vorfeld der Reflexion»

Ikemuras Arbeiten auf Papier fanden in diesem Umfeld schnell Anerkennung, so etwa 1981 durch die Verleihung der Preise der Stiftung für die Graphische Kunst der Schweiz und der Kiefer Hablitzel Stiftung sowie 1983 durch das Stipendium als Stadtzeichnerin von Nürnberg. Die 120 Zeichnungen aus den Jahren 1980–1987, die sich heute in der Sammlung des Basler Kupferstichkabinetts befinden, stellen nur einen kleinen Ausschnitt der Produktion Leiko Ikemuras in dieser Zeit dar.[9] Bis 1983 bleiben die Papierarbeiten, meist im Format A5 oder A4, eher klein. Sie sind linear mit Kohle ausgeführt, ab und zu kommen ein paar Schattierungen oder dünnere Linien mit Kugelschreiber, Kreide oder Farbstift dazu **(Kat. 9, S. 51, Kat. 16, S. 60, und Kat. 17, S. 60)**. Sie entstanden ohne spezifischen Zweck um ihrer selbst willen. Nur wenige Blätter sind konkrete Skizzen im Zusammenhang mit Gemälden.[10]

Die Arbeiten entstanden in rascher, prozesshafter Abfolge, die sich auch als eine Art Fliessen beschreiben lässt, denn es gibt kein Zurück, keine Korrektur, nur das nächste Blatt, auf dem Ikemura ganz neu ansetzt. Die Künstlerin beschreibt die Zeichnung als «Seelen-Seismograf», der ihre geistigen und seelischen Befindlichkeiten zu Papier bringe.[11] Der Zeichnungsprozess beinhaltet das Erfassen innerer Bilder: «Im Vorfeld der Reflexion da zeichne ich, denn die Zeichnung ist das Vehikel meiner vorbeiziehenden Bilder.»[12] Die Zeichnungen reflektieren nicht eine Idee, sondern entstehen in dem Moment, da ein Gedanke oder ein Bild erst im Entstehen begriffen ist. Hans-Jürgen Schwalm hat ihn sehr treffend als den schmalen Grat zwischen Finden und Erfinden bezeichnet, wo ein Gedanke sichtbar wird.[13]

Die zeichnende Hand ist nicht bloss ausführendes Instrument, sondern spielt spürbar ihren eigenen Part in diesem Prozess. Sie übt mal wenig, mal mehr Druck mit der Kohle aus, sodass das dünne Papier an manchen Stellen fast bis zum Zerreissen beansprucht wird **(Kat. 21, S. 63)**. Ikemura verstärkt Linien und betont eine Form oder eine

3   Leiko Ikemura, in: «‹Erotik in ihrer Ausstrahlung hat eine unaussprechbare Trauer.› Ein Gespräch mit Leiko Ikemura von Gerlinde Gabriel», in: Ausst.-Kat. Nürnberg 1984 (wie Anm. 1), S. 9–12, hier S. 12 (Hervorhebung im Original).

4   Leiko Ikemura, in: «‹Wir Menschen leben auch vom Ahnen.› Leiko Ikemura im Gespräch mit Alexander Pühringer», in: *Noëma Art Journal*, Nr. 39, 1995, S. 53–57, hier S. 54.

5   Siehe «Ikemura» im Saalblatt von Dieter Koepplin zur Ausstellung *Leiko Ikemura. Gemälde, Zeichnungen 1980–1987*, Museum für Gegenwartskunst des Kunstmuseum Basel (Archiv Kunstmuseum Basel): «Die Kunst des Haiku ist für mich allgemeingültig, meine Zeichnungen haben alle damit zu tun. Das Wesen des Haiku ist Poesie in knappster Form, vergänglichkeitsbewusst, fern von Gigantomanie und Prätention.»

6   *Zeichnen/Bezeichnen: Zeichnungen aus der Sammlung Mia und Martin Visser, Bergeyk*, Ausst.-Kat. Kunstmuseum Basel, Basel 1976.

7   Weitere Stationen der Ausstellung 1976/77: Staatliche Kunsthalle Baden-Baden, Graphische Sammlung der Albertina in Wien, Sonjia Henie-Niels Onstad Museum in Oslo und Tel Aviv Museum of Art.

8   *Mentalität: Zeichnung. Christian Ludwig Attersee, Anton Bruhin, Martin Disler, Markus Dulk, Helmut Federle, Heiner Kielholz, Claude

Sandoz, Hugo Suter, David Weiss,* Ausst.-Kat. Kunstmuseum Luzern, Luzern 1976. – Siehe auch Beat Wismer: «Über die Peripherie um Zentrum (und mitten im Herz). Ein Versuch über die Arbeit auf dem Papier in der Schweizer Kunst des 20. Jahrhunderts», in: *Im Reich der Zeichnung. Zeichnungen und Arbeiten auf Papier: Werke des 20. Jahrhunderts aus dem Aargauer Kunsthaus Aarau,* hrsg. von Stephan Kunz und Beat Wismer, Ausst.-Kat. Aargauer Kunsthaus, Aarau 1998, S. 8–15.

9   Die Zeichnungen gelangten durch Kauf und Schenkung zwischen 1982 und 1989 in die Sammlung, eine weitere Gruppe 1998/99.

10   Vgl. Dieter Koepplin, «Leiko Ikemura», in: *Räume heutiger Zeichnung. Werke aus dem Basler Kupferstichkabinett,* Ausst.-Kat. Staatliche Kunsthalle Baden-Baden, Tel Aviv Museum of Art, Baden-Baden 1985, S. 102.

11   Leiko Ikemura, in: Ikemura/Malsch 1998 (wie Anm. 2), S. 79.

12   Leiko Ikemura, in: Margarethe Jochimsen, «Sprung über die Zeit, aus einem Gespräch während einer langen Nacht», in: Ausst.-Kat. Bonn 1983 (wie Anm. 1), S. 64–70, hier S. 68.

13   Hans-Jürgen Schwalm, «Dazwischen», in: *Leiko Ikemura. Skulptur, Malerei, Zeichnung,* hrsg. von Hans-Jürgen Schwalm, Ausst.-Kat. Kunsthalle Recklinghausen, Pfalzgalerie Kaiserslautern, Ulmer Museum, Bielefeld 2004, S. 8–16, hier S. 9.

Drawing as Haiku and Site of Emptiness

Ikemura is Japanese, but she has found her own, fitting form of expression in the European tradition of drawing. At the same time, her work remains marked by Japanese influences. The synthesis she effects is so powerful and so much her own that it is barely possible to differentiate the "Japanese" and "European" characteristics from one another. From the start, Ikemura has published her drawings together with texts, thereby underscoring the relationship between her graphic work and poetry—in particular, haiku. In 1985, for instance, she published drawings in a book of Matsuo Bashō's haikus. Other projects followed.[14]

Ikemura's drawings of the 1980s were also repeatedly compared to the principles and aesthetic of haiku.[15] This extremely spare Japanese poetic form is known as the art of the frugal word; it is simple yet thoroughly complex.[16] Instead of describing or narrating, haiku is an art of suggestive still life. Ambivalence and openness, the both/and, are central characteristics. The interstice is as interesting as the form itself.[17] These qualities are not difficult to see in Ikemura's drawings. The artist herself has emphasized the connection and, tellingly, in 1983 introduced the illustration section of her Bonner Kunstverein exhibition catalog with a haiku by Yoshiwake Tairo and another poet.[18] This was the period when Ikemura was standing "At the Beginning of an Alphabet."[19] The haiku by Tairo reads, "In the lamplight / I burn / the frozen brush." The words are juxtaposed with an untitled work from 1980 painted with acrylic on paper, in which a person can be seen carrying a white house on their head through a gloomy terrain. Red flames shoot from the house on one side, as well as a brown tuft reminiscent of a paint brush. The text and image do not describe each other, but the two-page spread creates a coherent space of resonance.[20]

A year later, in 1984, in the catalog of the show at Kunsthalle Nürnberg, the eighteenth-century haikus make way for Ikemura's own poetry. She calls the portion of the catalog devoted to reproducing the drawings, "Fragment of a Diary." Interspersed among the illustrations, she places four poems that, despite their greater length, have a kinship with haiku.[21] The first expresses sadness and loneliness:

How can I
spit
the clouds out of my heart?
Nightly
I learnt the world
in the cold of the light
The oceanic worlds
smuggled
the longing of a stranger
Behold
the thundering clouds
how they conquer the sky
One morning
under my tears
will you awaken?

Ikemura's drawings and texts here stand side by side as autonomous statements that do not elucidate each other but are similar. She experiences the impulse and ductus of drawing as "an act of writing": both entail concentration and intimacy.[22] Since then she has published more of her own poetry.[23]

Ikemura's drawings are figurative. People, animals, plants, and houses are recognizable, even if they are simplified, distorted, or transformed through metamorphoses. Yet there are often also abstract elements that are difficult to interpret **(cat. 19, p. 62)**. Animate beings encounter, touch, or penetrate one another. What is represented is not to be understood narratively but rather evokes images of attraction, seduction, uprooting, forlornness, or threat—that is, physical and psychological states, moments of interpersonal relationships. Koepplin describes this as a process of realization and recognition that emerges on paper.[24]

14   Matsuo Bashō, *Hundertundelf Haiku,* selected, translated, and with an introduction by Ralph-Rainer Wuthenow, ill. Leiko Ikemura (Zurich: Amman Verlag, 1985). The book has been reprinted four times (1985, 1987, 1994, and 2009). See also Elisabeth Plessen, *Gedichte: Ich sah uns dort in der Ferne gehen,* Leiko Ikemura Aquarelle (Stuttgart: Radius Verlag, 2008).

15   Dieter Koepplin, "Acht Jahre künstlerischer Arbeit Leiko Ikemuras," in *Leiko Ikemura: Gemälde, Zeichnung 1980–1987,* 7.

16   Hortensia von Roda, "Tag, Nacht, Halbmond: Zeichnungen 1980–2007," in *Leiko Ikemura: Tag, Nacht, Halbmond,* exh. cat. (Zurich: Scheidegger & Spiess, 2008), 22.

17   Schwalm, "Dazwischen," 9.

18   *Leiko Ikemura* (1983), 4, 59.

19   Jochimsen, "Sprung über die Zeit," 3.

20   See also *Ancestors: Leiko Ikemura,* exh. cat. (St. Gallen: Kunstverein St. Gallen, 1984), with interspersed texts by Cesare Pavese, selected by Ikemura, as well as illustrations of two Peruvian and African objects from the Völkerkundemuseum München.

21   *Leiko Ikemura* (1983), 14, 20, 28, 40.

22   Alexander Pühringer, "Ein Gespräch mit Leiko Ikemura," in *Leiko Ikemura,* ed. Alexander Pühringer (Ostfildern: Hatje Cantz Verlag, 1995), 96.

23   See, for example, *Uminoko: Drawings and Poetries by Leiko Ikemura* (Kyoto: Aakaka Art Publishing, 2006). The picture book *Leiko Ikemura: Wild Cats and Domesticated Cats* (Zurich: Galerie und Edition Stähli, 1983) is also based on Ikemura's drawings; it has no text other than the title page and impressum, which the artist wrote by hand.

24   Dieter Koepplin, "Annäherung zweier Bilder," in *Leiko Ikemura: Stadtzeichnerin von Nürnberg 1983,* 10.

Energie durch die Verdichtung von Strichen **(Kat. 9, S. 51 und Kat. 22, S. 62)**. Dicke, tiefschwarze und dünnere Linien wechseln sich ab, werden auch ab und an ergänzt durch flächige Schattierungen, die nicht nur beschreibend sind **(Kat. 19, S. 62)**. Diese Linien vermitteln kein Zögern, nichts Provisorisches, keine flüchtigen Skizzen, sondern sind selbstbewusste, verdichtete Zeichnung.

Die Zeichnung als Haiku und Ort der Leere

Ikemura ist Japanerin, fand aber in der europäischen Tradition das ihr gemässe Ausdrucksmittel. Zugleich bewahrt ihr Werk auch die japanische Prägung. Die Synthese, die Ikemura realisiert, ist so stark und eigen, dass sich «japanische» und «europäische» Merkmale kaum voneinander trennen lassen. Indem die Künstlerin ihre Zeichnungen von Anfang an zusammen mit Texten veröffentlicht, unterstreicht sie die Verwandtschaft von Gedichten – insbesondere dem Haiku – und ihren graphischen Arbeiten. 1985 beispielsweise veröffentlichte sie Zeichnungen in einer Publikation von Matsuo Bashōs Haikus, weitere Projekte folgten.[14]

Ikemuras Zeichnungen der 1980er-Jahre wurden auch immer wieder mit dem Prinzip und der Ästhetik des Haikus verglichen.[15] Diese äusserst knappe Gedichtform Japans wird auch «Kunst des geizigen Wortes» genannt; sie ist sehr einfach und doch überaus komplex.[16] Anstatt zu beschreiben und zu erzählen, präsentiert sich der Haiku als eine Art suggestives Stillleben. Ambivalenz und Offenheit, das Sowohl-als-Auch sind zentrale Charakteristika; das Dazwischen ist so interessant wie die Form als solche.[17] Diese Merkmale erkennt man unschwer auch in Ikemuras Zeichnungen. Die Künstlerin wies selber darauf hin und leitete den Bildteil im Ausstellungskatalog

des Bonner Kunstvereins 1983 bezeichnenderweise mit einem Haiku von Yoshiwake Tairo ein; ein Haiku eines anderen Autors folgte weiter hinten im Katalog.[18] Es war die Zeit, als Ikemura «[a]m Anfang eines Alphabets» stand.[19] Der Haiku von Tairo lautet: «Am Lampenlichte / Liess den vereisten Pinsel / Ich nachts versengen.» Die Worte stehen einer mit Acryl auf Papier gemalten, unbetitelten Arbeit Ikemuras von 1980 gegenüber, auf der ein Mensch zu sehen ist, der ein weisses Haus auf dem Kopf durch eine düstere Gegend trägt. Aus dem Haus schiessen rote Flammen, aber auch ein braunes Büschel, das durchaus an die Borsten eines Pinsels erinnern könnte. Text und Bild beschrieben sich nicht gegenseitig, es entsteht aber ein stimmiger Resonanzraum auf der Doppelseite.[20]

Ein Jahr später, 1984, weichen im Katalog der Kunsthalle Nürnberg die Haikus aus dem 17. Jahrhundert eigenen Gedichten. Den Bildteil, der hier den Zeichnungen gewidmet ist, nannte Ikemura «Fragment eines Tagebuches», und sie platzierte im Wechsel mit Abbildungen vier eigene Gedichte, die trotz des grösseren Umfangs eine Verwandtschaft mit Haikus haben.[21] Das erste bringt Traurigkeit und Einsamkeit zum Ausdruck:

Wie kann ich
die Wolken aus meinem Herz
ausspucken?
Nächtlich
erfuhr ich die Welt
in der Kälte des Lichtes
Die ozeanischen Welten
schmuggelten
das Sehnen eines Fremden
Seht
die donnernden Wolken
wie sie den Himmel erobern
Eines Morgens
Unter meinen Tränen
wirst Du erwachen?

Ikemuras Zeichnungen und Texte stehen hier als eigenständige Äusserungen nebeneinander, die sich nicht gegenseitig erläutern, aber ähnlich sind. Sie empfindet Impuls und Duktus beim Zeichnen als «schreibend»: Beides beinhaltet Konzentration und Intimität.[22] Seitdem hat sie weitere Gedichte publiziert.[23]

Die Zeichnungen von Ikemura sind figurativ. Menschen, Tiere, Pflanzen und Häuser sind erkennbar, auch wenn sie vereinfacht, verzerrt oder durch Metamorphosen verfremdet sind. Doch finden sich oft auch schwer interpretierbare, abstrakte Elemente **(Kat. 19, S. 62)**. Die Lebewesen begegnen, berühren oder durchdringen einander. Das Dargestellte ist nicht narrativ zu verstehen, sondern

14 Matsuo Bashō, *Hundertundelf Haiku*, ausgewählt, übersetzt und mit einem Begleitwort versehen von Ralph-Rainer Wuthenow, Zeichnungen Leiko Ikemura, Zürich 1985 (weitere Auflagen 1985/1987/1994/2009). – Vgl. auch Elisabeth Plessen, *Gedichte. Ich sah uns dort in der Ferne gehen, Leiko Ikemura Aquarelle*, Stuttgart 2008.

15 Dieter Koepplin, «Acht Jahre künstlerischer Arbeit Leiko Ikemuras», in: Ausst.-Kat. Basel u.a. 1987 (wie Anm. 1), S. 7–21, hier S. 7.

16 Hortensia von Roda, «Tag, Nacht, Halbmond. Zeichnungen 1980–2007», in: *Leiko Ikemura. Tag, Nacht, Halbmond*, Ausst.-Kat. Museum zu Allerheiligen Schaffhausen, Zürich 2008, S. 17–26, hier S. 22.

17 Schwalm 2004 (wie Anm. 13), S. 9.

18 Ausst.-Kat. Bonn 1983 (wie Anm. 1), S. 4 und 59.

19 Margarethe Jochimsen, «Am Anfang eines Alphabets» (Vorwort), in: Ausst.-Kat. Nürnberg 1984 (wie Anm. 1), S. 3.

20 Siehe auch *Ancestors. Leiko Ikemura*, Kunstverein St. Gallen, St. Gallen 1984, mit Texten von Cesare Pavese sowie Abbildungen von zwei Objekten aus Peru und Afrika aus dem Völkerkundemuseum München, Texte und Bilder ausgewählt von der Künstlerin.

21 Ausst.-Kat. Bonn 1983 (wie Anm. 1), S. 13–44, Gedichte auf S. 14, 20, 28 und 40.

22 Alexander Pühringer, «Ein Gespräch mit Leiko Ikemura», in: Alexander Pühringer (Hrsg.), *Leiko Ikemura,* mit Texten von Gérard A. Goodrow, Kimio Jinno, Friedemann Malsch und Alexander Pühringer, Ostfildern 1995, S. 94–98, hier S. 96.

23 Siehe z. B. *Uminoko: Drawings and Poetries by Leiko Ikemura*, Kyoto 2006. Das Bilderbuch *Wild Cats and Domesticated Cats*, Galerie und Edition Pablo Stähli, Zürich 1983, basiert auf Zeichnungen und hat, abgesehen vom Titelblatt und dem Impressum in der Handschrift der Künstlerin, keinen Text.

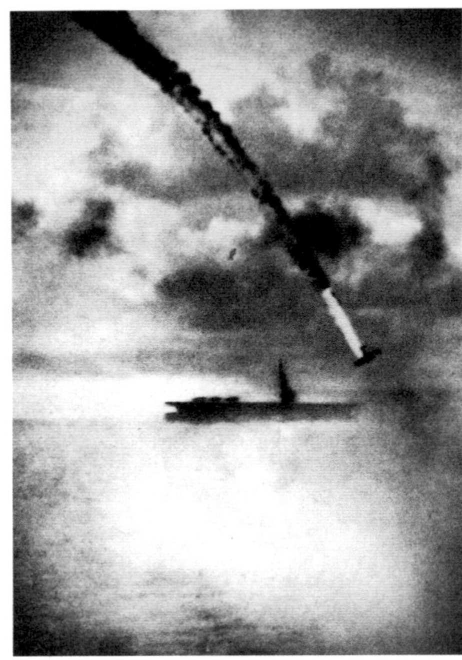

Abb. | Fig. 1 Reproduktion eines Pressefotos in dem Ausstellungskatalog | Reproduction of a press photo in the exhibition catalog *Leiko Ikemura. Stadtzeichnerin von Nürnberg 1983*

Roland Barthes's comments on the reception of the haiku are also applicable to Ikemura's drawing: it cannot be the aim of the reader/beholder to decipher the work completely—that would be to take a European approach that does not befit it: "for the work of reading which is attached to it [i.e., the haiku] is to suspend language, not to provoke it."[25]

In addition to the haiku-like economy of the depictions, the placement of figures and forms in empty space is, as Hortensia von Roda has also emphasized, a further essential characteristic of Ikemura's drawings.[26] Particularly in the drawings made from 1980 to 1985, a firm ground or horizon is seldom to be seen. Occasionally the drawings contain elements that suggest a vertical orientation (cat. 19, p. 62). The perspective, however, shifts freely, and the pictorial elements often seem to hover on the paper (cat. 15, p. 54, cat. 20, p. 59). Here, Koepplin sees an instantiation of the Japanese culture of detachment from the ego, for the Japanese painter—and Ikemura as well—does not understand him- or herself as a conqueror of space but rather, in disregarding central perspective, withdraws from the position of an individual subject.[27] East Asian drawing unfolds from multiple centers that are distributed over the entire page; the drawing spreads out over the empty and undefined space of the page without ever filling it up.[28] The forms or figures might be staggered in space but are also arranged in varying proportions. The emphasis is on the way the lines and ordered forms move with respect to one another in the open space of the page. The undefined space is, however, intuitively perceived as sky, water, or mist, despite consisting of empty surfaces. In the nonrational, "vegetatively organic" mode of seeing described here, the subject (the artist or beholder) implied in European drawing by its central perspective does not exist. This unreality of space in East Asian drawing is not in the service of the self-representation of one's own interiority but rather of the interpersonal, which is so difficult to grasp.[29] Ikemura is consequently not interested in self-portraits, and they are not found as such in her work, quite in contrast to contemporaries such as Disler, for whom the self-portrait plays a central role.[30]

Drawing as Memento Mori

A programmatic sheet dating from 1980 seems at first not to fit in with the charcoal drawings of the 1980s (cat. 1, p. 57). *Kamikaze* is executed in dispersion paint in a flat and painterly manner. Ikemura's characteristic strokes of charcoal are lacking here. A media image served the artist as model for the free arrangement of the scene. In 1984, she reproduced the photograph in the Nuremburg exhibition catalog as the prelude to a two-page photo collage (figs. 1–2). *Kamikaze* is an allegory for the unnecessary waste of human life, and it exemplifies the horror and meaninglessness of war, the consequences of which had shaped Ikemura's childhood in Japan. In her free interpretation of the image, she tips the horizon radically toward the bottom left and thus intensifies the drama and inevitability of the impending crash, but her clear composition lends the image a certain aesthetic quality.[31]

25 Roland Barthes, *Empire of Signs*, trans. Richard Howard (New York: Hill & Wang, Noonday Press, 1989), 72.

26 Von Roda, "Tag, Nacht, Halbmond," 17.

27 Koepplin, "Annäherung zweier Bilder," 10; Koepplin, "Acht Jahre künstlerischer Arbeit Leiko Ikemuras," 10.

28 See Philip Rawson, "Two Modes of Space," in *Drawing*, 2nd ed. (Philadelphia: University of Pennsylvania Press, 1987), 201–203.

29 Ikemura in Koepplin, "Acht Jahre künstlerischer Arbeit Leiko Ikemuras," 10: "I know that it is precisely this point, space, that is a conflict for me, because in the Japanese tradition our way of seeing is almost vegetatively organic. The beholder or artist is not the conqueror of space, of the horizon, but rather in Asia, by withdrawing from the ego, they have created an unreal space. I want the content to create a psychic space."

30 See, for example, Martin Disler, *Lefthanded Self-portrait*, 1985, watercolor on paper, 31.8 × 24 cm, Kunstmuseum Basel, Kupferstichkabinett, Inv. 1986.1.

31 See *Leiko Ikemura im Gespräch mit Friedemann Malsch*, 23–26.

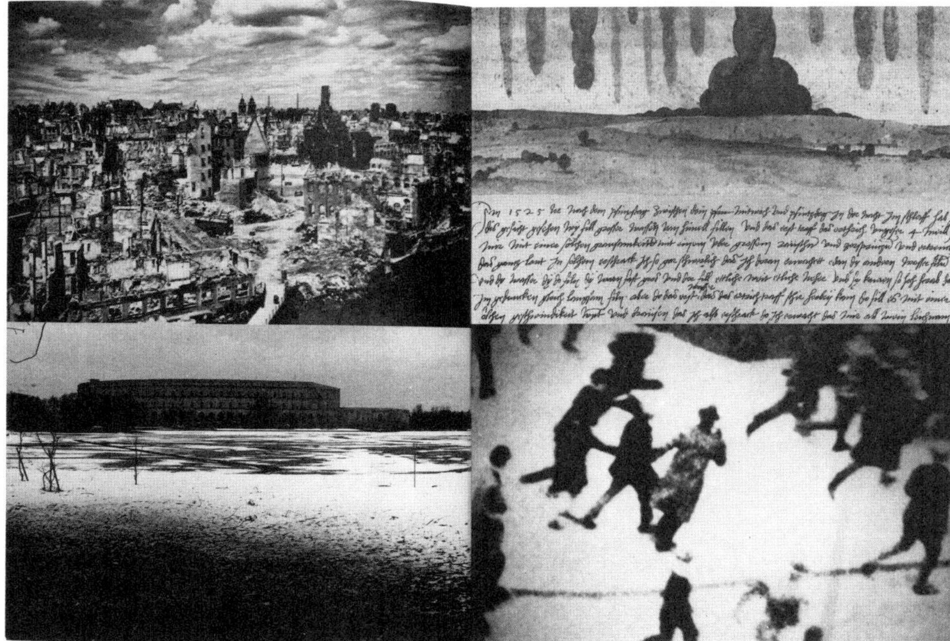

evoziert Vorstellungen von Anziehung, Verführung, Entwurzelung, Verlorenheit oder Gefährlichkeit, also körperliche und seelische Zustände, Momente zwischenmenschlicher Beziehungen. Koepplin umschreibt dies treffend als Prozess des Realisierens und Erkennens, der sich auf dem Papier abbilde.[24]

Was Roland Barthes in Bezug auf die Rezeption von Haikus schrieb, trifft auch auf Ikemuras Zeichnung zu: Es kann nicht das Ziel sein, sie restlos zu dechiffrieren, dies wäre ein europäischer Ansatz, der ihnen nicht gerecht würde. Sondern «die Lesbarkeit, die mit ihm [dem Haiku] verbunden ist, liegt darin, die Sprache in der Schwebe zu halten und nicht darin, sie zu provozieren».[25]

Neben der haiku-artigen Knappheit des Gezeichneten hat Hortensia von Roda die Platzierung der Figuren und Formen in der Leere als wesentliches Merkmal von Ikemuras Zeichnungen hervorgehoben.[26] Tatsächlich fällt auf, dass besonders in den Zeichnungen von 1980 bis 1985 selten ein fester Boden oder ein Horizont zu erkennen ist. Zuweilen enthalten die Zeichnungen Elemente, die eine vertikale Orientierung andeuten **(Kat. 19, S. 62)**. Die Perspektive wechselt allerdings ziemlich frei, und die Bildelemente scheinen oft auf dem Papier zu schweben **(Kat. 15, S. 54, Kat. 20, S. 59)**. Koepplin sieht hier die japanische Kultur der Ich-Entzogenheit verwirklicht,[27] denn der japanische Maler – ebenso Ikemura – verstehe sich nicht als Eroberer des Raums, sondern nehme sich als Individuum und Subjekt zurück, indem er die Zentralperspektive ausser Acht lasse. Die ostasiatische Zeichnung entfaltet sich ausgehend von mehreren Kernen, die über das Blatt verteilt sind, und verbreitet sich auf der leeren und undefinierten Fläche des Blattes, ohne diese je vollständig zu bedecken.[28] Die Formen oder Figuren können räumlich gestaffelt, aber auch in variierenden Grössenverhältnissen angeordnet sein. Die Betonung liegt darauf, wie die Linien und aneinandergereihten Formen sich im offenen Raum des Blattes bewegen. Der undefinierte Raum wird aber intuitiv als Himmel, Wasser oder Nebel wahrgenommen, obwohl es sich um leere Flächen handelt. Das in der europäischen Zeichnung durch die Zentralperspektive mitgedachte Subjekt (Künstler oder Betrachter) existiert in der eben beschriebenen, nicht rationalen, sondern «pflanzlich-organische[n] Sehweise» nicht. Diese Irrealität des Raumes in der ostasiatischen Zeichnung dient nicht der Darstellung des eigenen Innenlebens, sondern jener des schwer fassbaren Zwischenmenschlichen.[29] Es geht Ikemura also nicht um Selbstporträts, die man so in ihrem Werk nicht findet, ganz im Gegensatz zu den Zeitgenossen wie Martin Disler, bei denen das Selbstporträt eine zentrale Rolle spielt.[30]

24   Dieter Koepplin, «Annäherung zweier Bilder», in: Ausst.-Kat. Nürnberg 1984 (wie Anm. 1), S. 45–49, hier S. 10.

25   Roland Barthes, *Das Reich der Zeichen*, Frankfurt a. M. 1981, S. 98 (Übers. Michael Bischoff).

26   Roda 2008 (wie Anm. 16), S. 17.

27   Koepplin 1984 (wie Anm. 24), S. 10; Koepplin 1987 (wie Anm. 15), S. 10.

28   Vgl. «Two modes of space» in: Philip Rawson, *Drawing*, Philadelphia, 2. Auflage, 1987, S. 201–203.

29   Leiko Ikemura, in: Koepplin 1987 (wie Anm. 15), S. 10: «Ich weiss, dass genau dieser Punkt, der Raum, ein Konflikt für mich ist, weil unsere Sehweise in der japanischen Tradition gleichsam pflanzlich-organisch ist. Der Betrachter oder der Künstler ist nicht Eroberer des Raumes, des Horizonts, sondern in Asien hat man in der Ichentzogenheit einen irrealen Raum geschaffen. Ich will, dass der Inhalt einen psychischen Raum schafft.»

30   Siehe z. B. Martin Disler, *Linkshändiges Selbstbildnis*, 1985, Aquarell, 31,8 x 24 cm, Kunstmuseum Basel, Karl August Burckhardt-Koechlin-Fonds, Inv. 1986.1.

Although Ikemura constructed the large picture (120 × 90 cm) with a few simple forms, it has consolidated into something more complex. The image of the impending destruction is an allegory for the inevitability of suffering as such, which will affect the man in the airplane as much as those on the ship. In this archetypal situation there is neither good nor evil. As Ikemura emphasizes, such ambivalence and differentiation are possible only in art.[32] With this image, the artist takes up a theme that concerns her personally—the legacy of the war in Japan, which brought about a cultural crisis and drove a generation of fathers to despair or even suicide—and gives it a pictorial form that states in the most concise terms a universal concept, the Buddhist notion of "life as suffering."

The practically monumental drawing *Garten der Lüste* differs from Ikemura's earlier drawings **(cat. 92, pp. 132/33)**. Not only the misshapen branches but entire trees strive upward like flickering tongues of flame. The trees are a bit reminiscent of human shapes or ghosts wandering homeless—or, perhaps, fleeing from something—in a dark and hostile landscape. The title is undoubtedly a reference to the middle panel of Hieronymus Bosch's *The Garden of Earthly Delights,* which stands in stark contrast to Ikemura's apocalyptic landscape. Her Garden of Eden has been destroyed by the hand of man. The drawing was produced during her ten-month tenure in 1983 as the *Stadtzeichnerin* in Nuremberg. In Germany, she was confronted with the onerous legacy of the Second World War, which also called to mind her own childhood in Japan.[33] In her interviews, too, Ikemura has emphasized the significance of pain, the existential world-weariness and spiritual pain that, once it has been acknowledged, can also lead to catharsis and new vitality.[34] Pain does not necessarily mean suffering or masochism but can instead suggest the deeply anchored Japanese cultural attitudes of heightened sensibility to the past and acceptance of loss.[35] Do the inner and outer worlds meld here into a soul landscape? Such distinctions are not made nearly as clearly in the Japanese conception of life as they are in European thought. People and all other life-forms are part of an all-encompassing, circular movement, as Jochimsen notes.[36] They exist within a field of tension or, rather, in a state of hovering between all the poles, such as heaven and earth, life and death, past and future, male and female, the material and the spiritual. This also applies to Ikemura's work as a whole.

Despite the grief that accompanies pain and despite all the darkness, *Garten der Lüste* has something light and flowing, even seductively beautiful, about it. In Ikemura's work, this is not indicative of a contradiction. The short strokes drawn in charcoal form no sharp contours but rather caress the tree trunks and become embedded in the overall hatching. The sensual quality of the drawing evokes the feeling of a soft flow. At roughly 270 centimeters on each side, the drawing is almost superhuman in size and required immense physical effort. The artist has called attention to the function of the charcoal and the significance of the body: "Charcoal is the extension of the fingers, the extension of the body, with a softness and flexibility that the pencil doesn't have. A pencil is more like an instrument, relatively hard. Charcoal lets me work freely."[37] The lines on the paper are traces of a movement that was executed by the drawing hand. The lines are a "skeleton of thoughts" but also a "memory of the body"; namely, the body that translates the thoughts into movement.[38]

For the exhibition in Basel, as in Tokyo before, the sculpture *Memento Mori* (2012) will be placed on the floor on a low pedestal in front of the drawing *Garten der Lüste* **(cat. 92, pp. 132/33, cat. 93, p. 140)**. The sculpture, a recumbent figure in white, embodies the central aspects of Ikemura's artistic cosmos. The girlish being, which first becomes central in her art in the 1990s, is at once human and landscape, flower and shell, and radiates sensuality and fragility. The gouges on the upper body and the body openings, as well as the deep eye holes, invite contemplation of the fleetingness of life—as the title *Memento Mori* suggests. The figure exists in an interstitial space between earthly life and another world and epitomizes the fragility of earthly existence. The female figure could also be understood as a kind of self-portrait, as Johannes Hanssen suggests.[39]

32   Ibid., 24.

33   Ibid., 16.

34   Ibid., 28.

35   See Ikemura in Jochimsen, "Sprung über die Zeit," 64.

36   Ibid., 68.

37   Ikemura in Koepplin, "Acht Jahre künstlerischer Arbeit Leiko Ikemuras," 10.

38   *Leiko Ikemura im Gespräch mit Friedemann Malsch,* 75–78: "The lines are the skeleton of thoughts, visual thoughts, but also the memory of the body. They are translated by the hand into oscillating movement. It is not quite entirely automatism, which attempts to exclude consciousness."

39   Johannes Janssen, "Wellen Wesen Wolken," in *Leiko Ikemura—Zwischenwelten: Zeichnungen, Gemälde, Skulpturen,* exh. cat. (Bielefeld: Kerber Verlag, 2014), 17–18.

Die Zeichnung als Memento mori

Von 1980 datiert ein programmatisches Blatt, das zunächst ganz und gar nicht zu den oben besprochenen Kohlezeichnungen der 1980er-Jahre zu passen scheint **(Kat. 1, S. 57)**. *Kamikaze* ist mit Dispersionsfarbe flächig und malerisch ausgeführt, ohne Ikemuras charakteristische Kohlestriche. Das Pressefoto, das der Künstlerin als Vorlage für die freie Umsetzung der Szene diente, bildete sie 1984 im Nürnberger Ausstellungskatalog als Auftakt zu einer doppelseitigen Fotocollage ab **(Abb. 1–2)**. *Kamikaze* ist ein Sinnbild für die Verschwendung von Menschleben und verdeutlicht die Grausamkeit und Sinnlosigkeit des Krieges, dessen Folgen ihre Kindheit in Japan geprägt hatten. Ikemura neigt den Horizont stark nach links unten und steigert damit die Dramatik und Unausweichlichkeit des bevorstehenden Zusammenstosses, verleiht dem Werk aber durch die klare Komposition auch eine gewisse Ästhetik.[31]

Obwohl Ikemura das grosse Blatt (120 × 90 cm) mit wenigen und einfachen Formen gestaltet, verdichtet es sich zu hoher Komplexität. Es ist Sinnbild der bevorstehenden Zerstörung und für das unausweichliche Leiden schlechthin, das den Mann im Flugzeug genauso trifft wie jenen auf dem Schiff. Es gibt in dieser urtypischen Situation weder Gut noch Böse. Diese Ambivalenz und Differenzierung ist nur in der Kunst möglich, wie Ikemura betont.[32] Die Künstlerin bringt damit ein Thema, das sie persönlich beschäftigte – das Erbe des Krieges, das in Japan eine kulturelle Krise verursacht und die Vätergeneration zur Verzweiflung oder gar in den Selbstmord getrieben hatte – in eine Bildform, die ein universelles Konzept, das buddhistische «Leben ist Leiden» in aller Knappheit formuliert.

Auch die geradezu monumentale Zeichnung mit dem Titel *Garten der Lüste* von 1983 unterscheidet sich von den frühen Zeichnungen **(Kat. 92, S. 132/133)**. Wie züngelnde Flammen streben nicht nur verstümmelte Äste, sondern ganze Bäume in die Höhe. Ihre Wurzeln haben sich von der Erde gelöst. Ein wenig erinnern die Bäume an menschliche Wesen oder Geister, die heimatlos in einer düsteren und bedrohlichen Landschaft unterwegs – oder gar auf der Flucht sind. Der Titel erinnert unweigerlich an die mittlere Tafel des berühmten Triptychons von Hieronymus Bosch und steht im harten Kontrast zu Ikemuras apokalyptischer Landschaft. Der Garten Eden ist von Menschenhand zerstört worden. Ikemuras Zeichnung entstand während ihres zehnmonatigen Aufenthaltes als Stadtzeichnerin in Nürnberg 1983. In Deutschland war sie konfrontiert mit dem belastenden Erbe des Zweiten Weltkrieges, das zugleich die eigene Kindheit in Japan in Erinnerung rief.[33] Auch in Gesprächen betonte die Künstlerin die Bedeutung des Schmerzes, des Welt- und Seelenschmerzes, der – einmal zugelassen – auch zu Katharsis und neuer Vitalität führen kann.[34] Schmerz bedeutet nicht unbedingt Leiden oder Masochismus, sondern eine gesteigerte Sensibilität für Vergänglichkeit und Akzeptanz von Verlust, beides ist in der japanischen Kultur tief verankert.[35] Verschmelzen hier Innen- und Aussenwelt zu einer Seelenlandschaft? Dies ist eine Unterscheidung, die in der ostasiatischen Vorstellung vom Leben nicht so deutlich vorgenommen wird wie im europäischen Denken. Menschen und alle anderen Lebewesen sind Teil einer umfassenden grossen, kreisenden Bewegung, wie es Margarethe Jochimsen beschrieben hat.[36] Sie befinden sich in einem Spannungsfeld, besser: Schwebezustand zwischen allen Polen wie Himmel und Erde, Leben und Tod, Vergangenheit und Zukunft, dem Männlichen und Weiblichen, dem Sinnlichem und Geistigen. Dies trifft auch für Ikemuras ganzes Werk zu.

Trotz dieser den Schmerz begleitenden Trauer und trotz aller Finsternis hat die Zeichnung *Garten der Lüste* auch etwas Leichtes und Fliessendes, geradezu verführerisch Schönes, was in Ikemuras Werk keinen Widerspruch bedeutet. Die mit Kohle gezogenen, kurzen Striche bilden keine scharfe Kontur, sondern umschmeicheln die Baumstämme und werden eingebettet in flächige Schraffuren. Die sinnliche Qualität der Zeichnung suggeriert das Gefühl eines weichen Fliessens. Die Zeichnung ist mit etwa 270 cm im Quadrat von einer gleichsam übermenschlichen Grösse, die immensen Körpereinsatz gefordert hat. Die Künstlerin hat auf die Funktionsweise des Kohlestifts hingewiesen und die Bedeutung des Körpers betont: «Kohle ist die Verlängerung des Fingers, die Verlängerung

31 Vgl. Ikemura/Malsch 1998 (wie Anm. 2), S. 23–26.

32 Ebd., S. 24.

33 Siehe Leiko Ikemura, in: Ebd., S. 16.

34 Ebd., S. 28.

35 Vgl. Leiko Ikemura, in: Jochimsen 1983 (wie Anm. 12), S. 64.

36 Ebd., S. 68.

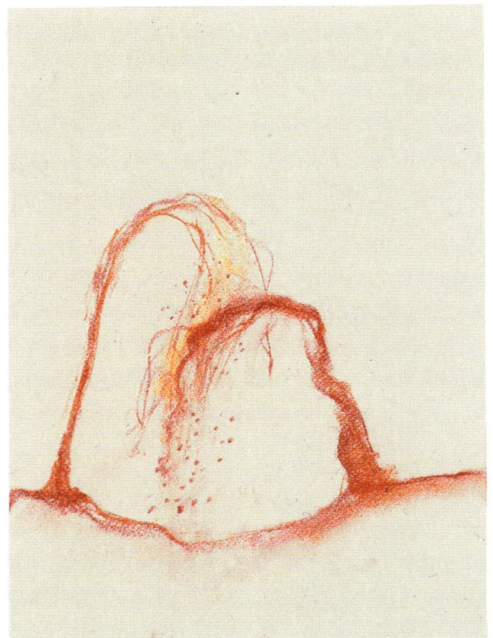
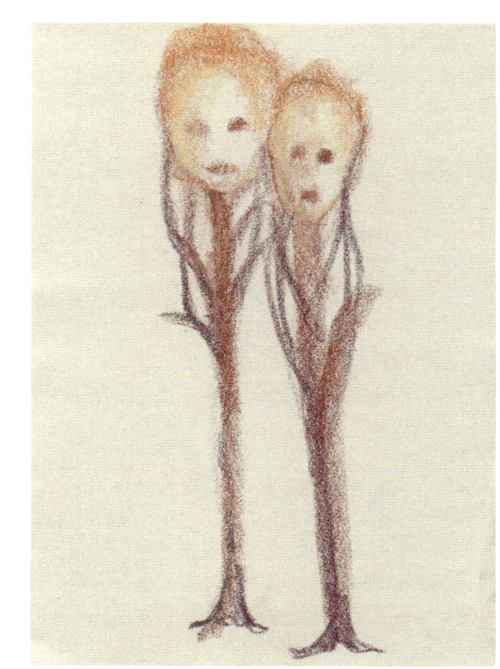

Abb. | Fig. 3 *Tree Love*, 2007,
Pastell auf Papier | pastel on paper,
40,5×29,5 cm, The National Museum
of Modern Art, Tokyo

Abb. | Fig. 4 *Tree Love, True Love*,
2007, Pastell auf Papier | pastel on
paper, 40,5×29,5 cm, The National
Museum of Modern Art, Tokyo

The sculpture, which radiates a deep sorrow, was produced a year after the tragedy at Fukushima.[40] The current exhibition's juxtaposition of the drawing *Garten der Lüste* with the sculpture *Memento Mori* makes clear that Ikemura sought with the latter to create a connection with the theme of war, which was strongly present in her early 1980s works. Willful destruction of the planet through human agency is the chief reason for the "unease of our existence."[41]

But both pieces are, as with all of Ikemura's works, multilayered, because the sensual and the power of the erotic also play a role in them. The trees have a human quality in the way they blaze up and move, while the recumbent figure has a mussel shell for a lower body and is thus half human, half animal. With this juxtaposition of tree and woman, two motifs are placed in immediate proximity that exist in a symbiotic relationship in many of her other works. Earlier drawings already introduce the merging of the two motifs; for example, the untitled drawing from November 1, 1983, shows a woman rooted to the ground with shoots growing out of her legs **(cat. 19, p. 62)**. Similarly, the two heads of a double figure from 1985 and the woman in the study for the painting *Verkündigung* (Annunciation) from the same year **(cat. 33, p. 72, cat. 35, p. 75)** are fused with a (tree) trunk. The linkage of woman and tree has numerous iconographic precedents, from Daphne's transformation into a laurel tree in Ovid's *Metamorphosis* to numerous images by modern artists, such as those of Giovanni Segantini and Paul Klee, to name just two.[42] Ikemura's depictions should not be interpreted symbolically, however, but as simply showing the merging of human being and tree. With her, there are also human trees or tree-like people, as in the series of drawings *Tree Love* from 2007 **(figs. 3–4)**.

Liberation from the Solid Line

Around 1985, Ikemura began to create somewhat larger and more elaborate sheets that are more spatially complex. At times, these depictions are explicitly anchored to the ground **(cat. 28, p. 66)**, but such anchoring is often also immediately offset by figures that hover or are flipped 180 degrees **(cat. 36, p. 73)**. In other drawings, a dynamic vortex nullifies any sense of orientation **(cat. 30, p. 67)**. Ikemura, from around 1985 onward, makes more thorough use of the sheet by structuring the transitional space with hatching and creating black surfaces **(cat. 29, p. 67)**. Color is only rarely mixed with the black charcoal—perhaps some green to suggest plants, or red for pain and blood **(fig. 5)**.

Step by step, Ikemura conquers space on paper and canvas. A fruitful interplay develops between her drawing and painting. The drawing becomes more painterly, and the painting emancipates itself from line: "The compulsion of the solid line is gone."[43] An unusual drawing from 1987 references the painting *Kriegsgöttin* (Goddess of War) from 1986 **(cat. 42, p. 83, cat. 43, pp. 80/81)**, but with the warlike mood giving way to a certain lightness. A red cross structures the surface but remains

40   Immediately following the catastrophe, Ikemura initiated the exhibition *Breaking News: Fukushima and the Consequences*, KW Institute for Contemporary Art, Berlin, June 9–July 17, 2011.

41   *Leiko Ikemura im Gespräch mit Friedemann Malsch*, 28.

42   For example, Giovanni Segantini, *Landschaft mit Frau im Baum*, ca. 1881 (unfinished), 68.5 × 104.5 cm, Sturzenegger-Stiftung, Museum zu Allerheiligen, Schaffhausen;

Giovanni Segantini, *Die bösen Mütter*, 1894, oil on canvas, 120 cm × 225 cm, Österreichische Galerie Belvedere, Vienna; and Paul Klee, *Jungfrau im Baum*, 1903/2, etching, Zentrum Paul Klee, Bern.

43   Ikemura quoted in Koepplin, "Acht Jahre künstlerischer Arbeit Leiko Ikemuras," 10.

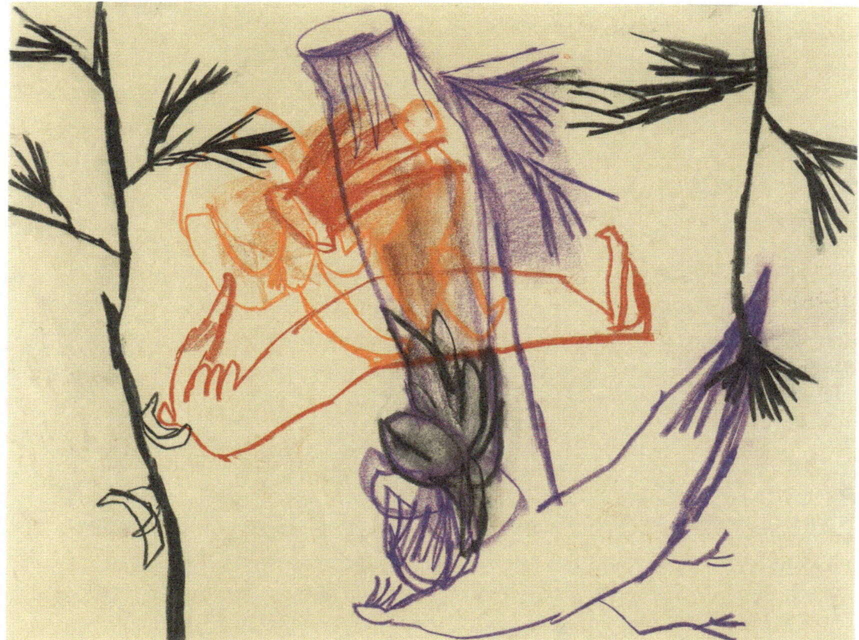

des Körpers, mit einer Weichheit und Flexibilität, die der Bleistift nicht hat. Bleistift ist eher wie ein Instrument, relativ hart. Kohle lässt mich frei arbeiten.»[37] Die Linien auf dem Papier sind Spuren einer Bewegung, die die zeichnende Hand ausgeführt hat. Linien sind das «Skelett der Gedanken», aber auch das «Gedächtnis vom Körper», nämlich dem ausführenden Körper, der sie in Schwingungen übersetzt.[38]

In der aktuellen Ausstellung in Basel wird wie in Tokio auf dem Boden vor der Zeichnung *Garten der Lüste* auf einem niedrigen Podest die Plastik *Memento mori* (2012) platziert, eine liegende Figur in Weiss **(Kat. 92, S. 132/133, Kat. 93, S. 140)**. Sie verkörpert alle zentralen Aspekte von Ikemuras künstlerischem Kosmos: Das mädchenhafte Wesen, das erst in den 1990er-Jahren ins Zentrum ihrer Kunst rückt, ist zugleich Mensch und Landschaft, Blume und Muschel, strahlt Sinnlichkeit und Zerbrechlichkeit aus. Die Kerben am Oberkörper und die Körperöffnungen sowie die tiefen Augenhöhlen lassen – wie es der Titel *Memento mori* suggeriert – an die Vergänglichkeit des Lebens denken. Die Gestalt befindet sich in einem Bereich zwischen irdischem Leben und einer anderen Welt und versinnbildlicht die Fragilität der Existenz auf Erden. Die weibliche Figur könnte auch als eine Art Selbstporträt verstanden werden, wie es Johannes Hanssen vorgeschlagen hat.[39]

Die Plastik, die eine tiefe Traurigkeit ausstrahlt, entstand ein Jahr nach dem Reaktorunfall von Fukushima.[40] Dass Ikemura die Zeichnung *Garten der Lüste* in der aktuellen Ausstellung mit dieser Plastik in Dialog setzt, stellt einen Zusammenhang mit dem Anfang der 1980er-Jahre stark präsenten Thema des Krieges in ihren Werken dar. Mutwillige Zerstörung des Planeten durch die Menschheit ist ein Hauptgrund für das «Unbehagen unserer Existenz».[41]

Aber beide Werke sind wie alle Arbeiten Ikemuras vielschichtig, denn auch das Sinnliche und die Kraft der Erotik spielen in ihnen eine Rolle: Die Bäume haben eine menschliche Qualität in ihrem Aufflammen und der Bewegung, während die liegende Figur einen Unterleib in Form einer Muschel aufweist, also halb Mensch, halb Tier ist. Mit dieser Gegenüberstellung von Baum und Frau werden zwei Motive in unmittelbare Nachbarschaft zueinander gerückt, die in vielen Werken eine Symbiose eingehen. Bereits frühe Zeichnungen haben das Baum und Frau vereinende Motiv eingeführt; eine unbetitelte Zeichnung vom 1. November 1983 zeigt eine Frau, die im Boden verwurzelt ist und aus deren Beine Triebe schlagen **(Kat. 19, S. 62)**. Ebenso sind die beiden Köpfe einer Doppelfigur von 1985 und die Frau in der *Studie zum Gemälde «Verkündigung»* aus demselben Jahr **(Kat. 33, S. 72, Kat. 35, S. 75)** eng mit einem (Baum-)Stamm verwachsen. Für die Verbindung von Frau und Baum gibt es viele ikonografische Vorbilder, von der Ovidischen Metamorphose Daphnes in einen Lorbeer bis zu zahlreichen Darstellungen der Moderne, hier seien nur Giovanni Segantini und Paul Klee erwähnt.[42] Ikemuras Darstellungen

37   Leiko Ikemura, in: Koepplin 1987 (wie Anm. 15), S. 10.

38   Leiko Ikemura, in: Ikemura/Malsch 1998 (wie Anm. 2), S. 75–78: «Die Linien sind das Skelett der Gedanken, visuelle Gedanken, aber auch Gedächtnis vom Körper. Sie werden durch die Hände in Schwingungen übertragen. Es ist nicht ganz der Automatismus, der das Bewusstsein auszuschliessen versucht.»

39   Johannes Janssen, «Wellen Wesen Wolken», in: *Leiko Ikemura – Zwischenwelten. Zeichnungen, Gemälde, Skulpturen*, hrsg. von Andrea Firmenich, Johannes C. B. Janssen, Andrea Sietzy, Ausst.-Kat. Museum Sinclair-Haus, Bad Homburg, Bielefeld 2014, S. 11–18, hier S. 17–18.

40   Leiko Ikemura initiierte unmittelbar nach der Katastrophe eine Ausstellung: *Breaking News. Fukushima and the Consequences*, KW Institute for Contemporary Art, Berlin, 09.06.–17.07.2011.

41   Leiko Ikemura, in: Ikemura/Malsch 1998 (wie Anm. 2), S. 28.

42   Vgl. Giovanni Segantini, *Landschaft mit Frau im Baum*, um 1881 (unvollendet, 68,5 × 104,5 cm, Sturzenegger-Stiftung, Museum Allerheiligen, Schaffhausen), *Die bösen Mütter*, 1894 (Öl auf Leinwand, 120 × 225 cm, Österreichische Galerie Belvedere, Wien), und Paul Klee, *Jungfrau im Baum*, 1902/03 (Radierung, Zentrum Paul Klee, Bern).

strangely immaterial—it is more surface than object. The female figures—one with her wings spread out on the cross and another embracing the neck of the horse she is riding—are transparent.[44]

As with Ikemura's paintings from this period, the process of production on paper is turbulent and reminiscent of the multilayered working-over of the canvas in works such as *Kriegsgöttin*. In the wake of these works, the paper exhibits a noticeable relief: wet and dry media, charcoal and chalk, watercolor and oil have been applied in multiple layers in primary colors and in white, and yet the result is a kind of transparency that allows the figures to hover. Clearly structured and impactful paintings such as *Vogelspinnen* (Tarantulas) from 1983 **(cat. 26, p. 71)** and *Verkündigung* from 1985 are followed by images of war and violence: *Kriegsgöttin* (1986), *Pearl Harbour* (1986), *Trojanisches Pferd* (Trojan Horse, 1986).[45] The conflicts, which are above all between man and woman, take place not only within the depiction but at the level of the material. The artist wrestles with the paint on the canvas. It is not a struggle for its own sake but an internal confrontation that culminates in a creative crisis that Ikemura will not overcome until 1989, during her stay in the mountains of the Swiss Canton of Grisons. The concentrated, smaller-format *Alpenindianer* (Alps Indians) of 1989/90 mark a new beginning.[46]

New Functions of Drawing

Ikemura has lived in Cologne since 1985. Her 1989 sojourn in Switzerland and a new professorship in Berlin that began in 1991 provided caesuras for the artist that inspired changes in her drawing that are indicative of a new concentration and calm—and perhaps a certain equanimity. The drawings were produced in parallel with sculptures and paintings but were not direct preparatory studies. Rather, they were a means to develop and clarify ideas. At first, hybrid ur-creatures appear that have at times more vegetative and at times more animal characteristics **(cat. 53–56, pp. 100, 103)**. They are anchored firmly to the ground and appear almost to be growing out of it. They are drawn in charcoal, but only a few strokes outline the creatures. Ikemura uses the flat of the charcoal for shading and then sets down just a few accents with the point. The flat and delicate application of the charcoal brings out the material qualities of the paper. Through the variation of pressure, direction, and angle, thickness, and length of the charcoal stick, varied structures are produced on the paper. The way in which the ur-creatures are drawn conveys the impression that they manifest themselves slowly, emerging into light as though they had always been there but first had to be given concrete form.

In the early 1990s Ikemura began to emphasize the specific qualities of drawing, sculpture, and painting much more strongly. Sculpture as a three-dimensional medium, the haptic quality of which is concentrated in the surface of the colored glazes she uses, supplements her painting and drawing, whose support plays an increasingly greater role.

The drawings made in 1993—which continue the stronger commitment to the line—are connected to the charcoal drawings of the 1980s but have a different character **(cat. 66–69, pp. 106/107)**. In contrast to the fragmented and incoherently assembled bodies of the previous decade's work, here there is always a creature—sometimes doubled (mother/child or child/cat)—that stands or sits at the center and constitutes a self-enclosed entity. These creatures have human features—footed heads, for example—and the horizontal line becomes the basis for the figures.

Flowing Watercolor and the Structure of Paper

Ikemura produced her first pure watercolor in 1986, but she did not begin to use watercolors regularly until the mid-1990s.[47] An untitled group of watercolors plays a central role primarily for its thematic, for here the ur-creatures and footed heads become girls **(cat. 74–85, pp. 118–122)**. They have clear contours, yet they appear as if they are still pupae or closed-up flowers about to bloom. They are reminiscent of the female figures Beuys painted in watercolor, even as they are completely different.[48] Ikemura's girls practically hover on the white page. One or even several little legs do not suffice to anchor them firmly. The thin lines seem more like rods that hold up the figures in a shadow puppet theater. But the girls nonetheless have a strong presence in their intense coloration and their contours, where the water color pigment has in part been concentrated. Although the contours seem like continuous lines, the artist has not drawn silhouettes. The fluidity of the paint medium, its movement in the mixing process, is reflected in the way the colors

44 See ibid., 18, where Koepplin relates the image to the double figure in the *Annunciation*.

45 For extensive commentary on *Vogelspinnen*, see Koepplin, "Annäherung zweier Bilder"; and Koepplin, "Acht Jahre künstlerischer Arbeit Leiko Ikemuras."

46 On the *Alpenindianer*, see Gérard A. Goodrow, "Ohne Titel," in Pühringer, *Leiko Ikemura*, 25–27; David Elliott, "The House beyond the Horizon," in *Leiko Ikemura: Poetics of Form*, exh. cat. (Reno: Nevada Museum of Art, 2016), 65.

47 See Koepplin, "Acht Jahre künstlerischer Arbeit Leiko Ikemuras," 7; and cat. no. 166, fig. 80 (collection of the Kupferstichkabinett of the Kunstmuseum Basel, Inv. 1987.83).

48 See Dieter Koepplin, *Joseph Beuys in Basel*, vol. 2, *Zeichnungen und Holzschnitte bis 1954* (Basel: Schirmer/Mosel, 2003), nos. 9, 30. Beuys's work, which Koepplin exhibited in Basel in 1969 and 1976 (among other times), has been both an inspiration and a source of friction for Ikemura.

sind nicht symbolistisch zu deuten, sondern zeigen die Verschmelzung von Mensch und Baum. Bei ihr gibt es auch menschliche Bäume oder baumhafte Menschen, so etwa in er Zeichnungsfolge *Tree Love* von 2007 **(Abb. 3–4)**.

Befreiung von der festen Linie

Ikemura begann um 1985, etwas grössere und elaboriertere Blätter zu schaffen, die räumlich vielschichtiger sind. Teilweise sind die Darstellungen fest im Boden verankert **(Kat. 28, S. 66)**, aber auch diese Bodenhaftung wird oft sogleich wieder aufgehoben durch schwebende oder um 180 Grad gedrehte Figuren **(Kat. 36, S. 73)**. In anderen Zeichnungen hebt ein dynamischer Sog jegliche räumliche Orientierung des Geschehens auf **(Kat. 30, S. 67)**. Ikemura nutzt das Blatt Papier nun intensiver, indem sie Zwischenräume mit Schraffuren strukturiert und schwarze Flächen schafft **(Kat. 29, S. 67)**. Farbe mischt sich nur selten mit der Kohle, etwa Grün im Zusammenhang mit Pflanzen oder Rot für Schmerz und Blut **(Abb. 5)**.

Ikemura erobert nun doch schrittwiese den Raum auf Papier und Leinwand, es kommt zu einer fruchtbaren Wechselwirkung zwischen Zeichnung und Malerei. Die Zeichnung wird malerischer, und die Malerei emanzipiert sich von der Linie: «Der Zwang der festen Linie ist weg.».[43] Eine aussergewöhnliche Zeichnung von 1987 bezieht sich auf das Gemälde *Kriegsgöttin* von 1986 **(Kat. 42, S. 83, Kat. 43, S. 80/81)**, doch hier weicht die kriegerische Stimmung einer gewissen Leichtigkeit. Das rote Kreuz strukturiert die Fläche, bleibt aber seltsam entmaterialisiert – es ist mehr Fläche als Gegenstand. Die weiblichen Figuren – jene mit ausgebreiteten Flügeln am Kreuz und jene, die den Hals des Pferdes umarmt, auf dem sie reitet – sind transparent.[44]

Wie auf den Leinwänden dieser Zeit ist der Entstehungsprozess auf dem Papier turbulent und erinnert an die vielschichtige Überarbeitung der Gemälde, insbesondere *Kriegsgöttin*. Das Papier weist infolgedessen ein starkes Relief auf: Nasse und trockene Materialien, Kohle und Kreide, Aquarell und Öl, wurden in den Grundfarben und Weiss mehrschichtig aufgetragen, und doch resultiert daraus eine Transparenz, die die Figuren schweben lässt. Zeichnen und Malen verdichten sich zu einem interaktiven Prozess.

Auf klar strukturierten und einprägsamen Gemälden wie *Vogelspinnen* von 1983 **(Kat. 26, S. 71)**[45] und *Verkündigung* von 1985 folgen Bilder zu Krieg und Gewalt: *Kriegsgöttin* (1986), *Pearl Harbour* (1986) oder auch *Trojanischer Krieg* (1986). Die Kämpfe, vor allem solche zwischen Mann und Frau, finden nicht nur im Bild statt, sondern auch auf der Ebene des Materials. Die Künstlerin ringt auf der Leinwand mit der Malerei. Es ist nicht ein Kampf um seiner selbst willen, sondern eine innere Auseinandersetzung, die in eine Schaffenskrise mündet, die Ikemura erst 1989 während des Aufenthaltes in den Bergen des Kanton Graubünden überwinden wird. Die *Alpenindianer* von 1989/90 markieren in den konzentrierten kleineren Formaten einen Neuanfang.[46]

Neue Funktionen der Zeichnung

Die Zäsur des Schweiz-Aufenthaltes der seit 1985 in Köln lebenden Künstlerin und die Professur in Berlin ab 1991 hatten auch im Bereich der Zeichnung Veränderungen zur Folge, die Ausdruck einer neuen Konzentration und Beruhigung sind, vielleicht auch einer Gelassenheit. Die Zeichnungen entstanden parallel zu Skulpturen und Gemälden, sind aber nicht direkte Vorstudien, sondern vielmehr ein Mittel, Ideen zu entwickeln und klären. Zunächst erscheinen hybride Urwesen, die mal mehr pflanzliche, dann wieder mehr tierische Merkmale haben **(Kat. 53–56, S. 100, 103)**. Sie sind fest im Boden verankert und scheinen fast aus dem Boden herauszuwachsen. Gezeichnet sind sie mit Kohle, aber nur wenige Linien umreissen die Wesen, vielmehr nutzt Ikemura die Kohle flächig, schattierend, um dann mit der Spitze wenige Akzente zu setzen. Durch den flächigen und zarten Auftrag der Kohle kommt die Qualität des Papiers zum Tragen. Variationen des Drucks, der Richtung und des Winkels bzw. der Dicke oder Länge des Kohlestifts lassen vielseitige Strukturen auf dem Papier entstehen. Die Art und Weise, in der die Urwesen gezeichnet sind, bringt zum Ausdruck, dass diese sich allmählich manifestieren, zum Vorschein kommen, so als wären sie schon immer da gewesen, als Idee, müssten aber noch konkrete Form erhalten.

In den frühen 1990er-Jahren begann Ikemura, die spezifischen Qualitäten von Zeichnung, Plastik und Malerei stärker zu betonen. Die Plastik als drei-

43   Leiko Ikemura, zit. nach Koepplin 1987 (wie Anm. 15), S. 10.

44   Ebd., S. 18; Koepplin bringt sie in Zusammenhang mit der Doppelfigur der *Verkündigung*.

45   Siehe die ausführlichen Texte Koepplin 1984 (wie Anm. 25) und Koepplin 1987 (wie Anm. 15).

46   Zu den *Alpenindianern* siehe: Gérard A. Goodrow, «Ohne Titel», in: Pühringer (Hrsg.) 1995 (wie Anm. 22), S. 23–30, hier S. 25–27; David Elliott, «The House Beyond the Horizon», in: *Leiko Ikemura. Poetics of Form*, Ausst.-Kat. Nevada Museum of Art, Donald W. Reynolds Center for the Visual Arts, Reno/Nevada, Reno 2016, S. 56–71, hier v.a. S. 65.

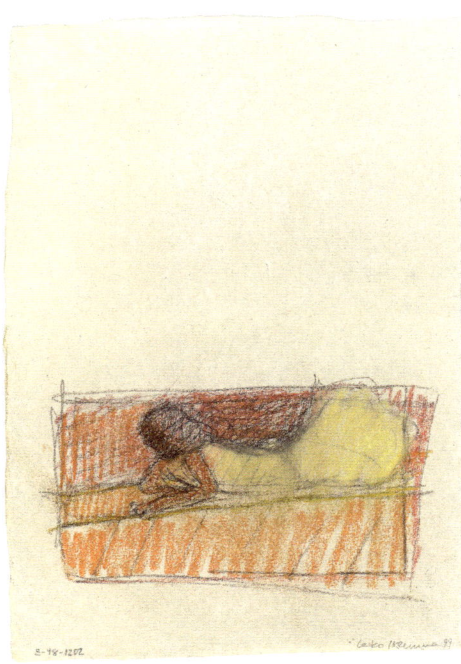
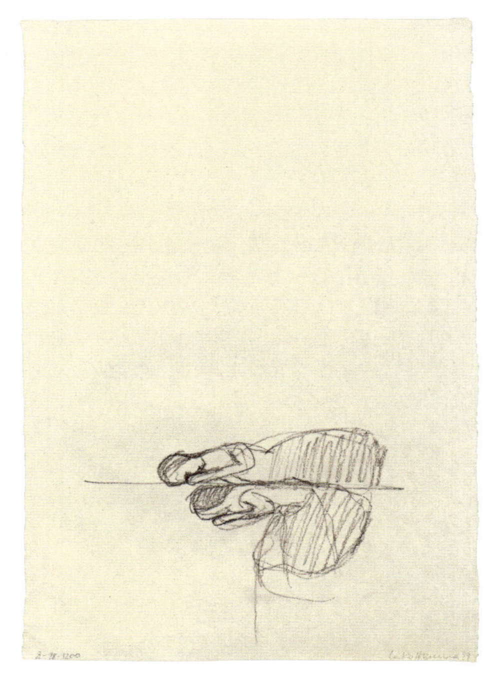

mix together on the surface, wet on wet. Where the color
is thin, the structure of the paper comes particularly to
the fore. The execution, however, owes less to a conscious
awareness of the medium than to the motif, which takes
on form but nonetheless remains "blurry."[49] Similar to
the ur-creatures and the footed heads, here it is not just
the visible form that is essential but the coming into being of the form, the actual becoming of the girl, less as
body than as a spiritual being.

The large and significant group of paintings and
sculptures of girls has been discussed extensively **(cat.
71–73, pp. 115–117, cat. 86–91, pp. 123–127, 129)**.[50] These works
are accompanied by watercolors and chalk drawings that
capture pictorial ideas for individual figures or entire
compositions **(figs. 6–7)**. Ikemura applied colored chalk
to handmade paper, which produces an effect akin to that
of the paintings. Since the early 1990s, she has been exe-
cuting the latter on rough canvas with a thin application
of color so that the structure of the canvas remains visible
and no illusion of a real world is produced. In the drawings, the gently applied chalk also lets the paper come to
the fore as a support.

The horizon, which plays a central role in the pictures of girls and the landscapes, is present in the drawings in the form of a line. In *Kamikaze* the horizon is produced through the separation of sea and sky, but in the
chalk studies a horizontal line suggests only a conceptual landscape, for the line does not even reach from one
edge of the page to the other **(fig. 7)**. The two hovering
figures are simultaneously held together and separated
by the line. In contrast to the ur-creatures or the footed
heads, they do not stand or lie on solid ground; rather,
the space is as undefined and unreal as in the drawings
of the 1980s. Only the notion of "above and below" provides orientation. All else remains merely suggested.
These sheets in particular make clear that, despite their

completely different appearance from the drawings of the
1980s, the terseness and poetry of haiku and the weight-
lessness and unreality of the pictorial space are equally
as actualized as in the earlier works.[51] In this way, the
synthesis Ikemura effects at the level of motif, content,
and execution continually manifests itself in ever new
and inspirational forms.

49 On this point, see *Leiko Ikemura im
Gespräch mit Friedemann Malsch*, 79–80.

50 See Doris von Drahten, "Horizontsüchtig,"
in *Leiko Ikemura: Les années lumières—Lichtjahre,* exh. cat. (Milan: Skira, 2001), 32–42; Doris
von Wilfried Dickhoff, "Präsenzmädchen," in
Leiko Ikemura: Skulptur, Malerei, Zeichnung,
exh. cat. (Bielefeld: Kerber Verlag, 2004), 94–98;
Renate Berger, "Woher—wohin? Tod und Auferstehung des Inneren Mädchens," in *Leiko
Ikemura: I-migration,* exh. cat. (Ostfildern:
Hatje Cantz Verlag, 2013), 145–153.

51 The same can be said of the more recent
series of drawings from 2008 with the head and
face motifs, which are executed in charcoal
(cat. 95–107, pp. 134–138, 141). See *Leiko Ikemura:
… and all of a sudden the wind is turning,*
exh.cat. (Berlin: Haus am Waldsee, 2016), 45–51.

dimensionales Medium, deren haptische Qualität sich in der Oberfläche der farbigen Glasuren konzentriert, ergänzt Malerei und Zeichnung, deren Träger zunehmend eine Rolle spielen.

Die wieder stärker der Linie verpflichteten Zeichnungen von 1993 schliessen zwar an die Kohlezeichnungen der 1980er-Jahre an, doch haben sie einen anderen Charakter (**Kat. 66–69, S. 106/107**). Im Zentrum steht oder sitzt jeweils ein Wesen, das eine in sich geschlossene Einheit bildet, anders als die fragmentierten und inkohärent zusammengesetzten Körper des vorhergehenden Jahrzehnts. Die Kreaturen haben menschliche Züge – es sind Kopffüssler –, und die horizontale Linie wird zur Basis der Figuren.

Papierstruktur und fliessende Wasserfarbe

Das erste reine Aquarell schuf Ikemura 1986,[47] doch setzte sie Wasserfarbe erst Mitte der 1990er-Jahre regelmässig ein. Eine unbetitelte Werkgruppe von Aquarellen spielt 1996 zunächst motivisch eine zentrale Rolle, denn hier werden aus den Urwesen und den Kopffüsslern Mädchen (**Kat. 74–85, S. 118–122**). Sie haben deutliche Umrisse, doch erscheinen sie wie verpuppt oder wie geschlossene Blüten, die sich erst entfalten werden. Sie erinnern an die weiblichen Figuren, die Joseph Beuys mit Wasserfarbe gemalt hat, sind aber zugleich auch ganz anders.[48] Ikemuras Mädchen schweben geradezu auf dem weissen Papier, ein oder auch mehrere Beinchen genügen nicht für eine feste Verankerung. Die dünnen Linien wirken eher wie die beweglichen Stäbe von Schattenfiguren. Dennoch haben die Mädchen eine starke Präsenz dank der intensiven Farbigkeit und der Umrisse, die sich dort abzeichnen, wo sich die Pigmente der Wasserfarbe zum Teil konzentriert haben. Obwohl die Kontur wie eine durchgehende Linie wirkt, handelt es sich nicht um von der Künstlerin gezogene Silhouette. Die Farben mischen sich auf einer Fläche nass in nass, die Flüssigkeit des Malmittels und dessen Bewegung beim Vermischen sind deutlich erkennbar. An Stellen mit dünnerem Farbauftrag kommt die Struktur des Papiers besonders stark zur Geltung. Die Ausführung ist indessen weniger einer Medienreflexion geschuldet als dem Motiv, das Form annimmt, aber trotzdem «verschwommen» bleibt.[49] Ähnlich wie bei den Urwesen und den Kopffüsslern ist hier nicht nur die sichtbare Form wesentlich, sondern das Zustandekommen der Form, das eigentliche Werden der Mädchen, weniger als Körper denn als spirituelle Wesen.

Die grosse und bedeutende Gruppe der Mädchenbilder und -plastiken wurde oft und ausführlich besprochen (**Kat. 71–73, S. 114–117, Kat. 86–91, S. 123–127, 129**).[50] Sie wird begleitet von Aquarellen und Kreidezeichnungen, die Bildideen für einzelne Figuren oder ganze Kompositionen festhalten (**Abb. 6–7**). Hier verwendete Ikemura farbige Kreide auf Büttenpapier, wobei der Effekt demjenigen der Gemälde verwandt ist. Letztere führt sie seit den 1990er-Jahren auf grober Leinwand und mit dünner Farbe aus, sodass die Leinwandstruktur sichtbar bleibt und keine Illusion einer realen Welt aufkommt. Auch in den Zeichnungen lässt die weich aufgetragene Kreide das Papier als Träger zur Geltung kommen.

Der Horizont, der bei den Mädchenbildern und Landschaften eine zentrale Rolle spielt, ist in der Zeichnung in Form einer Linie präsent. In *Kamikaze* entsteht diese durch die Abgrenzung des Meeres vom Himmel, in den Kreidestudien ist sie aber eine horizontale Linie, die nur im Ansatz eine Landschaft andeutet, denn sie ist nicht einmal von einem Blattrand zum anderen durchgezogen (**Abb. 7**). Die beiden schwebenden Figuren werden von der Linie zusammengehalten und zugleich getrennt. Anders als die Urwesen oder die Kopffüssler stehen oder liegen sie nicht auf festem Boden, sondern der Raum ist wieder so undefiniert und unreal wie in den Zeichnungen der 1980er-Jahre. Die einzige Orientierung besteht in Oben und Unten, alles andere bleibt Andeutung. Gerade diese Blätter verdeutlichen, dass hier die Knappheit und Poesie der Haikus, die räumliche Schwerelosigkeit und der irreale Bildraum ebenso verwirklicht sind wie in den völlig anders anmutenden früheren Zeichnungen der 1980er-Jahre. Weitere Beispiele liessen sich anführen.[51] So kommt die Synthese, die Leiko Ikemura auf der motivischen, inhaltlichen und der die Ausführung betreffenden Ebene verwirklicht, zu immer neuen und inspirierenden Ausprägungen.

47   Siehe Koepplin 1987 (wie Anm. 15), S. 7, und Kat. Nr. 166, Abb. 80 (die Arbeit befindet sich im Kupferstichkabinett des Kunstmuseum Basel, Inv. 1987.83).

48   Vgl. Dieter Koepplin, *Joseph Beuys in Basel*, Bd. 2, *Zeichnungen und Holzschnitte bis 1954*, München 2006, Nr. 9 und 30. – Beuys' Werk, das Dieter Koepplin 1969, 1976 und weitere Male in Basel ausstellte, war für die Künstlerin Inspiration, aber auch Reibungsfläche.

49   Siehe dazu Leiko Ikemura, in: Ikemura/ Malsch 1998 (wie Anm. 2), S. 79–80.

50   Siehe dazu Doris von Drahten, «Horizontsüchtig», in: *Leiko Ikemura. Les années lumières – Lichtjahre,* Ausst.-Kat. Musée cantonal des Beaux-Arts, Lausanne, Mailand 2001, S. 32–42; Wilfried Dickhoff, «Präsenzmädchen», in: *Leiko Ikemura. Skulptur, Malerei, Zeichnung,* Ausst.-Kat. Recklinghausen/Kaiserslautern/ Ulm 2004 (wie Anm. 13), S. 94–98; Renate Berger, «Woher – wohin? Tod und Auferstehung des Inneren Mädchens», in: *Leiko Ikemura. i-migration,* Ausst.-Kat. Staatliche Kunsthalle Karlsruhe, Ostfildern 2013, S. 145–153.

51   Dasselbe lässt sich zu den neueren Zeichnungsserien mit den Kopf- und Gesichtsmotiven von 2008 feststellen, die mit Kohle ausgeführt sind (Kat. 95–107, S. 134–138, 141). Vgl. *Leiko Ikemura … und plötzlich dreht der Wind,* Ausst.-Kat. Haus am Waldsee, Berlin, Köln 2016, Abb. S. 45–51.

Leiko Ikemura and the Genesis of Images

Mitsue Nagaya

Introduction

Leiko Ikemura has worked in a wide variety of media over the past forty years: painting, sculpture, drawing, watercolor, prints, and photography. This is a reflection of her openness to diverse media, but also of the urgent motivation driving her art, which relates strongly to the well-known words of Paul Klee: "Art does not reproduce the visible; it makes visible."[1]

What Klee attempted to "make visible" is a matter of some debate, but for the moment we can call them potential images, something not yet visible, inexpressible in words and lacking even definite form. Ikemura is inspired by the capabilities of various media to make such potential images visible, finding the images she seeks amid chaotic vortexes of imagery. Or she is guided by what images reveal and seeks to bring these revelations into the realm of recognizable form without sacrificing their rich uncertainty.

One category of things that is difficult to "make visible" comprises those things that constantly change. The orientation of Ikemura's artistic practice toward representation of "things that constantly change" has been discussed extensively from various angles.[2] As human beings, we establish various boundaries for the sake of expediency—between life and death, reality and fiction, this world and the next, East and West, image and word—and Ikemura no doubt went through considerable conflict and struggle with these. However, from the 1990s onward her work has appeared almost to negate these boundaries or to transcend them, seemingly without effort, like a rabbit freed from gravity, leaping through the air in a single bound.[3] What made this possible seems to be the uncertainty of the images, or the process of instilling images with a wealth of other potential images.

Uncertainty and Ambiguity of Images

Ikemura's works can create a shadowy, indefinable atmosphere while striking the viewer as soft and modest. All the works are strongly characterized by uncertainty and ambiguity.[4] Take, for example, *White Head with Trees* (2017) **(cat. 94, p. 139)**. The facial expression looks simultaneously peaceful and sad. The figure could be awake or asleep or even dead. The trees that grow out of the head can be seen as embodying the world of this person's imagination or as implying that life will continue after their death. The facial expression, simple but open to various interpretations, and the fantastical image of trees growing out of the head, evoke all manner of things.

Meanwhile, in addition to ambiguous and fantastical images, from the early years of her career to today Ikemura has frequently concealed images within images or used double images. Over the last ten years, her approach to inserting images into other images has become more complex.

The series *Cosmicscapes*, begun in 2008, is a group of majestic panoramas influenced by an East Asian animistic worldview. In *Genesis* and *Tokaido* (both 2015) **(cat. 108–110, pp. 144–151)**, this takes the form of people's faces lurking in mountains in the distance, a reclining figure that appears to be dreaming melting into the shoreline, long hair hanging from an enormous floating

1   Paul Klee, "Schöpferische Konfession," in *Tribüne der Kunst und der Zeit: Eine Schriftensammlung*, vol. 13 (Berlin: Erich Reiß Verlag, 1920), 28–40.

2   *Leiko Ikemura: Transfiguration*, exh. cat. (Tokyo: National Museum of Modern Art; Tsu: Mie Prefectural Art Museum, 2011).

3   Leiko Ikemura was inspired by Shiniche Nakazawa, *Nousagi no hashiri* [The hare's run]

(Tokyo: Chuokoronsha, 1989). See also Keisuke Mori, "The 'Jumping' Method—Leiko Ikemura's Hares and Sculptures," in *Leiko Ikemura: Ceramic Sculptures and Related Works* (Shizuoka: Vangi Sculpture Garden Museum and NOHARA, 2014).

4   Regarding the ambiguity and indeterminacy of images, see Dario Gamboni, *Potential Images: Ambiguity and Indeterminacy in Modern Art* (London: Reaktion, 2002).

Leiko Ikemura und die Entstehung der Bilder

Mitsue Nagaya

Einleitung

Leiko Ikemura arbeitet seit vierzig Jahren in einer Vielfalt von Medien: Malerei, Skulptur, Zeichnung, Aquarell, Druckgraphik und Fotografie. Dies spiegelt ihre künstlerische Offenheit, veranschaulicht aber auch die treibende Kraft hinter ihrem Schaffen, das eng verbunden ist mit der berühmten Aussage Paul Klees: «Kunst gibt nicht das Sichtbare wieder, sondern Kunst macht sichtbar.»[1]

Es ist viel darüber diskutiert worden, was Klee «sichtbar machen wollte», aber ich sehe darin eine Andeutung potenzieller Bilder, solcher, die nicht beschrieben werden und keine definitive Form haben, etwas, das nicht in Worten ausgedrückt werden kann und auch keine definitive Form hat. Ikemura lässt sich von den Möglichkeiten der verschiedenen Medien inspirieren, um solche erwünschten, potenziellen Bilder sichtbar zu machen, indem sie diese im chaotischen Strudel des Visuellen findet. Oder sie lässt sich durch das inspirieren, was Bilder preisgeben, und überführt diese Offenbarungen in den Bereich des Sichtbaren, ohne damit den Reichtum des Ungewissen aufzugeben.

Eine Schwierigkeit bei dieser Art von «Visualisierung» besteht darin, das «sich stets Wandelnde» darzustellen. Die Fokussierung Ikemuras auf die Darstellung des «sich stets Wandelnden» ist bereits aus verschiedenen Blickwinkeln betrachtet worden.[2] Als menschliche Wesen etablieren wir aus Gründen der Zweckmässigkeit zahlreiche Abgrenzungen zwischen Leben und Tod, Realität und Fiktion, Diesseits und Jenseits, Orient und Okzident, Wort und Bild, und Ikemura hat sich ohne Zweifel damit auseinandergesetzt. Seit den 1990er-Jahren jedoch negiert ihr Werk diese Abgrenzungen scheinbar mühelos oder transzendiert sie, wie ein Hase, der plötzlich der Schwerkraft entkommt und in einem grossen Bogen durch die Luft springt.[3] Es scheint, als wäre dies gerade durch die Mehrdeutigkeit der Bilder möglich geworden oder mithilfe ihrer Methode, Bilder mit einem Reichtum an weiteren potenziellen Bildern auszustatten.

Unbestimmtheit und Ambiguität der Bilder

Ikemuras Arbeiten vermitteln mitunter eine schattenhafte, undefinierbare Atmosphäre, die die Betrachter sanft und zurückhaltend berührt. Ihr Hauptmerkmal ist eine schwer definierbare Unbestimmtheit und Ambiguität.[4] Ein Beispiel hierfür ist ihre Skulptur *White Head with Trees* (2017) **(Kat. 94, S. 139)**: Der Gesichtsausdruck scheint sowohl friedlich als auch traurig, möglicherweise wachend oder aber schlafend, wenn nicht tot. Die Bäume, die aus seinem Schädel wachsen, verkörpern die imaginäre Welt dieser Person oder lassen sich als Andeutung interpretieren, dass es ein Leben nach dem Tod für diesen Menschen gibt. Angesichts eines zwar einfachen, aber vielseitig interpretierbaren Antlitzes und einer phantasmagorischen Darstellung von Bäumen, die aus einem Kopf herauswachsen, können wir unserer Vorstellungskraft freien Lauf lassen.

Neben der Mehrdeutigkeit und dem Fantastischen in ihren Werken zieht sich die Methode, im Bild ein weiteres Bild zu verbergen, das sogenannte Doppelbild, wie

1   Paul Klee, «Schöpferische Konfession», in: *Tribüne der Kunst und der Zeit. Eine Schriftensammlung*, Bd. 13, Berlin 1920, S. 28–40.

2   *Leiko Ikemura. Transfiguration*, Ausst.-Kat. The National Museum of Modern Art, Tokio, Mie Prefectural Art Museum, Tsu, Tokio 2011.

3   Inspiration fand Ikemura in dem Buch von Shinichi Nakazawa, *No-usagi no hashiri* (Wie ein Feldhase läuft), Tokio 1989. Vgl. Keisuke Mori, «The Jumping Method – Leiko Ikemura's Hares and Sculptures», in: *Leiko Ikemura: Ceramic Sculptures and Related Works*, Shizuoka, Vangi Sculpture Garden Museum und NOHARA, 2014.

4   Zur Ambiguität und Unbestimmtheit der Bilder siehe Dario Gamboni, *Potential Images: Ambiguity and Indeterminacy in Modern Art*, London 2002.

head becoming a road, and a mass at the roots of a giant tree resembling both a knob of the tree and a crouching person. People and animals are quiet, breathing presences within natural elements such as mountains, trees, rocks, and watersides, suggesting a pantheistic vision of Genesis. However, despite the majestic scale of the paintings, they never proclaim their presence loudly. The viewer's surprise at discovering these creatures integrated into landscapes is like that of finding unexpected images in the moving, shape-shifting clouds overhead. Some viewers may not even notice the human and animal figures.

This is one example of how Ikemura's imagery is ambiguous enough to be seen in completely different ways by different viewers. A single work may contain multiple images. While these images may be particularly approachable for Japanese grounded in the religious context of Shinto, in which mountains, waterfalls, stones, and so forth are divine presences, Ikemura's inclusion of such specific collective memories is premised on the activation of human memory and imagination.

In *The Anthropology of Images,* Hans Belting discusses human skulls with plaster added to transform them into ritual objects for ancestor worship, unearthed in the Jordan Valley village of Jericho and dating from circa 7,000 BCE, as the first humanlike images. The fleshless skulls re-fleshed with lime and clay, with shells placed on their eyes, are images "that gaze back at us for the first time with human faces."[5] These eventually evolved into the mask as manifestation of the absent dead and as ritual object. Whether modified skulls or masks, the images functioned as real objects that enabled the living to interact with the dead.

Later, in ancient Greece, and most famously articulated by Plato in his metaphor of the cave, the idea emerged that images are mere "shadows of shadows," substitutes for visible realities that are themselves substitutes for higher ideals. With this, in Western society at least, a fertile tradition of primal images inextricably bound up with the human body and encompassing the entirety of life and death was lost from the mainstream of visual arts. During the Renaissance, the mimetic aspects of the image were yet further emphasized.

The various abstract art movements that emerged in the early twentieth century, including surrealism, which focused on the human unconscious, can be seen as protests against the rigid norms governing art from the Renaissance onward. Ikemura is in the company of numerous artists, including Klee, in probing and questioning the dichotomies that continue to hold sway over our view of images to this day. The more blurred the boundaries between polarities become—that is, between visible and invisible, real and virtual, abstract and figurative, reproducible and nonreproducible—the more ambiguous and primal images become.

The ambiguity of the images encourages us to use our imagination when viewing them, activating our own memories and actively involving ourselves in the image. This is precisely because of the various dichotomies the images are imbued with; that is, the invalidation of any decisive recognition of what something represents or resembles transforms the work into a field of experience where images are nothing more than images. Henri Bergson says, "there is for images merely a difference of degree, and not of kind, between being and being consciously perceived," indicating the strong relationship between images and perception.[6] The virtual "is latent until actualized by perception."[7] With this premise, it is easy to understand why primal images, inseparably tied to the processes of life itself, were never perceived as anything less than fully real. Ikemura's images invite us to consider images in a new way.

Again and again in Ikemura's work we find images that become images only through the agency of the viewer's imagination. Ikemura alone does not create these images; viewers, too, engage in their creation through the act of seeing. *Genesis,* the title of one of her *Cosmicscape* paintings **(cat. 108–110, pp. 144–151)**, describes the primal landscape of image generation and is also the story of the creation of the world.

5   Hans Belting, *An Anthropology of Images: Picture, Medium, Body* (Princeton, NJ: Princeton University Press, 2011), 90.

6   Henri Bergson, *Matter and Memory,* trans. N.M. Paul and W.S. Palmer (New York: Zone Books, 1990), 37.

7   Anne Friedberg, *The Virtual Window: From Alberti to Microsoft* (Cambridge, MA: MIT Press, 2006), 142.

ein roter Faden durch ihr gesamtes Œuvre. In jüngster Zeit ist ihre Art und Weise, weitere Bilder ins Bild einzuschleusen, sogar noch komplexer geworden.

Ihre 2008 begonnene Werkgruppe *Cosmicscapes* stellt ein grandioses Panorama dar, das von der animistischen Weltauffassung Ostasiens geprägt ist. In *Genesis* und *Tokaido* (beide 2015) **(Kat. 108–110, S. 144–151)** verbergen sich menschliche Gesichter in der fernen Berglandschaft, oder eine liegende Träumende verschmilzt mit dem Strand. Das lange Haar eines schwebenden, riesenhaften Kopfes wird zu einer Strasse, während ein Ballen an einer Baumwurzel als knorriger Auswuchs oder als eine zusammengekauerte menschliche Gestalt gedeutet werden kann. Menschen und Tiere treten still atmend in Naturelementen wie Bergen, Bäumen oder Stränden zutage und verkörpern eine pantheistische Vorstellung der Genesis, aber trotz des beeindruckenden Formats der Leinwand drängen sie sich niemals auf. Die Überraschung bei der Entdeckung der mit der Landschaft verschmolzenen Kreaturen gleicht dem Erstaunen, mit dem wir bizarre Gebilde in vorüberziehenden, sich wandelnden Wolkenformationen auftauchen sehen. Bei flüchtiger Betrachtung mögen sie ganz unbemerkt bleiben.

Dies sind zwei Beispiele für die Uneindeutigkeit von Ikemuras Bildsprache, die unterschiedlichste Interpretationen zulässt, ebenso wie für die Vielzahl von Bildern, die ein Werk enthalten kann. Es ist eine Bildwelt, die japanischen Betrachtern leichter zugänglich sein mag, wenn sie im Shintoismus verwurzelt und daher vertraut sind mit Bergen, Wasserfällen und Felsen als Objekten des Glaubens. Doch auch ohne diesen Hintergrund wird bei jeglicher Bildrezeption das kollektive Gedächtnis, die menschliche Erinnerung und Vorstellungskraft aktiviert.

In seiner Schrift *Bild-Anthropologie* erwähnt Hans Belting bearbeitete Totenschädel aus Jericho im Jordantal von um 7000 v. Chr. als Kultgegenstände der Totenverehrung und beschreibt sie als früheste Zeugnisse menschlicher Abbilder. Die blanken Schädel, die mit Kalk und Lehm und deren Augenhöhlen mit Muschel-

schalen bedeckt wurden, wandeln sich zur Darstellung, die «uns zum ersten Mal mit menschlichen Gesichtern anblicken».[5] Später entwickelte sich daraus die Form der Maske, die als rituelles Requisit abwesende Tote vergegenwärtigt. Ob nun Schädel oder Maske, derartige Bildnisse erzeugen eine Art Wirklichkeit, um eine lebendige Kommunikation mit den Toten zu gewährleisten.

In späteren Epochen wie der griechischen Antike weist uns das berühmte «Höhlengleichnis» von Platon darauf hin, dass Bilder nur «Schatten von Schatten» sind, Platzhalter für die sichtbare Wirklichkeit, die wiederum lediglich Stellvertreter ist für Ideen.

In der Folge ging in der abendländischen Kultur die fruchtbare Wirklichkeit von Bildern, die tief mit dem menschlichen Körper verknüpft waren und die Ganzheit von Leben und Tod beinhalteten, im Strom der bildenden Künste verloren. In der Renaissance wurde der mimetische Aspekt der Darstellung noch stärker betont.

Der Anfang des 20. Jahrhunderts aufkommende Surrealismus, der sich dem Unbewussten zuwandte, sowie die späteren, abstrakten Kunstströmungen können als Auflehnung gegen das strikte Regelwerk gesehen werden, das seit der Renaissance die Kunst bestimmte. Wie unzählige andere Künstler, allen voran Paul Klee, rüttelt Ikemura an den mannigfaltigen Dichotomien, die die Bilderwelt beherrschen und immer noch starken Einfluss ausüben. Je mehr die Grenze zwischen Gegensätzen wie dem Sichtbaren und Unsichtbaren, Realen und Virtuellen, Abstrakten und Konkreten, Abgebildeten und Nichtabgebildeten verschwimmt, desto mehrdeutiger und archaischer erscheinen ihre Bilder.

Die Mehrdeutigkeit der Bilder fordert uns dazu heraus, unsere Vorstellungskraft wirken zu lassen, unser Gedächtnis zu mobilisieren und uns damit aktiv an der Realisierung des Bildes zu beteiligen. Erst dadurch wird es in einen einzigen Erfahrungsraum verwandelt, wo es nichts darstellt, das sich ausserhalb des Bildes befindet, denn die verschiedenen Gegensätze und die Konvention, dass es sich um ein Abbild von etwas handelt, verlieren ihre Gültigkeit. Gemäss Henri Bergson gilt, «daß für die Bilder zwischen *sein* und *bewußt wahrgenommen sein* ein schlichter Unterschied des Graduellen und nicht des Wesens besteht».[6] Das Bild ist aufs Engste mit der Wahrnehmung des Betrachters verknüpft. Es ist eine potenzielle Existenz, die erst in Erscheinung tritt, wenn sie durch Wahrnehmung zu einer Realität wird.[7] Man könnte auch sagen, es besteht kein auffälliger Unterschied im Bewusstsein bei einer realen oder virtuellen Erfahrung. Unter dieser Voraussetzung ist gut nachvollziehbar, warum die Wirklichkeit von Urbildern, die unmittelbar mit

5   Hans Belting, *Bild-Anthropologie. Entwürfe für eine Bildwissenschaft,* München 2001, S. 150.

6   Henri Bergson, *Materie und Gedächtnis,* Hamburg 2015, S. 39 (Übers. Margarethe Drewsen; Hervorhebung im Original).

7   Anne Friedberg, *The Virtual Window: From Alberti to Microsoft,* Cambridge (MA) 2006, S. 141.

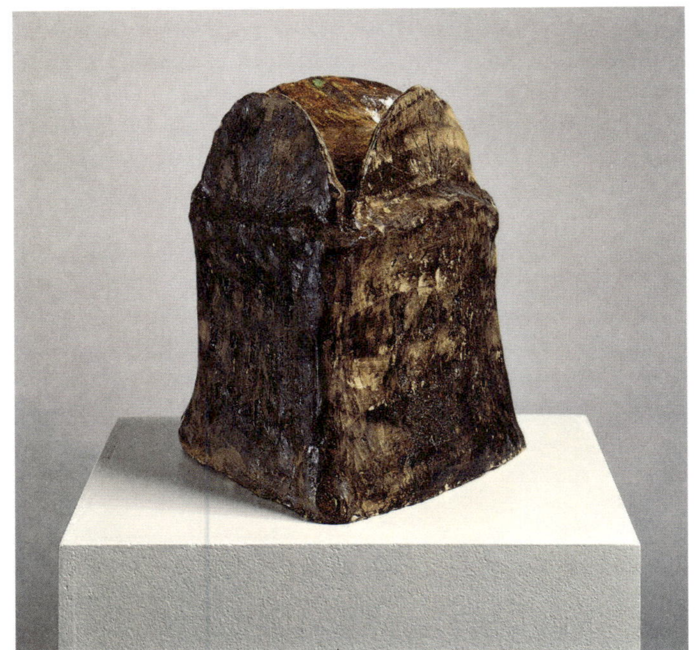

Abb. | Fig. 1 *Haus-Frau* | House-Wife, 1991, Terrakotta, glasiert | terra-cotta, glazed, 21,5 × 21 × 22,5 cm, ShugoArts Gallery, Tokyo

The Generation of Images

Entering the Image   Ikemura's work transcends the dualism of images and restores their original function. She has explored this theme explicitly at least since the 1990s. In the late 1980s she received major impetus for further development from two sources. One was her encounter with a new material, clay.

Wächter (Guard, 1987) **(cat. 48, p. 87)** is an early example of Ikemura's work in this medium. She kneaded clay and shaped its irregular masses by hand, searching for images. Out of its malleable mass came organic creatures, buildings such as houses, and hybrid shapes that fuse the two **(cat. 49, p. 90, and fig. 1)**. Sculpting is a medium in which the action of forming is strongly affected by physical sensation. This makes it very close to drawing, which directly reflects the movements of the hand. Both give improvised form to images that well up in the mind.

Soon after beginning to work with clay, Ikemura began to produce hybrid creatures such as *Stehende Figur in Petrolblau* (Standing Figure in Petrol Blue, 1990/91) **(cat. 57, p. 102)** and *Hase-Frau* (Hare-Woman, 1990/91) **(cat. 60, p. 105)**. In drawing, Ikemura had begun with improvisational rendering of deformed people, animals, and plants **(e.g., cat. 20, p. 59, cat. 37, p. 76, cat. 32, p. 69)**, and as her sculptures came to reflect a similar approach, similar fantastic life-forms began to appear again in her drawings. In a series of charcoal drawings **(cat. 53–56, pp. 100, 103)**, landscapes are superimposed on the figures of animals. Another series depicts humorous creatures alone **(cat. 66–69, pp. 106–107)**. The multilayered ambiguity woven into these images leads us into our own memories and imagination.

Another major late-1980s turning point came in 1989, when Ikemura spent about six months in a quiet Alpine village in Switzerland. There she painted the nine works in the *Alpenindianer* (Alps Indians) series **(cat. 50–52, pp. 93–97)**. In this series Ikemura succeeded in conveying an abstract vision based on her spectacular natural surroundings. In addition to the majestic Alps, however, she also drew inspiration from East Asian landscape painting. The composition of *Skifahrer auf dem Malojasee* (Skier on Maloja Lake, 1990) **(cat. 52, p. 97)** is based on the landscape painting of Sesshū Tōyō **(fig. 2)**, the Japanese Zen monk who pioneered a unique style of ink wash painting.[8] However, the borrowing of the composition is not the only important factor. The landscape painting that developed in China in conjunction with Taoism and the philosophy of yin and yang and the five elements and was later transmitted to Japan together with Zen Buddhism depicts idealized, spiritual scenery that transcends everyday reality. For Ikemura, the essential point must have been taking actual experiences of being in the midst of the majestic Alps and transforming them into internal visions comparable to East Asian landscape painting.

About twenty years later, Ikemura began working on the series of *Cosmicscapes* that at first glance appear even more closely related to East Asian landscapes. That they have roots in the *Alpenindianer* series is easy to infer, but the two also differ fundamentally in size. *Genesis* and *Tokaido* are large enough to envelop the viewer's body (190 × 290 cm). Ikemura, who produced large-scale paintings in the 1980s **(cat. 26, p. 71, cat. 43, pp. 80/81, cat. 35, p. 75)**, had distanced herself from that mode by 1989. The

8   Kenjiro Hosaka, ed., "Long Interview with Leiko Ikemura," in *Leiko Ikemura: Transfiguration*, 219.

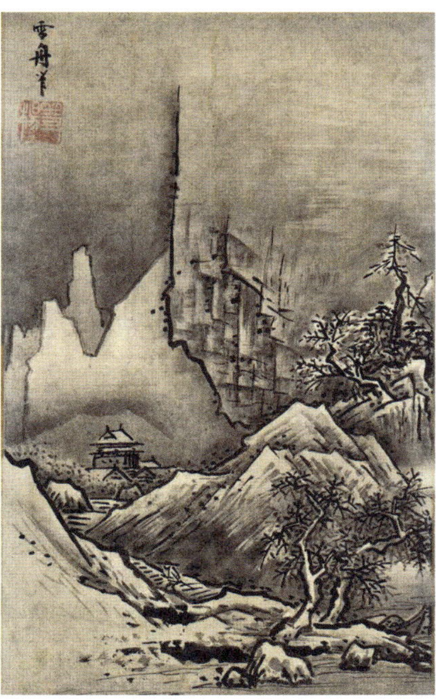

Abb. | Fig. 2 Sesshū Tōyō, *Herbst-Winter-Landschaft* (Detail, Muromachi-Zeit Ende 15. Jh./Anfang 16. Jh.) | Autumn and Winter Landscape (detail, Muromachi period, late 15th c./early 16th c.) | Tusche auf Papier | india ink on paper, 47,7 × 30,2 cm, The Tokyo National Museum

dem Leben verknüpft sind, niemals infrage gestellt wurde. Die von Ikemura präsentierten Bildwelten verlangen eben diese Betrachtungsweise.

Werfen wir vor diesem Hintergrund erneut einen Blick auf die Gemälde der *Cosmicscapes* **(Kat. 108–110, S. 144–151)**. Wir entdecken dort nach und nach Formen und Gestalten, und zwar erst mittels unserer Imagination. Ikemura hat das Bild nicht allein erschaffen, sondern der Betrachter trägt durch die Tätigkeit des Schauens dazu bei. *Genesis* – so lautet auch der Titel dieser Bildserie – stellt die Urlandschaft für die Entstehung der Bilder dar, die zugleich die Geschichte der Schöpfung der Welt ist.

Die Erschaffung der Bilder

Eintreten ins Bild Ikemura überwindet den Dualismus der Bilder und gibt ihnen ihre ursprüngliche Funktion zurück. Dezidiert verfolgt sie diese Strategie mindestens seit den 1990er-Jahren. In den späten 1980er-Jahren erhielt sie zwei wichtige Impulse, die ihre weitere Entwicklung vorantrieben. Der erste war die Begegnung mit einem neuen Material, dem Ton.

Wächter (1987) **(Kat. 48, S. 87)** ist ein frühes Exemplar der Tonarbeiten. Sie knetet die Masse und gestaltet den unförmigen Klumpen mit den Händen, auf der Suche nach bildhaften Formen. So entstehen nicht nur organische Lebewesen aus den wandlungsfähigen Tonklumpen, sondern auch Formen wie Häuser oder auch Hybride, in denen beides ineinander verschmilzt **(Kat. 49, S. 90, Abb. 1)**. Im Medium der Plastik ist das Modellieren des Tons stark von der physischen Empfindung beeinflusst. Damit steht es dem Zeichnen sehr nah, das die Bewegungen der Hand unmittelbar wiedergibt, beide bringen Bilder, die vor dem inneren Auge aufsteigen, spontan in eine Form.

Sobald Ikemura mit dem Material Ton zu arbeiten begonnen hatte, schuf sie hybride Wesen, wie sie *Stehende Figur in Petrolblau* (1990/91) **(Kat. 57, S. 102)** und *Hase-Frau* (1990/91) **(Kat. 60, S. 105)** repräsentieren. Schon in ihren frühen Zeichnungen und Skizzen hat die junge Künstlerin Menschen, Tiere und Pflanzen frei gestaltet und transformiert **(z.B. Kat. 20, S. 59, Kat. 37, S. 76, Kat. 32, S. 69)** nun tauchten derartige Fabelwesen auch in ihren skulpturalen Arbeiten auf. In einer Serie von Kohlezeichnungen **(Kat. 53–56, S. 100, 103)** überlagern sich Tiergestalten und Landschaftsformationen, während in einer weiteren Gruppe solche grotesken Kreaturen für sich dargestellt sind **(Kat. 66–69, S. 106, 107)**. Die Vielschichtigkeit dieser Bilder weckt unsere Erinnerungen sowie die Imagination.

Ein weiterer Wendepunkt war für Ikemura die Möglichkeit, sich 1989 für etwa ein halbes Jahr in einem abgeschiedenen Dorf in der Schweiz aufzuhalten. Dabei entstand die Serie *Alpenindianer* mit neun Gemälden **(Kat. 50–52, S. 93–97)**. In dieser Werkreihe gelang es ihr, die Anregungen der grandiosen Natur aus ihrer neuen Umgebung in abstrakte Formen umzusetzen. Anregungen dafür fand sie nicht nur in der erhabenen Berglandschaft, sondern sie schöpfte auch aus der fernöstlichen Landschaftsmalerei, Shanshui. *Skifahrer auf dem Malojasee* (1990) **(Kat. 52, S. 97)** soll auf einer Komposition Sesshūs **(Abb. 2)** beruhen, eines japanischen Zen-Priesters, der einen einzigartigen Stil der Tuschemalerei entwickelte.[8] Entscheidend ist jedoch nicht allein die Anlehnung an vorhandene Kompositionen – auch in der chinesischen Malerei,

8   Kenjiro Hosaka (Hrsg.), «Long Interview with Leiko Ikemura», in: Ausst.-Kat. Tokio/Tsu 2011 (wie Anm. 2), S. 219.

Girls series, for example, was painted in the late 1990s on canvases of appropriate size for an intimate and modest atmosphere. In the 2000s she again began producing large works like the *Cosmicscapes,* of which she said, "When making a large painting like this in the studio, I first lay it on the floor, then I literally get inside the picture. The first thing I do is make a construction so I can get on top of the picture and work inside it. The horizontality lets me incorporate accidental factors like bleeding and spreading. This stage comes before the generation of recognizable 'forms.' After that, I stand the painting against the wall and continue working with oil paint."[9]

Ikemura literally gets inside the scene, reacts sensitively to accidental effects, and seizes on images that emerge. She becomes part of the world of images generated on the canvas. The work is no longer subordinate to the artist as creator; instead, work and artist are fully integrated, subverting the conventional relationship between the former as a personal expression of the latter.

In a 1998 interview, Ikemura addressed the simplistic and sentimental themes of "me," saying, "The self, what people think of as 'me,' is an illusion, full of holes and far more disjointed and fluid than people think."[10] The statement shows that Ikemura stands in opposition to a discourse on the generation of images through mimesis (i.e., the idea that objects and ideas exist beforehand and that images are merely expressions of these). Ikemura has said, "It is not a question of expression. What I want to paint are not things. It is something connected to my self and my body, and I believe that that connection is a boundless source of energy. Creativity does not mean summoning up images in my head; it means experiencing connections between myself and the world through painting and drawing, which I may experience, for example, through trees. I think it is through this process that the picture emerges."[11] Ikemura is someone possessed by images, a medium or mediator for images, her work a natural outgrowth of this process.

When viewing the images that Ikemura presents, they might seem at first sight to be vague and undefined, so we mobilize our own memory, consciousness, and emotions. In doing so, we are already at one with the image. The scene that emerges depends on the viewer. The ostensibly vague and uncertain images we see in Ikemura's works encourage us to unite ourselves with them, to receive them through an experience rich in latent possibility. The creation of images occurs when Ikemura herself coalesces with them and the viewer does as well.

Where Images Are Born   In discussing Ikemura's creation of images, the role of language cannot be overlooked. Ikemura is multilingual, fluent in Spanish, German, and English, as well as her native Japanese, and also someone steeped in literature. This seems essential to her generation of images.

Ikemura states that the experience of moving to new countries and learning languages from square one allowed her "to face the world in a more immediate way."[12] She consciously moves back and forth between the two zones of word and image. This is not a back-and-forth based on mimesis but a way to assimilate herself into the myriad of images that rain down from, or rise up from, or which she herself finds in the vast spaces where neither form nor language exist. The "self = image," whether it is converted into words or evolves in the direction of images, seems to be the sole source of Ikemura's creative production.

Giorgio Agamben discusses the state of infancy, defined as the period prior to linguistic activity, which may be an effective supplementary line of thought for considering the genesis of images.[13] For Agamben, infancy is not a temporary condition that speechless infants overcome as soon as they acquire language: "Infancy and language seem to refer back to one another in a circle, in which infancy is the origin of the language and language is the origin of infancy."[14] That is, infancy is always accompanied by linguistic activities and vice versa, the two complementing each other. If we view infancy in terms of its relationship with images, images are, without a doubt, generated in the state that exists prior to the emergence of language. Ikemura's work may exist at such a threshold.

9   Tokyo National Research Institute for Cultural Properties, ed., "Teidan: Katachi no seisei wo megutte—Ikemura Leiko no baai" [Tripartite talk: On the genesis of forms: In the case of Leiko Ikemura], http://www.tobunken.go.jp/japanese/ikemura/ikemura3.html (accessed November 30, 2018).

10   Gisela Neven Du Mont and Wilfried Dickhoff, eds., *Leiko Ikemura im Gespräch mit Friedemann Malsch,* Kunst heute Nr. 20 (Cologne: Kiepenheuer & Witsch, 1998), 59.

11   Tokyo National Research Institute for Cultural Properties, "Teidan."

12   Hosaka, "Long Interview with Leiko Ikemura," 206.

13   Giorgio Agamben, *Infancy and History: The Destruction and Experience* (Brooklyn: Verso, 1993).

14   Ibid., 48.

die sich in Verbindung mit dem Daoismus und der Philosophie der Fünf-Elemente-Lehre sowie dem Yin-und-Yang-Prinzip entwickelte und zusammen mit dem Zen-Buddhismus Einzug in Japan hielt, gibt es spirituelle Landschaften jenseits der Alltagsrealität. Das Entscheidende lag für Ikemura offenbar vielmehr darin, ihre tatsächlichen Erlebnisse inmitten der überwältigenden Alpenlandschaft als innere Vision zu gestalten, die Züge der Shanshui-Malerei aufweist.

Rund 20 Jahre später begann Ikemura, sich mit den kosmischen Landschaften, den sogenannten *Cosmicscapes* zu befassen, die auf den ersten Blick der Shanshui-Malerei noch näher stehen. Man könnte meinen, dass sie ihren Ausgang mit den *Alpenindianern* nahmen, doch unterscheiden sich die Serien in einem wesentlichen Punkt: den Bildformaten. Die Gemälde *Genesis* und *Tokaido* sind so gross (190×290 cm), dass sie den Betrachter überragen. Schon in den 1980er-Jahren schuf Ikemura grossformatige Leinwandbilder **(Kat. 26, S. 71, Kat. 43, S. 80/81, Kat. 35, S. 75)**, rückte jedoch 1989 wieder davon ab. In ihren Formaten entsprechen die Mädchenporträts der intimen und harmonischen Stimmung der Bilder. Ikemura beschreibt ihre Arbeitsweise auf grossen Leinwänden wie bei den «kosmischen Landschaften» wie folgt: «Wenn ich solche grossen Arbeiten im Atelier male, lege ich sie erst auf den Boden und trete buchstäblich in das Bild ein. Als Erstes bereite ich die Struktur vor, mit der ich das Bild anlege, und male mich dann hinein. Durch die horizontale Lage entstehen zufällige, verschwommene, verlaufene Farben, Elemente, die ich dann zum Ausgangspunkt nehme für die ‹Form›-Findung. Danach stelle ich die Arbeit an die Wand und arbeite mit Ölfarben weiter.»[9]

Ikemura begibt sich regelrecht in ihre Landschaft, reagiert sensibel auf zufällige Effekte und hält erscheinende Gestalten fest. Sie wird Teil dieser Bildwelt, die auf der Leinwand entsteht. Das Werk ist nicht mehr der schaffenden Künstlerin untergeordnet, sondern wird eins mit ihr. Das herkömmliche Verhältnis zwischen einem Künstler und seinem Werk als Ausdruck der Persönlichkeit wird unterlaufen.

In einem Interview von 1998 reflektiert Ikemura das häufig vereinfachte, sentimentale Thema des «Ich»: «‹Ich› ist porös, ein Phantasma, das ist viel gebrochener, fliessender, als man denkt.»[10] Mit dieser Aussage erhebt Ikemura explizit Einwand gegen das Konzept der Generierung von Bildern durch Mimesis und gegen den Gedanken, dass die zur Darstellung gelangenden Sujets und Ideen bereits in den Künstlern existieren. In einem anderen Gespräch sagt sie: «Es ist keine Frage des Ausdrucks. Was ich malen will, sind nicht Dinge. Sondern es ist mit meinem Selbst und meinem Körper verbunden, und diese Verbindung ist eine unerschöpfliche Energiequelle. Kreativität heißt nicht, sich Bilder vorzustellen, sondern erst im Akt des Malens und des Zeichnens entsteht die Verbindung zwischen mir und der Welt. Diese kann ich zum Beispiel mittels eines Baumes erleben. Das ist der Prozess, durch den Bilder entstehen.»[11] Womöglich also ist Ikemura ein Medium, das von Bildern ergriffen wird und diese vermittelt, sodass ihr Werk natürlich aus diesem Prozess erwächst.

Wenn wir vor Ikemuras auf den ersten Blick vagen und undeutlichen Bildern stehen, aktivieren wir unsere persönlichen Erinnerungen, unser Bewusstsein und unsere Sinne. In diesem Moment sind auch wir schon mit ihren Bildern vereint. Die Landschaft, die in den Augen der Betrachter erscheint, wird je nach Sichtweise unterschiedlich sein. Die scheinbar nebelhaften und undefinierten Szenen laden uns ein, uns mit ihnen zu verbinden und sie als ein Erlebnis voller latenter Möglichkeiten zu betrachten. Die Erschaffung von Bildern geschieht, indem die Künstlerin mit der Bildwelt verschmilzt und es ihr der Betrachter nachtut.

Der Entstehungsort von Bildern Wenn wir über Ikemuras Schaffensprozess nachdenken, müssen wir auch die Rolle der Sprache einbeziehen. Man kann sich gut vorstellen, dass ihre Sprachbegabung – ausser ihrer Muttersprache Japanisch beherrscht sie auch fliessend Spanisch, Deutsch und Englisch – sowie ihre literarische Bildung eine nicht unbedeutende Auswirkung auf die Bildgenerierung haben.

9 Tokyo National Research Institute for Cultural Properties (Hrsg.), «Teidan: Kaachi no seisei wo megutte – Ikemura Leiko no baai (Tripartite talk: On the Genesis of forms: in the case of Leiko Ikemura)», Tokyo-Bunka-Kenkyûjo, Tokio 2011, http://www.tobunken.go.jp/japanese/ikemura/ikemura3.html (Abruf 30.11.2018).

10 *Leiko Ikemura im Gespräch mit Friedemann Malsch* (Kunst heute Nr. 20), hrsg. von Gisela Neven DuMont und Wilfried Dickhoff, Köln 1998, S. 59.

11 Tokyo National Research Institute (wie Anm. 9).

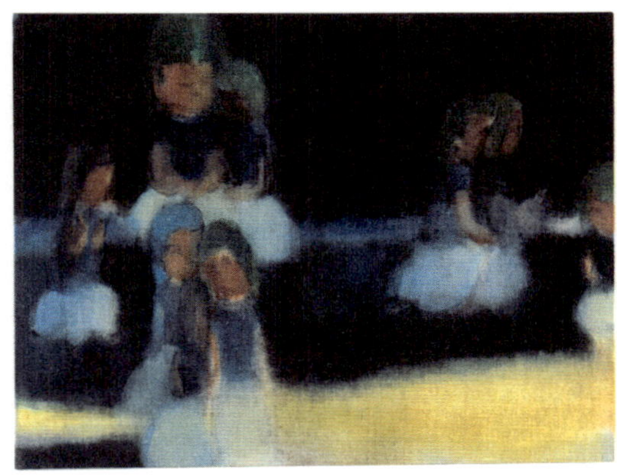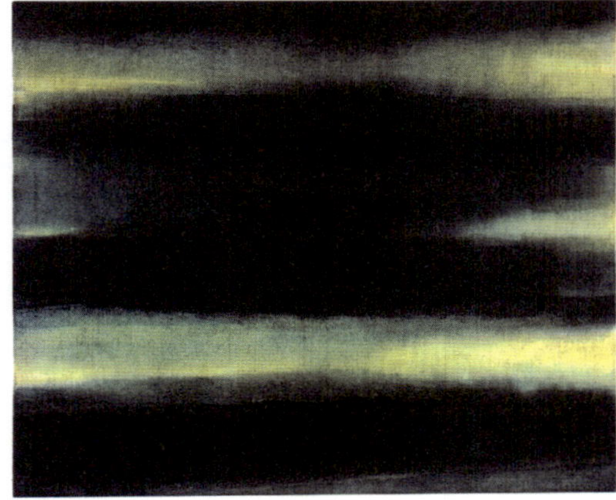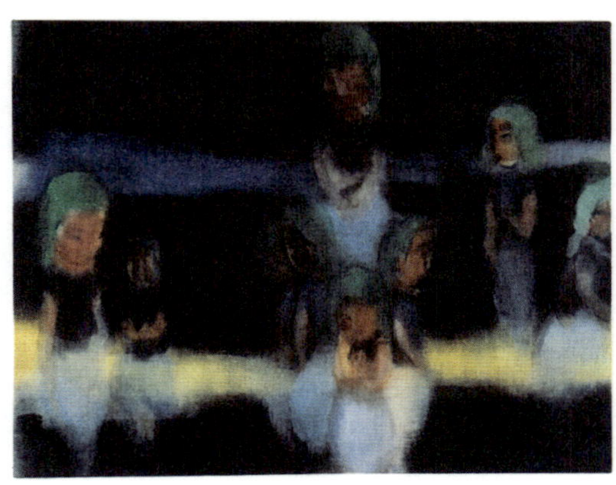

Ikemura's monochromatic backgrounds seem like zones where images are not yet clearly recognized but definitely exist in latent form, are on the verge of being generated. Ambiguous spaces often appear in Ikemura's drawings and paintings. Take, for instance, the *Girls*, whose figures adopt a variety of poses against black or monochromatic backgrounds **(cat. 88–91, pp. 124–127)**. The images appear to be emerging, descending, or transforming, in a zone like that of the infantile consciousness.

In the *Girls* paintings, a horizon line floats amid the monochromatic landscape, evoking natural elements such as the earth and sea, and prompting various interpretations. In the paintings of adolescent girls, the horizon line can be interpreted as representing the boundary between childhood and adulthood that the girls are poised to cross, thus symbolizing the various dichotomies we have established for our convenience. For Ikemura, though, images may emerge beyond such established concepts, definitions, and constraints.

Consider, for example, the triptych *Ocean* (2000/01) **(figs. 3–5)**. For the artist, who grew up near the coast, the sea was a familiar presence, both giving life and threatening death but also fascinating her as another world, one that transcends the cycles of our own. The *Ocean* series is set at night, after the sun has set and the curtain of night has fallen, the distant horizon disappearing into the pitch-black darkness. A band of light appears instead of a horizon line, and the ghosts of the girls appear as if beckoned by it. This is a scene that can appear only when the boundary between sky and sea has been invalidated.

Generation of Images and "Mother" Motif The horizon implies something else as well; namely, death. Ikemura was strongly affected by the horizontal compositions of Hans Holbein's *Dead Christ in the Tomb* (1521/22) **(fig. 6)** and Swiss painter Ferdinand Hodler's depiction of his dying partner **(fig. 7)**.[15] *Memento Mori* (2013) **(cat. 93, p. 140)** seems like Ikemura's response to such earlier examples, but it adopts a unique viewpoint. The already decaying woman's body conveys not so much grieving over death as a powerful expression of life and death as part of the great cycle of nature. The simple horizontal form and tranquil whiteness have a purity that is even refreshing.

The images of a decaying female figure in *Memento Mori* seem to be based on that of *Motherscape* (2000/01) **(fig. 8)**. There, a mother and daughter lie in the valley with a majestic mountain landscape in the background. The mother, already dead, is decaying and returning to the earth, and a similarly shaped girl lies on top of her like a cell separating from the mass of her mother. The work seems to render visible the process of images separating from images and generating new ones.

15   Hosaka, "Long Interview with Leiko Ikemura," 216.

Sie beschreibt ihre Erfahrungen, wenn sie – bedingt durch einen Ortswechsel – mit einer ihr unbekannten Sprache konfrontiert wird: «Vorübergehend die Sprache zu verlieren, ist so, als würde man mit der Welt unmittelbar in Berührung kommen.»[12] Ikemura bewegt sich bewusst zwischen den Bereichen Wort und Bild. Selbstverständlich basiert dieses Hin und Her nicht auf Mimesis, wo eins das andere repräsentiert, sondern es ist ein Prozess, sich auf die Bilder einzulassen, die in dem grossen Raum, in dem weder Form noch Sprache existieren, auf sie einströmen, in ihr aufsteigen oder die sie dort selber findet. Die Gleichung Selbst = Bild scheint der Quell ihres Schaffens zu sein, ob es nun sprachliche oder bildnerische Form erlangt.

Im Zusammenhang mit dem Entstehungsort von Bildern ist der Begriff «Infanzia» aus der Soziologie der Kindheit von Giorgio Agamben hilfreich (lat. infans = sprachlos; Phase vor der sprachlichen Handlung).[13] Das Infans-Stadium ist kein vorübergehender Zustand, den Kleinkinder durch das Erlernen von Sprache überwinden. «Kindheit und Sprache scheinen demnach in einem Zirkel aufeinander zu verweisen, in dem die Kindheit der Ursprung der Sprache und die Sprache der Ursprung der Kindheit ist.»[14]

Mit anderen Worten, Infanzia wird immer von sprachlicher Aktivität begleitet und umgekehrt – sie ergänzen sich. Stellt man nun den Vergleich mit Bildern her, so müsste der Ort, an dem diese entstehen, dem vorsprachlichen Stadium entsprechen.

In dieser Zone, in der nichts deutlich zu erkennen ist, existieren mit Sicherheit latente, potenzielle Bilder, die jederzeit in Erscheinung treten können. Diesem Ort entspricht der monochrome Grund in Ikemuras Arbeiten. In vielen ihrer Zeichnungen und Gemälde tauchen solche uneindeutigen Räume auf. In den Mädchenbildern beispielsweise **(Kat. 88–91, S. 124–127)** stehen die Figuren in verschiedensten Haltungen vor schwarzem oder einfarbigem Hintergrund. Die Bilder scheinen in einem Bereich aufzusteigen, herabzusteigen oder sich zu verwandeln, der dem kindlichen Bewusstsein entspricht. Die

im monochromen Hintergrund schwebenden horizontalen Linien sind ein wichtiger Bestandteil der Mädchenbilder. Sie evozieren nicht nur Naturelemente wie den Erdboden oder das Meer, sondern verweisen auch auf andere Dinge. Bezogen auf die als Jugendliche dargestellten Mädchen kann eine solche horizontale Spur die Grenze zwischen Kind und Erwachsener bedeuten, die sie gerade überschreiten. Darüber hinaus kann sie auch als Symbol für verschiedenste Dualismen gelten, die wir uns zurechtgelegt haben. Für Ikemura steigen die Bilder vielleicht am Horizont auf, indem sie sich über die etablierten Konzepte, Definitionen und Einschränkungen hinwegsetzen.

Als Beispiel wäre die *Ozean* betitelte dreiteilige Arbeit von 2000/01 zu nennen **(Abb. 3–5)**. Ikemura wuchs nahe der Küste auf. Das Meer war einerseits der Inbegriff des Lebens und barg zugleich tödliche Gefahr. Andererseits faszinierte es sie auch als ein Symbol für eine Welt jenseits der uns vertrauten. Die *Ozean*-Serie handelt vom nächtlichen Meer. Nach Sonnenuntergang lässt die Nacht ihren Schleier herab, und die weit entfernte Horizontlinie löst sich im stockfinsteren Schwarz auf, wird unsichtbar. In diesem Augenblick erscheinen anstelle der Horizontlinie Lichtbänder gleich einer Vision. Als würden sie von diesem Licht angelockt, schweben die Mädchen wie Geister herbei. Es ist eine Szenerie, die erst in Erscheinung tritt, wenn die Grenze zwischen Himmel und Meer ungültig geworden ist.

Die Entstehung der Bilder und das «Mutter»-Motiv

Ein anderer Aspekt, auf den die Horizontlinie verweist, ist der Tod. Ikemura berichtet, wie stark sie beeindruckt war von den Kompositionen aus horizontalen Linien in dem Werk *Der tote Christus im Grab* (1521/22) **(Abb. 6)** von Hans Holbein d. J. oder auch von Ferdinand Hodlers Darstellungen seiner sterbenden Lebensgefährtin **(Abb. 7)**.[15] *Memento mori* (2013) **(Kat. 93, S. 140)** scheint Ikemuras Antwort auf diese Motive zu sein. Hier offenbart sich jedoch eine sehr persönliche Perspektive. Der bereits verwesende weibliche Leichnam ist stärker von der Sichtweise geprägt, dass der Tod lediglich ein Teil des Kreislaufs der Natur ist, und nicht vom Schmerz über den Tod. Die schlichte, horizontal ausgerichtete Komposition und das ruhige Weiss strahlen sogar eine Art Frische aus.

Die Figur der verwesenden Frau in *Memento mori* scheint auf die Darstellung der toten Mutter in *Motherscape* (2000/01) **(Abb. 8)** zurückzugehen. Vor dem Hintergrund einer grandiosen Berglandschaft liegen Mutter und Tochter in einem Tal. Der verfallende Leichnam der Mutter ist im Begriff, zur Erde zurückzukehren, während die

12 Hosaka (Hrsg.) 2011 (wie Anm. 8), S. 206.

13 Giorgio Agamben, *Kindheit und Geschichte. Zerstörung der Erfahrung und Ursprung der Geschichte*, Frankfurt a. M. 2001.

14 Ebd., S. 71.

15 Hosaka 2011 (wie Anm. 8), S. 216.

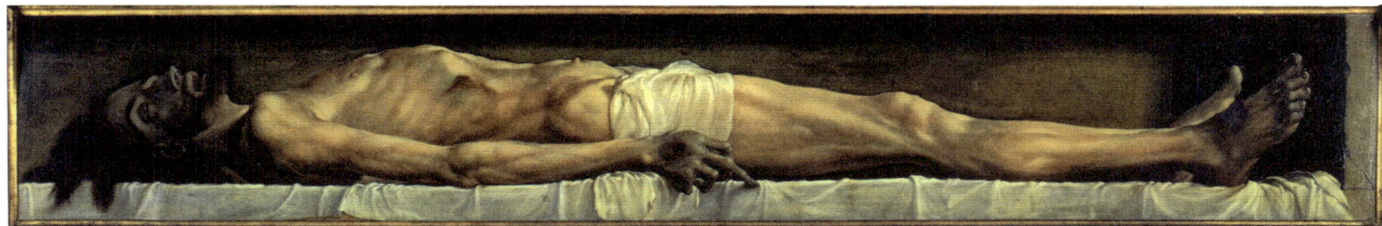

Throughout her career Ikemura has produced many works in which images overlap, including people integrated with trees and double images of rocks and people, sometimes breaking apart and sometimes generating new images. While absorbed in producing plant specimens nearly a century earlier, Klee observed the process of plants' germination from seeds, differentiation into leaves, stems, and roots, and growth and transformation at astonishing speeds, and he found therein a model for his own art production. Klee not only used vegetation as subject matter, but he used techniques reminiscent of the great chain of organic life, cutting pictures up, including their backing materials and all, joining parts together, or transferring images from one surface to another. He invalidated the traditional differentiation between works' content and form, integrating them by making the structure and generation of his images analogous to living organisms.

The mother-image seems to be an archetype of image creation for Ikemura, just as vegetation was for Klee. In the 1980s, Ikemura depicted conflict-filled scenes of mothers and children. *Unerwünschtes Kind* (Unwanted Child, 1982) **(fig. 9)** shows a mother turning her face away from her dead child, and an untitled 1984 drawing **(cat. 44, p. 86)** shows a naked mother raising her arms above her head, as if refusing to hold the child who desperately clings to her. These depictions seem to convey anxieties and ambivalence about sexual issues, motherhood, or mother figures.

However, after turning points in the late 1980s, in the 1990s Ikemura entered a new creative period, and her images of mothers and children also changed. Simple, primal sculpted figures of mothers and children appeared, including mothers holding small children to their bosoms, inspired by the artist's cat Miko **(fig. 10, cat. 73, p. 117)**. These figures often have the hollow interiors of their bodies exposed, revealing a paradoxical aspect of existence: the need for an internal void in order to have a shape. This conveys in a formal manner the emptiness and anxiety that can lurk within the bond between parents and children and is a major feature of Ikemura's sculpture in general, including her images of girls, such as *Hockende (Sich auf die Augen stützend)* (Squatting [Leaning on Eyes], 1997) **(cat. 87, p. 129)**.

Ikemura addresses the theme of mothers and children in a manner that starkly contrasts the images on this theme that have appeared throughout art history. Joining the numerous iconic images of the Virgin and Child overflowing with love and tenderness, which embody the teaching of Christ, are Egon Schiele's mother smothering her son with love by restraining him in an overly strong embrace, Paula Modersohn-Becker's mother and child rooted in the earth, expressing a paean to life, and Käthe Kollwitz's heartrending image of a mother seeking to shelter her child from the horror of war—all are inspired by something fundamentally different than Ikemura's works. The unique quality of her mother-and-child images can be seen as a manifestation of the "generation" inherent in images themselves, as aspects of generation and transformation that encompass even the world's emptiness.

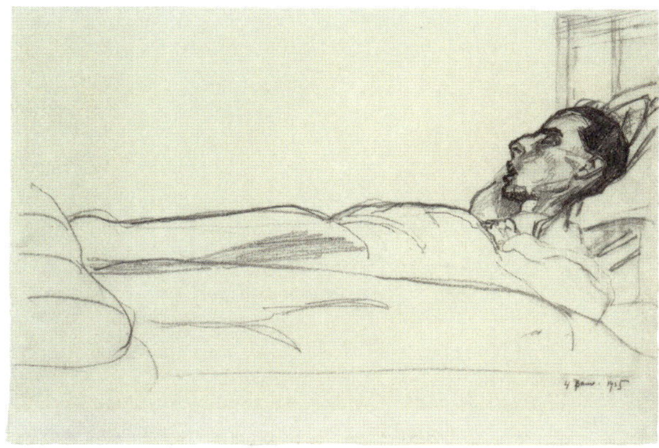

Abb. | Fig. 7 Ferdinand Hodler, *Die sterbende Valentine Godé-Darel* | Valentine Godé-Darel on Her Deathbed, 1915, Bleistift auf Papier | pencil on paper, 29,6 × 44,5 cm, Kunstmuseum Basel, Kupferstichkabinett, erworben 1943, Inv. 1943.58

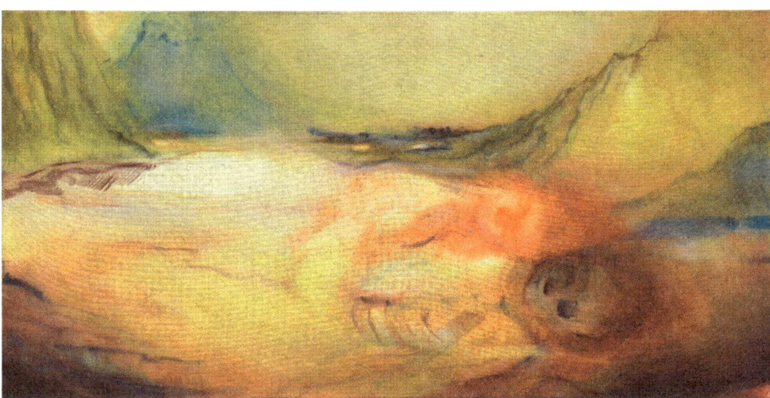

Abb. | Fig. 8 *Motherscape*, 2011/15, Öl auf Jute | oil on jute, 90 × 180 cm, Besitz der Künstlerin / Galerie Mikael Andersen

ähnlich gestaltete Tochter auf ihr liegt und sich wie durch Zellteilung von ihr abspaltet. Diese Arbeit erscheint wie eine Veranschaulichung des Vorgangs, durch den sich ein Bild von einem anderen ablöst, damit ein neues Bild entstehen kann.

In zahlreichen Werken Ikemuras, von den Anfängen bis zu ihren jüngsten Arbeiten, finden sich weitere Doppelbilder von menschlichen Gestalten. Solche, die sich mit einem Baum vereinen, oder menschliche Wesen in Felsen, wobei die Darstellungen sich manchmal selbstständig machen oder daraus neue Bilder entspringen.

In diesem Zusammenhang möchte ich noch einmal auf die Verfahrensweise von Paul Klee eingehen. Er war ein leidenschaftlicher Pflanzensammler und beobachtete, wie Samen aufkeimten und sich zu Blättern, Stielen und Wurzeln weiterentwickelten, wie eine Pflanze rasch heranwuchs und sich dabei transformierte. Darin sah er ein Modell seiner eigenen Bildproduktion. Er verwendete Pflanzen nicht nur als Motiv, sondern arbeitete mit einer Methode, die an die Grundordnung alles Lebendigen aus der Naturphilosophie erinnert: Klee schnitt Figuren und Formen inklusive deren Träger aus seinen Werken, fügte sie neu zusammen oder fertigte Abdrücke davon. Er hob die traditionelle Trennung von Form und Inhalt in der Kunst auf, indem er Struktur und Entstehungsprozess seiner Bilder gleichsetzte mit jenen lebendiger Organismen.

So wie die Pflanze für Klee ein archetypisches Sinnbild der Bildentstehung darstellte, scheint dies für Ikemura das Mutter-Motiv zu sein. In den 1980er-Jahren stellte sie konfliktbeladene Mutter-Kind-Beziehungen dar. *Unerwünschtes Kind* (1982) **(Abb. 9)** zeigt eine Mutter, die den Blick von der Leiche ihres Kindes abwendet, und auf einer unbetitelten Zeichnung aus dem Jahr 1987 ist eine nackte Mutter zu sehen, die ihre Hände weit über den Kopf streckt, um nicht ihr Kind in den Arm nehmen zu müssen, das sich verzweifelt an sie klammert **(Kat. 44, S. 86)**. In diesen Darstellungen scheinen sich Ängste und ambivalente Gefühle in Bezug auf Sexualität, Mutterschaft und Mutterfiguren zu offenbaren.

Allerdings erfahren die Darstellungen von Müttern und Kindern nach dem Wendepunkt der späten 1980er-Jahre eine deutliche Transformation. Nun treten einfach und urtümlich geformte Mutter-Skulpturen auf, die ihre Kinder – die von Ikemuras Katze Miko inspiriert sind – im Arm halten **(Abb. 10 und Kat. 73, S. 110)**. Diese Keramiken stellen oft ihr hohles Körperinneres zur Schau und führen dadurch die Paradoxie des Daseins vor Augen, die in der Notwendigkeit einer inneren Leere besteht, um eine äussere Form anzunehmen. Derartige Hohlräume sind ein wesentliches Merkmal der Skulpturen Ikemuras, auch bei Mädchenfiguren wie *Hockende (Sich auf die Augen stützend)* (1997) **(Kat. 87, S. 129)**. Bei den Mutter-Kind-Skulpturen verweist der Hohlraum auf die angstbesetzte Kehrseite der symbiotischen Beziehung.

Ikemuras Behandlung des Mutter-Kind-Themas unterscheidet sich grundlegend von bekannten Vorbildern aus der Kunstgeschichte. Die Madonna als Sinnbild der christlichen Barmherzigkeit, die Mütter Egon Schieles, die mit übertriebener Liebe den Sohn an sich zu

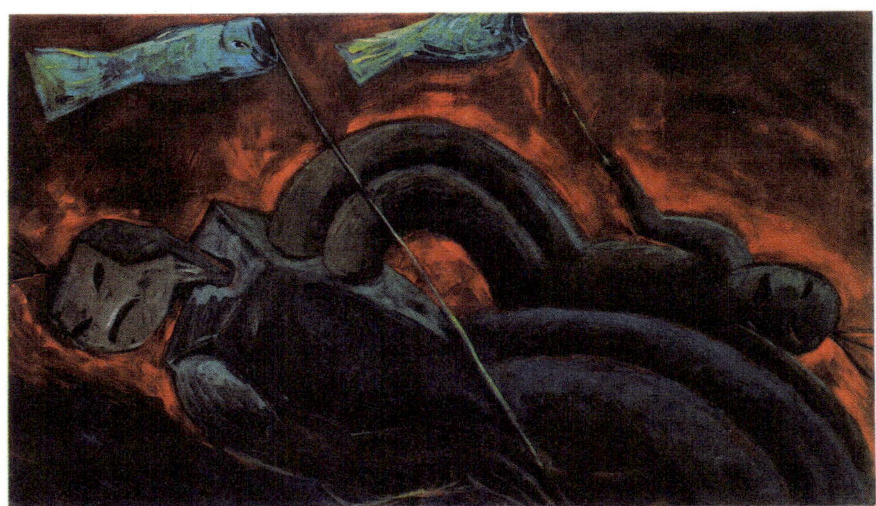

Abb. | Fig. 9 *Unerwünschtes Kind |
Unwanted Child*, 1982, Acryl auf Leinwand |
acrylic on canvas, 120 × 210 cm, Privatsammlung Basel

Ikemura recalls a turning point around 1990, when she "sought to eliminate the narrative element and make a new start by returning to the source of life itself."[16] Ikemura's images of girls, her most characteristic works of the 1990s, were a manifestation of this new start, but the mother figures that appeared at the same time also played a part in this exploration of the primal and can be seen as a breakthrough after the gender-conscious emotional expression of the 1980s. An atmosphere of mourning and prayer flows into *Usagi Kannon* (2012) **(cat. 116, p. 157)**, inspired by the artist's shock over the 2011 Tōhoku earthquake and tsunami, and *Motherscape* and the series of *Cosmicscapes* share the common ground of a primeval landscape.

Conclusion

Because images brim with potential, they continue to guide the unpredictable process of life. When images are in concert with our own inner memories and intentions, their latent power opens up new horizons of existence. If Ikemura herself is synchronized with the images she discovers, then we, the viewers, are synchronized with Ikemura through her images.

Contemporary society, founded on the control and organization of people and nature, is continually disrupted not only by natural disasters but by all sorts of human-made calamities, such as nuclear accidents. Ikemura's images—fantastical hybrid creatures, young girls, mothers with children, figures from nature, the primeval world that contains all of life and its manifestations—convey a powerful philosophy of acceptance and embrace of the diversity of those being born into this world, or to be born in the future, just as they are. The introspective world of her work—quiet, modest, and immersed deeply in its own distinctive vision—is in this sense keenly critical of the world and society surrounding us today. This vision rewards the viewer richly with revelations that only Ikemura, with a keen sensibility honed in the real between word and image, can convey.

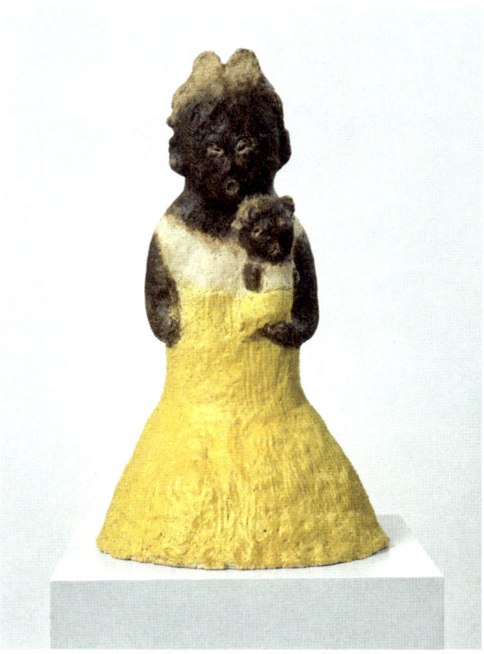

fesseln suchen, die erdverbundenen Mutterfiguren von Paula Modersohn-Becker als Hymne auf das Leben, die anrührende Darstellung von Müttern, die ihre Kinder vor den Schrecken des Krieges bewahren wollen, bei Käthe Kollwitz – mit all diesen haben Ikemuras Darstellungen nichts gemein. In der Originalität ihrer Interpretation des Themas könnte man sogar die Manifestation von Genese und Transformation – und damit verbunden das «Entstehen» aus den Werken selbst – erkennen, einschliesslich der darin enthaltenen Welt der Leere.

Ikemura erinnert sich an den Wendepunkt um 1990: «Ich versuchte neu zu starten, indem ich das Erzählerische ausschaltete und den Ursprung des Lebens aufsuchte.»[16] Ihre Mädchenbilder, die ihre für die 1990er-Jahre repräsentativsten Werke sind, waren Ausdruck dieses Neuanfangs. Doch auch die Mutterfiguren, die gleichzeitig in ihrem Werk auftauchen, spielten eine Rolle in dieser Erkundung des Ursprünglichen und können als Durchbruch nach den gender-bewussten, emotionalen Darstellungen der 1980er-Jahre gesehen werden.

Das Thema Mütterlichkeit findet sich auch in ihrem Trauer und Gebet symbolisierenden Skulptur *Usagi Kannon* (2012) **(Kat. 116, S. 157)** wieder, die aus ihrer Betroffenheit über die Katastrophe von Fukushima hervorging, während *Motherscape* und die Serie der *Cosmicscapes* die Urlandschaft als gemeinsame Grundlage haben.

Schluss

Da Bilder unendliches Potenzial bergen, können sie den unvorhersehbaren Verlauf des Lebens begleiten. Die latente Kraft der Bilder eröffnet einen neuen Horizont des Daseins, wenn diese mit unseren Erinnerungen und Intentionen zusammenklingen. Wenn wir Leiko Ikemura als vereint sehen mit den Bildern, die sie entdeckt, so sind wir durch ihre Bilder mit der Künstlerin in Einklang.

Die heutige Gesellschaft, die sich durch ihre Beherrschung und Systematisierung von Mensch und Natur definiert, wird nicht allein durch Naturkatastrophen, sondern auch durch menschengemachte Katastrophen erschüttert, wie beispielsweise Unfälle in Atomkraftwerken. Ikemuras vielseitige Bildwelt, die sie mit hybriden Wesen, fantastischen Kreaturen, Mädchen, Mutter-Kind-Darstellungen und Naturwesen geschaffen hat, ebenso wie die archaische Welt, die alles Leben beinhaltet, und dessen vielfältige Erscheinungen: All dies wird von der kraftvollen Grundidee getragen, die Dinge in ihrer Vielfalt so zu akzeptieren, wie sie sind, ganz gleich, ob sie schon in der Welt sind oder noch zur Welt kommen werden. Es ist eben diese stille, bescheidene und selbstreflexive Bildwelt, die tief in ihrer ganz eigenen Vision versunken zu sein scheint, durch die Ikemura deutliche Kritik an der Gegenwart übt. So gesehen, sind diese Werke reich an Offenbarungen, die allein Ikemura, die zwischen Bildsprachen und Worten ihre Sinne zu schärfen pflegt, zu vermitteln vermag.

16 Ebd., S. 48.

being silent —
A Letter to Leiko

Stefan Kraus

Dear Leiko,

Over the past two decades we have discussed your work at your studio now and then, as well as presenting our dialogue several times in public, and now you have asked me to write about your work. But speech and text are different forms, and, to be honest, if I had the choice I'd rather remain silent this time. That strikes me as indispensable as a first reaction to art in general, but it is especially important for me with regard to your work. In any case, being silent with art means more to me than talking about it. Because only silence creates the conditions in which we become capable of saying something, allowing the right words to find us, rather than the other way around, ensuring that in the act of seeing and subsequent reflection, words come together that we didn't know beforehand. Might remaining silent be a communicable form that speaks of an artistic work? I don't know. But I am sure that silence can be shared as a connecting and expressive experience with your works in the same way it can be shared with a familiar person at special moments. In such moments, it creates something of substance and is far more than a state of helplessness.

There are as many ways of being silent as there are reasons to do so, and they can all be found in your work. When I think of your sculptures, which you shape out of clay with your hands like pots, then my first impulse is a silence of curiosity and an inclination to approach them, to walk round them, to visually scan their surfaces, which are full of details, full of handwritten traces that form a whole only when looked at this way. But at the same time, it is a silence touched by the unshielded vulnerability, the deformation of crippled limbs, and the traces of violence that are troublingly paired here with beauty. It is a bashful silence because, since your earliest drawings, the hints of erotic fantasies have been so unveiled and open; a baffled silence in the face of the fragment, the seemingly unfinished, whose state remains beyond words. It is a silence of pain at the sight of the eyes punched into the soft material, the abrupt incisions in the finely worked bodies, and the sealed mouths that allow no words. It can be a weary silence that shares an expression of exhaustion with your sculptures, while, in the face of graceful plant and animal forms in the process of becoming or decaying, it becomes a tense silence of expectation. Looking at the girlish figures and their exquisite colored glazes, the perception of pain connects with a silence of quiet joy, like being in the company of alien beings who act as friendly guides. But your sculptures are passive, their sole purpose is to expose themselves to our gaze. In keeping with Buddhist tradition, their actions are directed wholly inward. With this self-focused autonomy, they embody a state of personality formation that reminds me of children at play, lost to the world. Do you remember how quickly words destroyed the space dreamed up by the imagination, a space taken for real? Is it not generally the case that words, more than speaking about the reality of the artwork, transport unrelated content that restricts their ability to translate the specificity of what has been perceived? Do words with their fixing not rob your works of the floating ambivalence that characterizes them?

Of course, as someone who writes about art, words are more or less my only choice, and I have long since returned to them here. But in order to say something that stands in meaningful relation to your work, they must be chosen with reference to their provisional quality. Because they are merely tools to approach a medium whose actual meaning is conveyed visually. With your haikus, you yourself have chosen a path via the open form of poetry that depends on the reader's interpretative contribution. And, whereas in speech, words remain malleable and fleeting, changing to follow possible ways of seeing

schweigen –
Ein Brief an Leiko

Stefan Kraus

Liebe Leiko,

nachdem wir in den vergangenen zwei Jahrzehnten immer wieder einmal im Atelier über Deine Arbeit gesprochen und den gemeinsamen Dialog auch mehrfach öffentlich geführt haben, hast Du mich um einen Text gebeten, der sich mit Deiner Arbeit beschäftigt. Doch Rede und Text sind zweierlei Form – und ehrlich, wenn ich als Kunstvermittler die Wahl hätte, würde ich diesmal lieber schweigen. Das scheint mir als erste Reaktion auf Kunst im Allgemeinen unabdingbar zu sein, doch ist es mir gegenüber Deinen Werken besonders wesentlich. Jedenfalls bedeutet mir das Schweigen mit Kunst noch mehr als das darüber Reden. Denn erst das Schweigen schafft die Voraussetzung dafür, dass wir sprachfähig werden und zulassen, dass nicht wir die passenden Worte finden, sondern diese uns, dass sich im Akt des Sehens und in der nachsinnenden Reflexion solche Worte fügen, die wir nicht zuvor schon gewusst haben. Ob das Schweigen auch eine mittelbare Form sein kann, die Auskunft über eine künstlerische Arbeit gibt? Ich weiss es nicht. – Ich bin aber sicher, dass man das Schweigen als verbindende und ausdrucksstarke Erfahrung mit Deinen Werken ebenso teilen kann wie man es in besonderen Momenten mit einem vertrauten Menschen teilt. Dann schafft es durchaus Inhalt und ist weit mehr als nur ein Zustand der Hilflosigkeit.

Es gibt so viele Arten wie Gründe des Schweigens, und sie alle finden sich in Deinen Werken wieder. Wenn ich an Deine Skulpturen denke, die Du wie Gefässe aus Ton mit den Händen formst, dann ist es im ersten Impuls ein Schweigen der Neugierde und der Zuneigung, die es erfordern, sich ihnen anzunähern, sie zu umkreisen, um mit den Augen tastend über ihre Oberflächen zu fahren, die voller Details sind, voller handschriftlicher Spuren, die sich erst in der Betrachtung zu einem Ganzen fügen. Doch im gleichen Augenblick ist es ein betroffenes Schweigen, ob der schutzlosen Verletzlichkeit, der de-

formierten Glieder und der Spuren von Gewalt, die sich darin auf verstörende Weise mit Schönheit paaren. Es ist ein Schweigen aus Scham, weil seit Deinen frühen Zeichnungen die Andeutungen erotischer Fantasien so unverborgen offen liegen; ein Schweigen aus Ratlosigkeit gegenüber dem Fragment, dem scheinbar Unfertigen, dessen Zustand noch vor den Worten bleibt. Es ist ein Schweigen des Schmerzes beim Anblick der in das weiche Material eingestochenen Augen, der unvermittelten Cuts, die in die fein bearbeiteten Körper einschneiden, und der verschlossenen Münder, die keine Begriffe zulassen. Ist es zuweilen ein mattes Schweigen, das den Ausdruck der Erschöpfung mit deinen Skulpturen teilt, so wandelt es sich angesichts der Anmutung von Tieren und Pflanzenformen, die im Werden oder auch im Vergehen begriffen sind, zu einer gespannten Erwartung. Bei der Betrachtung Deiner mädchenhaften Figuren und ihrer exquisiten farbigen Glasuren verbindet sich die Wahrnehmung des Schmerzes mit einem Schweigen in stiller Freude, als würde man sich in einer Gesellschaft fremder Wesen aufhalten, die uns freundlich begleiten. Doch Deine Skulpturen sind passive Akteure, deren Bestimmung allein darin besteht, sich unseren Blicken auszuliefern. Ihre Handlung ist – buddhistischer Lehre entsprechend – ganz nach innen gerichtet. Mit dieser auf sich selbst bezogenen Autonomie verkörpern sie einen Zustand der Persönlichkeitsbildung, die mich an das selbstvergessene Spiel der Kinder erinnert. Weisst Du noch, wie schnell Worte den mit der Fantasie erträumten, wie für die Wirklichkeit angenommenen Raum zerstört haben? Ist es nicht allgemein so, dass Worte, weit mehr als etwas über die Wirklichkeit des Kunstwerks auszusagen, davon unabhängige Inhalte transportieren, die ihre Möglichkeit der spezifischen Übersetzung des Wahrgenommenen einschränken? Gehen mit der Festlegung der Worte nicht jene schwebenden Ambivalenzen verloren, die Deine Werke auszeichnen?

and experiencing, always subject to being tried and tested and discarded, in writing—especially with the finality of print—they run a greater risk of being unambiguous, putting them at odds with your work. In that work, you effortlessly bring opposites together while leaving this connection as open as possible, allowing for personal impressions and evaluations. Which is why the concrete coincides with the abstract, the real with the surreal, the lasting with the temporary, the monumental with the intimate, and the conscious with the unconscious. But the alliance of beauty and pain seems to me to be the most important of all the supposed opposites you sustain in your work, in order not to end up in the realm of kitsch. I want to find different words and, with the letter, a different form. A form that now seems as anachronistic as your works, which add up to a statement making no distinction between past and present, presence and memory, dream and reality, fragility and strength, life and death.

The world of experience reflected in this work leads from a childhood in Japan to Europe, first for a period of study in Spain and then, before you settled in Germany, several years in, of all places, Switzerland. There could hardly be a greater contrast than that between your early work, with its unbridled chaotic energy, and any form of civic order. Your ego exploded in these years, you once told me, referring to the expressive force of your early paintings and drawings. We also spoke about how the country of your birth and that of your voluntary exile are linked by recent history. The upheavals of World War II have inscribed themselves into the memory of both Japan and Germany. Both their attempts to mask the tragedy they had suffered with a facade of growing prosperity and their tangled dealings with collective guilt were experienced by you in all their dubiousness and abysmal falsehood. You catapulted yourself out of your own society in search of possibilities for an artistic processing of trauma, trod in the footsteps of Goya and El Greco, followed Matisse, Picasso, and Kirchner, stepped into the shoes of Joseph Beuys, then emancipated yourself from these models with feminist radicalism, leaving them all behind like a shed cocoon. Both fascinated and repelled, you reveled in the brutal and passionate drama of medieval Europe, not least in an attempt to overcome the insurmountable nightmare of Hiroshima and Nagasaki. Reduced to black and white, your early chemigrams look like nightmares manifesting as pictures, like projections from the shadowy realm of our consciousness that connect the animal and the abstract in ways that cannot be named. To get closer to holistic thinking and feeling, you dreamed your way into creatures, sprouted wings, settled on trees and rocks, casting a furtive glance at the world from a sitting or reclining position. This has remained your viewpoint to this day.

You didn't need Fukushima to see the brutality with which we ignore creation, behaving on this earth as if plenty more were held in reserve. On the contrary, it hit you so hard that you were unable to make art for some time. Instead, you joined forces with others and became politically active by curating a group show. One year later, you made a five-part series of large-format landscape paintings that refer to Fukushima, expressing not only the longing for all wounds to be healed in an Eden-like unity of human beings and nature, but also the toxic whiff of ecological disaster and the apocalyptic mood it creates. It seems to me that the disaster of Fukushima, which (contrary to what waning media interest might suggest) stigmatizes your country like a bleeding open wound, brought you closer to your roots in a Japanese aesthetic. Your painting is characterized by the flowing lightness of gestural marks, freely wielded brushstrokes modeled on the calligrapher's sure command of pen and

Sicher, als Kunstvermittler und Autor habe ich fast keine andere Wahl als die der Worte, bei denen ich längst wieder angekommen bin. Doch um etwas auszusagen, das mit Deinem Werk in einer sinnstiftenden Relation steht, wollen sie mit dem Hinweis auf ihre Vorläufigkeit gewählt sein. Denn sie sind nur Werkzeuge der Annäherung an ein Medium, dessen eigentlicher Sinn sich visuell vermittelt. Du selbst wählst mit Haikus den Weg über die offene Form der Lyrik, die auf die interpretierende Leistung des Lesers angewiesen ist. Und während die Worte beim Reden formbar und flüchtig bleiben, der wechselnden Empfindung möglicher Sicht- und Wirkungsweisen folgen, während sie darin ausprobiert, geprüft und wieder verworfen werden können, steht das Schreiben – zumal mit der Endgültigkeit des Gedruckten – in der weit grösseren Gefahr der Eindeutigkeit und damit in einem unmittelbaren Widerspruch zu Deinem Werk. Denn mit scheinbarer Leichtigkeit verbindest Du darin Gegensätzliches und lässt diese Verbindung so weit als möglich offen, um individuelle Eindrücke und Wertungen zu ermöglichen. Deshalb fällt das Konkrete mit dem Abstrakten zusammen, das Reale mit dem Surrealen, das Bleibende mit dem Flüchtigen, das Monumentale mit dem Intimen und das Bewusste mit dem Unbewussten. Der Bund von Schönheit und Schmerz aber scheint mir der Wesentlichste aller vermeintlichen Gegensätze zu sein, die Du in Deiner Arbeit aushältst, um nicht im Kitsch zu landen. Ich möchte andere Worte und mit dem Brief eine andere Form dafür finden. Eine Form, die ebenso aus der Zeit gefallen zu sein scheint wie Deine Werke. Denn sie kennen keinen Unterschied zwischen Vergangenheit und Gegenwart, Präsenz und Erinnerung, zwischen Traum und Wirklichkeit, Fragilität und Stärke, Leben und Tod.

Der Erfahrungsraum, der sich darin spiegelt, führt von einer Kindheit in Japan nach Europa, zunächst für einen Studienaufenthalt in Spanien und dann – noch vor Deiner Beheimatung in Deutschland – für einige Jahre in die Schweiz. Ausgerechnet in die Schweiz, denke ich, denn einen grösseren Gegensatz als Dein vor ungebremster und chaotischer Energie überbordendes Frühwerk zur jeder Form der bürgerlichen Ordnung vermag ich mir kaum vorzustellen. Dein «Ich» sei in diesen Jahren explodiert, meintest Du einmal mit Bezug auf die expressive Wucht der frühen Bilder und Zeichnungen. Wir kamen auch darauf zu sprechen, dass es zwischen dem Land Deiner Herkunft und dem Deines frei gewählten Exils eine Verbindung über die nicht allzu ferne Geschichte gibt. Die Verwerfungen des Zweiten Weltkriegs haben sich in das Gedächtnis dieser Gesellschaften eingeschrieben. Deren Versuch, einerseits die erlittene Tragödie mit einer Fassade des wachsenden Wohlstands zu überspielen wie andererseits die Verstrickung in kollektive Schuld, hast Du in seiner ganzen Fragwürdigkeit und bodenlosen Falschheit erlebt. Du hast Dich aus der eigenen Kultur herauskatapultiert, um nach Möglichkeiten der künstlerischen Bewältigung vorhandener Traumata zu forschen, bist auf Goyas und El Grecos Spuren gewandelt, Matisse, Picasso und Kirchner gefolgt, auch in die Haut eines Joseph Beuys geschlüpft, um Dich mit feministischer Radikalität von allen Vorbildern zu emanzipieren und sie hinter Dir zurückzulassen wie einen abgestossenen Kokon. Du hast Dich so fasziniert wie abgeschreckt an der brutalen Passionsdramatik des europäischen Mittelalters berauscht, wohl auch im Versuch, den nicht zu bewältigenden Albtraum von Hiroshima und Nagasaki zu überwinden. Reduziert auf Schwarz und Weiss, wirken Deine frühen Chemigramme wie bildgewordene Albträume, wie Projektionen aus dem Schattenreich unseres Bewusstseins, das Kreatürliches mit Abstraktem unbenennbar verbindet. Um dem ganzheitlichen Denken und Fühlen näherzukommen, hast Du Dich in Kreaturen hineingeträumt, Dir Flügel wachsen lassen, hast Dich auf Bäumen und Felsen niedergelassen und beobachtest die Welt sitzend wie liegend mit lauerndem Blick. Dies ist bis heute Deine Perspektive.

ink achieved by constant repetition. In the combinations of oil and tempera that you pile up in countless layers, mixed with pure pigments, on unprimed canvas or rough jute, you have succeeded in transferring the transparency of watercolors to large formats. With multiple washes of color, you create pictorial spaces where details of landscapes or figures take shape with hints of outlines, while the task of identifying the specifics is left to the viewer. As is often the case in painting, a lack of focus is the actual quality of what is portrayed. In their composition and their many-layered depth, your most recent pictures in particular recall the landscapes of Japanese woodcut printing, as perfected by Hokusai and Hiroshige.

With detours via medieval Europe, German romanticism, and Western classical modernism, you have returned to the nature religion of your home country, a religion that manifests itself, among others, in popular worship at sacred sites and shrines. Shintoism has one if its centers in the prefecture where you were born. Fine art and literature contain many examples of people finding themselves by moving away and experiencing the unfamiliar. In one of our conversations, you rightly referred to yourself as "cosmopolitan," knowing that globalization remains a purely economic factor only as long as one pretends to be able to overlook the cultural traditions of specific regions. As panoramas of mythical landscapes and as accounts of personified nature, your paintings are disconcertingly untimely. With emphatic insistence, they call for a rethinking of our purely empirical attitudes, bringing spirituality back into play in our secular age. They strike me as proposals for a new religion that combines the oldest traditions of animist thinking with the consciousness of a present that thinks only in fragments and bases everything on the individual. A religion that is aware of the loss of paradise and that wishes to reconcile us with maltreated nature and its creatures, not by masking the almost unbearable ills and the damage done, but by integrating them into art as an aesthetic of pain, presenting them as trophies of a life that is authentic, albeit far from ideal. Here, rather than being projected into some metaphysical zone beyond our world, faith focuses on an expanded experience of all worldly phenomena. Your sculpture and painting are animated by your struggle to reconcile opposites. In them, more than ever, I experience an awe of the world that leaves me speechless.

Du hast Fukushima nicht gebraucht, um die Brutalität zu erkennen, mit der wir die Schöpfung ignorieren und uns auf dieser Erde verhalten, als gäbe es noch etliche davon in Reserve. Im Gegenteil, es hat Dich so schwer getroffen, dass Du für eine Weile unfähig warst, künstlerisch zu arbeiten. Du hast Dich stattdessen im Verbund mit anderen und mit den Möglichkeiten der bildenden Kunst in einer von Dir kuratierten Gruppenausstellung politisch betätigt. Mit einem fünfteiligen Gemälde-Zyklus grosser Landschaften, der ein Jahr später entstand, hast Du auf Fukushima Bezug genommen und der Sehnsucht nach Heilung aller Wunden, nach der paradiesischen Einheit von Mensch und Natur darin ebenso Ausdruck gegeben wie dem giftigen Hauch des ökologischen Abgrundes und der Endzeitstimmung, die er produziert. Mir scheint, die Katastrophe von Fukushima, die – anders als das abnehmende Medieninteresse daran suggeriert – Deine Heimat stigmatisiert, wie eine offene, blutende Wunde, hat Dich Deinen Wurzeln in der japanischen Ästhetik noch nähergebracht. Deine Malerei kennzeichnet die fliessende Leichtigkeit gestischer Farbaufträge, deren frei geführte Pinselschwünge die durch stete Wiederholung erlangte Sicherheit der Tuschpinselzeichnung zum Vorbild haben. In der Verbindung von Öl- und Temperafarben, die Du in etlichen Lagen und vermischt mit reinen Pigmenten auf ungrundierte Leinwände oder auf grobe Jute schichtest, ist es Dir gelungen, die lasierende Transparenz des Aquarells in das grosse Format zu übertragen. Mit den wässrigen Verläufen der Farblagen realisierst Du Bildräume, in denen sich mit angedeuteten Konturen landschaftliche oder figurale Details herausbilden, deren konkrete Erkennbarkeit dem Betrachter vorenthalten bleibt. Die Unschärfe bildet – wie so oft in der Malerei – die eigentliche Qualität des Dargestellten. In ihrer Komposition und mehrschichtigen Tiefe erinnern gerade Deine jüngeren Gemäldezyklen an die narrative Dichte der Emaki, jener auf Querrollen ausgebreiteten Bilderzählungen, und an die Landschaftsdarstellungen des japanischen Holzschnitts, die Hokusai und Hiroshige zur Meisterschaft führten.

Mit dem Umweg über das europäische Mittelalter, die deutsche Romantik und die westliche klassische Moderne bist Du zur Naturreligion Deiner Heimat zurückgekehrt, die sich gerade auch in der volkstümlichen Verehrung heiliger Orte, der sogenannten Schreine offenbart. Der Shintoismus hat in der Präfektur Deiner Geburt eines seiner Zentren. Es gibt zahlreiche Beispiele von Künstlern und Literaten, deren Identitätsfindung sich erst über die Entfernung und das Fremde vollzogen hat. In einem unserer Gespräche hast Du Dich zu Recht als «Kosmopolitin» bezeichnet, wohl wissend, dass Globalisierung nur so lange ein Wirtschaftsfaktor bleibt, wie man sich einbildet, über die kulturellen Traditionen der Regionen hinwegsehen zu können. Als Panoramen mythischer Landschaften und als Zeugnisse personifizierter Natur sind Deine Gemälde auf eine irritierende Weise unzeitgemäss. Mit eindringlicher Beharrlichkeit fordern sie ein Überdenken unserer sich nur am Faktischen orientierenden Haltung ein und bringen in einer säkularen Zeit die Spiritualität erneut ins Spiel. Sie erscheinen mir wie die Entwürfe zu einer neuen Religion, die älteste Traditionen animistischer Vorstellungen mit dem Bewusstsein einer nur noch in Fragmenten denkenden und vom Individuum ausgehenden Gegenwart verbindet. Einer Religion, die um den Verlust des Paradieses weiss und uns mit der geschundenen Natur und der deformierten Kreatur versöhnen möchte, indem sie die kaum auszuhaltenden Abgründe und die erlittenen Verletzungen nicht kaschiert, sondern als Ästhetik des Schmerzes in die Kunst einarbeitet und sie wie Trophäen eines nicht idealisierten, aber authentischen Lebens präsentiert. Der Glaube wird darin nicht in einen metaphysischen, jenseitigen Bereich projiziert, sondern er richtet sich auf die erweiterte Erlebbarkeit aller diesseitigen Phänomene. Skulptur und Malerei sind von Deinem Ringen um eine Versöhnung der Gegensätze beseelt. Ich erlebe darin mehr denn je ein grosses Staunen vor der Welt, das mich sprachlos macht.

Prelude to Reflection

In the early 1980s, Leiko Ikemura communicates emotional and physical states as well as interpersonal relationships in drawings that are small but all the more powerfully expressive, though at times ungainly. She draws without hesitation or correction with a soft and fluid charcoal pencil. She tells no stories but rather creates snapshots of her interior world. These are not preparatory studies for paintings. They are haiku-like notes that are entirely self-contained. Not until 1985 do the drawings become larger and more dense. Hatching is added. This makes the drawings seem more composed but still impulsive and expressive.

The groundbreaking *Kamikaze* (1980) points in the direction Ikemura's art will take. Executed in a flat, painterly manner in dispersion paint, the work on paper is inspired by a press photograph that the artist interprets freely. It is a symbol for the unnecessary waste of human life and highlights the atrocity and meaninglessness of war, the consequences of which marked Ikemura's childhood in Japan. By tipping the horizon unnaturally toward the left, Ikemura heightens the drama and emphasizes the inevitability of the impending crash. The scene heralds pain and lasting injury.

Im Vorfeld der Reflexion

In kleinen, aber umso kraftvolleren, expressiven und manchmal auch sperrigen Zeichnungen bringt Leiko Ikemura Anfang der 1980er-Jahre emotionale und körperliche Zustände sowie zwischenmenschliche Beziehungen zum Ausdruck. Mit dem weichen und beweglichen Kohlestift zeichnet sie ohne zu zögern und ohne zu korrigieren. Sie erzählt keine Geschichten, sondern schafft Momentaufnahmen ihrer Gedankenwelt. Es sind keine Vorstudien für Gemälde, sondern Haiku-ähnliche Notizen, die in sich abgeschlossen sind. Erst um 1985 werden die Zeichnungen grösser und dichter. Schraffuren kommen hinzu. Die Arbeiten wirken stärker durchkomponiert, aber immer noch impulsiv und ausdrucksstark.

Kamikaze (1980) ist wegweisend für Ikemuras Kunst. Das mit Dispersionsfarbe flächig und malerisch ausgeführte Werk auf Papier ist inspiriert von einem Pressefoto, das sie frei umgesetzt hat. Es ist ein Sinnbild für die Verschwendung von Menschenleben und verdeutlicht die Grausamkeit und Sinnlosigkeit des Krieges, dessen Folgen Ikemuras Kindheit in Japan prägten. Indem sie den Horizont unnatürlich nach links neigt, steigert sie die Dramatik und betont die Unausweichlichkeit des bevorstehenden Zusammenpralls. Die Szene kündigt Schmerz und bleibende Versehrtheit an.

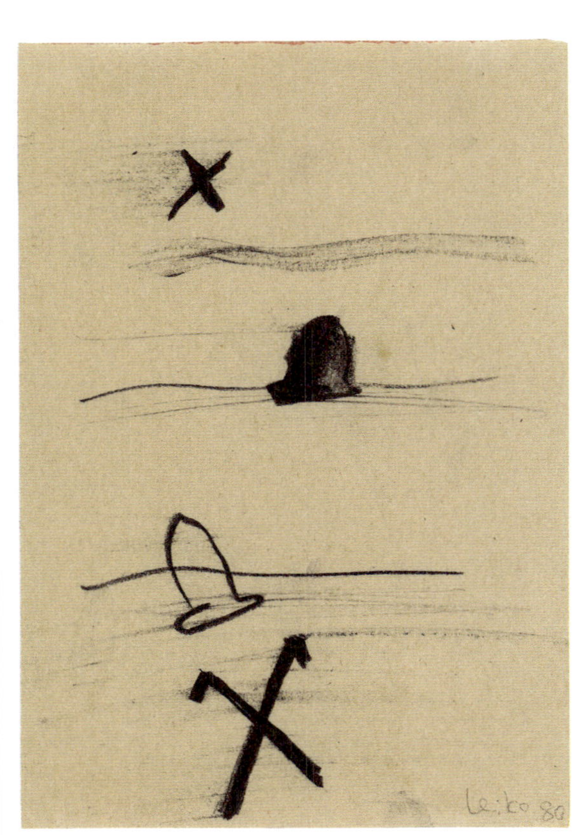

Ohne Titel | Untitled, 1980
Bleistift und Kohle
auf Papier | Pencil and
charcoal on paper,
21×14,7 cm
[Kat. | cat. 2]

Ohne Titel | Untitled, 1981
Kohle auf Papier |
Charcoal on paper,
21×29,7 cm
[Kat. | cat. 10]

Ohne Titel | Untitled, 1981
Kohle auf Papier |
Charcoal on paper,
14,7×21 cm
[Kat. | cat. 8]

*In einem Hotel in
Moskau* | In a Hotel in
Moscow, 1981
Kohle auf Papier |
Charcoal on paper,
21×14,7 cm
[Kat. | cat. 5]

Ohne Titel | Untitled, 1981
Kohle auf Papier |
Charcoal on paper,
21×14,7 cm
[Kat. | cat. 6]

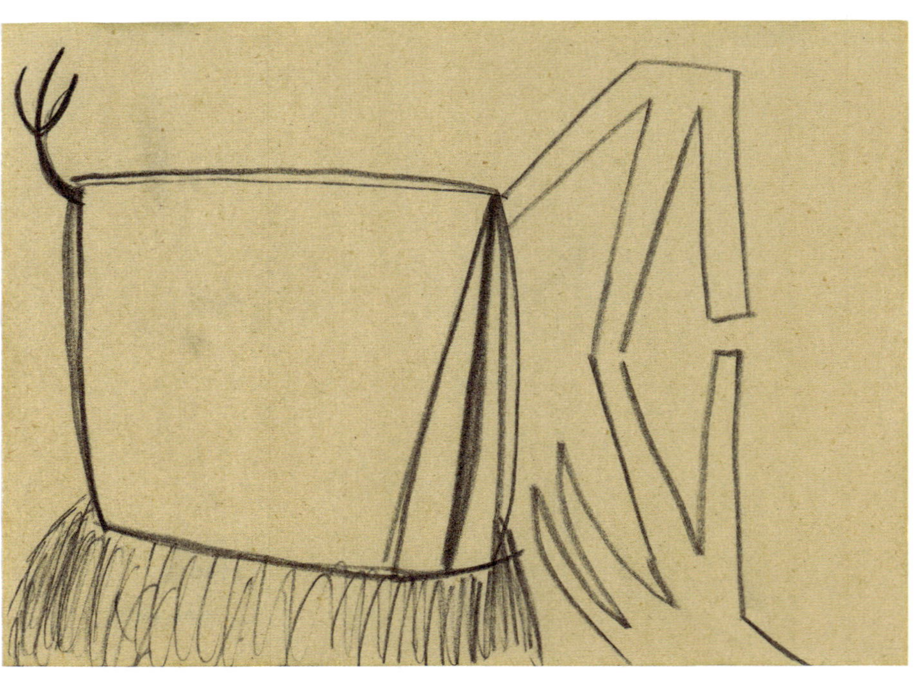

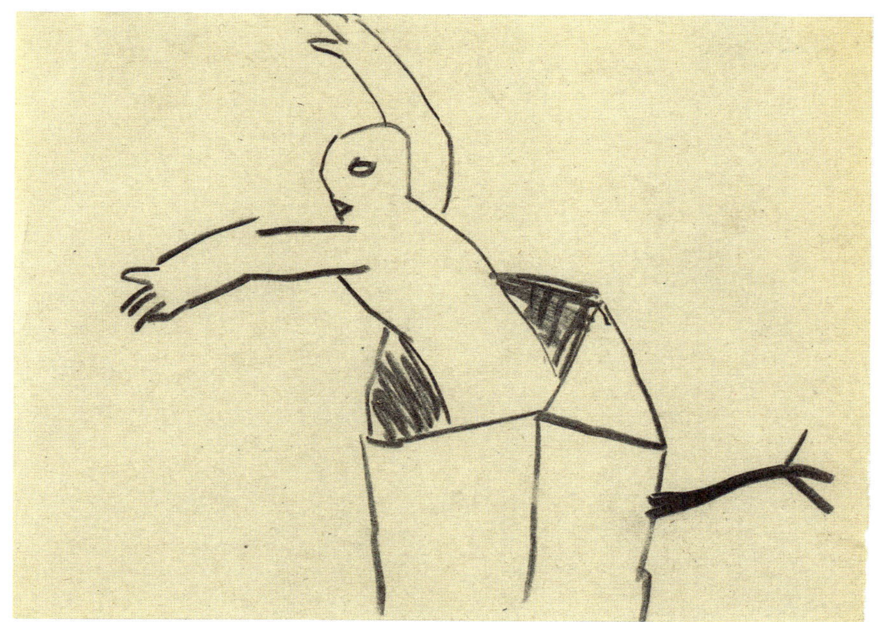

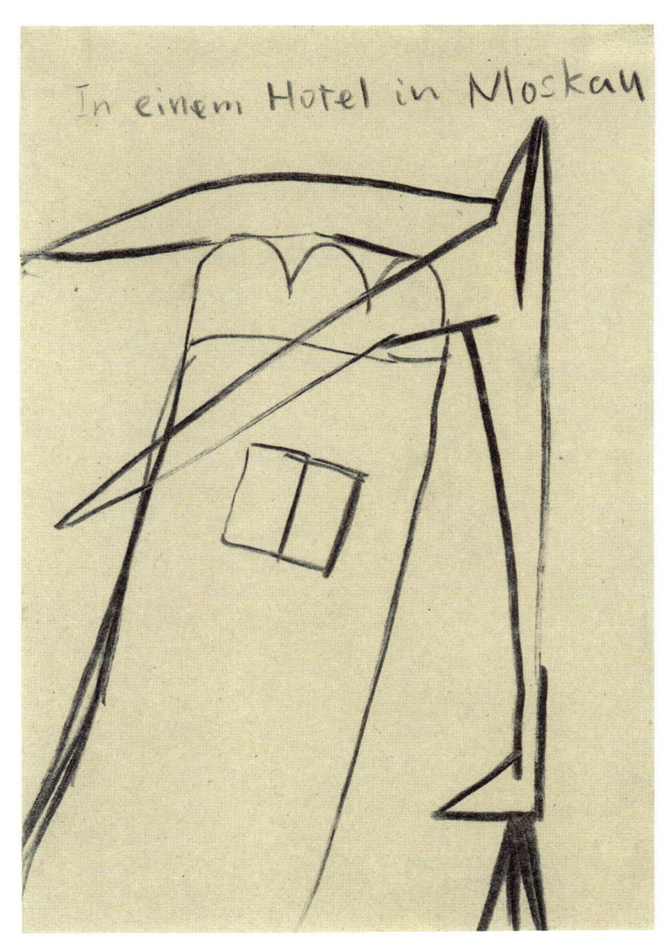
In einem Hotel in Moskau

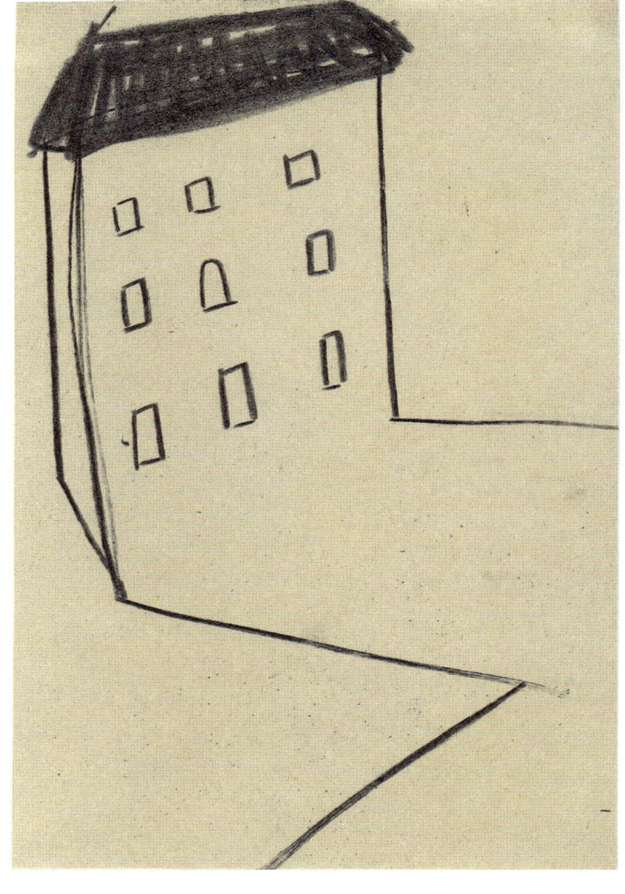

Ohne Titel | Untitled, 1981
Kohle auf Papier |
Charcoal on paper,
21×14,7 cm
[Kat. | cat. 7]

Ohne Titel | Untitled, 1981
Kohle auf Papier |
Charcoal on paper,
21×29,7 cm
[Kat. | cat. 9]

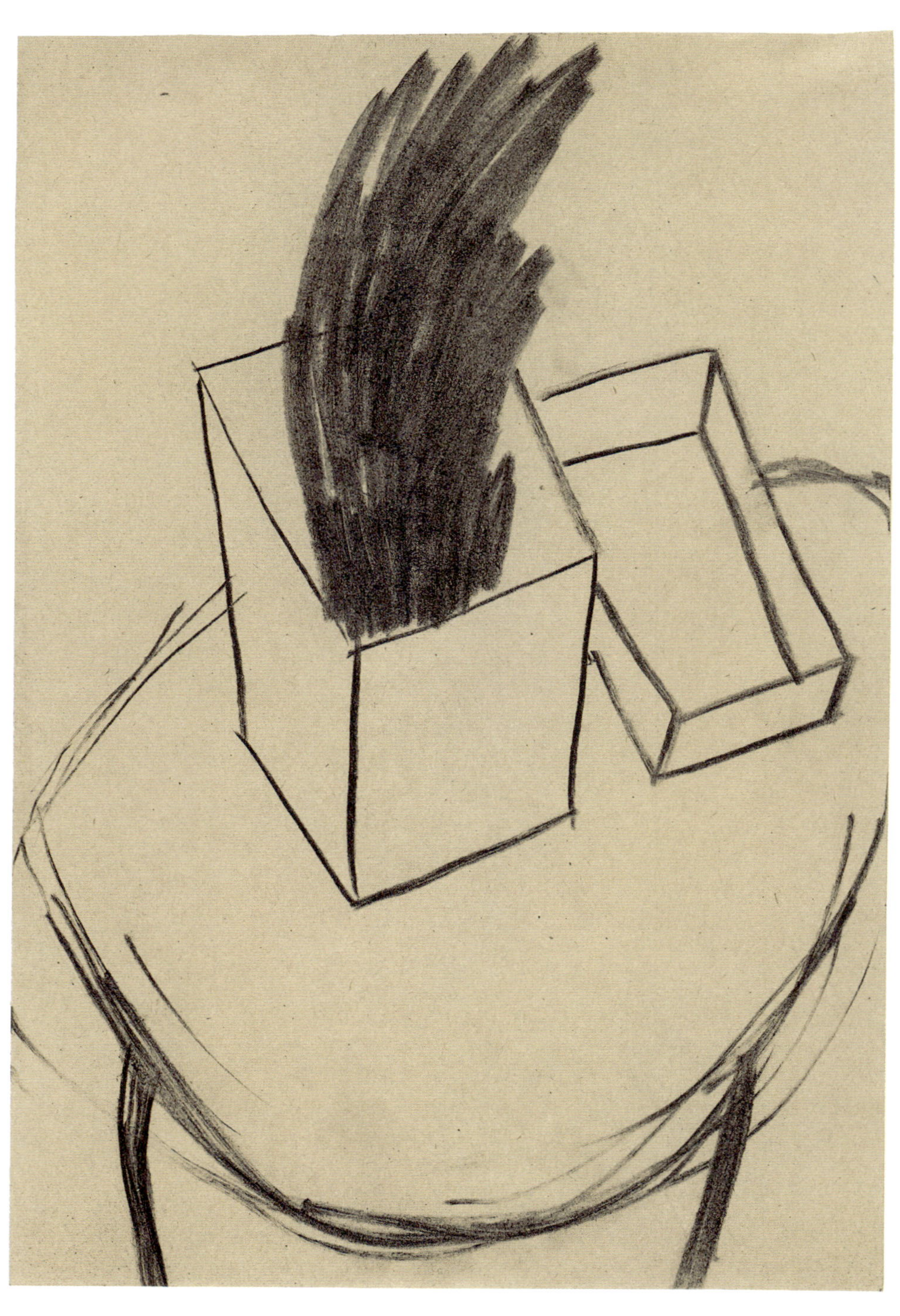

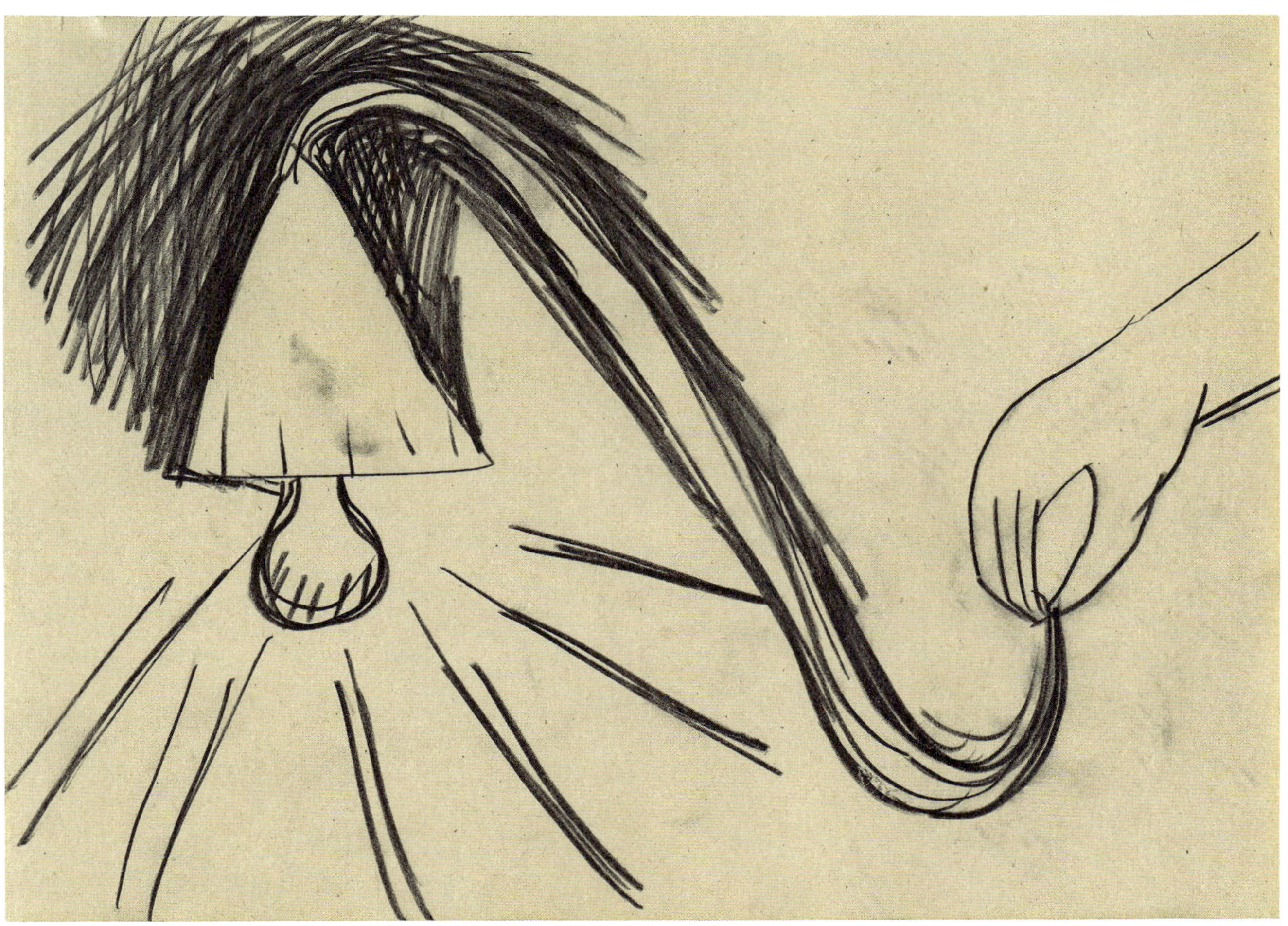

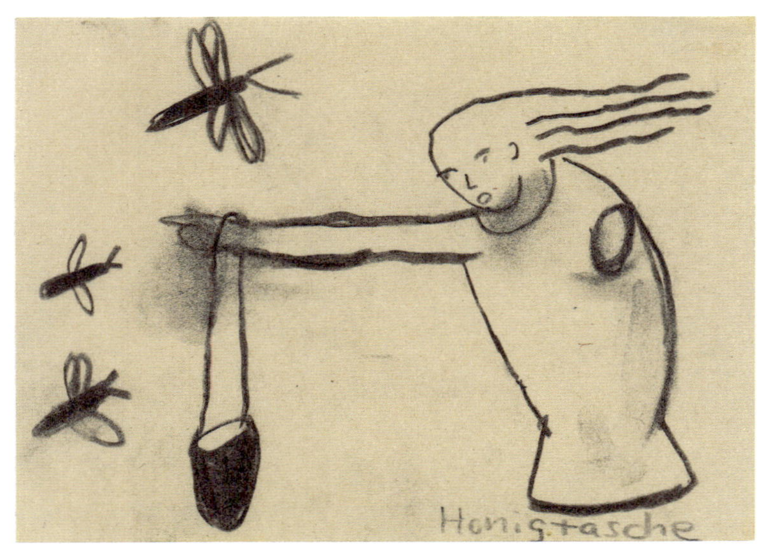
Honigtasche

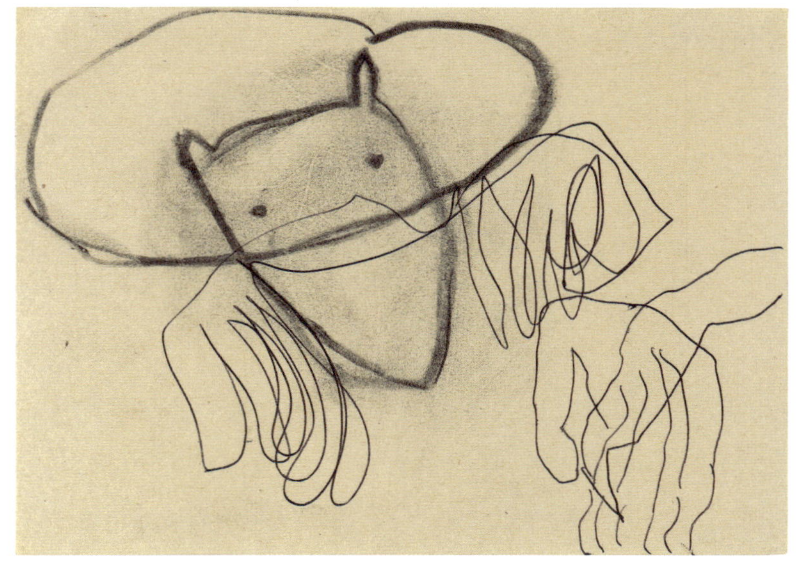

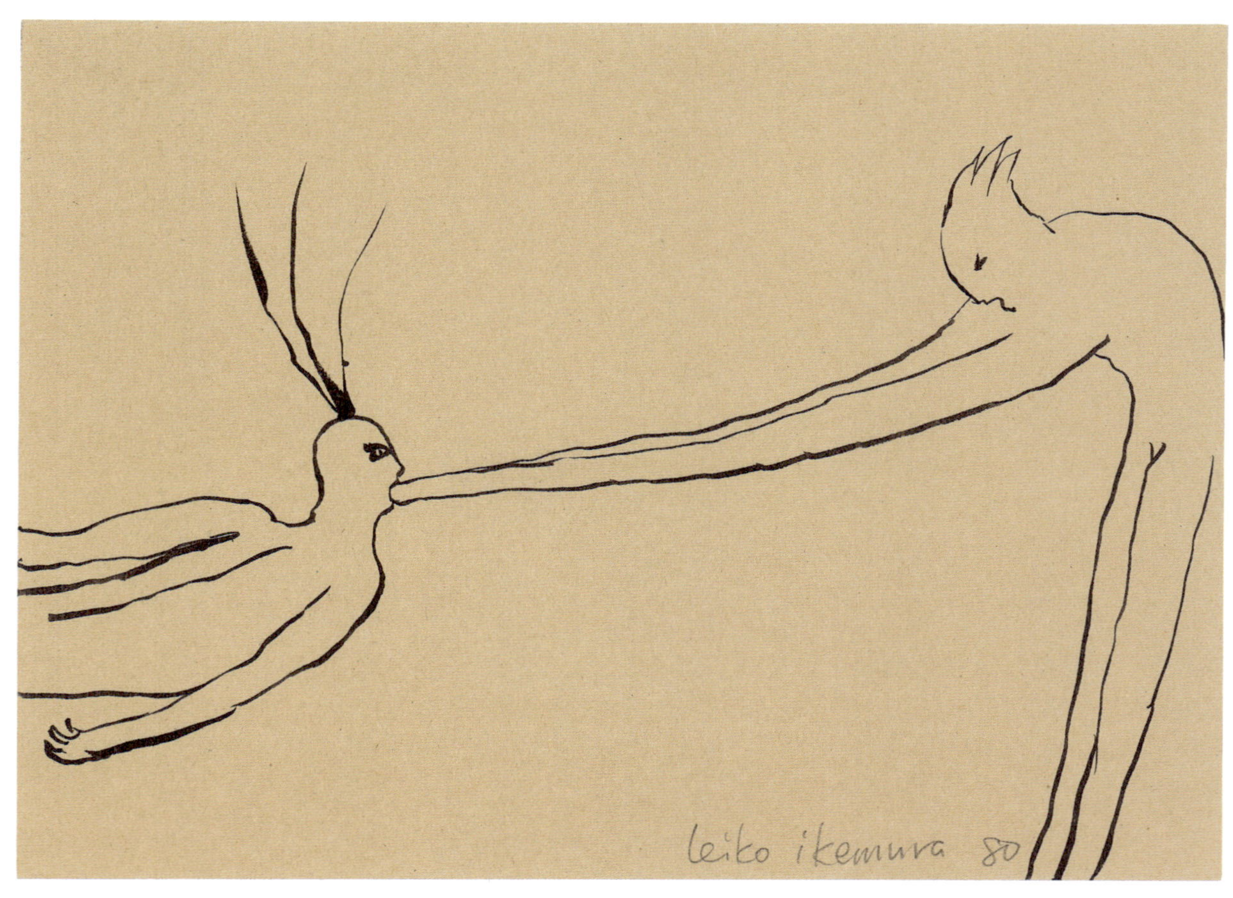
leiko ikemura 80

Honigtasche | Honey
Bag, 1983
Kohle auf Papier |
Charcoal on paper,
14,8 × 21 cm
[Kat. | cat. 13]

Ohne Titel | Untitled, 1983
Kohle und schwarzer
Kugelschreiber auf
Papier | Charcoal and
black pen on paper,
14,8 × 21 cm
[Kat. | cat. 14]

Ohne Titel | Untitled, 1980
Tusche auf Papier |
India ink on paper,
14,7 × 20,9 cm
[Kat. | cat. 3]

Die Kastrierten |
The Castrated, 1982
Kohle auf Papier |
Charcoal on paper,
32 × 24 cm
[Kat. | cat. 11]

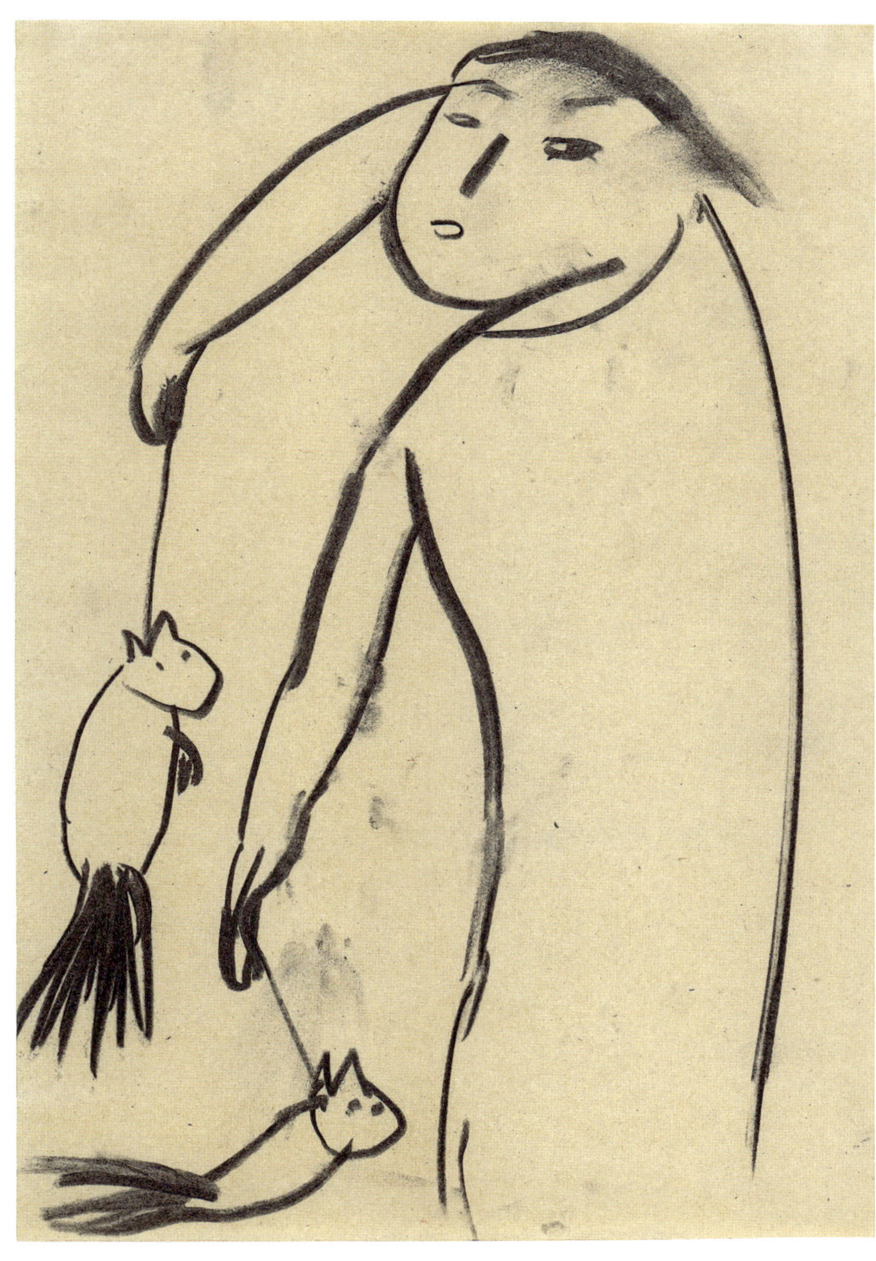

Ohne Titel | Untitled, 1982
Kohle auf Papier |
Charcoal on paper,
21 × 29,6 cm
[Kat. | cat. 12]

Ohne Titel | Untitled, 1983
Kohle auf Papier |
Charcoal on paper,
36 × 47,9 cm
[Kat. | cat. 18]

Ohne Titel | Untitled, 1983
Kohle auf Papier |
Charcoal on paper,
14,8 × 21 cm
[Kat. | cat. 15]

No me gustas tù!, 1981
Kohle auf Papier |
Charcoal on paper,
21 × 29,6 cm
[Kat. | cat. 4]

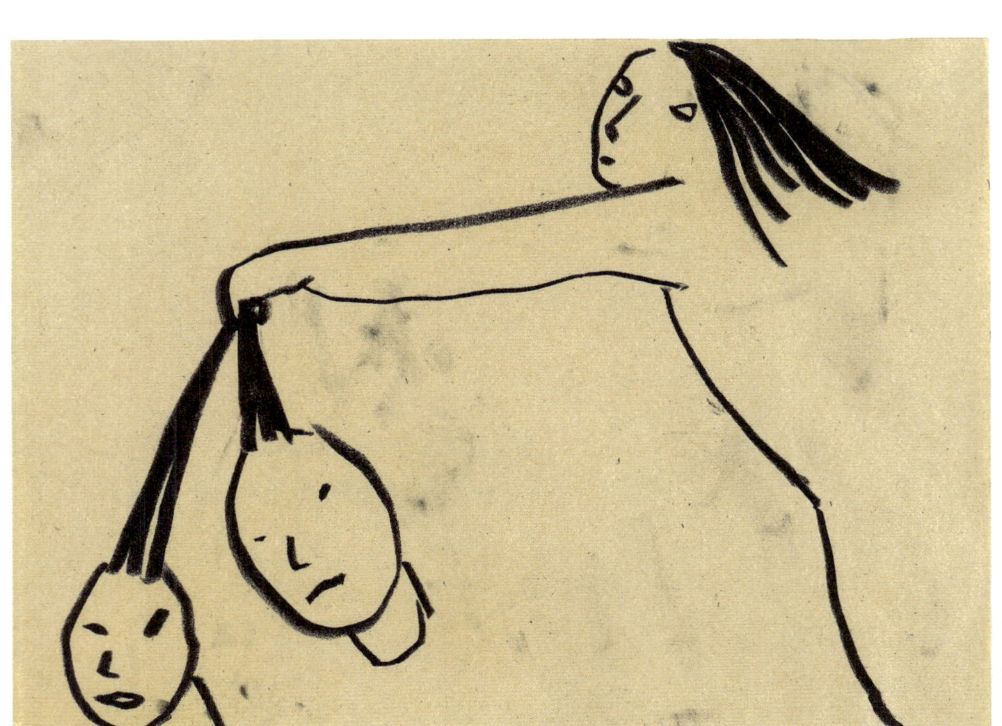

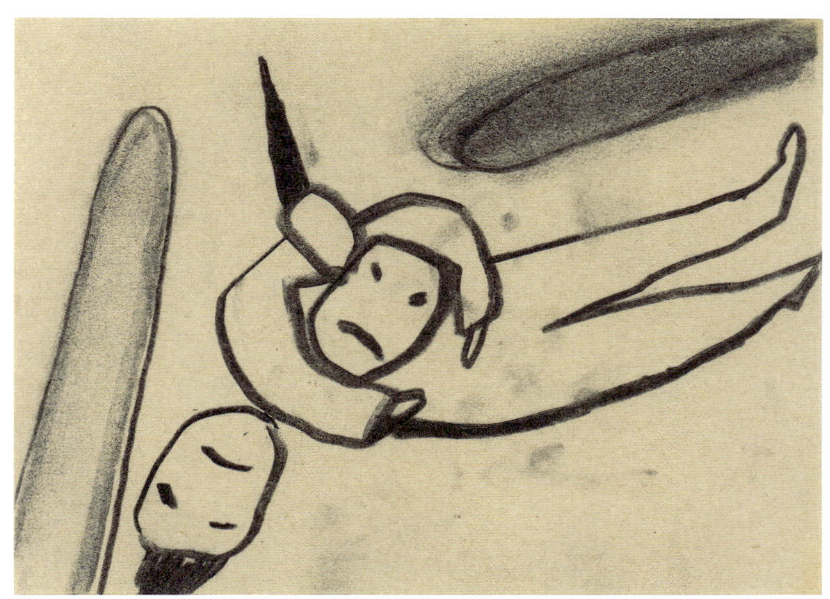

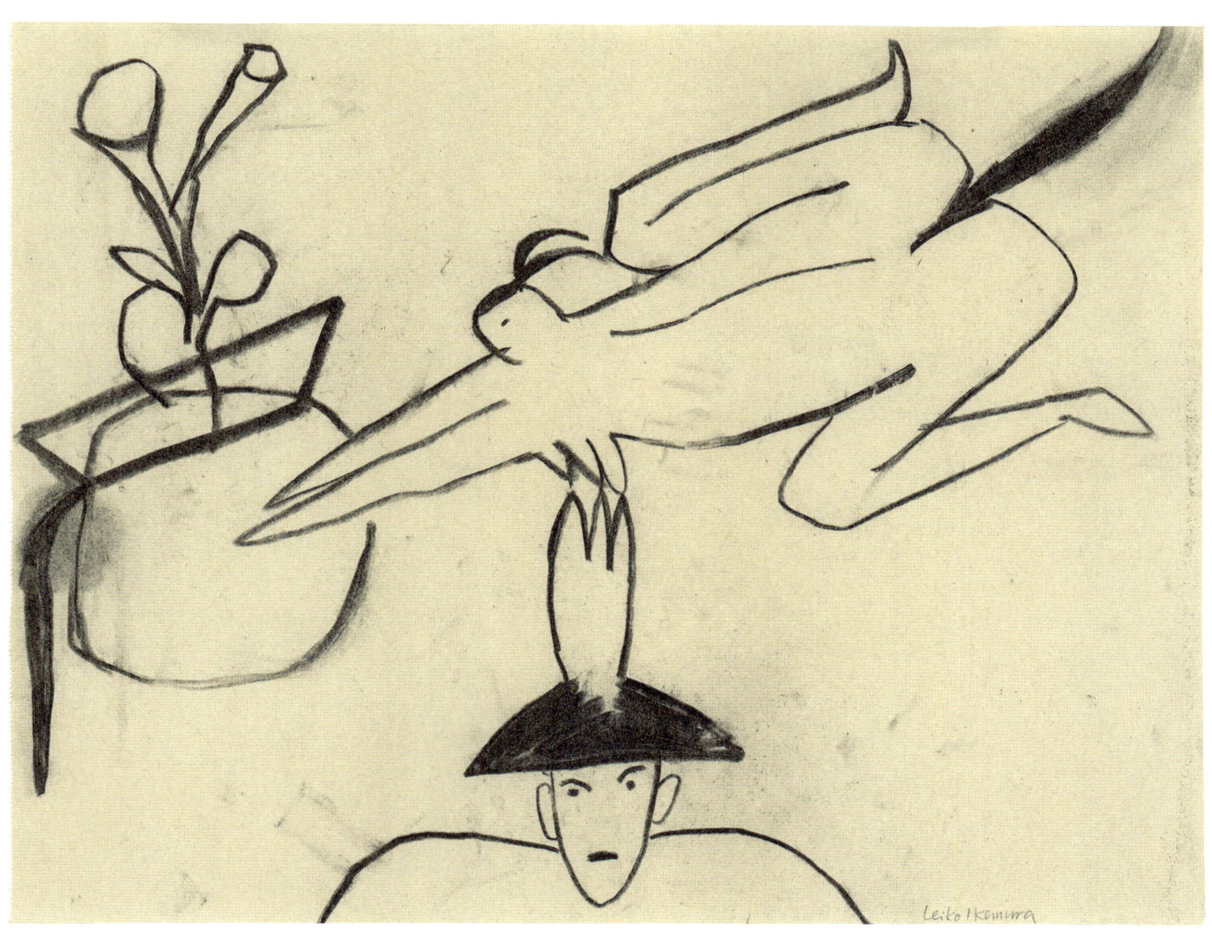

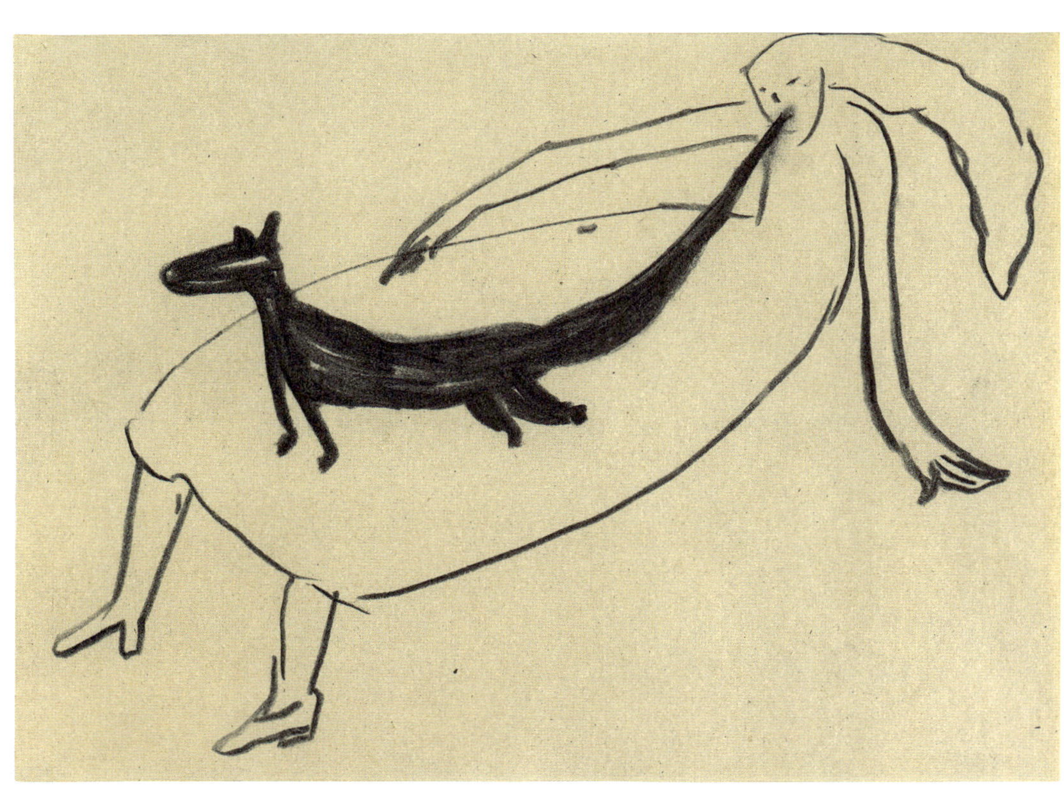

Kamikaze, 1980
Dispersionsfarbe auf
Papier | Dispersion paint
on paper, 120 × 90 cm
[Kat. | cat. 1]

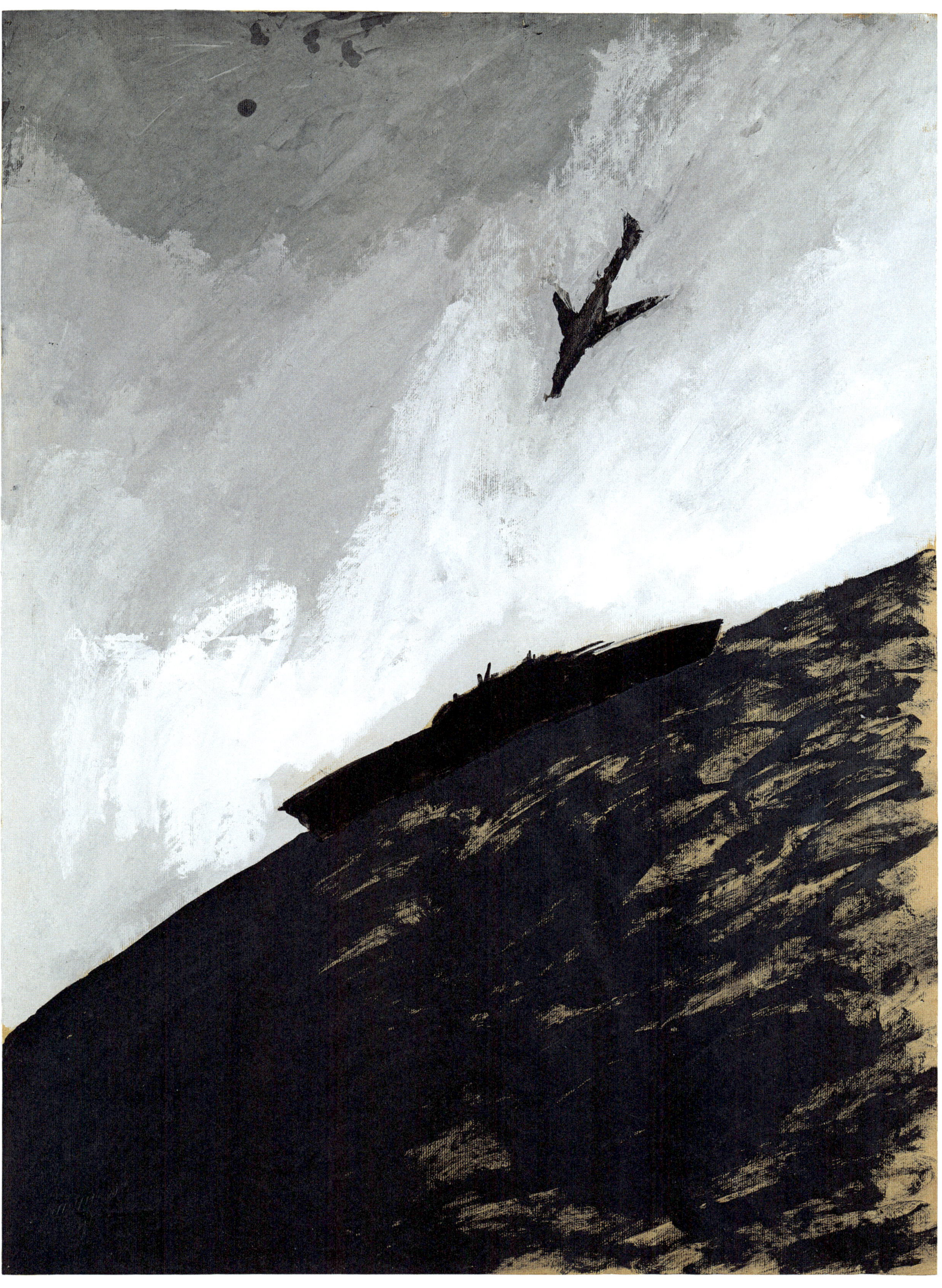

Ohne Titel | Untitled, 1984
Kohle auf Papier |
Charcoal on paper,
42,1×29,6 cm
[Kat. | cat. 24]

Ohne Titel | Untitled, 1984
Kohle auf Papier |
Charcoal on paper,
42,1×29,6 cm
[Kat. | cat. 23]

Ohne Titel | Untitled, 1983
Kohle auf Papier |
Charcoal on paper,
29,7×41,9 cm
[Kat. | cat. 20]

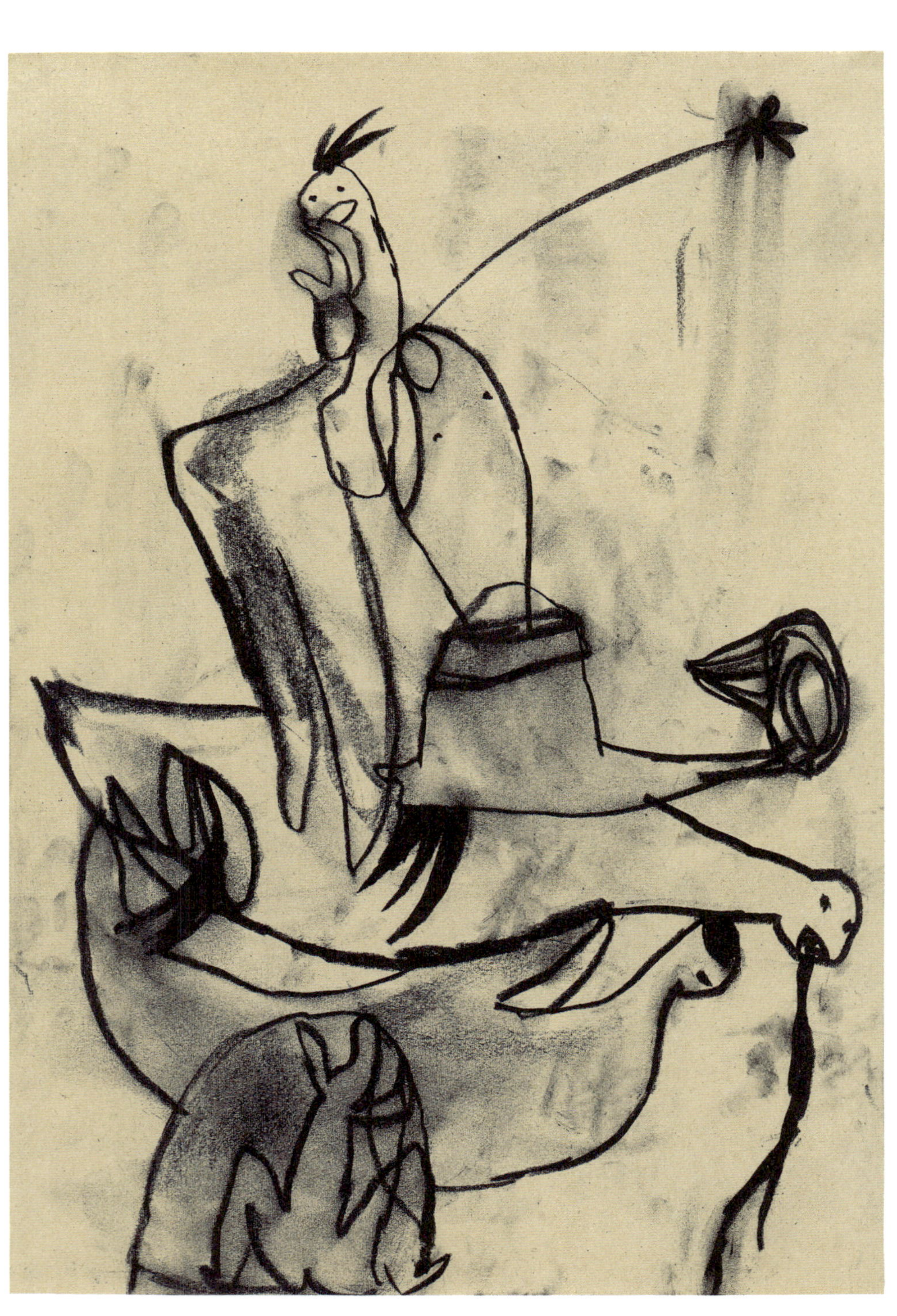

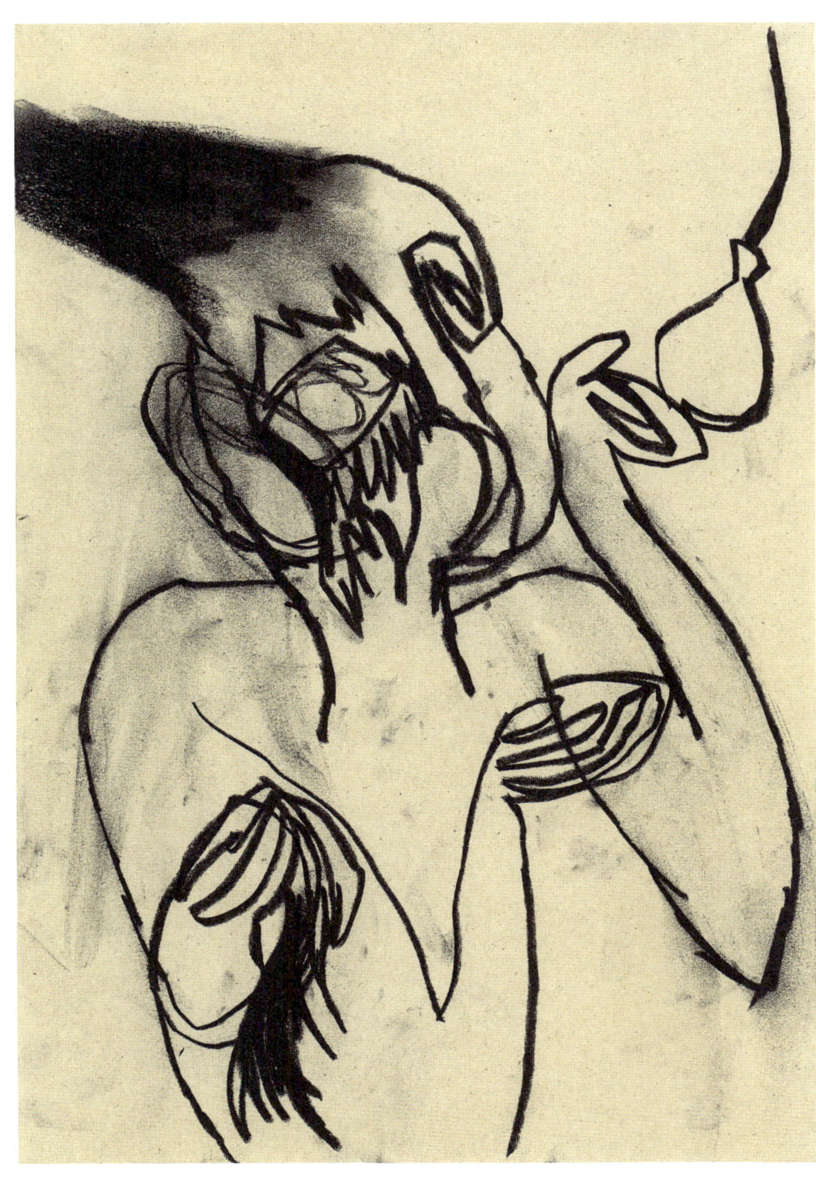

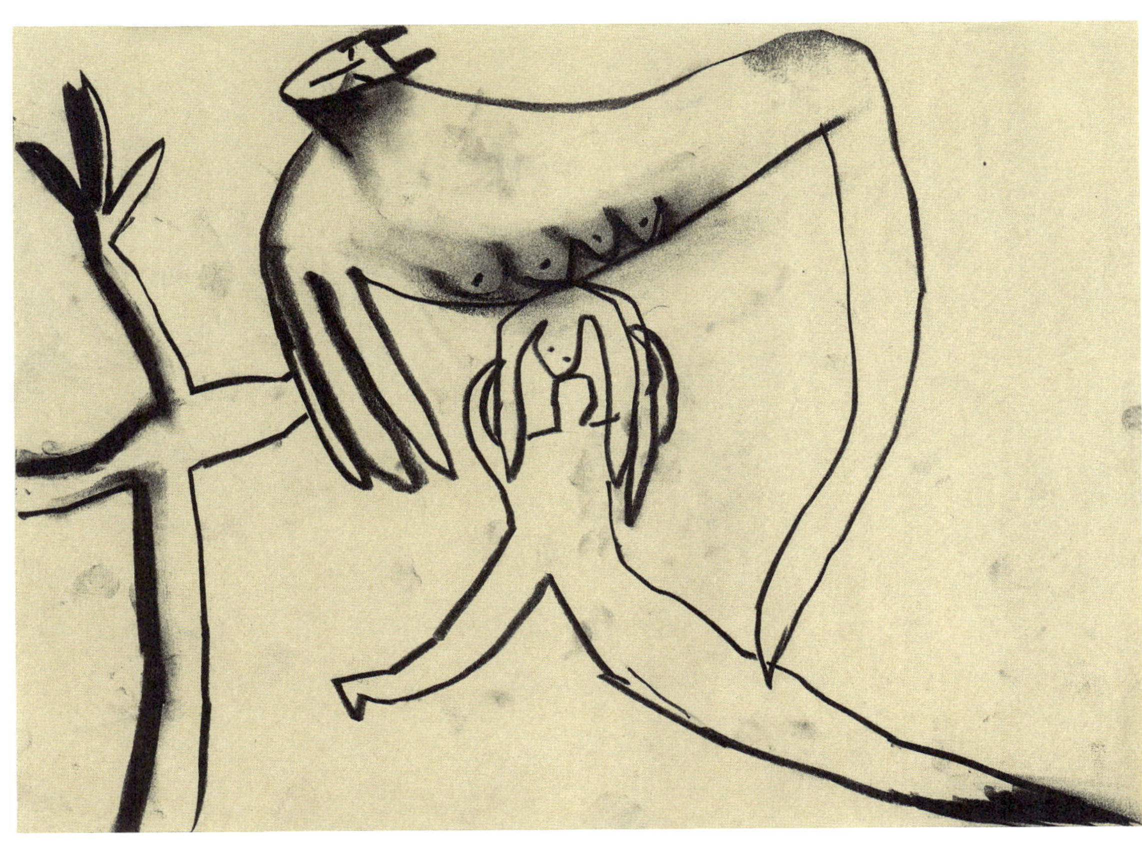

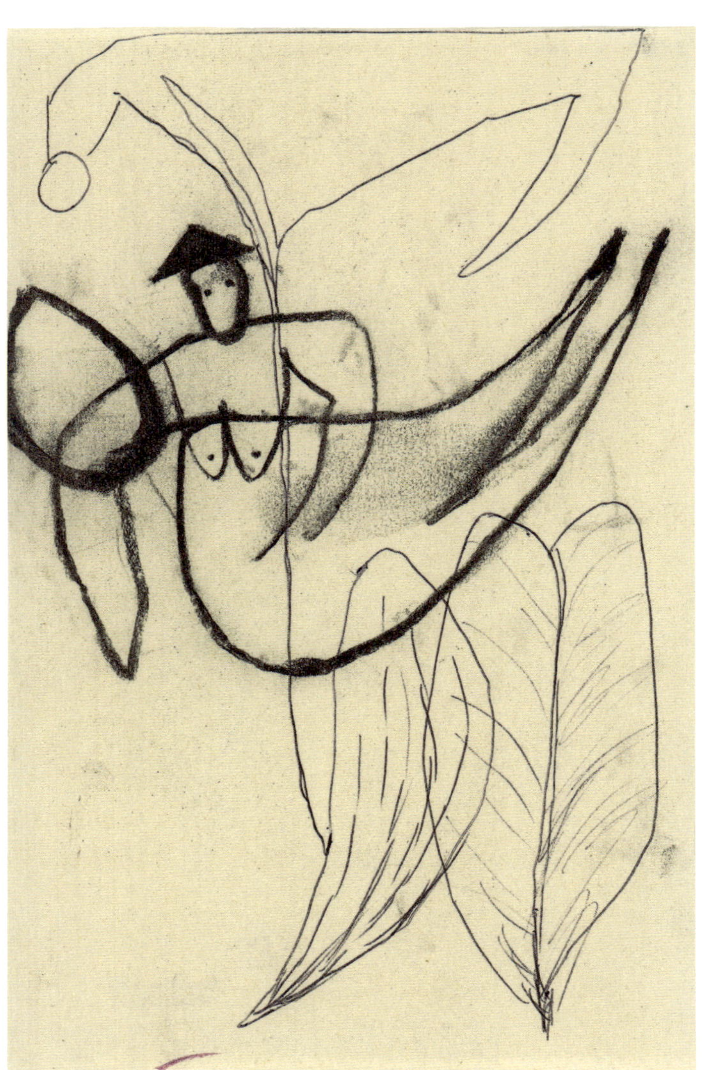

Ohne Titel | Untitled, 1983
Kohle und schwarzer
Kugelschreiber auf Papier |
Charcoal and black
pen on paper, 24×16 cm
[Kat. | cat. 16]

Ohne Titel | Untitled, 1983
Kohle und grüne Fett-
kreide auf Papier |
Charcoal and green
oil chalk on paper,
29,6×41,9 cm
[Kat. | cat. 17]

Ohne Titel | Untitled, 1984
Kohle auf Papier |
Charcoal on paper,
42,1×29,6 cm
[Kat. | cat. 25]

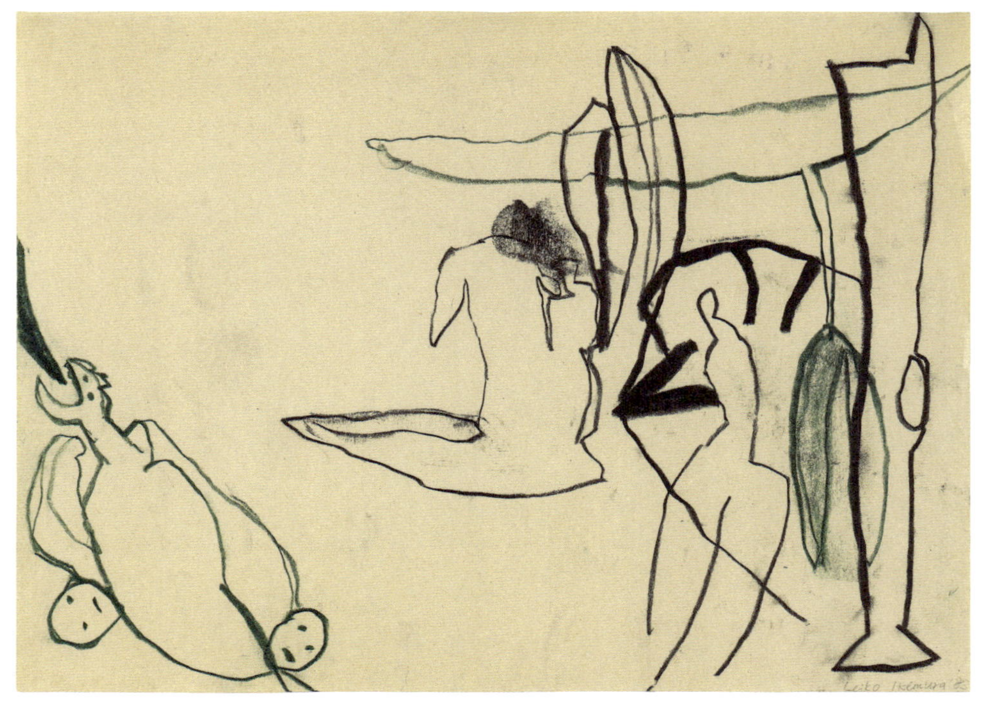

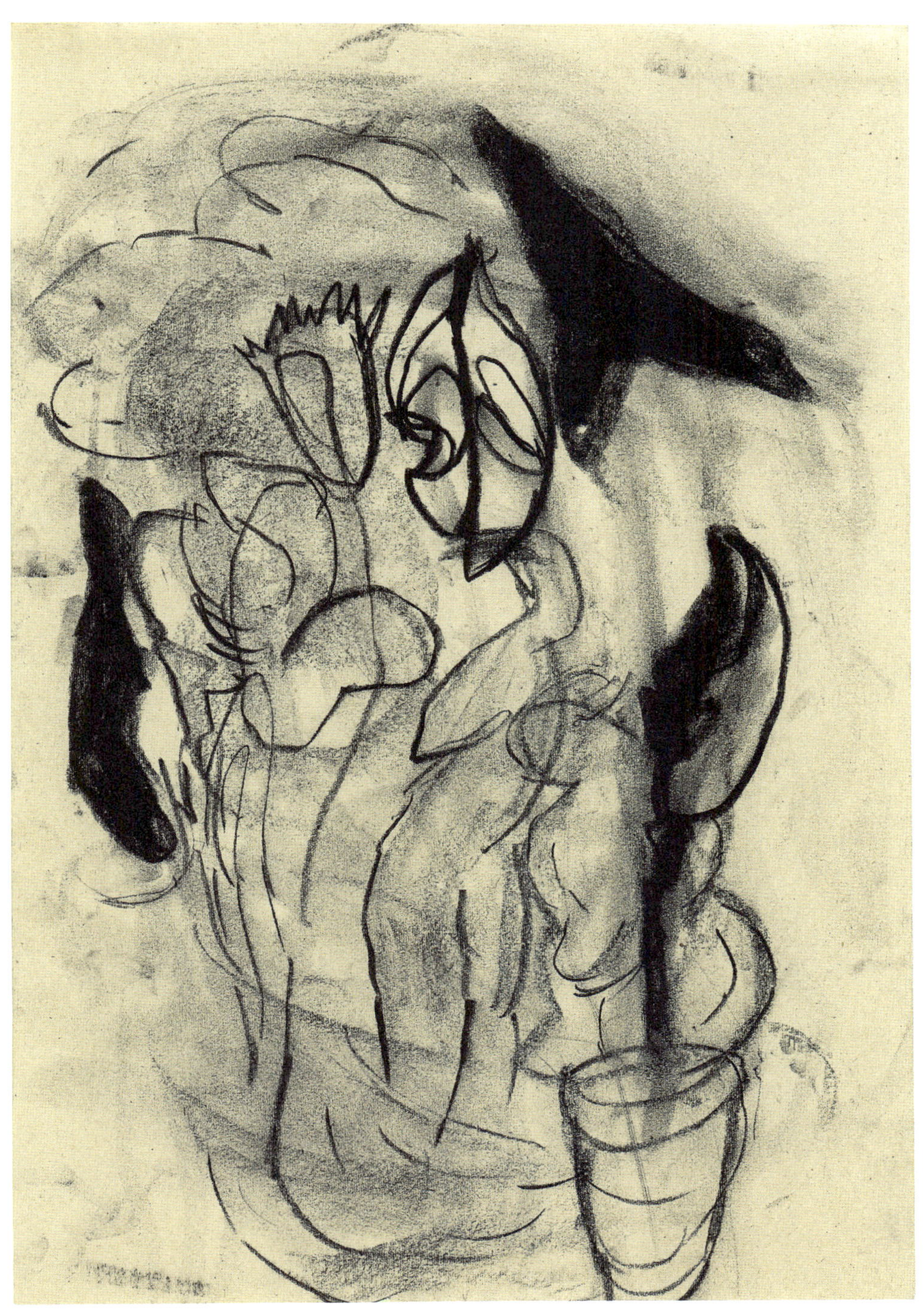

Ohne Titel | Untitled, 1983
Kohle auf Papier |
Charcoal on paper,
29,7 × 41,9 cm
[Kat. | cat. 19]

Ohne Titel | Untitled, 1984
Kohle auf Papier |
Charcoal on paper,
42,1 × 29,6 cm
[Kat. | cat. 21]

Ohne Titel | Untitled, 1984
Kohle auf Papier |
Charcoal on paper,
29,8 × 42,1 cm
[Kat. | cat. 22]

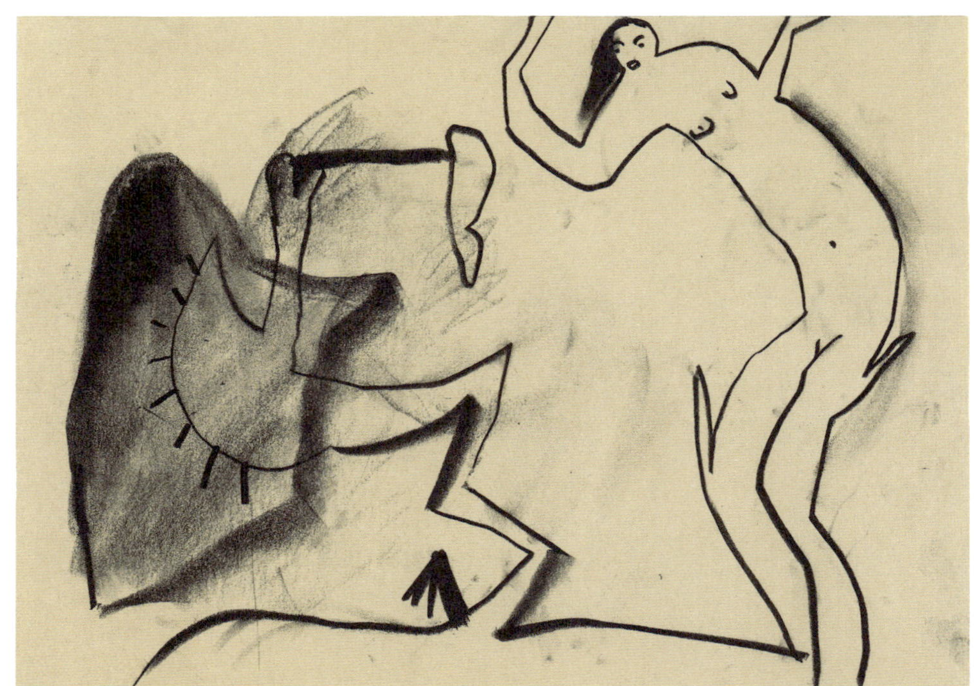

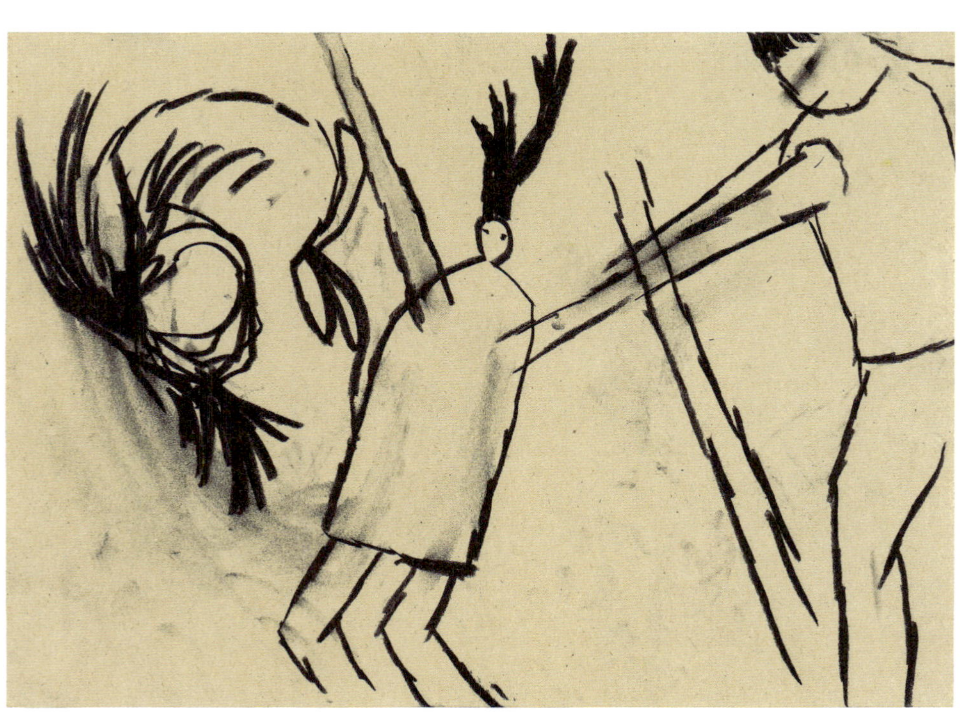

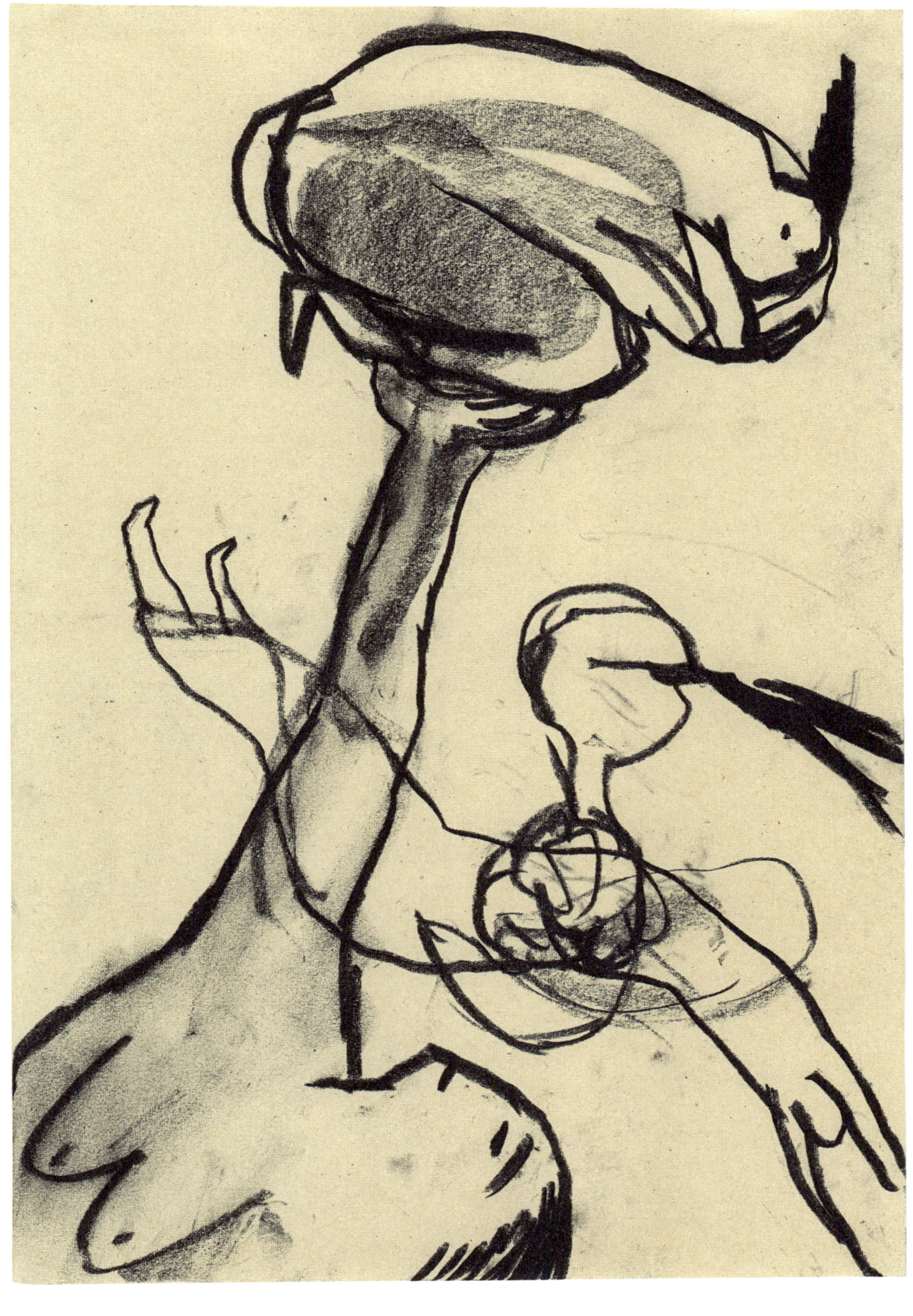

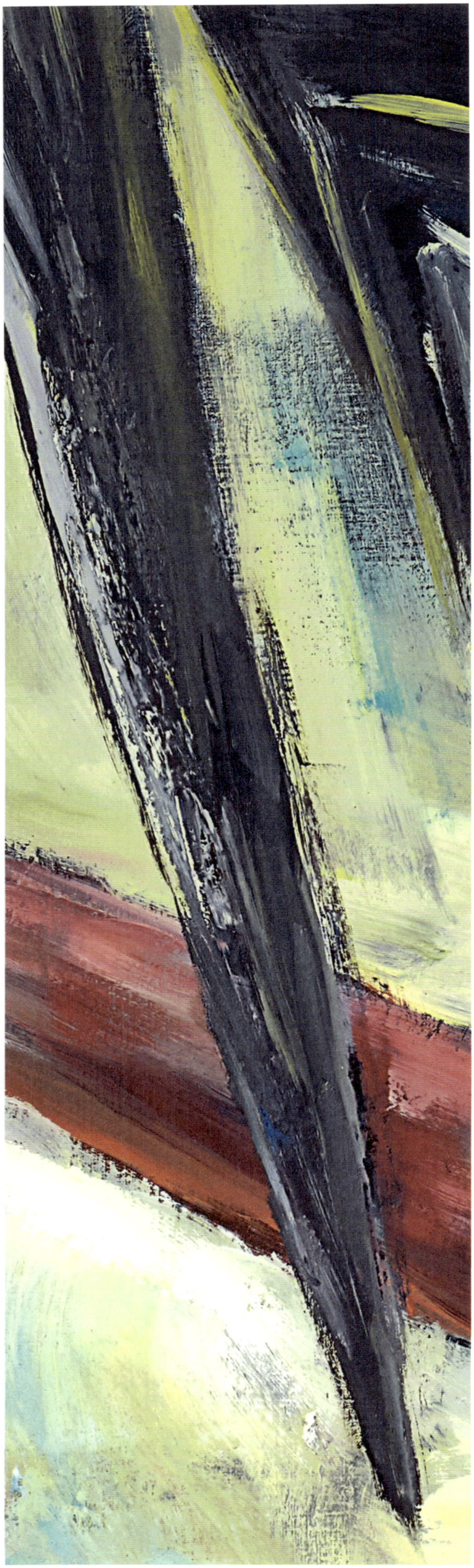

Spiders and a Goddess of War

In her painting, Ikemura wrestles initially with resistance. Line also plays an important role. Large-format paintings such as *Vogelspinnen* (Tarantulas) from 1983 not only demonstrate her ambition but show her sovereign confidence. In its radical frontal orientation, the image, which is loaded with tension, confronts the beholder directly. The spiders, their human facial features making an uncanny impression, are frozen in their movement and yet ready to spring into action at any time.

In 1986/87, themes of aggression and even war become dominant. Ikemura now uses color in her drawings; blood-red above all. The brutality of what she represents is paralleled by a drawing process whose intensity is manifest on the paper. The archaic quality of the pictorial world is even more heightened. The drawing *Schlacht (Kriegsgöttin)* (Battle [Goddess of War], 1985) is executed in a seemingly childish style, but the naivete is misleading. Ikemura breaks taboos by thematizing female aggression.

Comparing *Vogelspinnen* with the painting *Kriegsgöttin* (Goddess of War, 1986) vividly demonstrates Ikemura's development in painting during the mid-1980s: the "compulsion of the solid line" is gone; instead the brushstroke is clearly visible and the coloration more complex, which also makes the effect of space more pronounced. The artist becomes more aware of the physicality of color, its double role as vehicle and material.

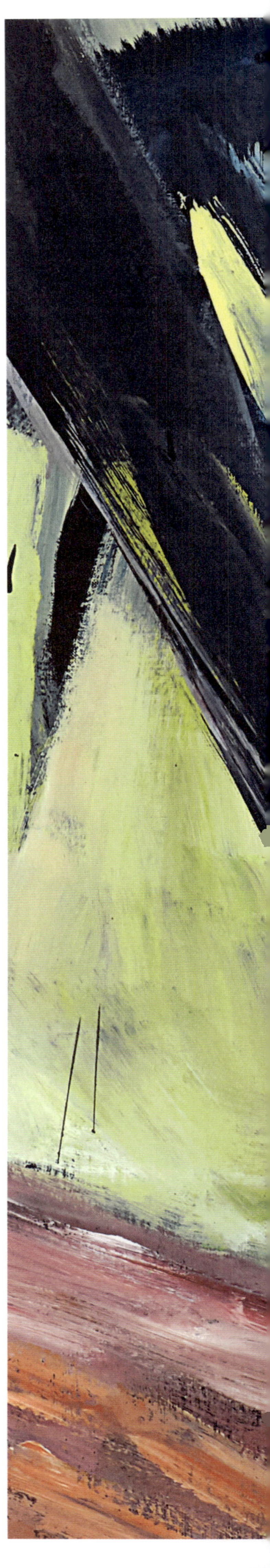

Spinnen und eine Kriegsgöttin

In der Malerei ringt Ikemura anfangs mit Widerständen. Grossformatige Bilder wie *Vogelspinnen* von 1983 verdeutlichen nicht nur ihre Ambitionen, sondern zeigen bereits ihre Souveränität. Die Linie spielt in dieser Zeit auch auf der Leinwand eine wichtige Rolle. Durch die radikal frontale Ausrichtung ist der Betrachter unmittelbar mit dem Bild konfrontiert. Die Spinnen, die aufgrund ihrer menschlichen Gesichtszüge unheimlich wirken, sind in ihrer Bewegung eingefroren und doch jederzeit zur Aktion bereit, wodurch das Bild mit grosser Spannung aufgeladen wird.

1986/87 werden die Themen Aggression und Krieg im Schaffen Ikemuras dominant. Zudem verwendet sie in den Zeichnungen nun auch Farbe, vor allem Rot ist sehr präsent. Die Brutalität des Dargestellten findet eine Parallele in der Intensität des Zeichnungsprozesses, die sich auf dem Papier manifestiert. Das Archaische prägt ihre Bildwelt noch stärker als zuvor. Das Blatt *Schlacht (Kriegsgöttin)* von 1985 ist in einem kindlich anmutenden Stil ausgeführt, doch das Naive täuscht. Indem sie auch die Aggressivität der Frau thematisiert, bricht Ikemura Tabus.

Der Vergleich von *Vogelspinnen* mit dem Gemälde *Kriegsgöttin* (1986) macht die Entwicklung in der Malerei Mitte der 1980er-Jahre anschaulich: Ikemura hat sich vom «Zwang der festen Linie» gelöst, stattdessen wird der Pinselstrich deutlicher sichtbar und die Farbigkeit komplexer, so entsteht auch eine ausgeprägtere räumliche Wirkung. Die Farbe und ihre Doppelrolle als Mittel und Material rücken stärker ins Bewusstsein der Künstlerin.

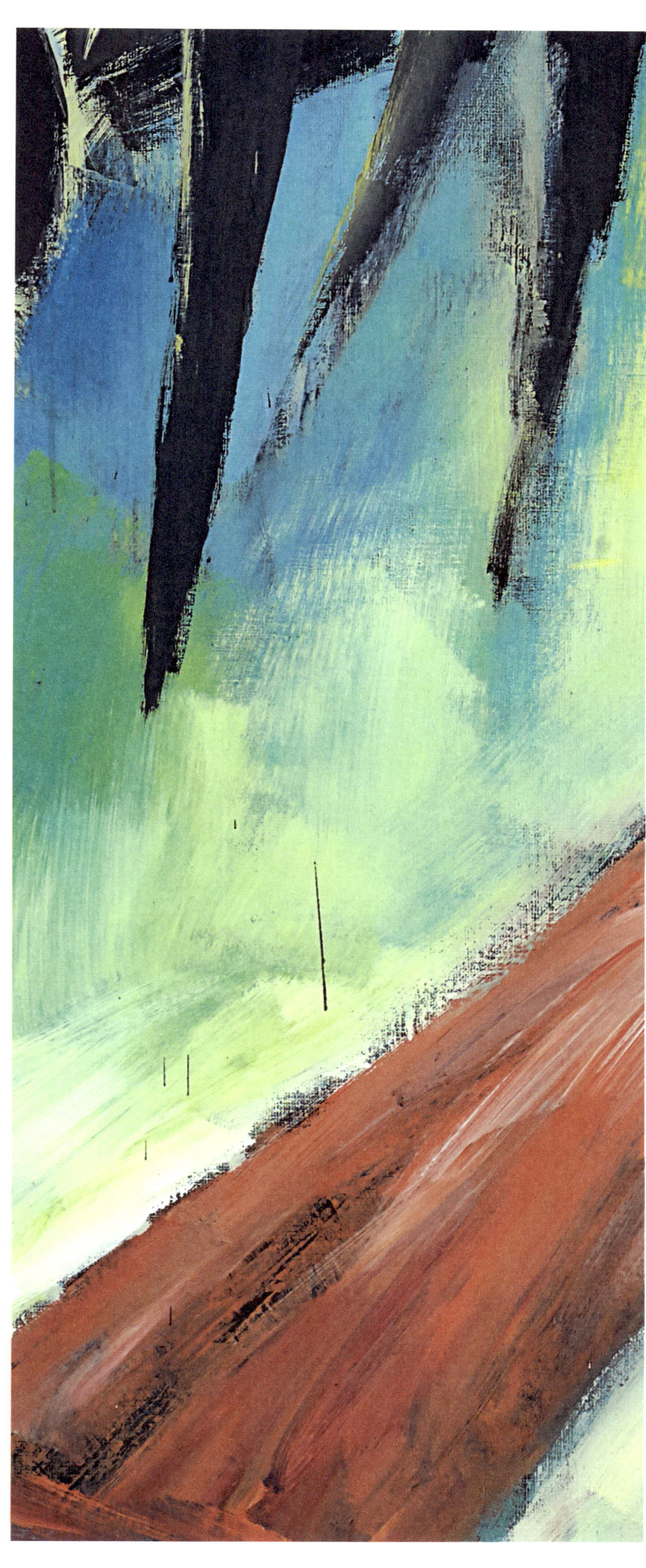

Ohne Titel | Untitled, 1985
Kohle auf Papier |
Charcoal on paper,
47,9 × 36 cm
[Kat. | cat. 27]

Ohne Titel | Untitled, 1985
Kohle auf Papier |
Charcoal on paper,
47,9 × 36 cm
[Kat. | cat. 29]

Ohne Titel | Untitled, 1985
Kohle auf Papier |
Charcoal on paper,
47,9 × 36 cm
[Kat. | cat. 28]

Ohne Titel | Untitled, 1985
Kohle auf Papier |
Charcoal on paper,
47,9 × 36 cm
[Kat. | cat. 30]

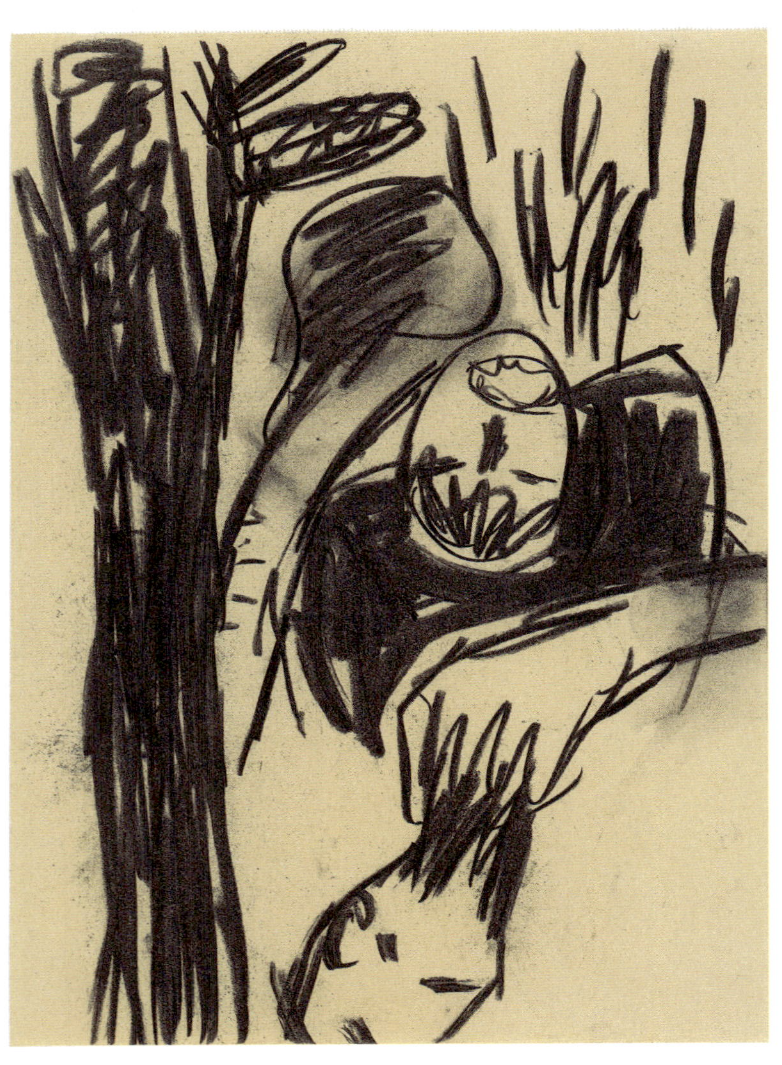

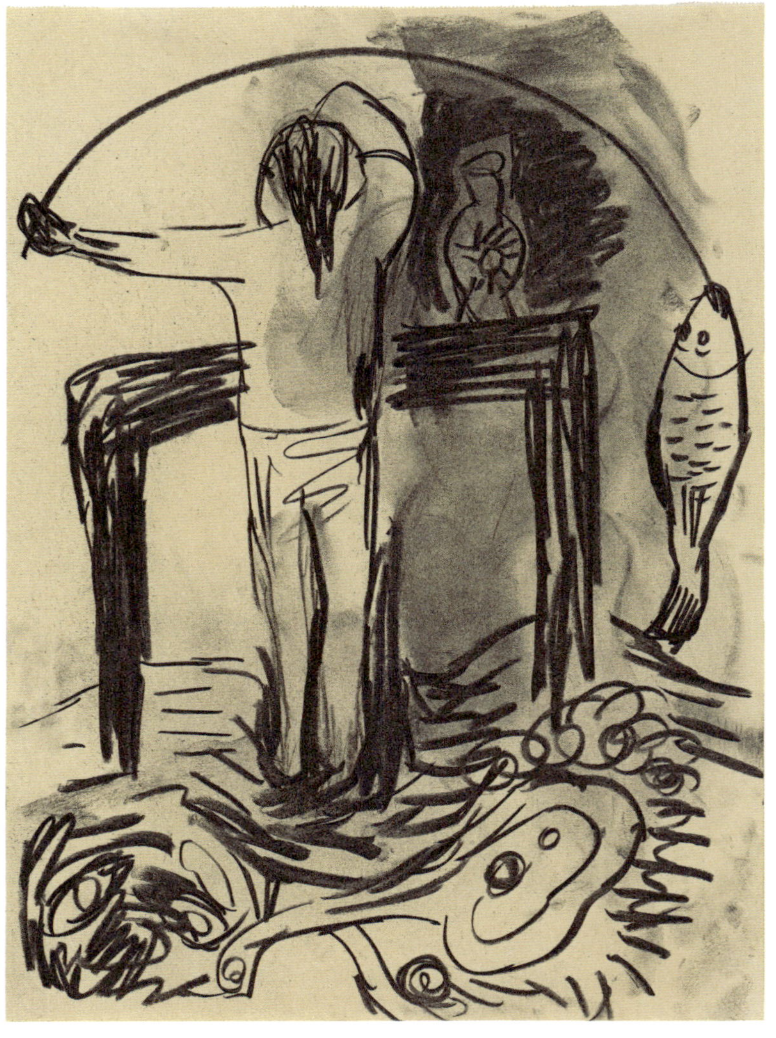

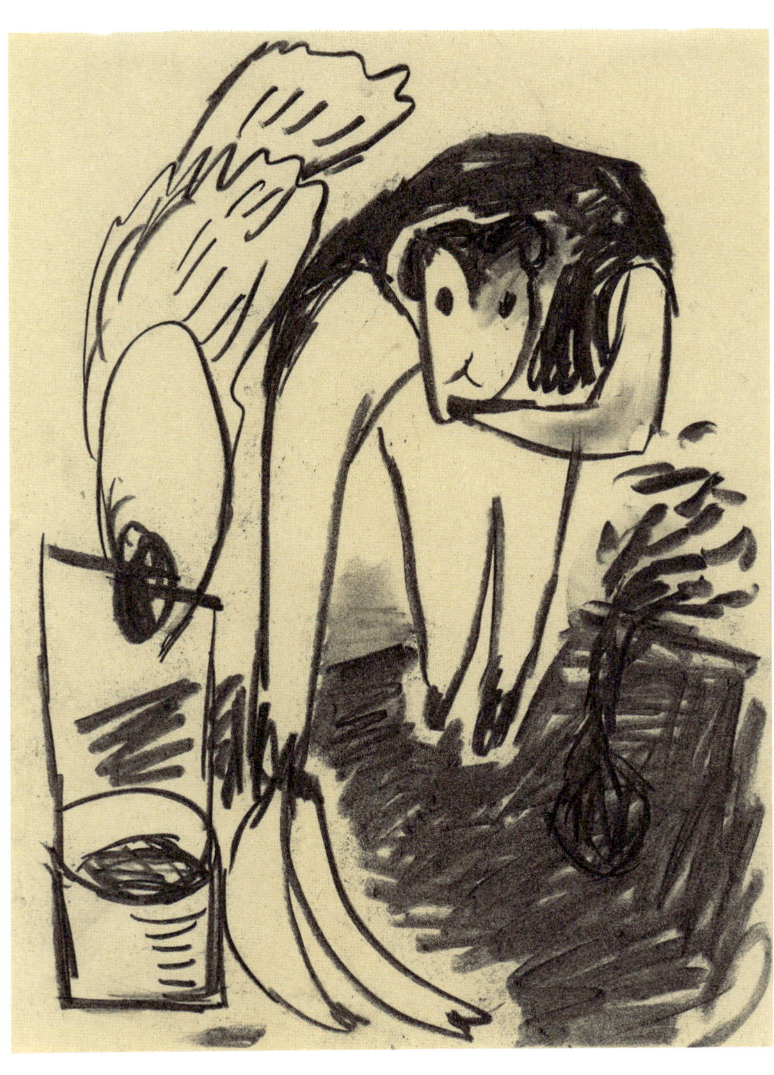

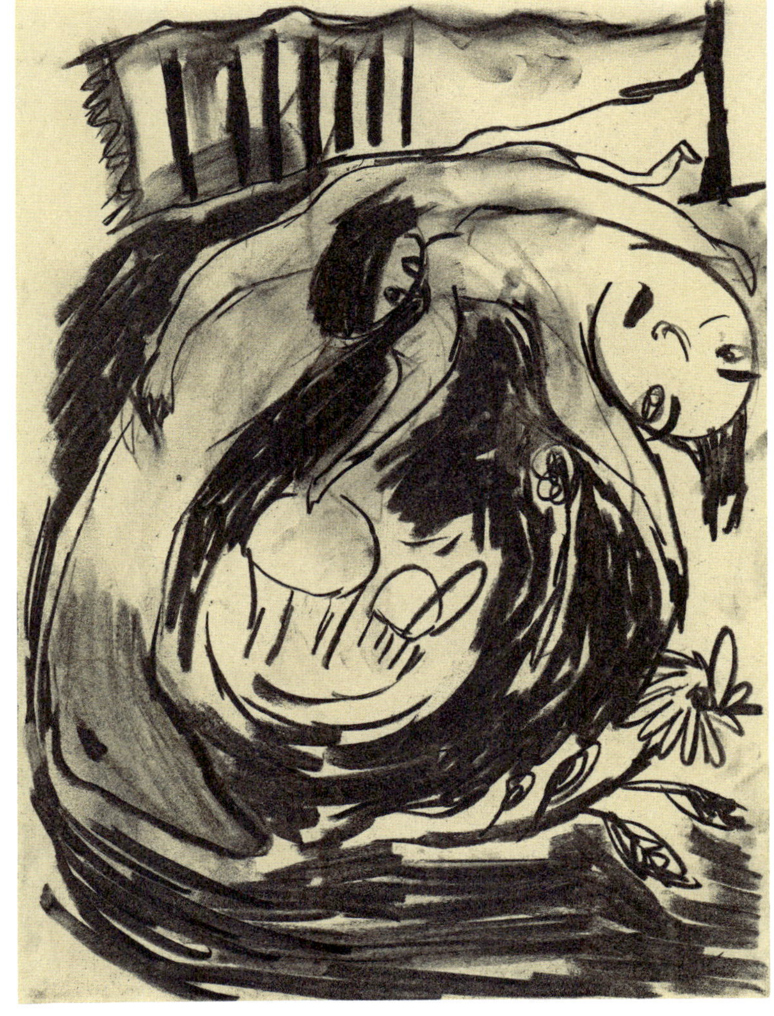

Ohne Titel | Untitled, 1985
Kohle auf Papier |
Charcoal on paper,
47,9 × 36 cm
[Kat. | cat. 31]

Ohne Titel | Untitled, 1985
Kohle und Bleistift
auf Papier | Charcoal
and pencil on paper,
42,1 × 29,7 cm
[Kat. | cat. 32]

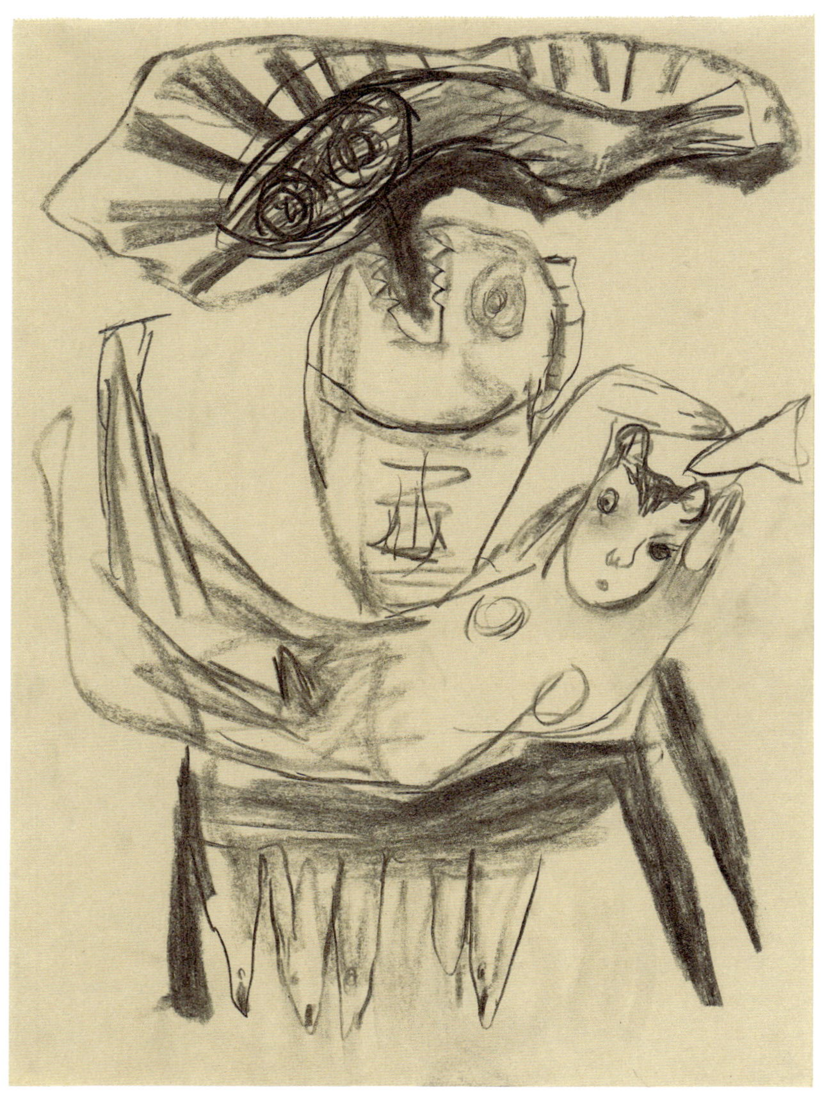

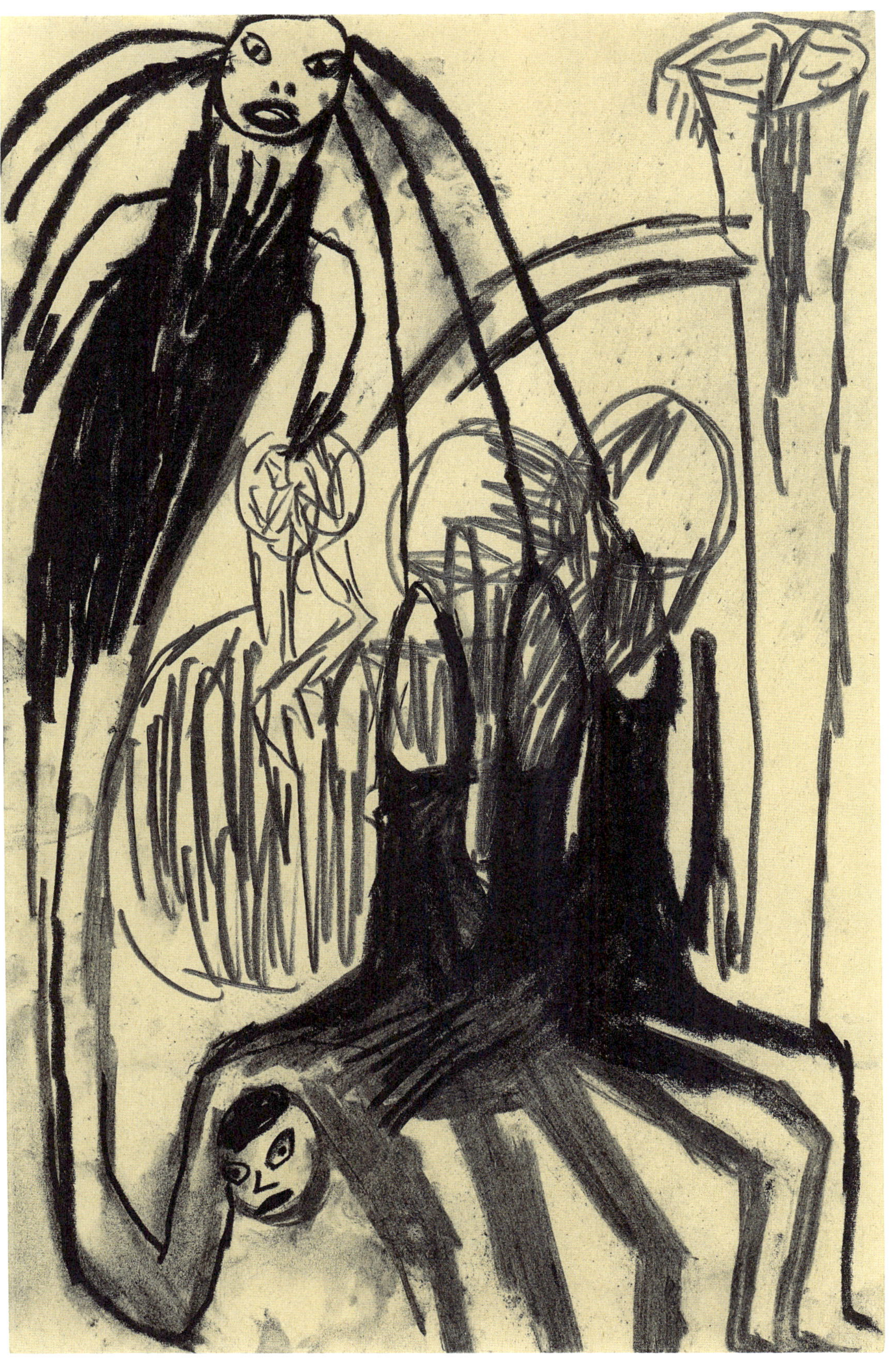

Vogelspinnen |
Tarantulas, 1983
Acryl auf Leinwand |
Acrylic on canvas,
179×199 cm
[Kat. | cat. 26]

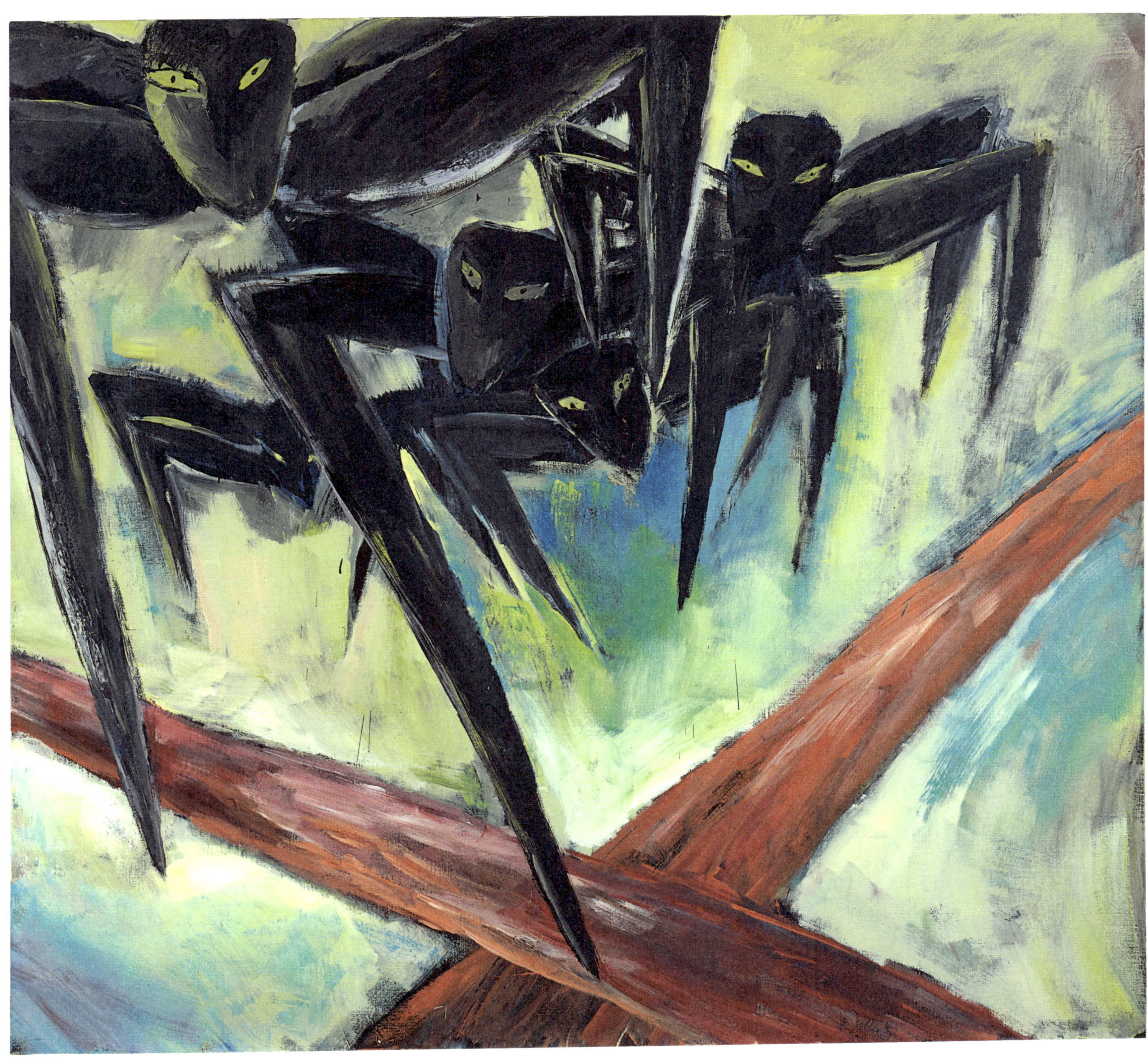

Ohne Titel | Untitled, 1985
Kohle auf Papier |
Charcoal on paper,
42,1 × 29,8 cm
[Kat. | cat. 33]

Studie zum Gemälde
Verkündigung | Study
for the painting
Annunciation, 1985
Kohle auf Papier |
Charcoal on paper,
42 × 29,8 cm
[Kat. | cat. 34]

Ohne Titel | Untitled, 1985
Kohle und farbige Kreide
auf Papier | Charcoal
and color chalk on paper,
47,9 × 36 cm
[Kat. | cat. 36]

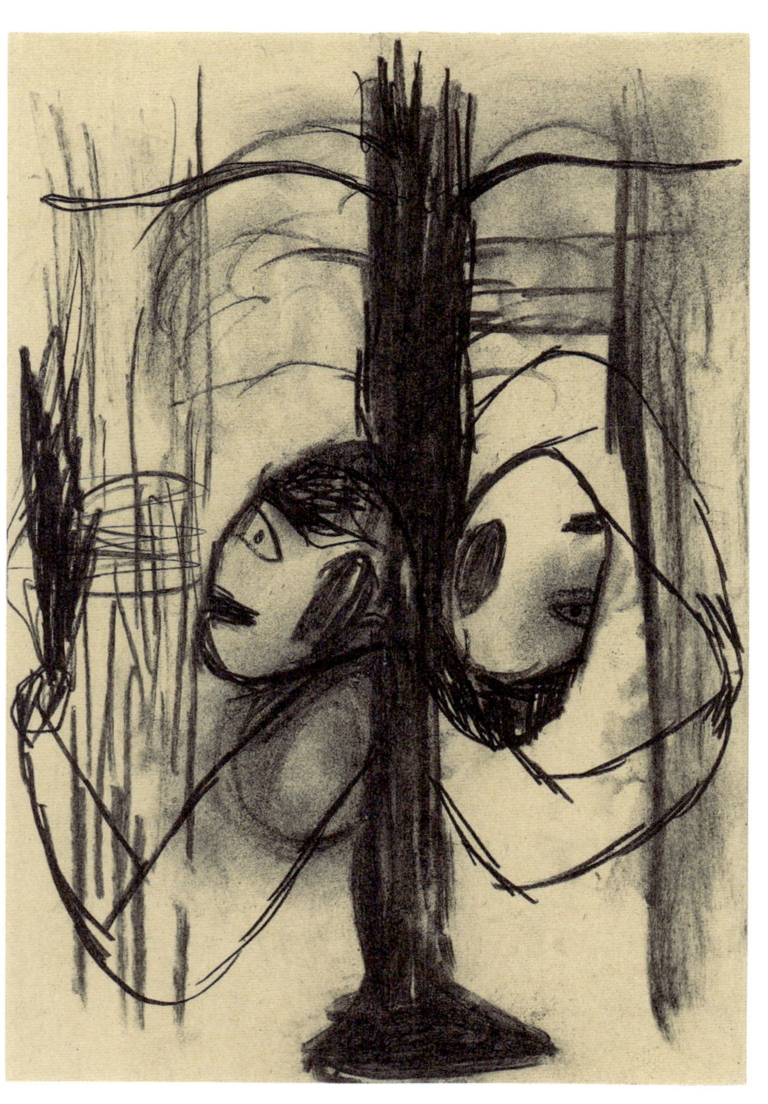

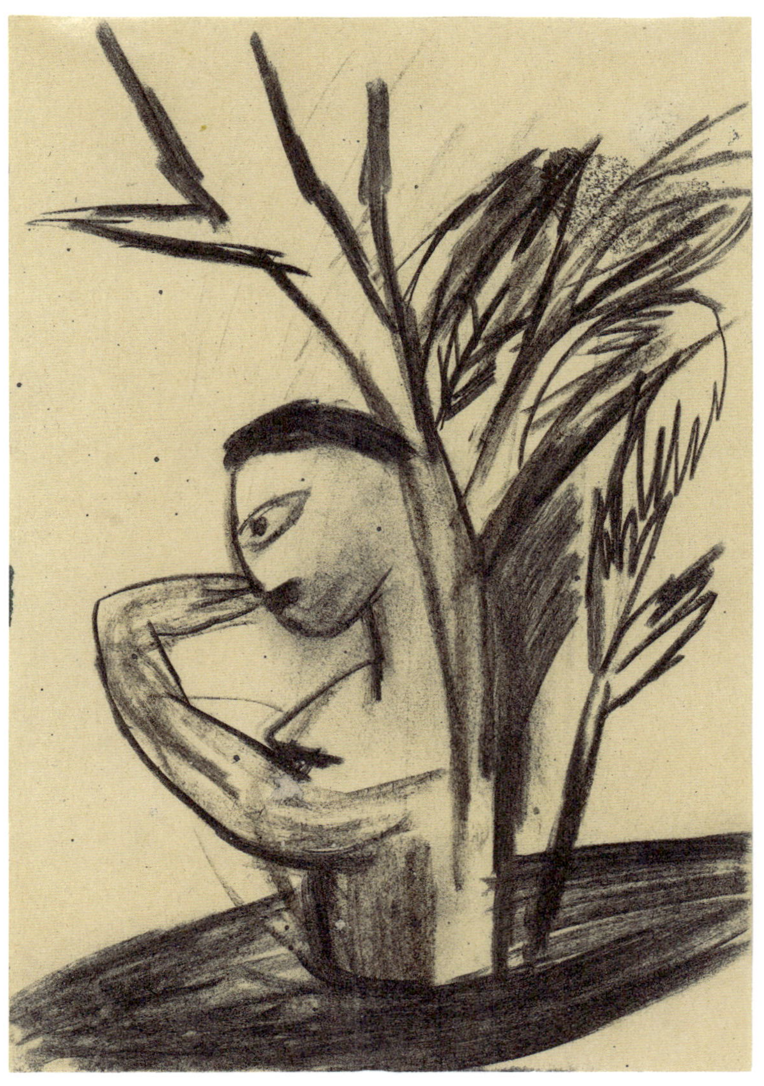

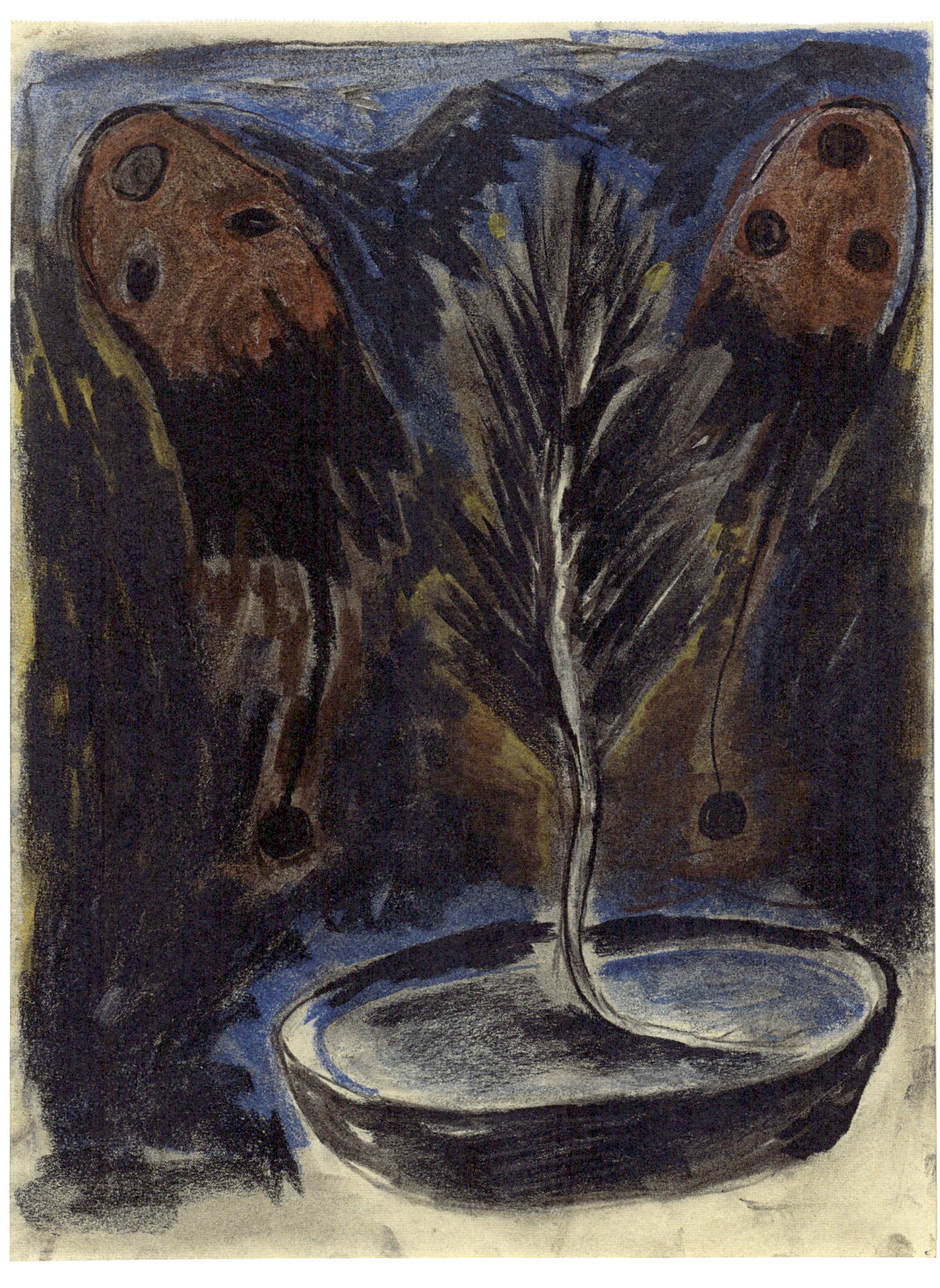

Verkündigung |
Annunciation, 1985
Acryl auf Leinwand |
Acrylic on canvas,
210 × 240 cm
[Kat. | cat. 35]

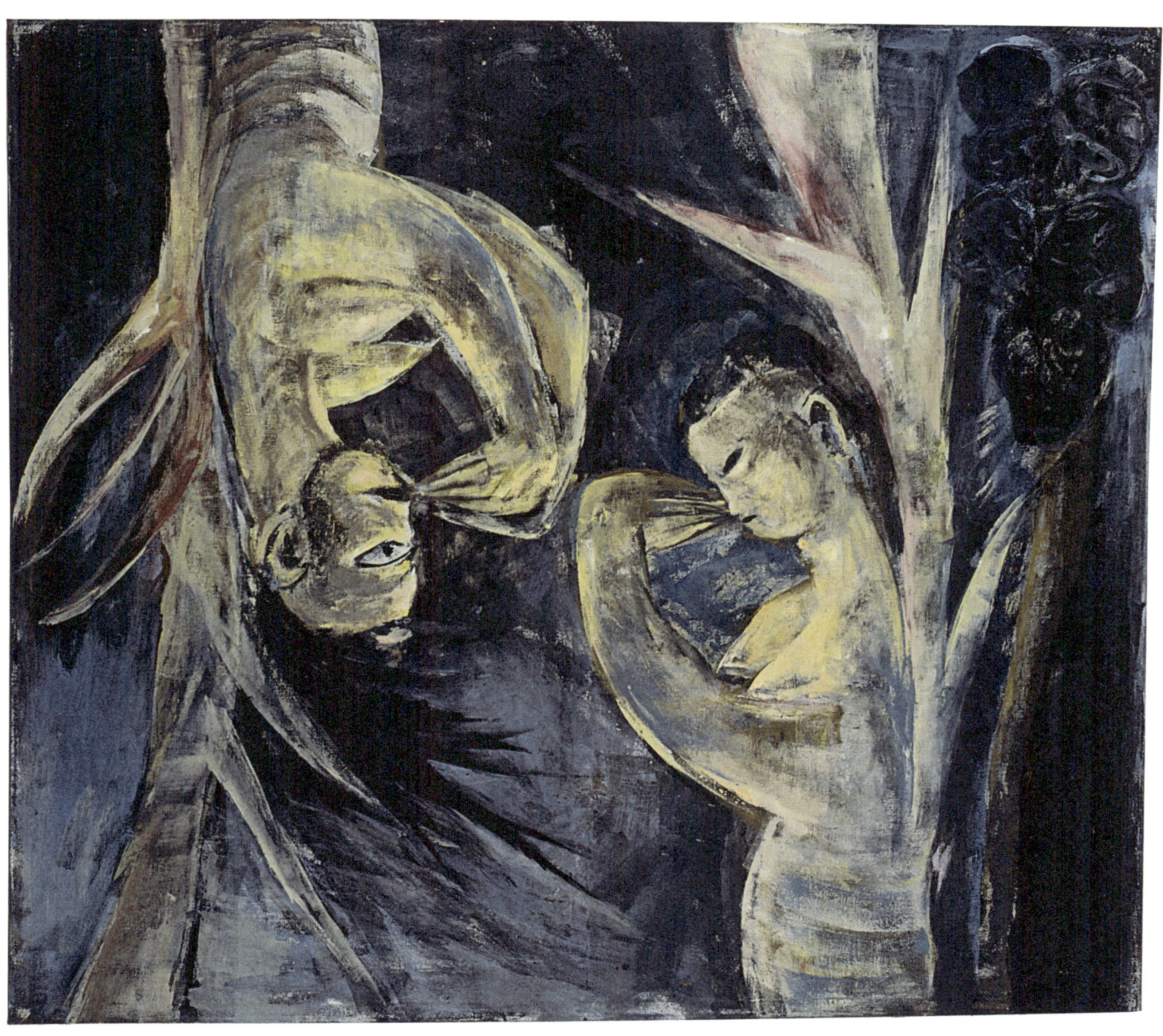

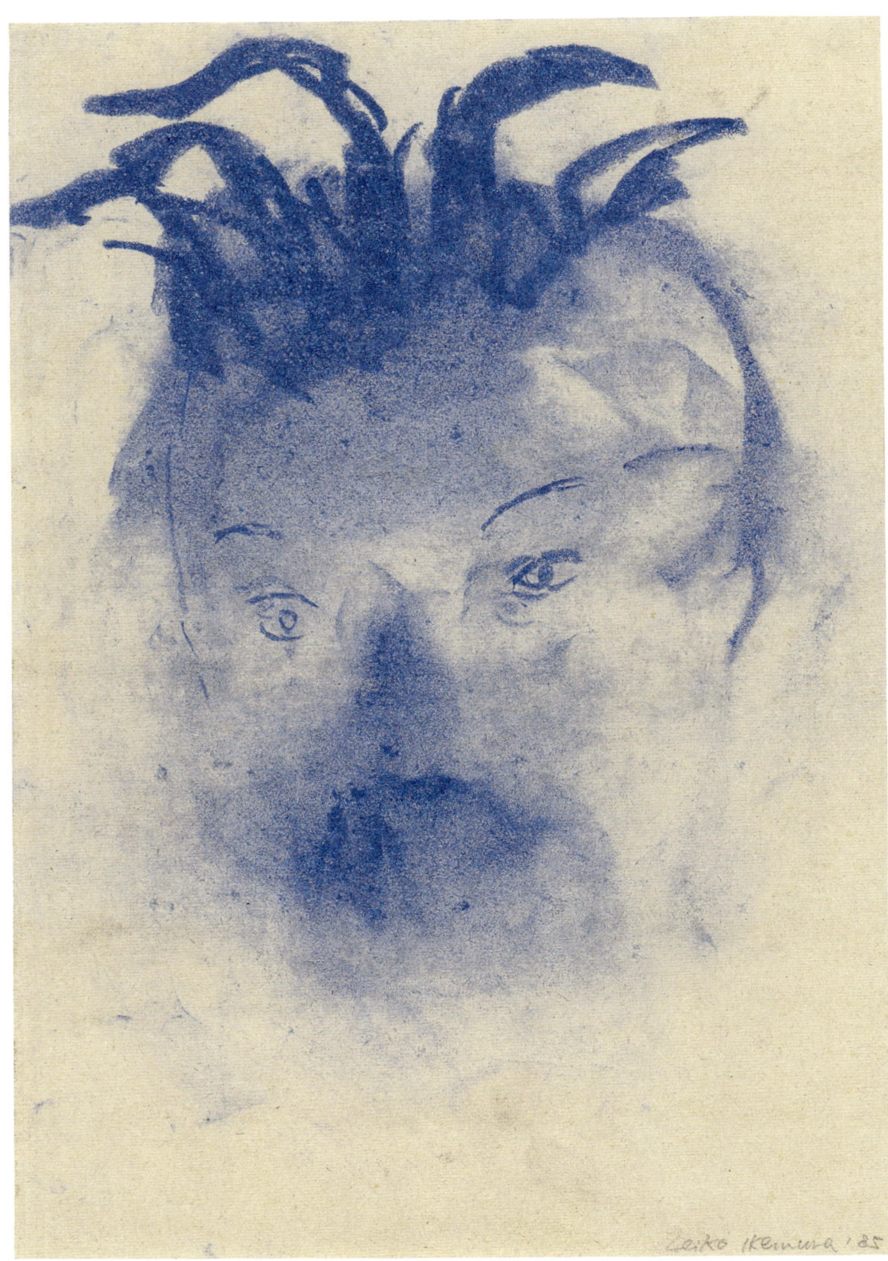

Blauer Kopf | Blue Head,
1985
Blaue Kreide auf Papier |
Blue chalk on paper,
29,8 × 21 cm
[Kat. | cat. 37]

Trojanisches Pferd |
Trojan Horse, 1986
Kohle auf Papier |
Charcoal on paper,
48 × 36 cm
[Kat. | cat. 38]

Ohne Titel | Untitled, 1986
Kohle und Pastellkreide
auf Papier | Charcoal
and pastel on paper,
56,1 × 42 cm
[Kat. | cat. 40]

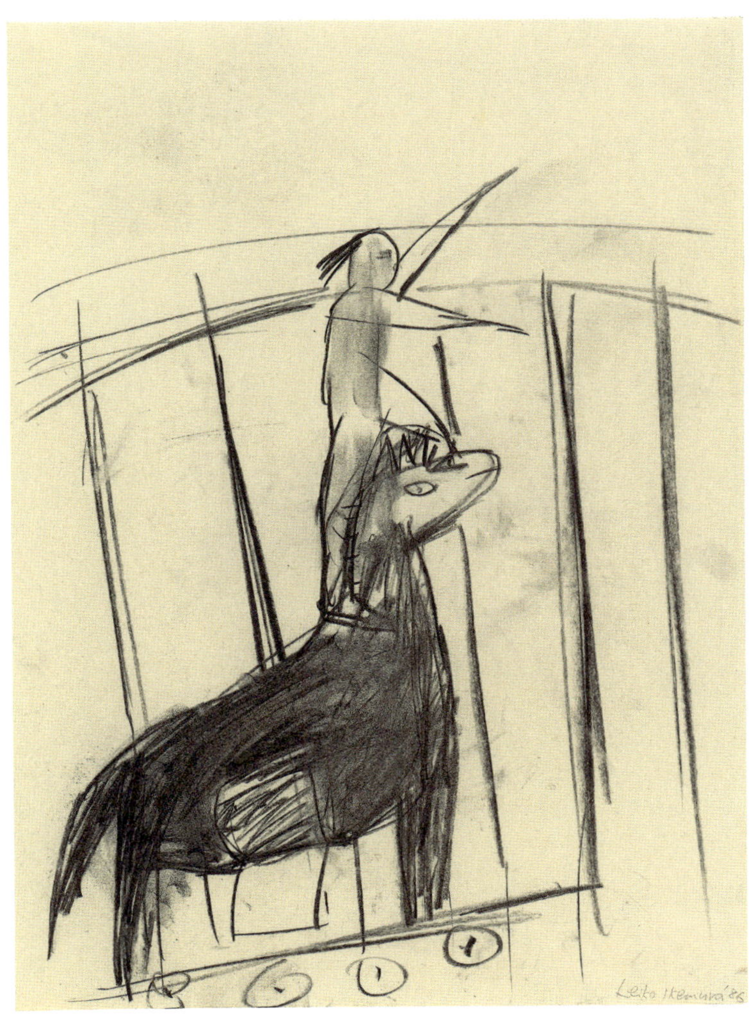

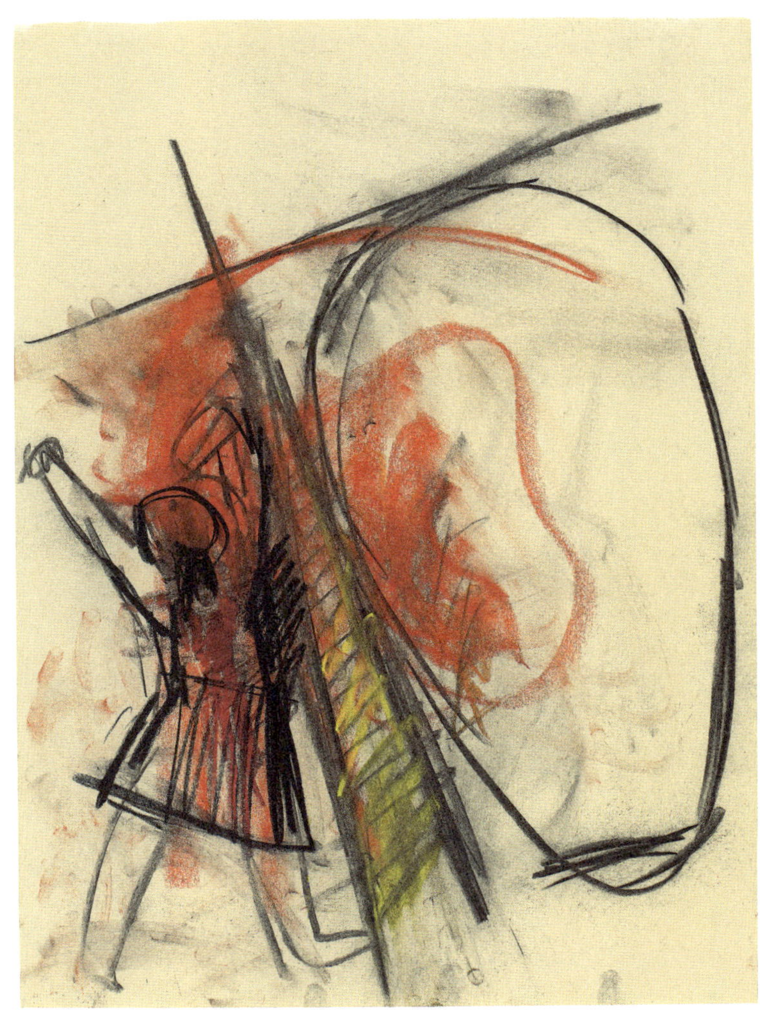

Ohne Titel | Untitled, 1986
Kohle, Bleistift und
Farbstift auf Papier |
Charcoal, pencil,
and crayon on paper,
29,9 × 39,9 cm
[Kat. | cat. 41]

Schlacht (Kriegsgöttin) |
Battle (Goddess of War),
1985
Kohle und Pastellkreide
auf Papier | Charcoal
and pastel on paper,
21 × 29,7 cm
[Kat. | cat. 39]

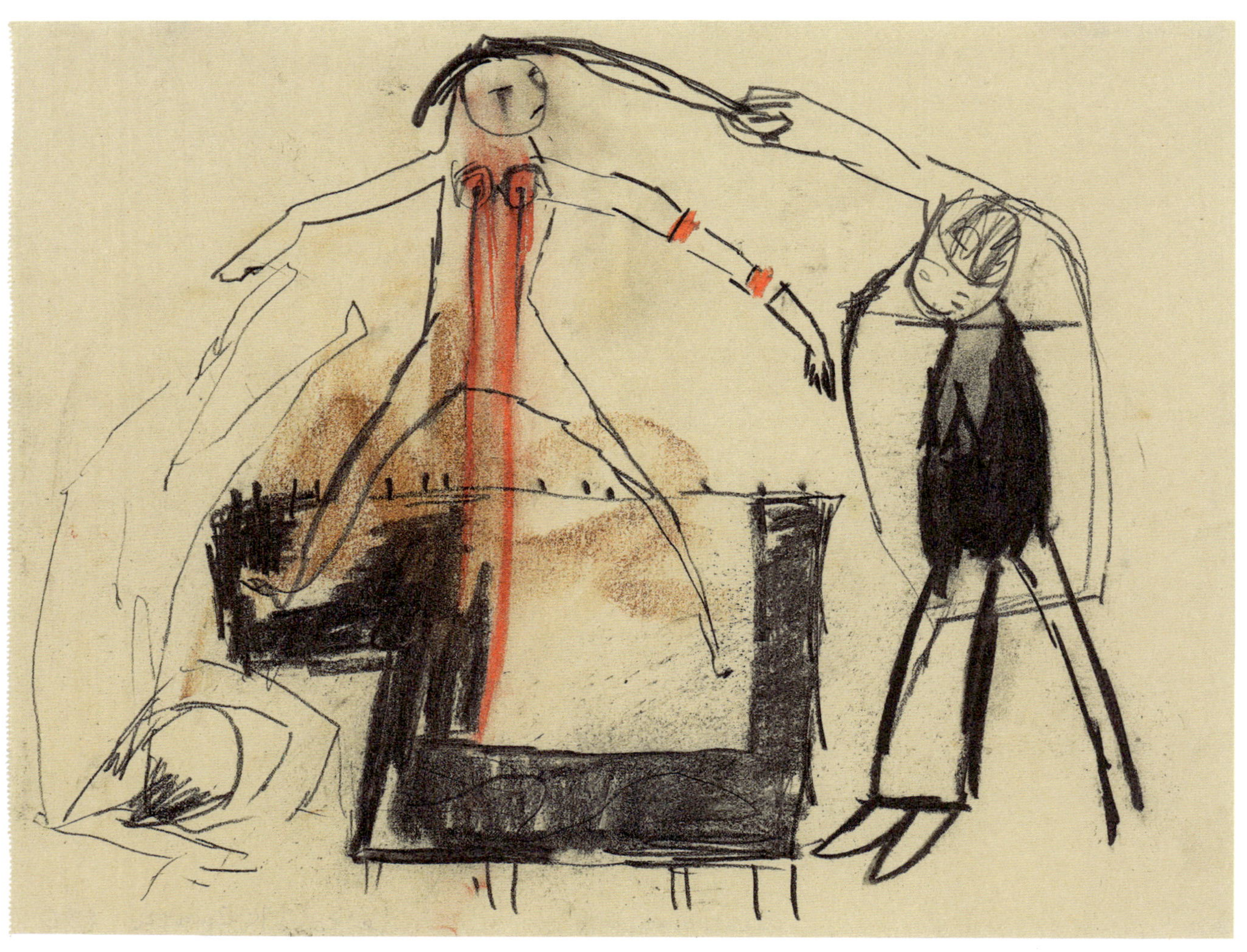

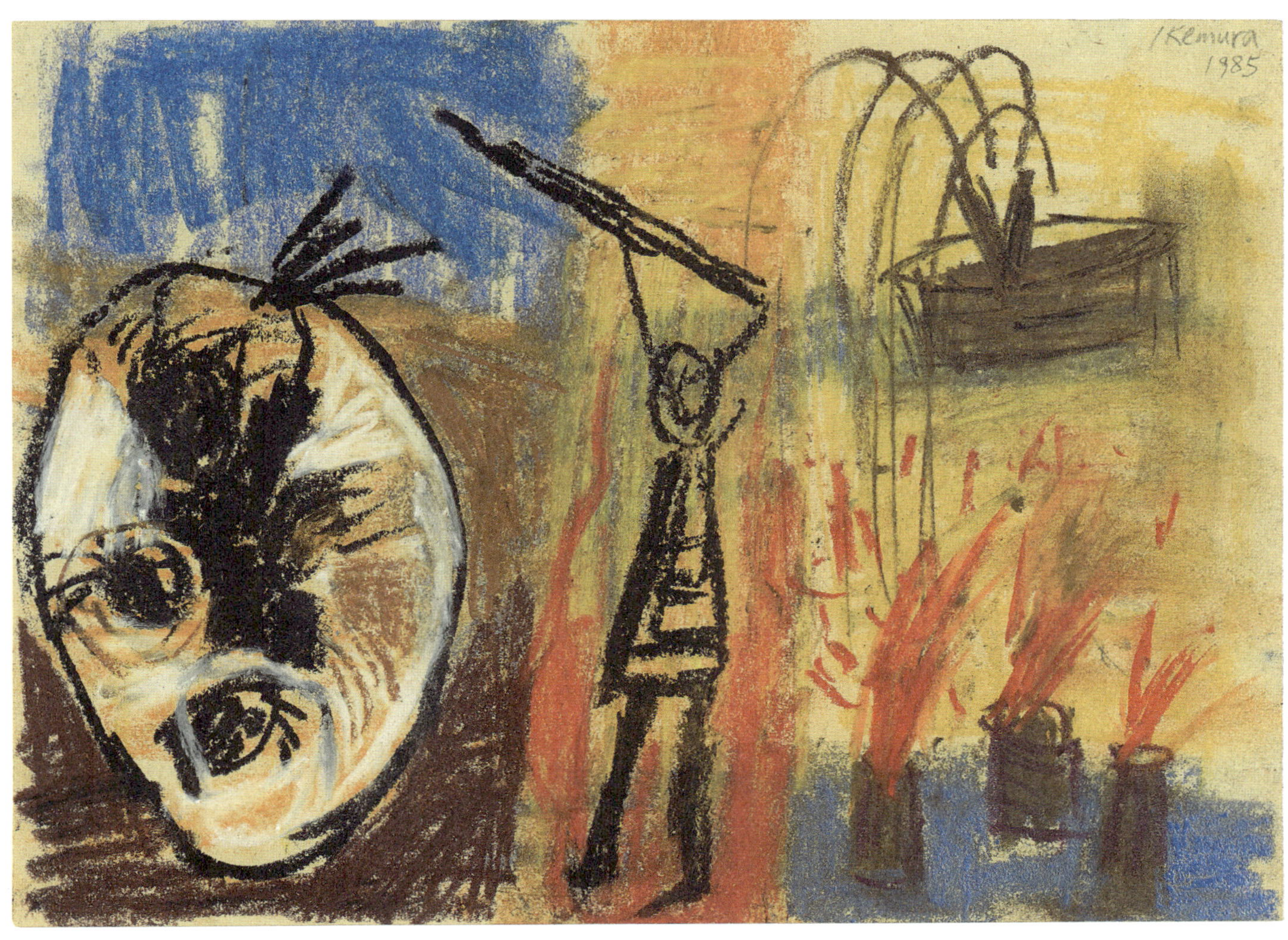
IKemura
1985

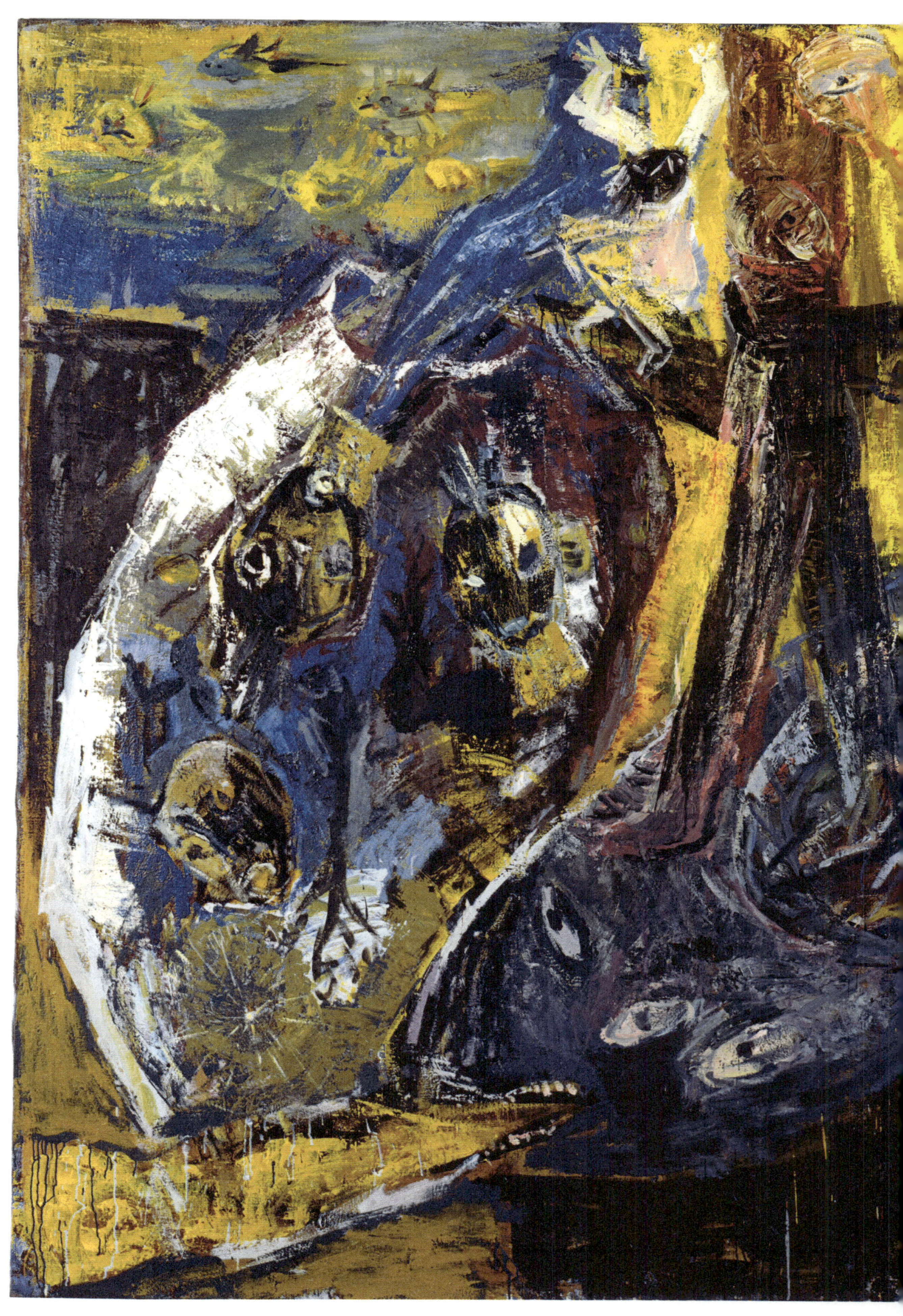

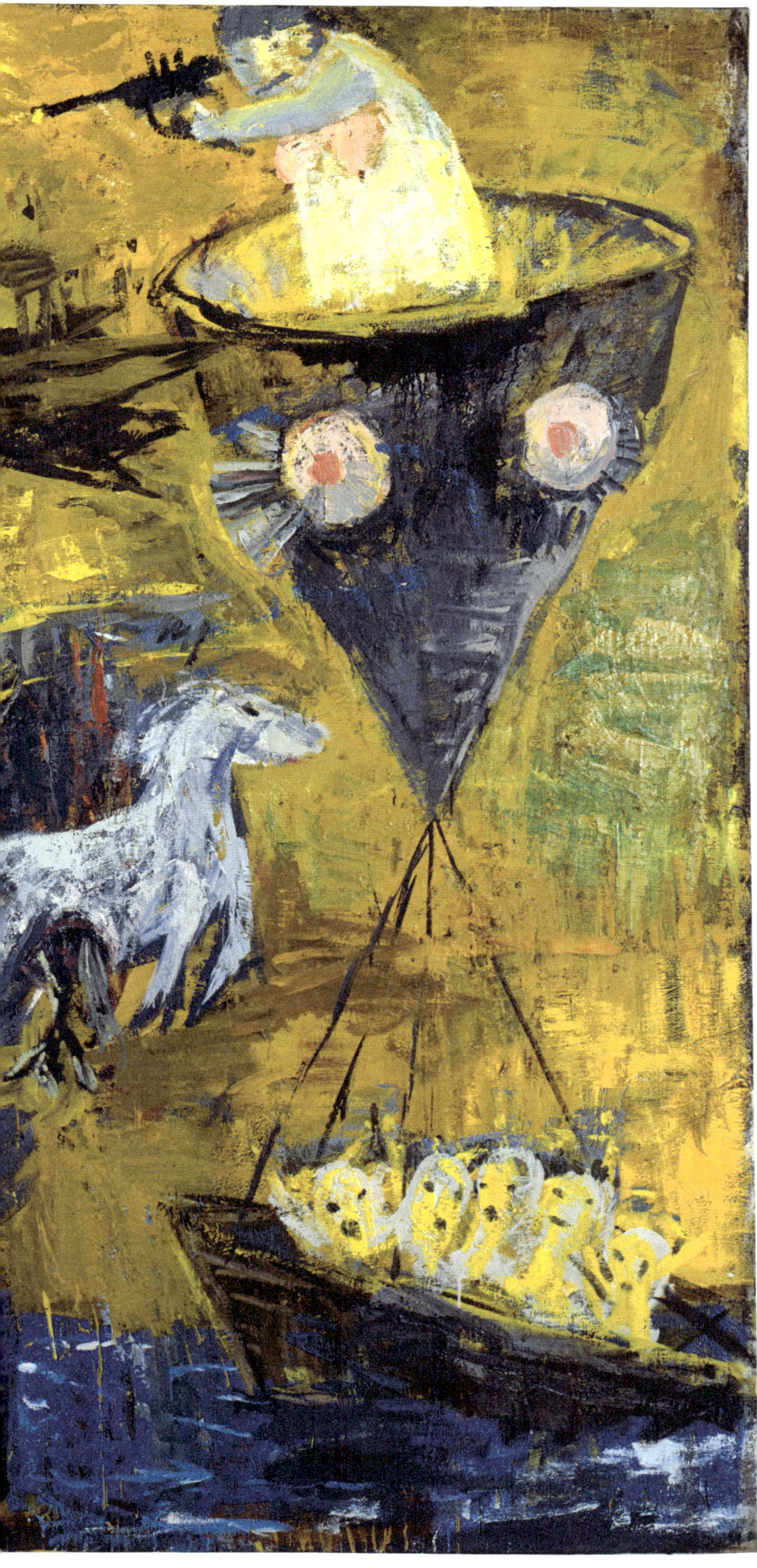

Ohne Titel | Untitled, 1987
Kohle, Aquarell, Kreide
und Öl auf Papier |
Charcoal, watercolor,
chalk, and oil on paper,
59,7 × 79,8 cm
[Kat. | cat. 42]

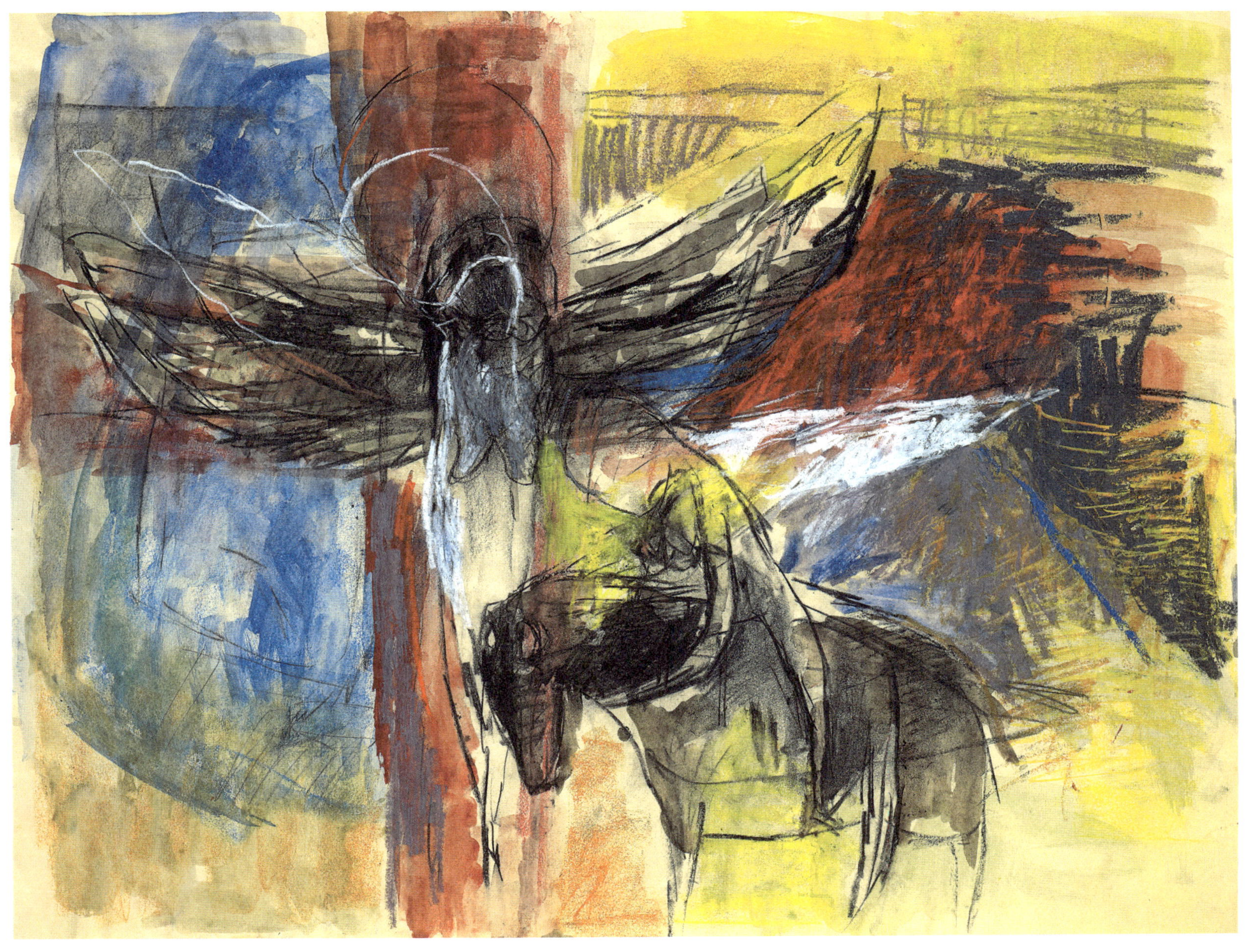

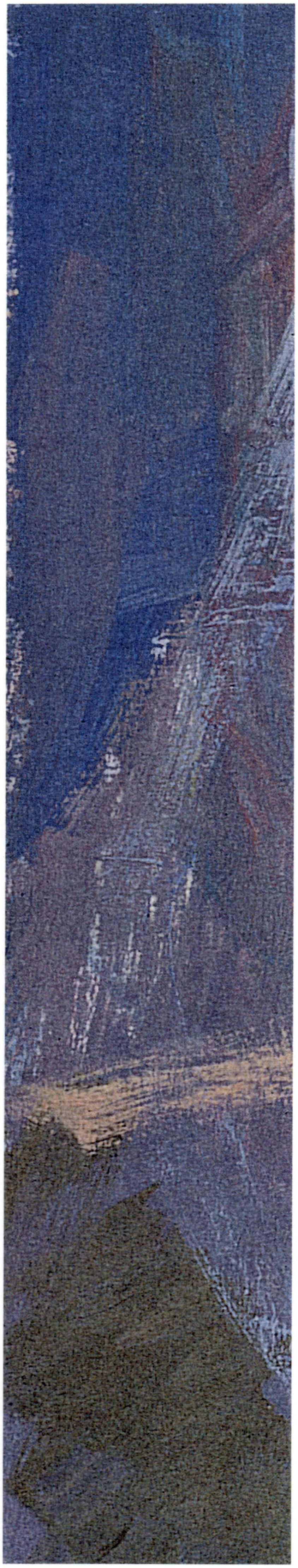

Alps Indians and Painterly Thinking

Ikemura's understanding of painting has already begun to emerge in paintings such as *Kriegsgöttin,* but she has not yet attained on canvas the effortlessness that she experiences in drawing. Her dissatisfaction with this culminates in a crisis in 1987. At first she produces dense, large-format drawings that take up themes of mother and child and resonate with Christian iconography. These are less expressive and more distinctly constructed than the earlier sheets. Concurrently, Ikemura also produces clay figures, which mark the beginning of her engagement with her rootedness in Japanese culture. The *Wächter* (Guard, 1987) and *Ahnenhaus* (Ancestral House, 1989) bring together important motifs that are symbols less of stability than of constant change and the lack of boundaries between the mundane and the spiritual world.

During a studio residency in the Canton of Grisons in 1989, Ikemura undertakes a radical change of style. In 1989/90, using more fluid color and a broad brush, she paints the series *Alpenindianer* (Alps Indians). She finds inspiration in the mountains, which also play an important mythological role in Japan and make human beings seem small and insignificant in the face of nature. She is stimulated by her engagement with space in Paul Cézanne and the Chinese monk and painter Sesshū. In the *Alpenindianer* the contours disappear; color alone gives rise to the sense of space in the image. Figure and landscape meld into a single continuum.

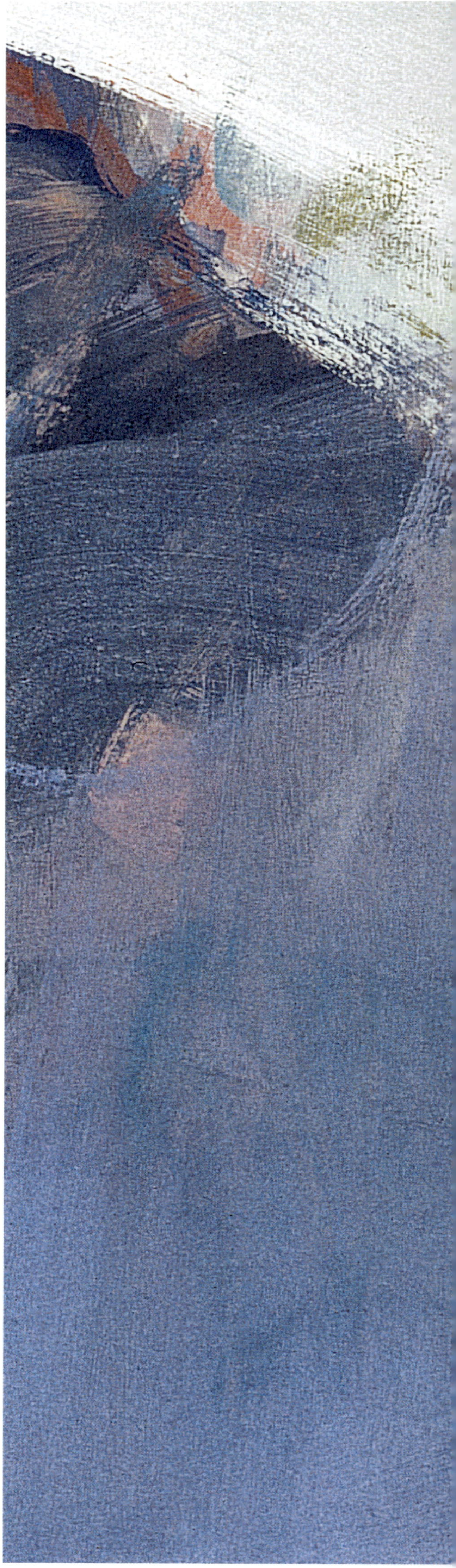

Alpenindianer und das malerische Denken

Ikemuras Verständnis von Malerei hat sich mit Gemälden wie *Kriegsgöttin* bereits abgezeichnet, trotzdem hat sie die Leichtigkeit, die sie im Zeichnen erlebt, auf der Leinwand noch nicht erreicht. Die Unzufriedenheit darüber kulminiert 1987 in einer Krise. Es entstehen zunächst grossformatige und dichte Zeichnungen, die etwa das Mutter-Kind-Thema aufnehmen und christliche Ikonografie anklingen lassen. Sie sind weniger expressiv und stärker konstruiert als die frühen Blätter. Zeitgleich entstehen ungebrannte Tonfiguren, die den Anfang der Beschäftigung mit der eigenen Verwurzelung in der japanischen Kultur markieren. *Wächter* (1987) und *Ahnenhaus* (1989) vereinen wichtige Motive, die weniger Symbole für die Beständigkeit sind als für den steten Wandel und die Grenzenlosigkeit zwischen der alltäglichen und der spirituellen Welt.

Während eines Atelieraufenthaltes im Kanton Graubünden 1989 vollzieht Ikemura einen radikalen Stilwechsel. Mit breitem Pinsel und flüssigeren Farben malt sie 1989/90 die Werkgruppe *Alpenindianer*. Die Berge, die den Menschen klein und unbedeutend erscheinen lassen und auch in der japanischen Mythologie eine wichtige Rolle spielen, inspirieren sie. Anregung findet sie ausserdem in der Auseinandersetzung mit Raum bei Paul Cézanne und dem chinesischen Maler und Mönch Sesshū. In *Alpenindianer* verschwinden die Konturen, allein die Farbe lässt Räumlichkeit im Bild entstehen. Figur und Landschaft verschmelzen zu einem Kontinuum.

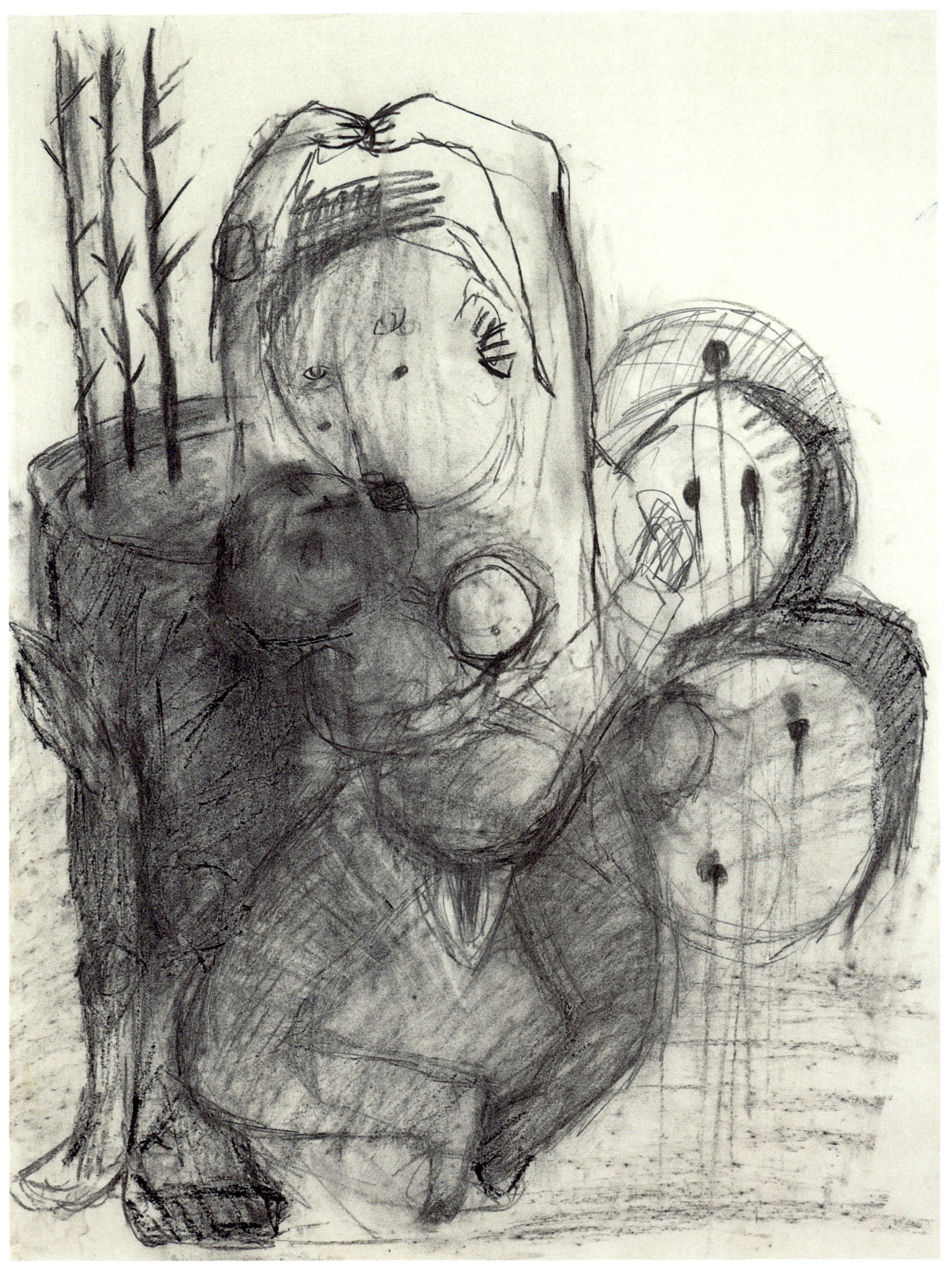

Ohne Titel | Untitled, 1987
Kohle und Ölkreide
auf Papier | Charcoal
and oil chalk on paper,
79,8 × 59,8 cm
[Kat. | cat. 44]

Wächter | Guard, 1987
Ton, ungebrannt | Clay,
unfired, 29 × 16 × 28,5 cm
[Kat. | cat. 48]

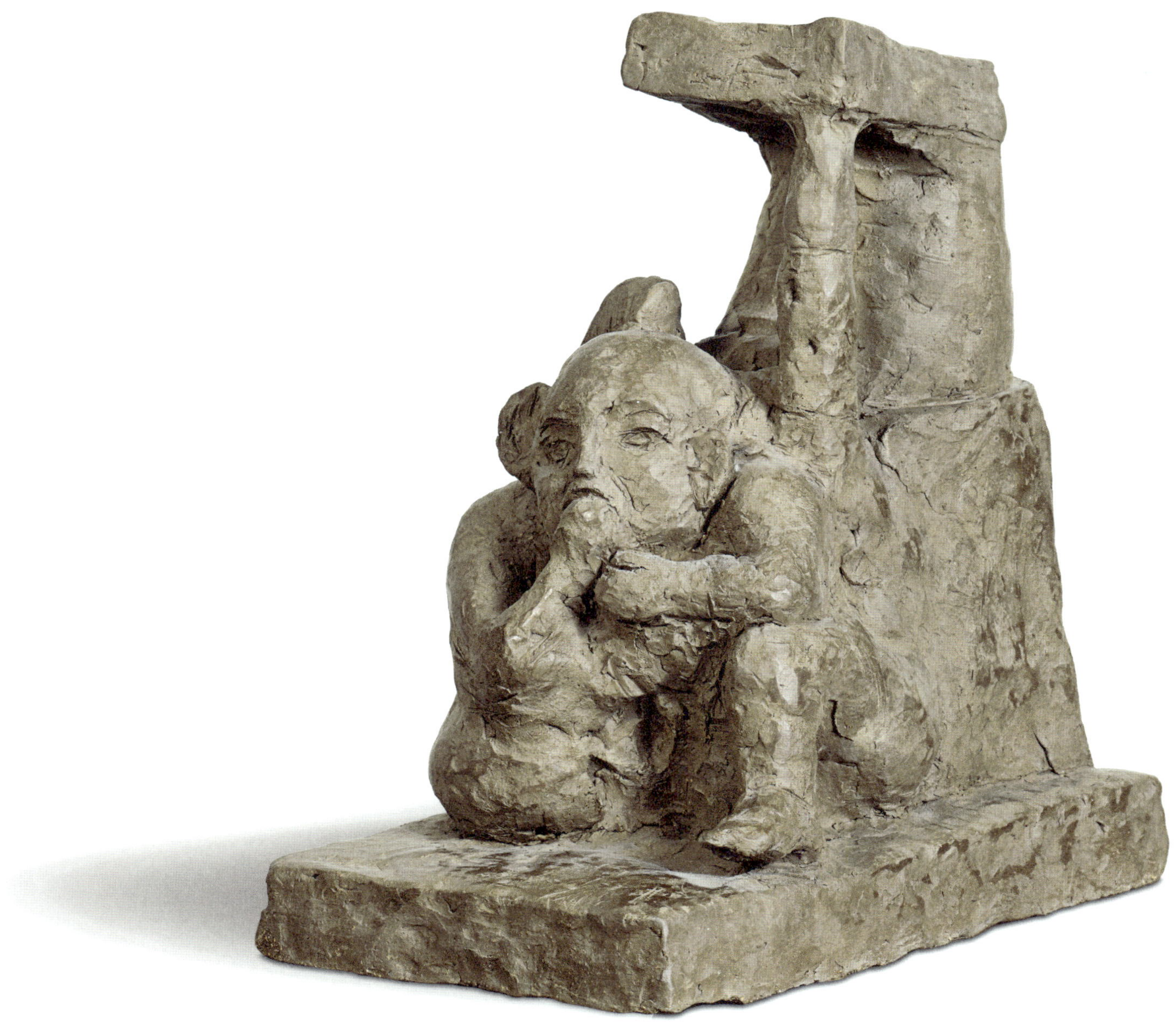

Ohne Titel | Untitled, 1987
Kohle, Wasserfarbe
und Kreide auf Papier,
auf Leinwand aufge-
zogen | Charcoal,
watercolor, and chalk
on paper, mounted
on canvas, 80 × 59,6 cm
[Kat. | cat. 45]

Ohne Titel | Untitled, 1987
Kohle, Wasserfarbe
und Kreide auf Papier,
auf Leinwand aufge-
zogen | Charcoal,
watercolor, and chalk
on paper, mounted
on canvas, 80 × 59,6 cm
[Kat. | cat. 45]

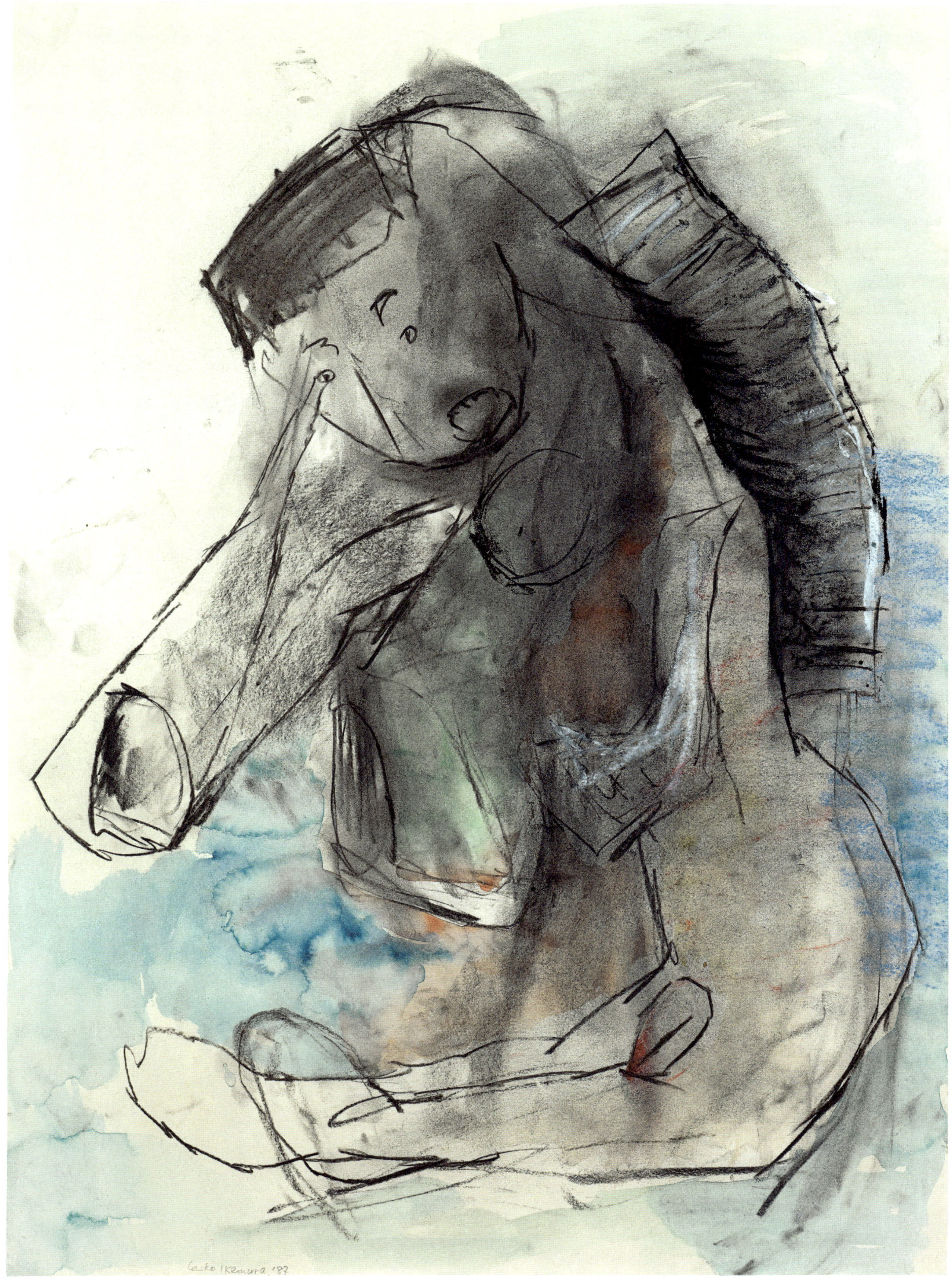

Ahnenhaus | Ancestral
House, 1989
Ton, ungebrannt | Clay,
unfired, 33 × 18 × 31 cm
[Kat. | cat. 49]

Ohne Titel | Untitled, 1987
Kohle auf Papier |
Charcoal on paper,
80 × 59,7 cm
[Kat. | cat. 46]

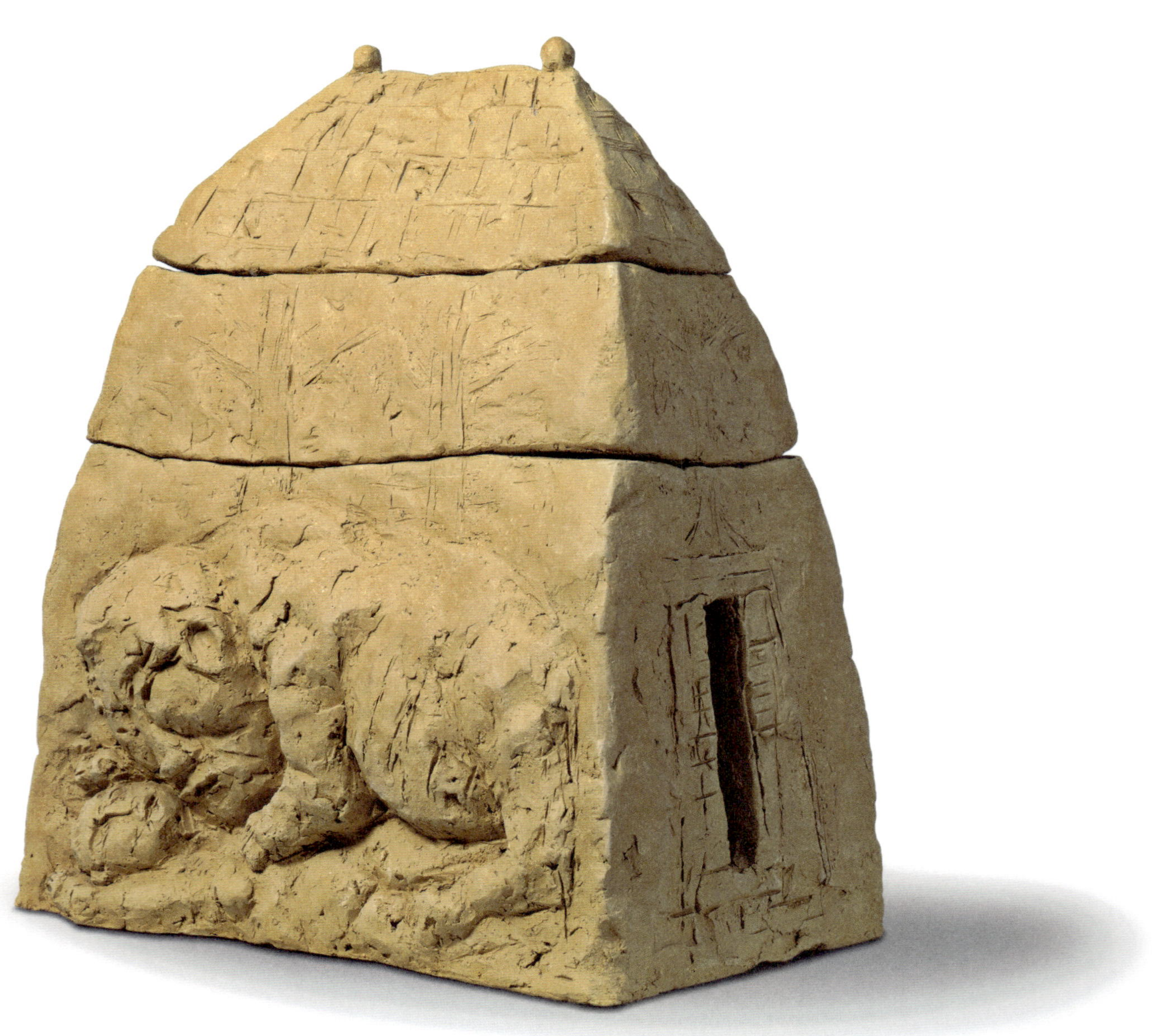

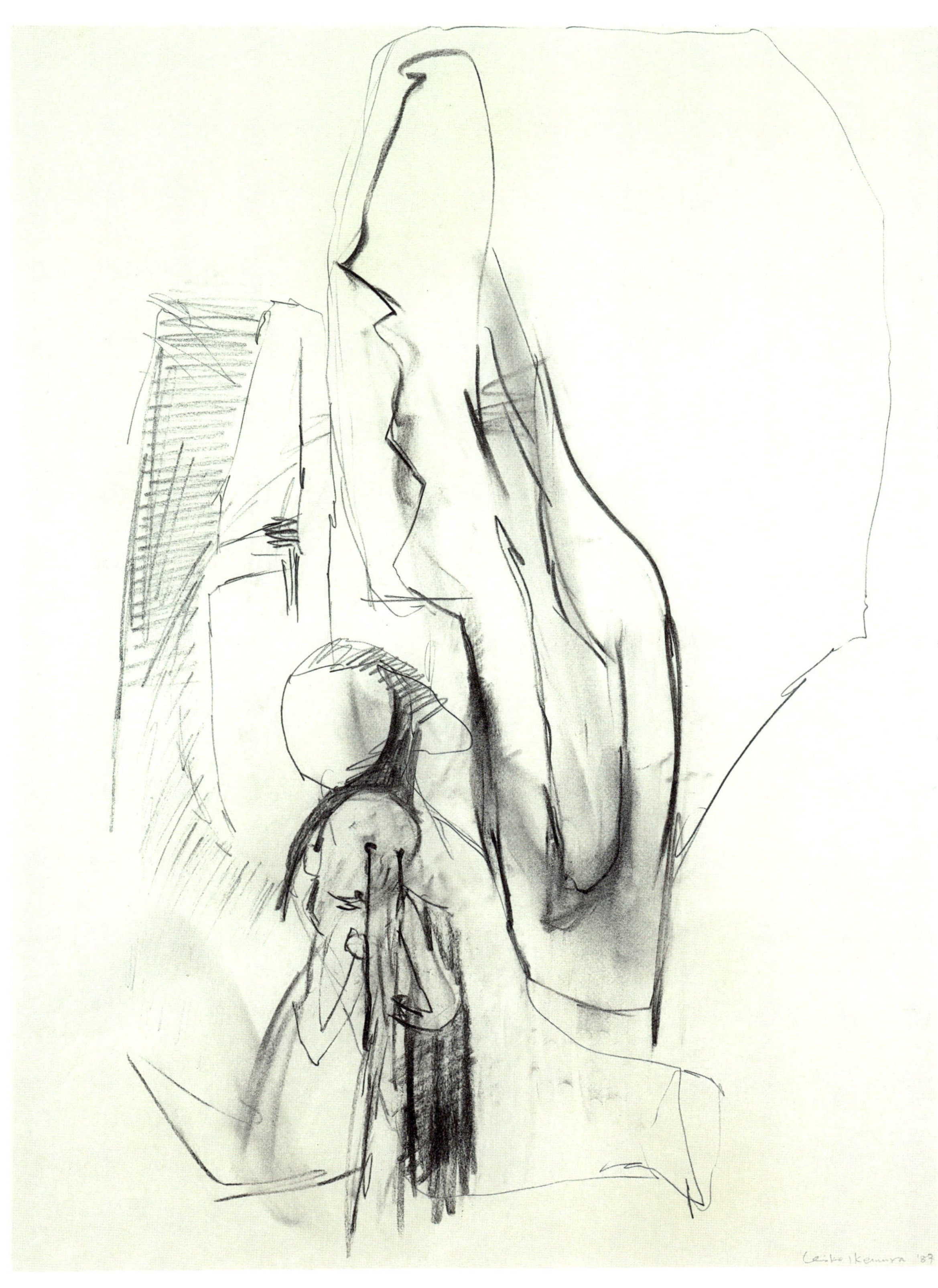

Ohne Titel | Untitled, 1987
Kohle und Bleistift
auf Papier | Charcoal
and pencil on paper,
79,9 × 59,9 cm
[Kat. | cat. 47]

Alpenindianer |
Alps Indians, 1989
Acryl auf Leinwand |
Acrylic on canvas,
127 × 88,5 cm
[Kat. | cat. 50]

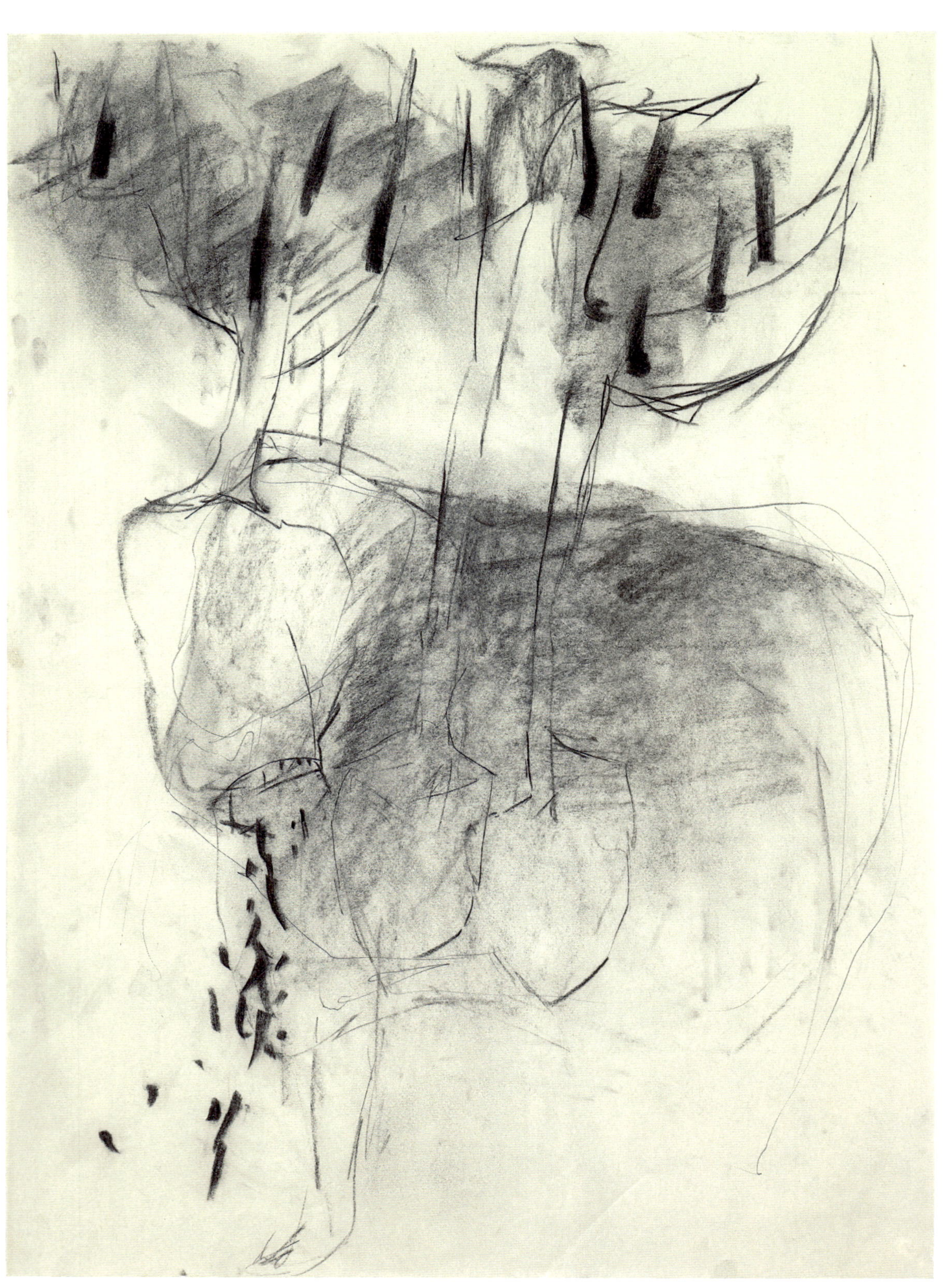

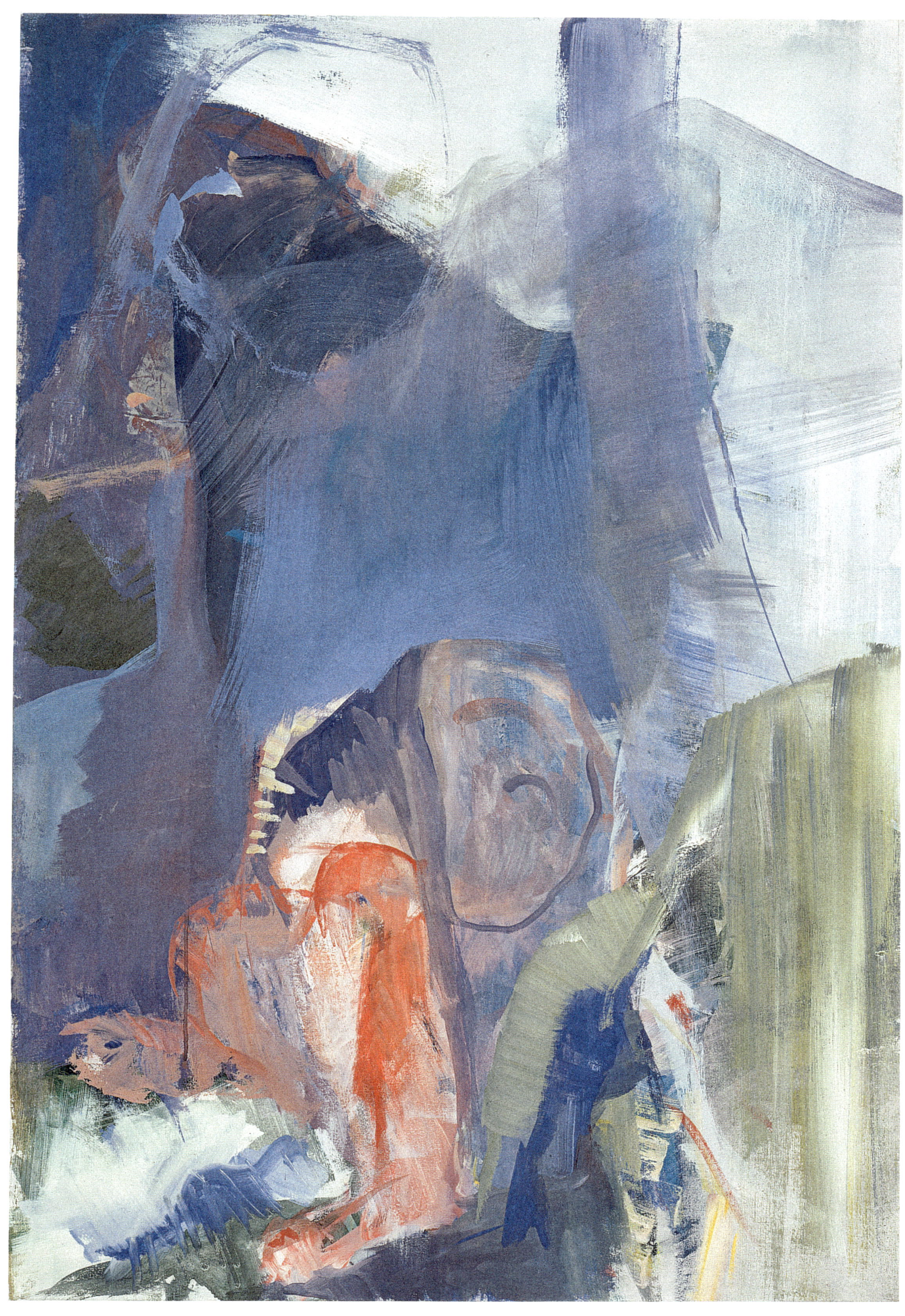

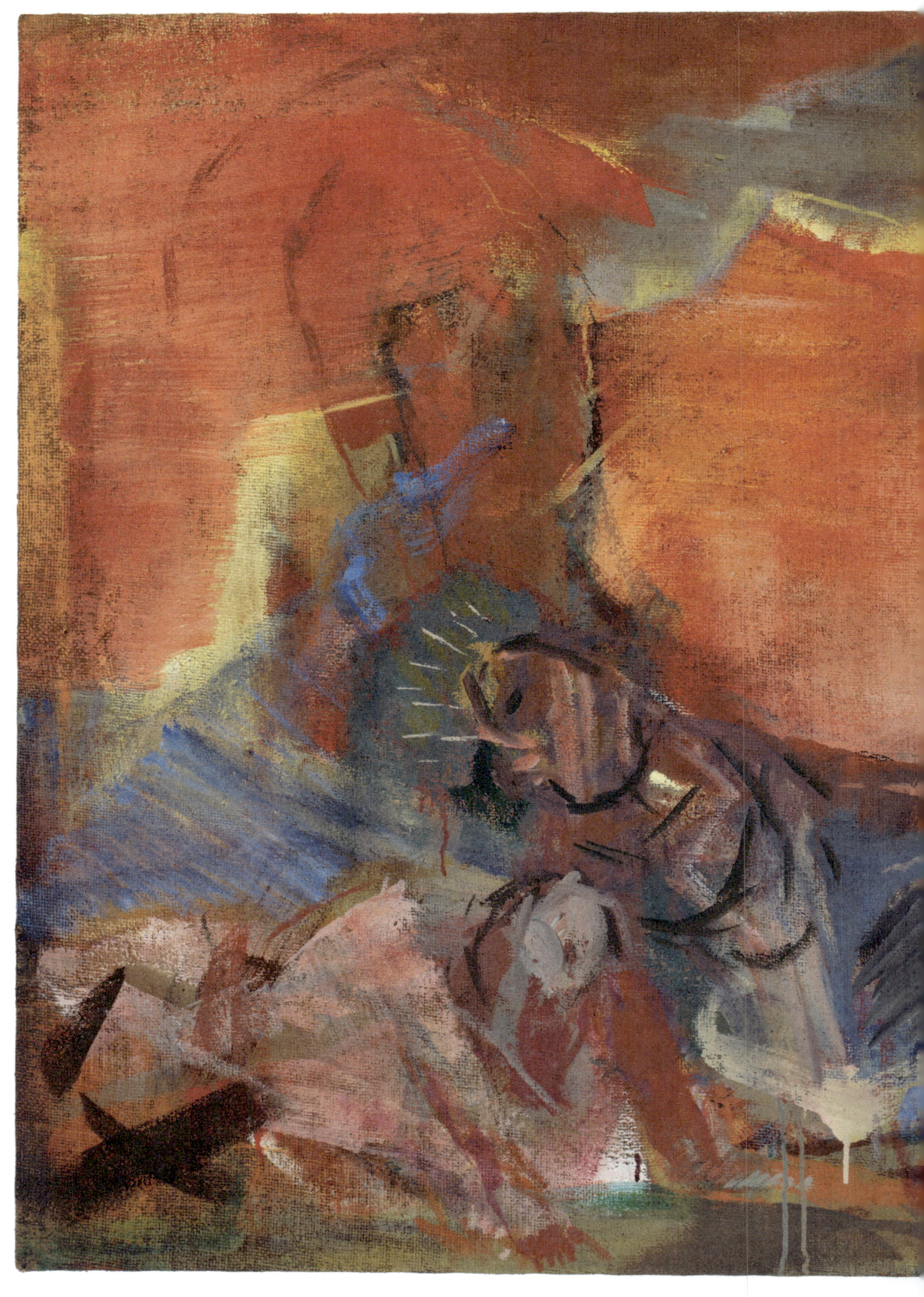

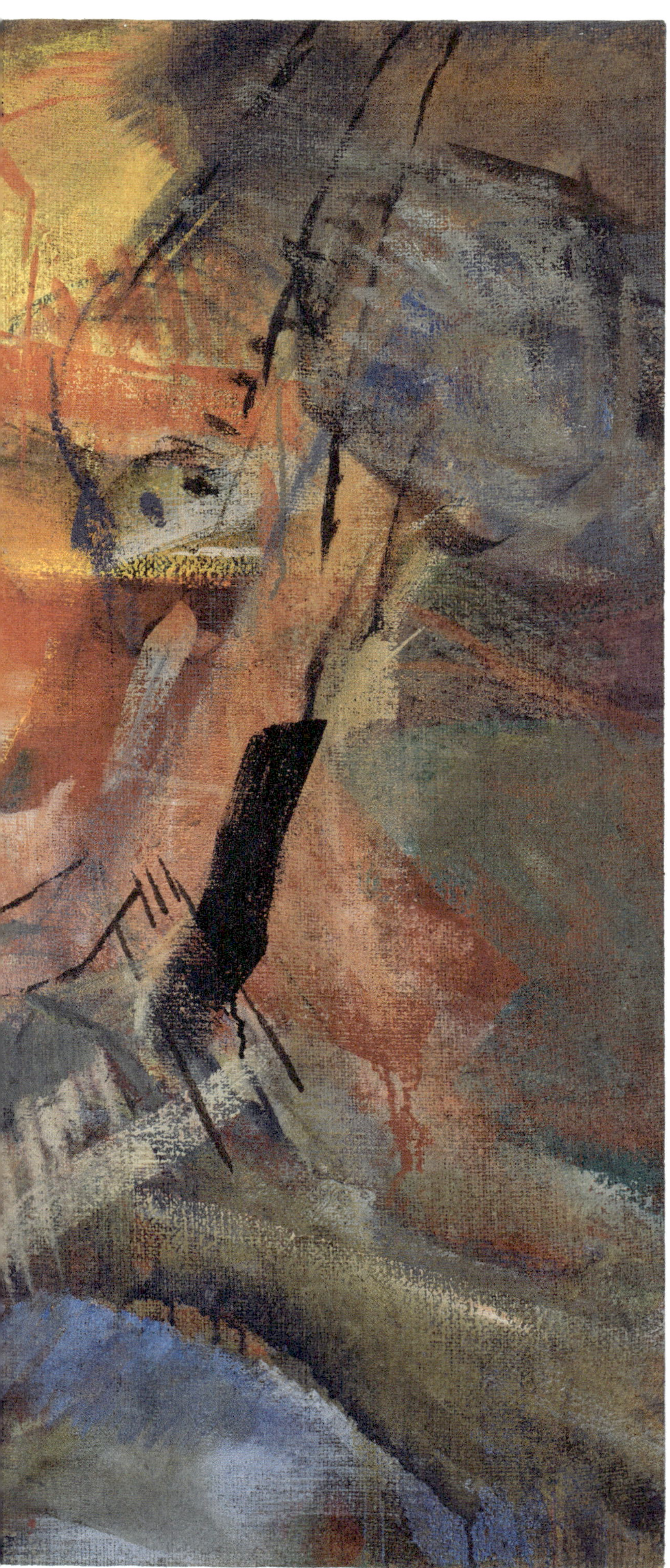

Rot | Red, 1989
Acryl auf Leinwand |
Acrylic on canvas,
103 × 124,5 cm
[Kat. | cat. 51]

Skifahrer auf dem Malojasee | Skier on
Maloja Lake, 1990
Tempera auf Leinwand |
Tempera on canvas,
120 × 94 cm
[Kat. | cat. 52]

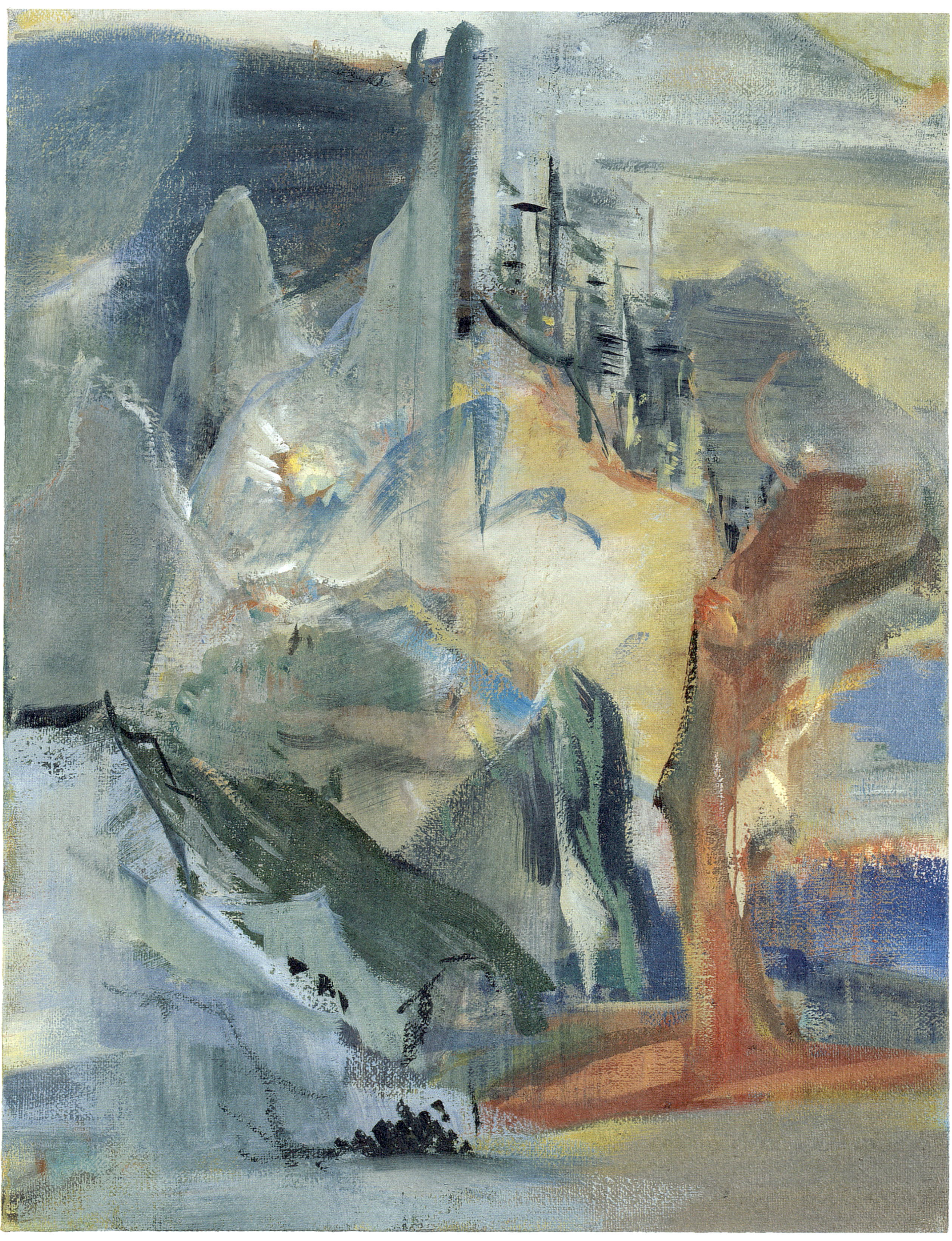

Hybrid Mythical Creatures

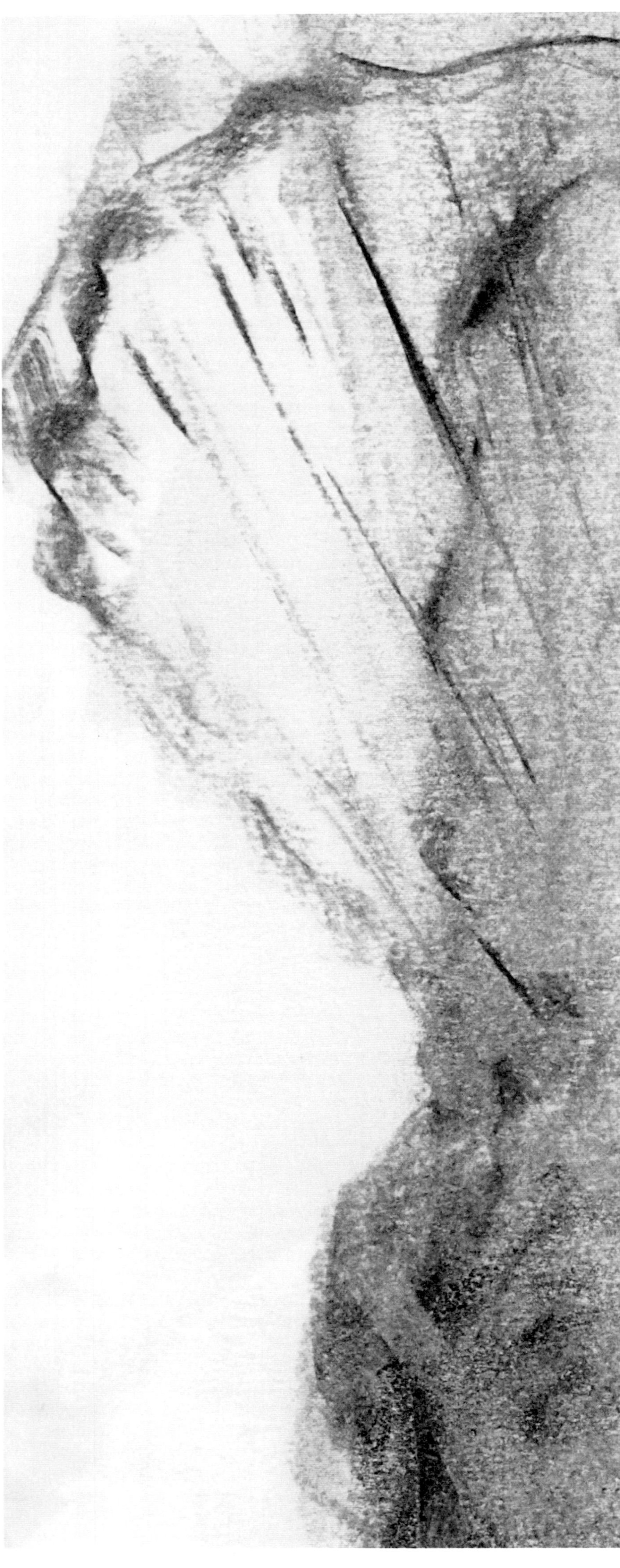

The early 1990s are a time of new departures and clarity for Leiko Ikemura. Thematically, this entails contemplation of the origins of life and originary ancestors. She invents raw, archaic-seeming mythical creatures and now begins to emphasize the specific qualities of each medium. While in the delicate drawings she thematizes the growth of the originary beings with the aid of searching lines made with a soft charcoal pencil, in the sculptures her focus is on bringing out their massive corporeal presence. Although this work is related to her unfired clay sculptures of the 1980s, now Ikemura emphasizes the sensuality of the surface with colored glazes and lends the figures a great sense of plasticity.

Oscillating between human, animal, and plant, the mythical creatures are firmly anchored to the ground. Ikemura uses the charcoal flatly, for shading, and then defines the contours of the figure with a few lines and sets a few accents with the point. The delicate application of the powdery coal brings forth the quality of the paper. Varying the pressure, the direction, the angle, and the width or length of the charcoal stick creates multifaceted structures on the paper.

The cast bronze *Hase-Frau* (Hare-Woman) of 1990/91 has the ears of a hare. They rest directly above the breasts of the torso, which emerges out of an architectonic base. The base evokes the skirts of Ikemura's later sculptures of girls. Although the hybrid ur-creatures are mostly androgynous, their appearance suggests a female being.

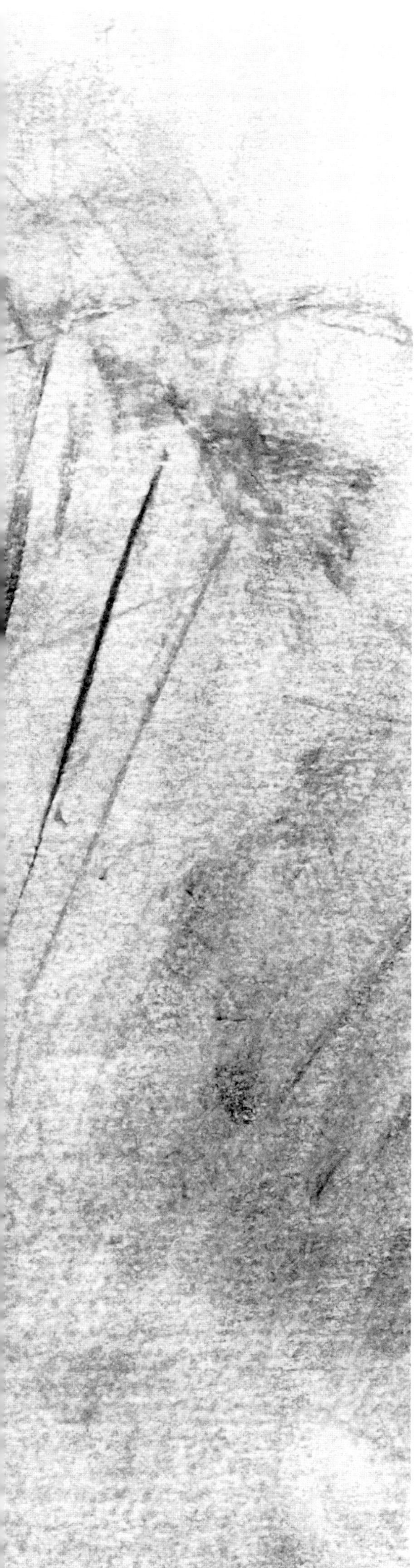

Hybride
Fabelwesen

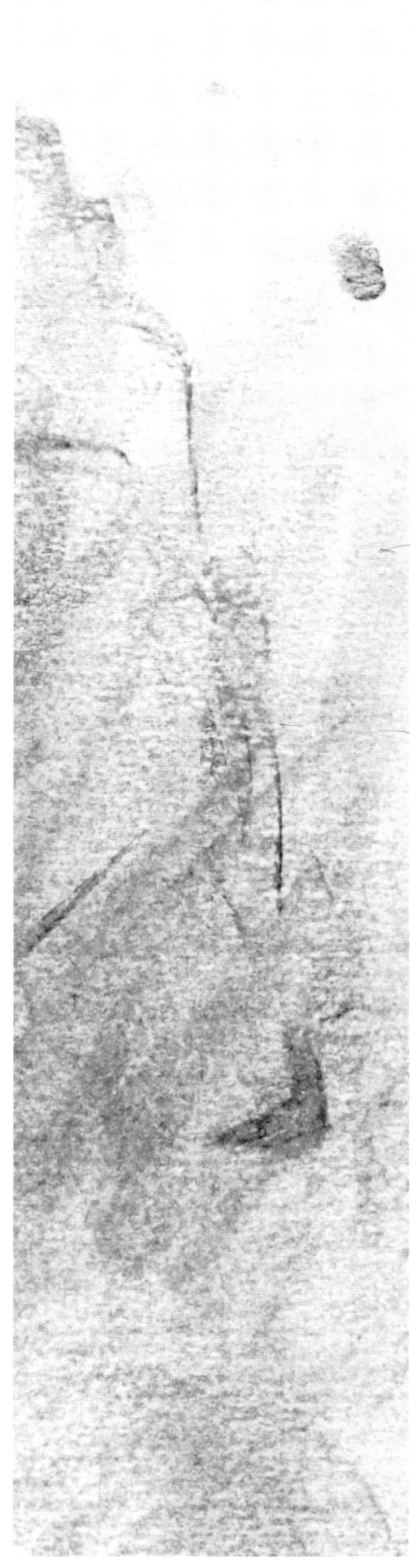

Die frühen 1990er-Jahre sind für Leiko Ikemura die Zeit des Aufbruchs und der Klärung. Damit geht thematisch die Besinnung auf die Ursprünge des Lebens und die Urahnen einher. Sie erfindet rohe, archaisch anmutende Fabelwesen und beginnt, die spezifischen Qualitäten ihrer Medien zu betonen. Während sie in den feinen Zeichnungen das Wachsen von Urwesen mithilfe der suchenden Linie des weichen Kohlestifts thematisiert, legt sie den Fokus in den Skulpturen auf die Herausarbeitung der massiven körperlichen Präsenz. Zwar knüpft Ikemura an die ungebrannten Tonplastiken der 1980er-Jahre an, doch hebt sie nun mit farbiger Glasur die Sinnlichkeit der Oberfläche hervor und verleiht den Figuren grosse Körperhaftigkeit.

In den Zeichnungen erscheinen Fabelwesen, die zwischen Mensch, Tier und Pflanze oszillieren und fest im Boden verankert sind. Ikemura nutzt die Kohle flächig, schattierend, um dann mit wenigen Linien die Figur zu umreissen und mit der Spitze wenige Akzente zu setzen. Durch den zarten Auftrag der pudrigen Kohle kommt die Qualität des Papiers zum Tragen. Veränderungen des Drucks, der Richtung und des Winkels beziehungsweise der Dicke oder Länge des Kohlestifts lassen vielseitige Strukturen auf dem Papier entstehen.

Die Ohren der 1990/91 in Bronze gegossenen Figur *Hase-Frau* gleichen denen eines Hasen. Sie ruhen oberhalb der Brüste direkt auf dem Oberkörper, der wiederum aus einem architektonisch anmutenden Sockel emporwächst. Dieser lässt bereits die Röcke der Mädchenplastiken anklingen. Die hybriden Urwesen sind zwar meist androgyn, doch kündigt sich hier das Erscheinen weiblicher Wesen an.

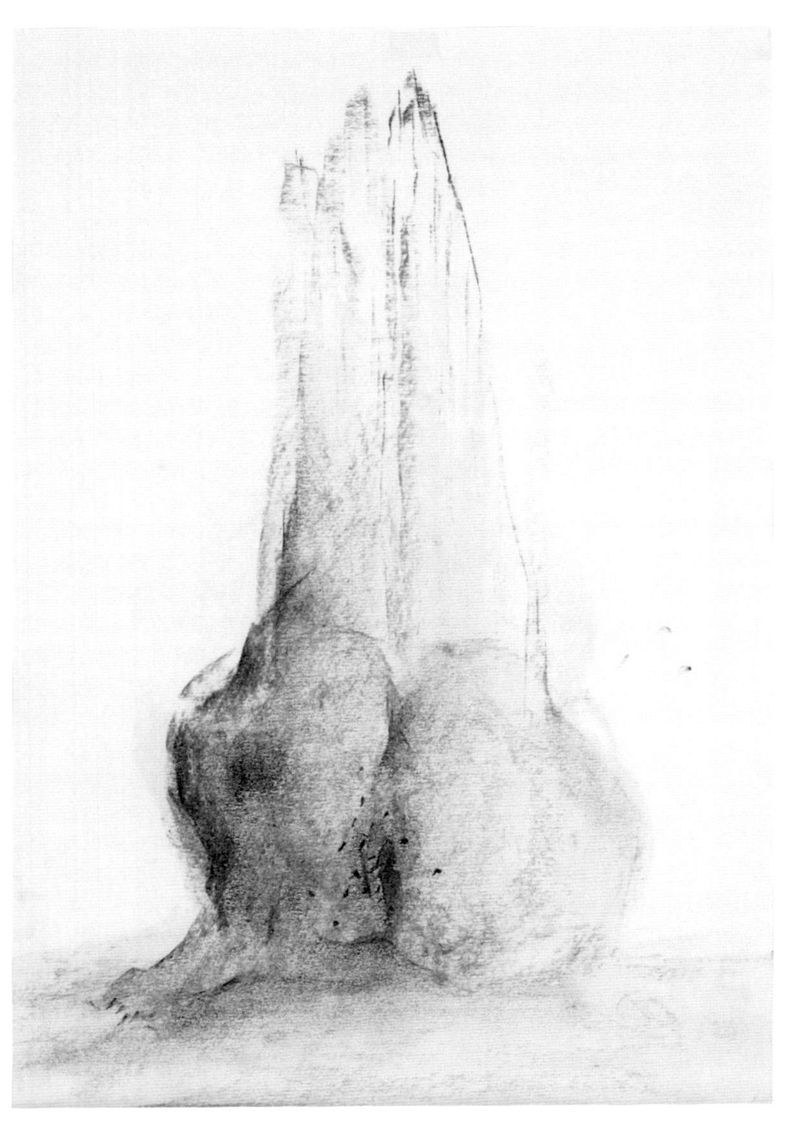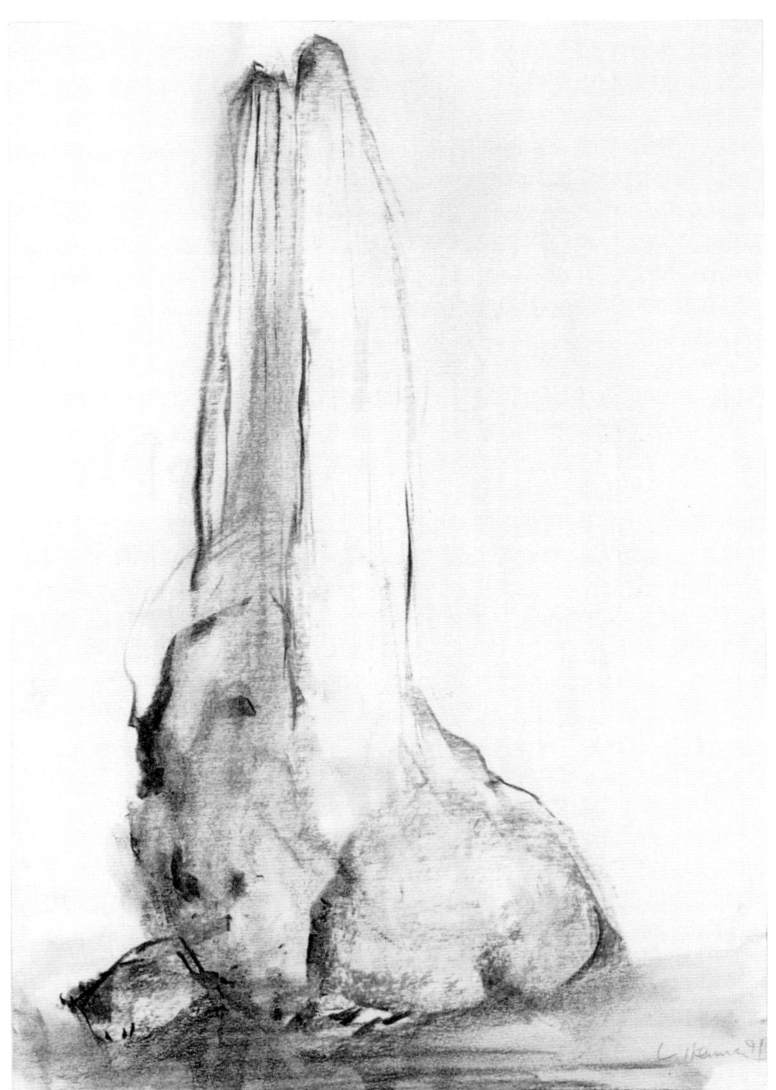

Ur 8, 1990
Kohle auf Papier |
Charcoal on paper,
42,0×29,7 cm
[Kat. | cat. 53]

Ha, 1991
Kohle auf Papier |
Charcoal on paper,
42,0×29,7 cm
[Kat. | cat. 56]

Grüne Ohren lang |
Green Ears Long, 1993
Terrakotta, glasiert |
Terra-cotta, glazed,
19×16×41 cm
[Kat. | cat. 61]

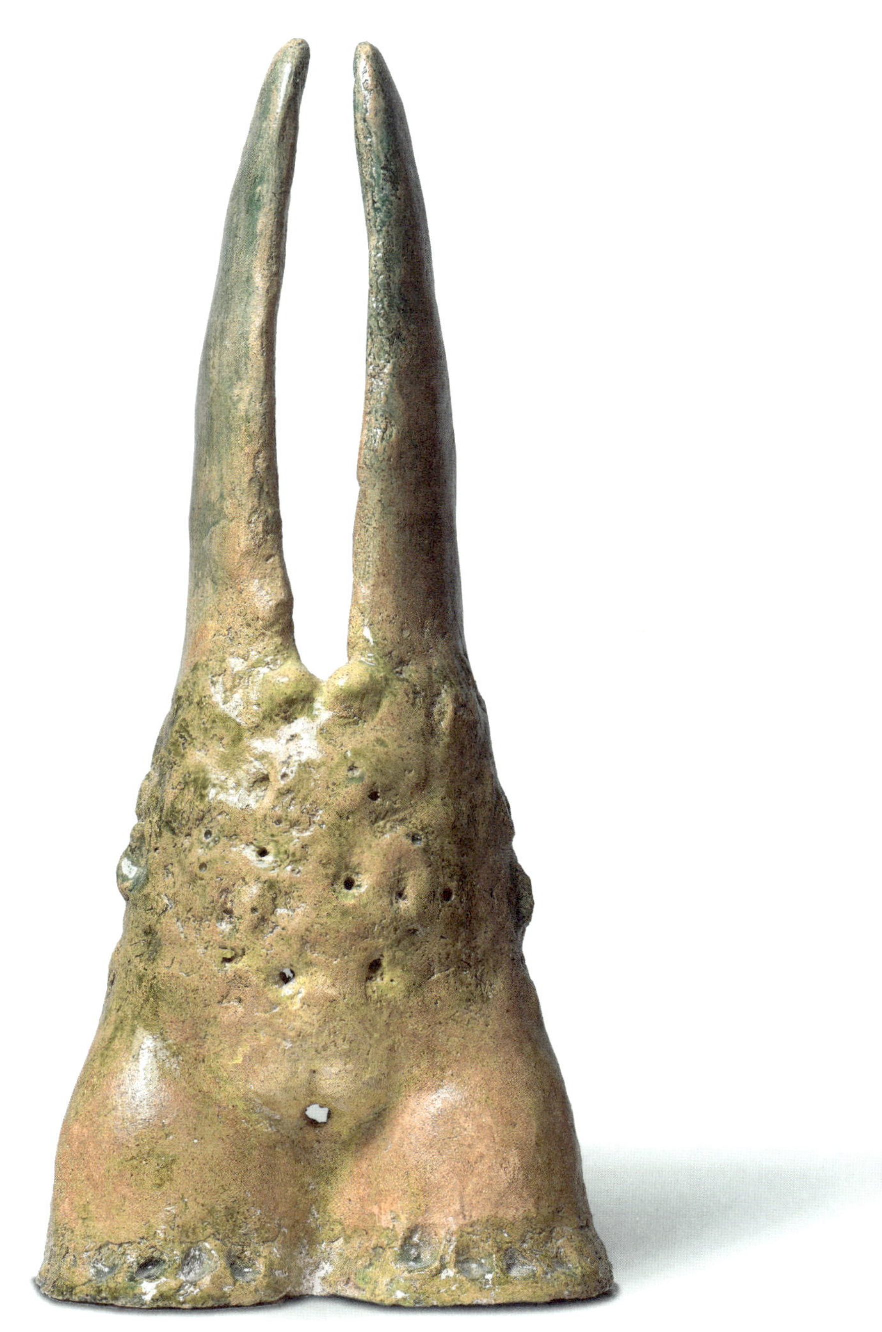

Türkises Baby | Turquoise
Baby, 1994
Terrakotta, glasiert |
Terra-cotta, glazed,
17 × 13 × 43 cm
[Kat. | cat. 59]

*Stehende Figur in Petrol-
blau* | Standing Figure in
Petrol Blue, 1990/91
Terrakotta, glasiert |
Terra-cotta, glazed,
20 × 10 × 40 cm
[Kat. | cat. 57]

Ur 11, 1990
Kohle auf Papier |
Charcoal on paper,
42,0 × 29,7 cm
[Kat. | cat. 55]

Ur 9, 1990
Kohle auf Papier |
Charcoal on paper,
42,0 × 29,7 cm
[Kat. | cat. 54]

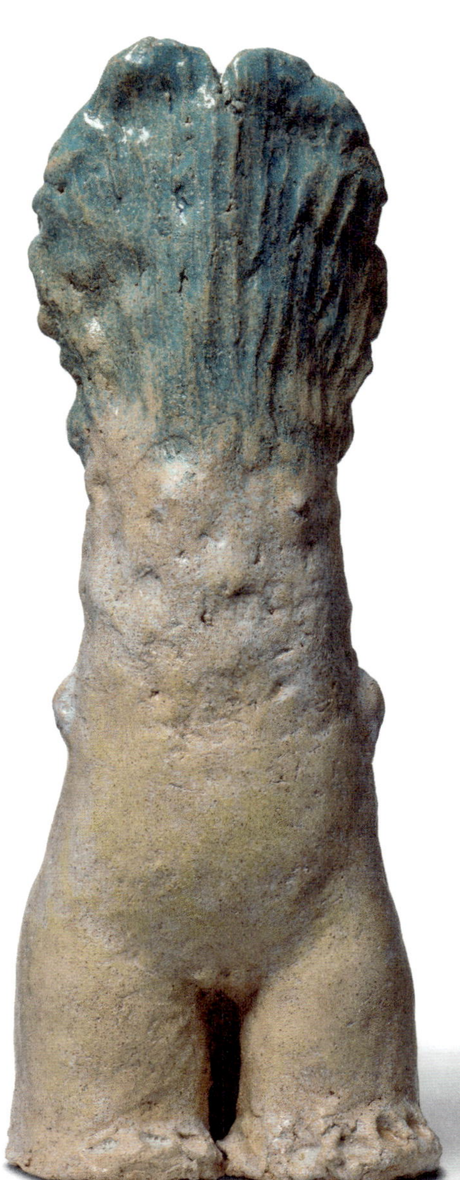

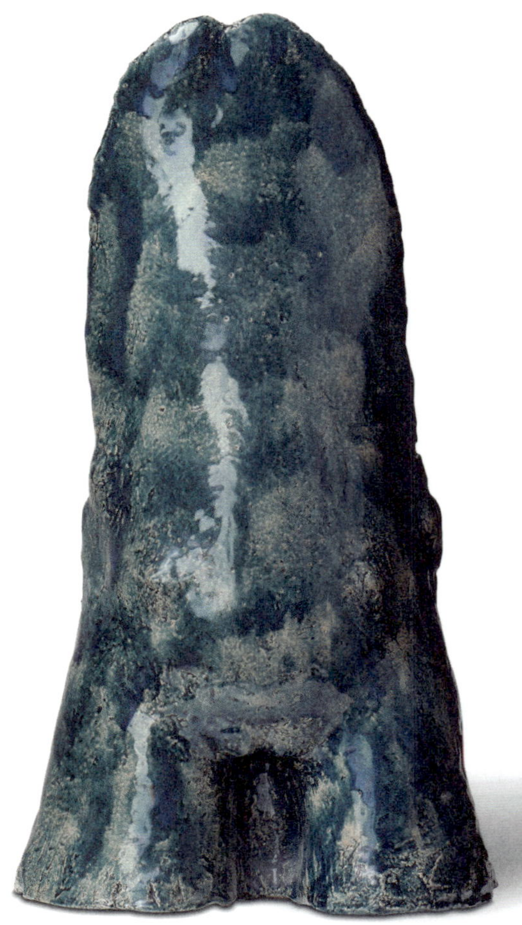

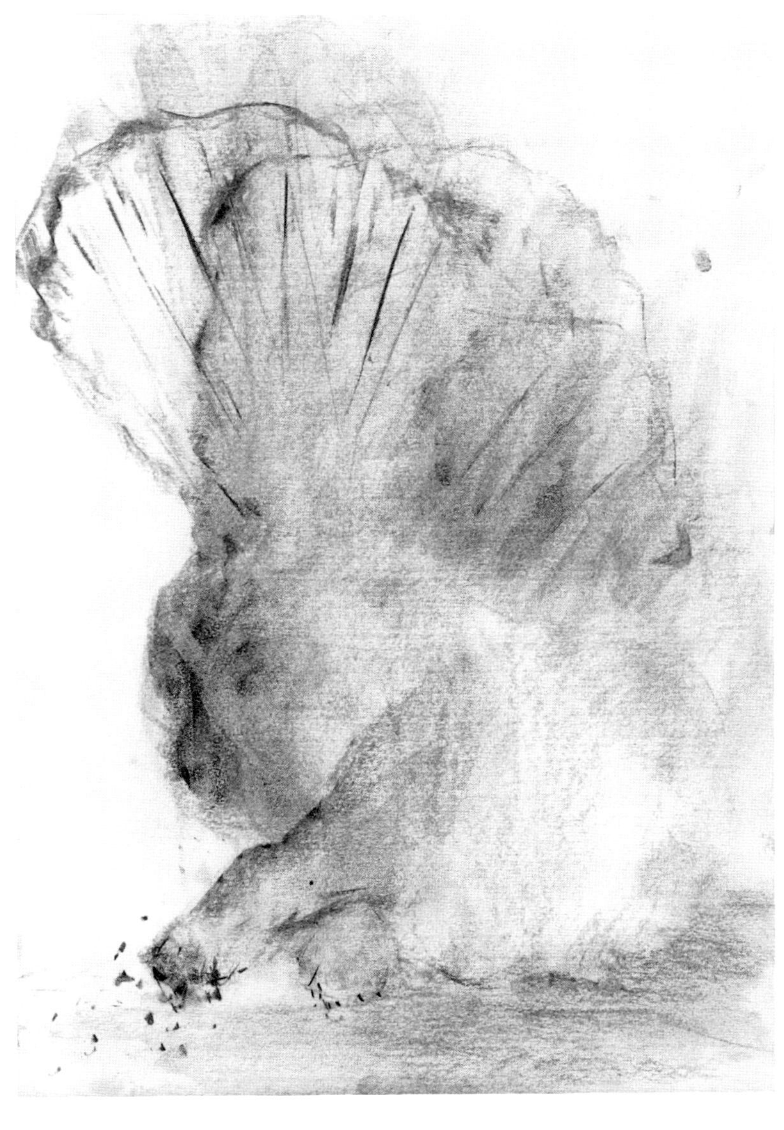

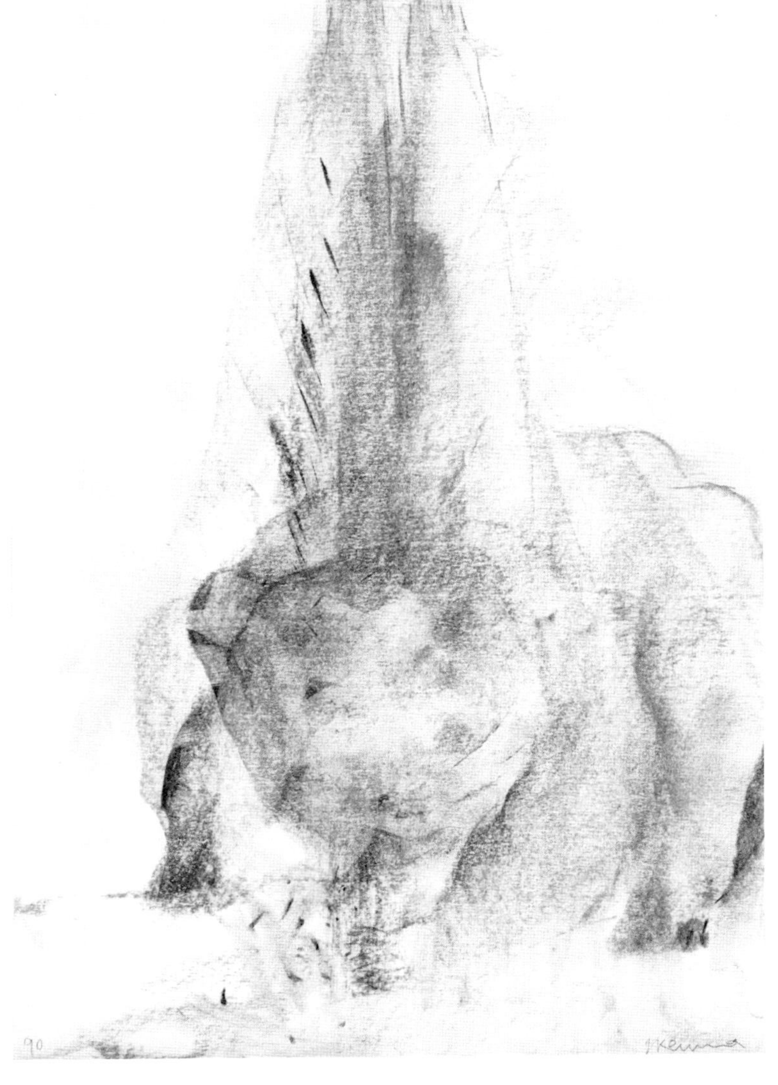

Ur, 1992
Bronze, 27,5 × 23 × 47 cm
[Kat. | cat. 58]

Hase-Frau | Hare-
Woman, 1990/91
Bronze, 19 × 19 × 58 cm
[Kat. | cat. 60]

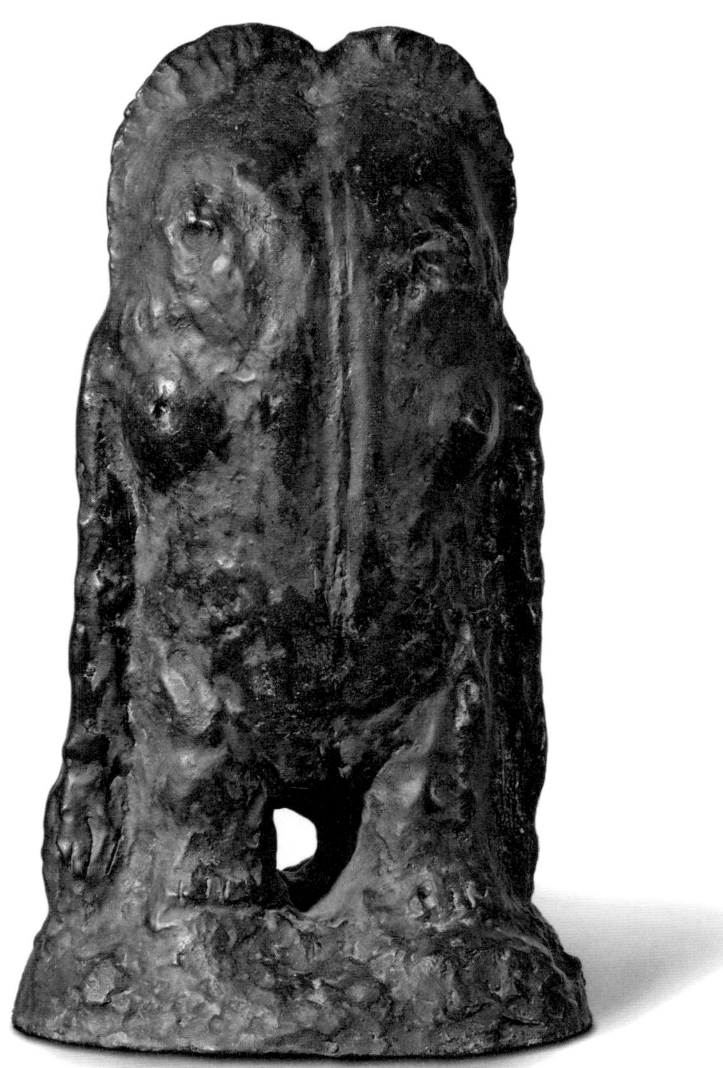

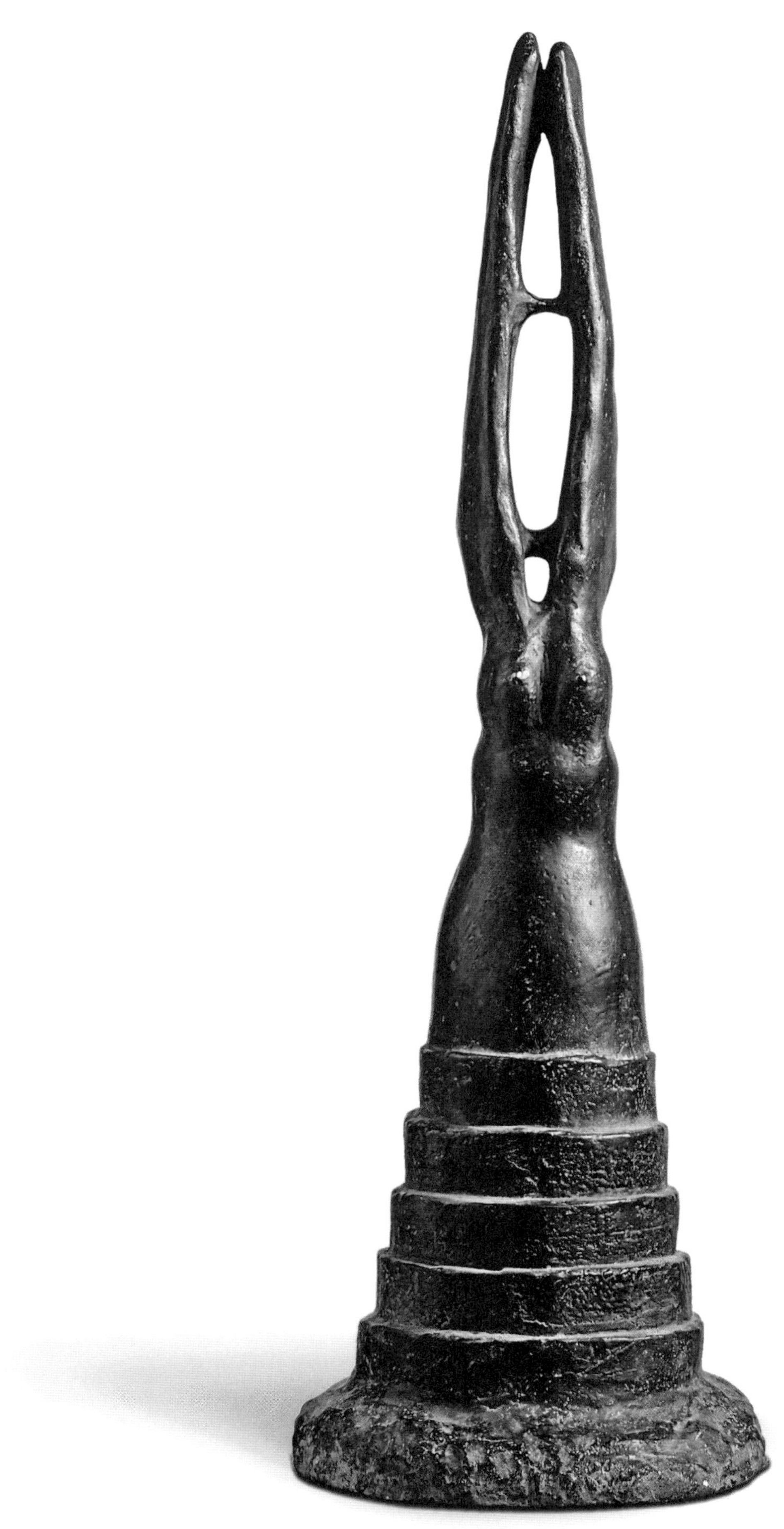

Alone, 1993
Kohle und Pastell auf
Papier | Charcoal
and pastel on paper,
42 × 29,5 cm
[Kat. | cat. 67]

W-Boy, 1993
Kohle und Pastell auf
Papier | Charcoal
and pastel on paper,
43 × 30,5 cm
[Kat. | cat. 66]

Alone, 1994
Kohle und Pastell auf
Papier | Charcoal
and pastel on paper,
43,5 × 30,5 cm
[Kat. | cat. 68]

Inclined, 1994
Kohle und Pastell auf
Papier | Charcoal
and pastel on paper,
43,5 × 30,5 cm
[Kat. | cat. 69]

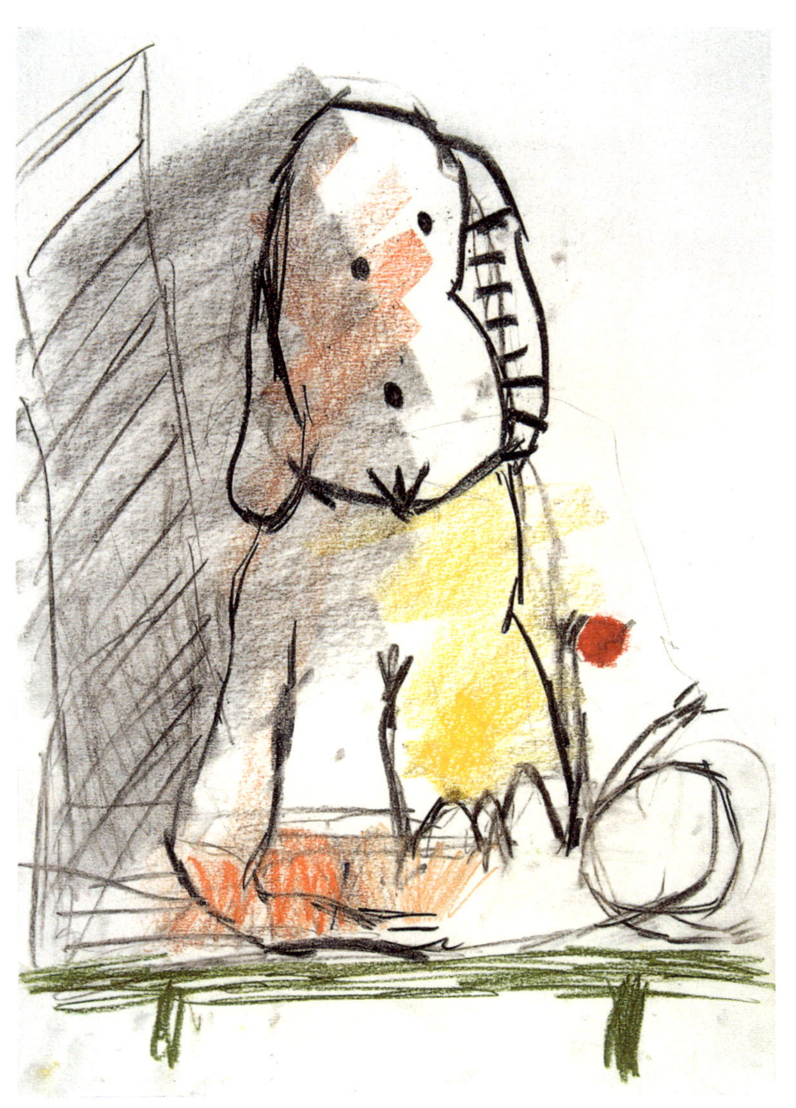

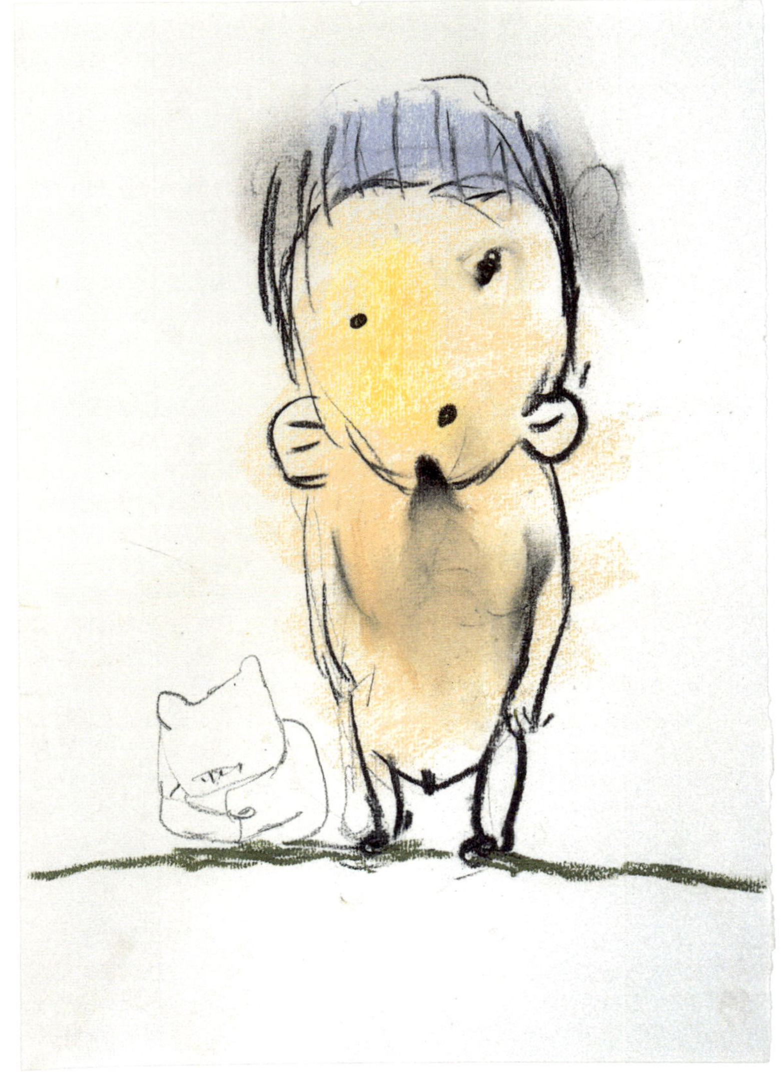

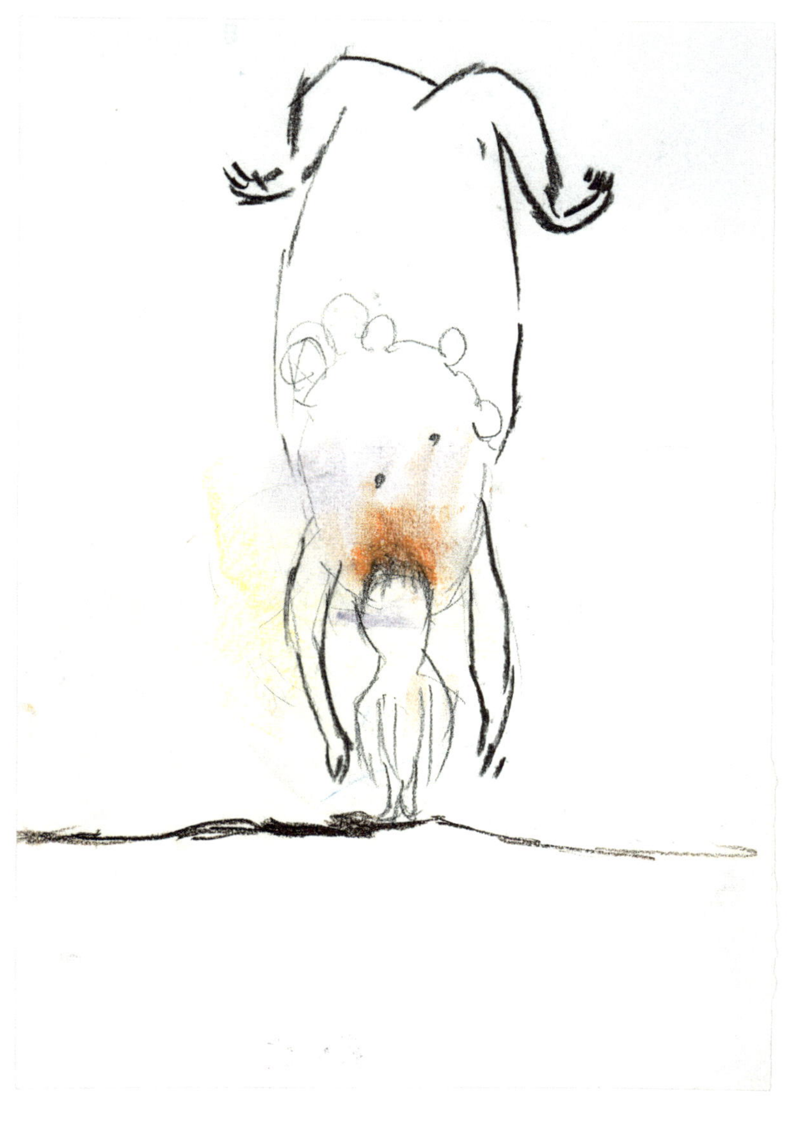

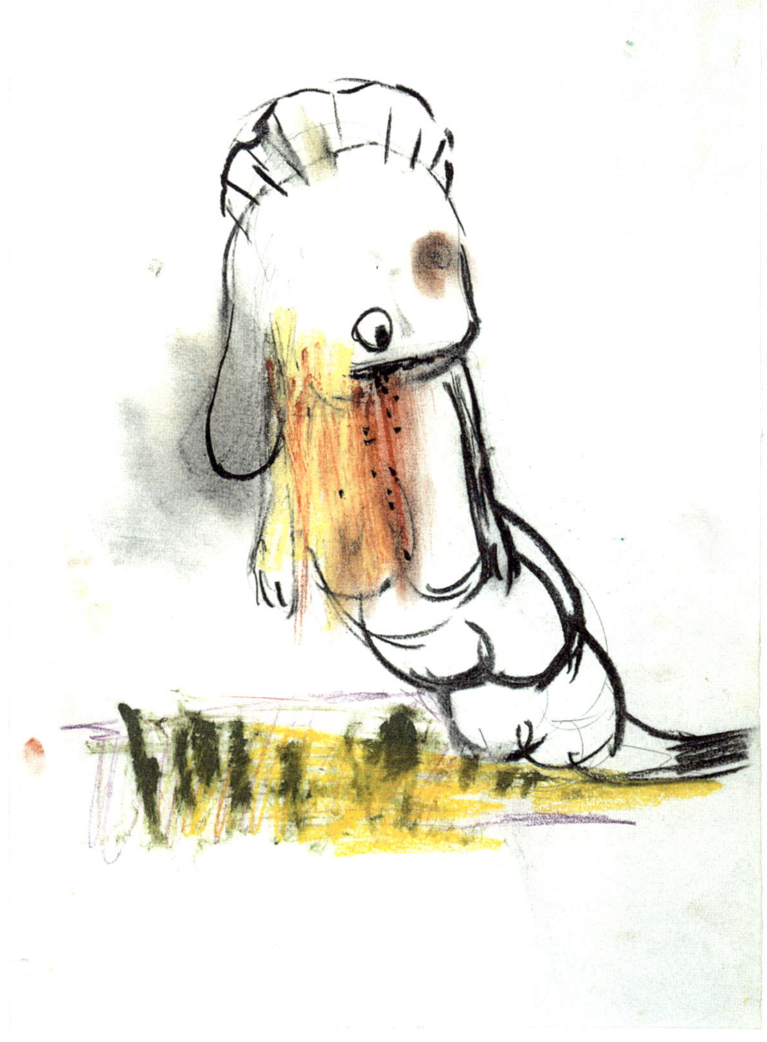

Doppelfigur | Double Figure, 1993
Öl auf Leinwand | Oil on canvas, 50 × 36 cm
[Kat. | cat. 65]

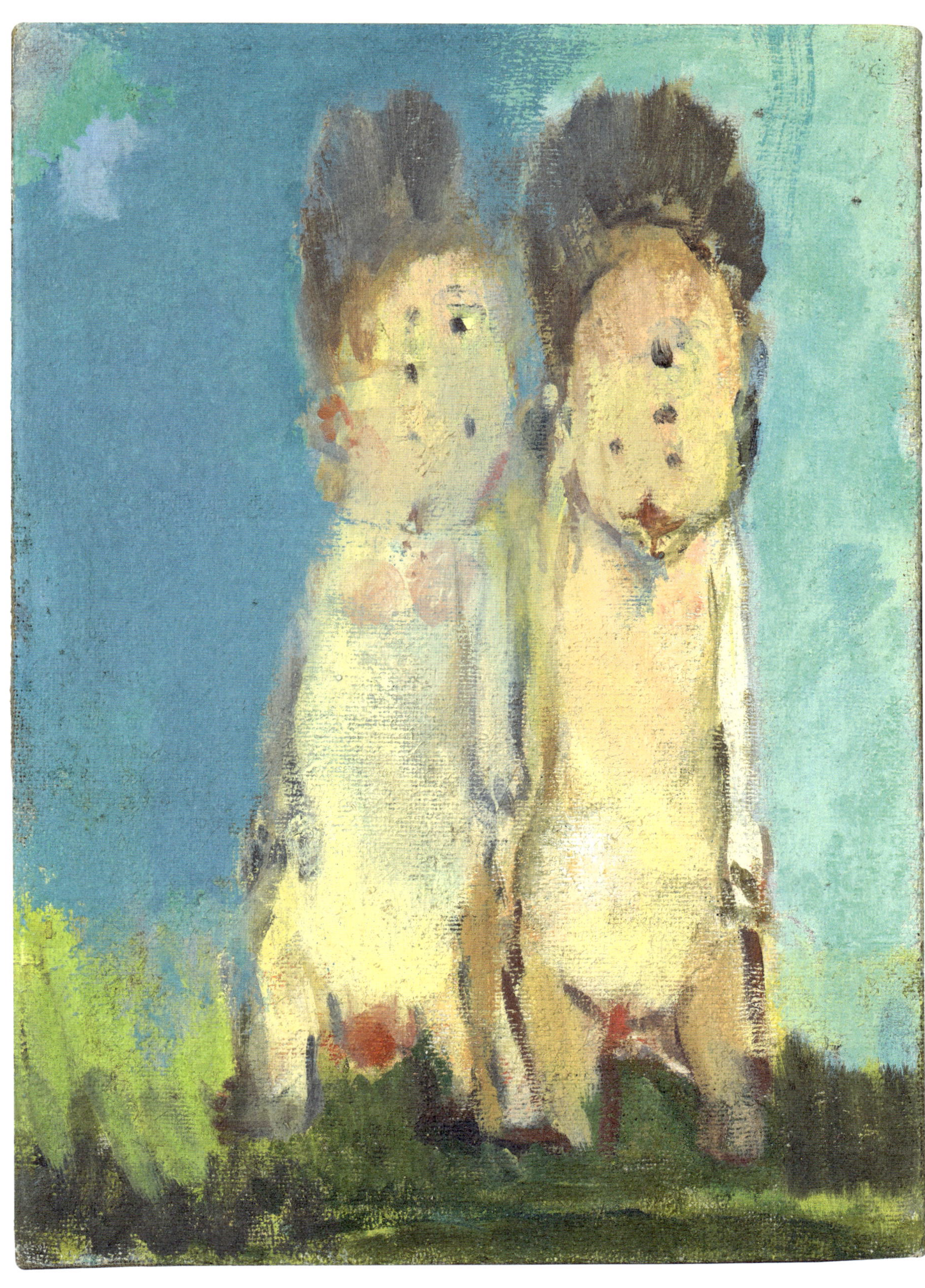

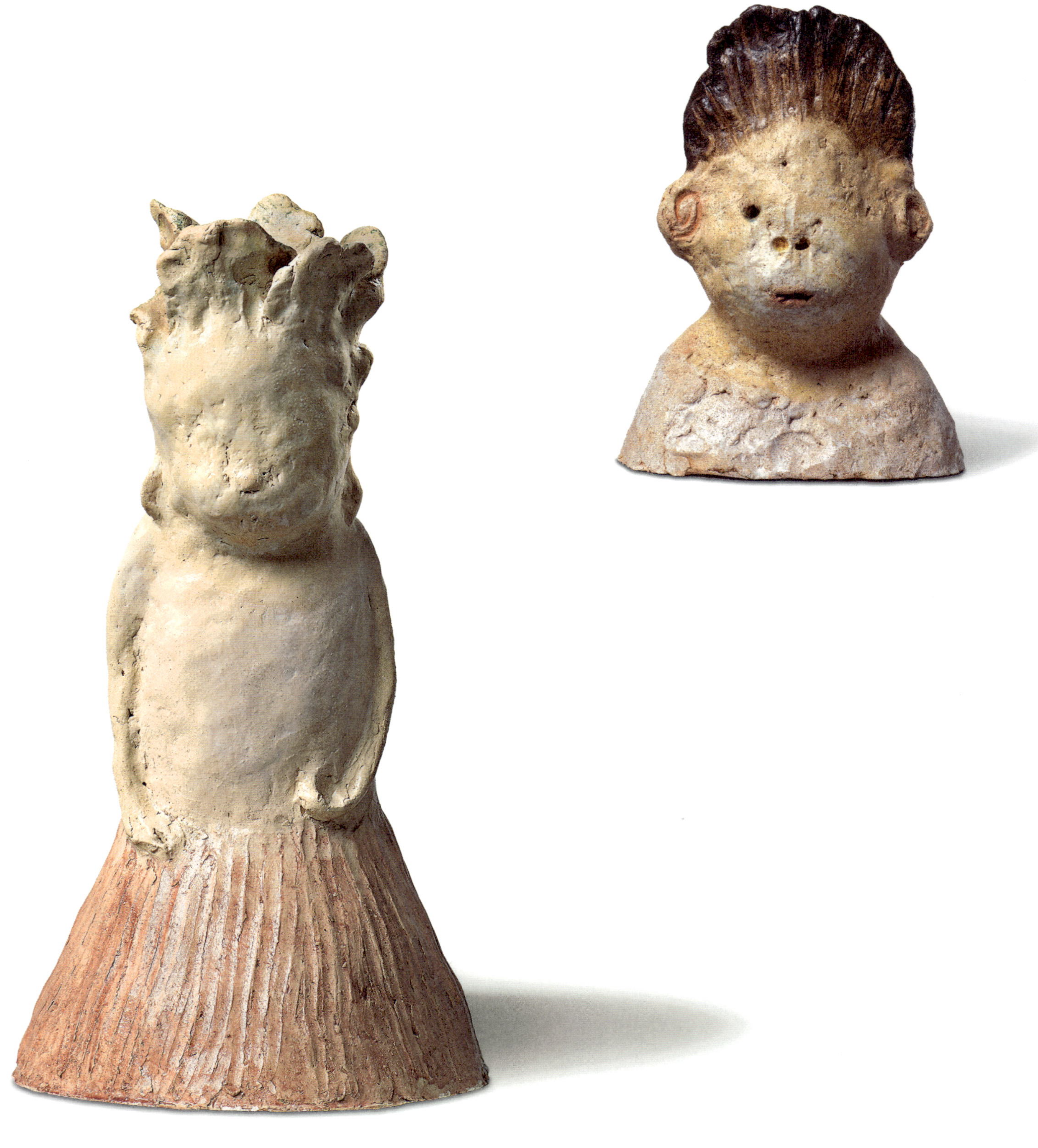

*Stehende in einem
rosa Rock* | Standing in a
Pink Skirt, 1994
Terrakotta, glasiert |
Terra-cotta, glazed,
25×25×49,5 cm
[Kat. | cat. 62]

Einäugiges Baby |
Single-Eyed Baby, 1994
Terrakotta, glasiert |
Terra-cotta, glazed,
30×23×16 cm
[Kat. | cat. 63]

*Black Miko in Blue
Dress*, 1995
Terrakotta, glasiert |
Terra-cotta, glazed,
29×26×55,5 cm
[Kat. | cat. 64]

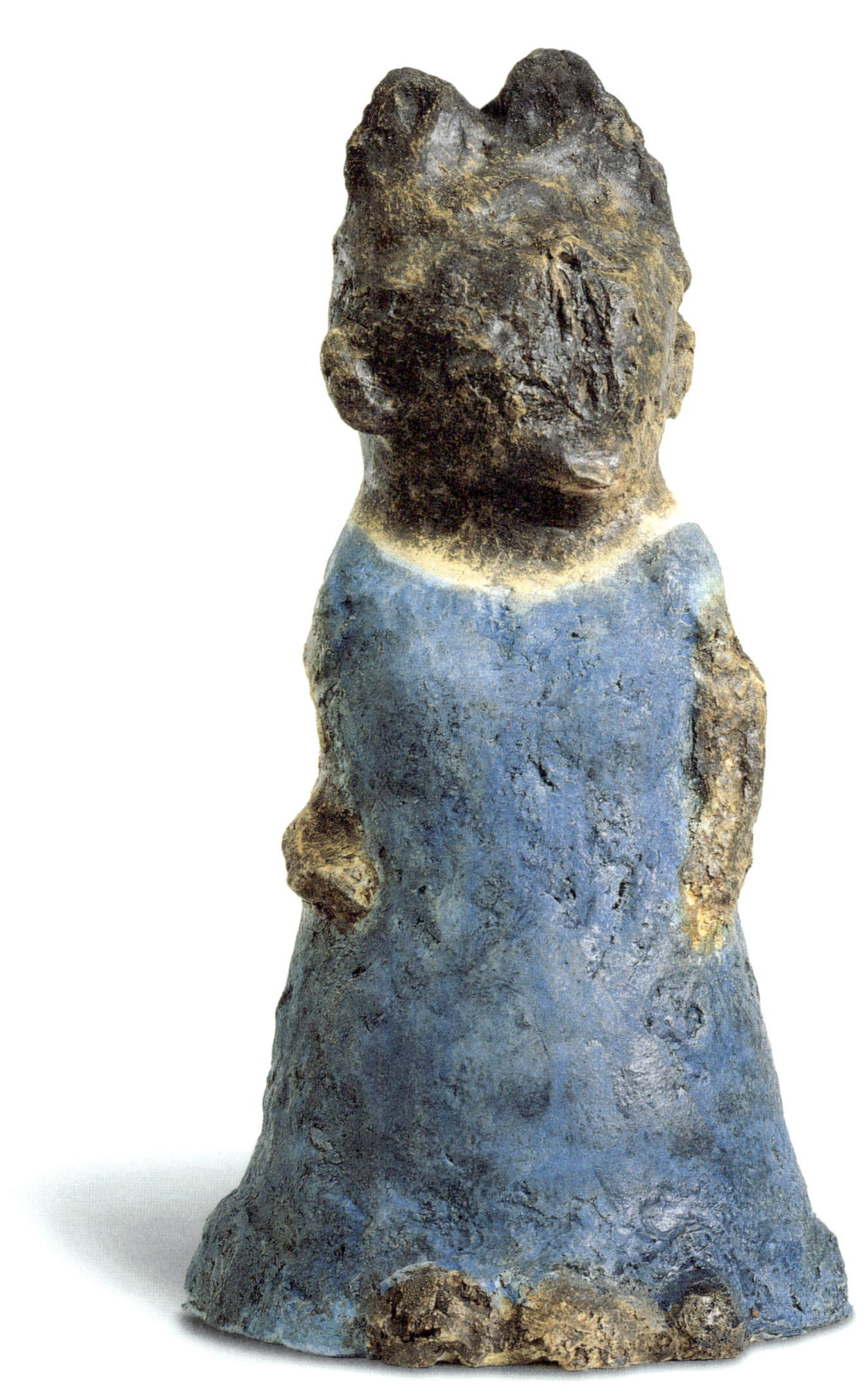

Girls Between Worlds

Around the mid-1990s, Ikemura's pictorial world is taken over by girls. They appear caught between different worlds. Hovering, standing, lying, or diving, they evade more precise characterization, for their facial features and their age remain indeterminate. Only their skirts make them into female creatures. They appear in a fleeting state of innocence and loneliness on the horizon—in the zone between heaven and earth—where they can be seen but not reached.

The paintings are executed flatly. The canvasses practically soak up the paint, so that the materiality of the support is emphasized. No illusion is created here; the painterly gesture is neutralized. In the sculpture, the girls are stylized into vessels for the soul. The sculptures in particular make clear that the theme is multilayered and ambivalent—and thus anything other than harmless. The *Gelbe Figur mit drei Armen* (Yellow Figure with Three Arms, 1996), for instance, with its hands digging into its eye sockets and mouth, suggests a latent eroticism and an appetite for violence and (self-)destruction.

The *Shadow Girl* series of 1996 is executed in watercolor, wet on wet, so that although the girls' silhouettes are clearly visible, lending them form, they still remain "blurred." As with the ur-creatures, the moment in which the form comes into being is as essential as the visible form itself. The becoming of the girls as spiritual beings is more important than their corporeality.

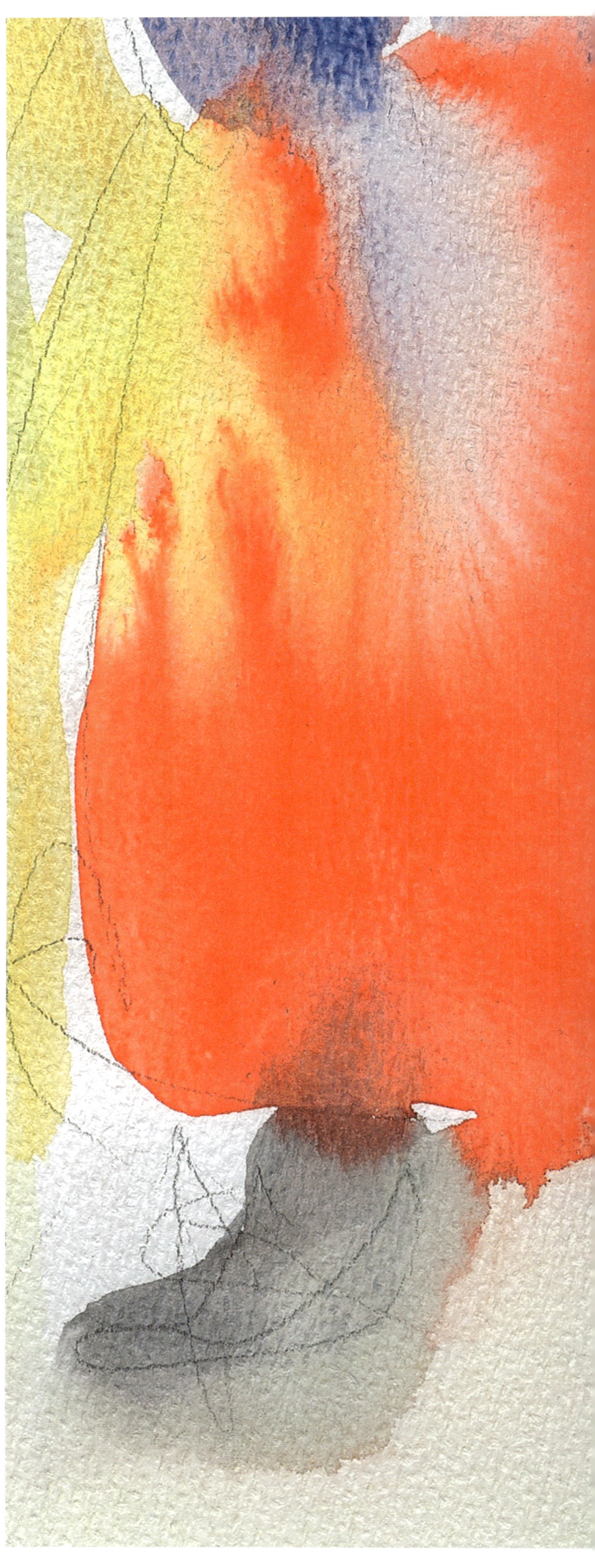

Mädchen in Zwischenwelten

Gegen Mitte der 1990er-Jahre erobern Mädchen Ikemuras Bildwelt. Sie scheinen in Zwischenreichen zu existieren. Schwebend, stehend, liegend oder ins Meer eintauchend entziehen sie sich genauerer Charakterisierung, denn ihre Gesichtszüge und ihr Alter bleiben unspezifisch, nur der Rock macht sie zu weiblichen Wesen. Sie erscheinen im flüchtigen Zustand von kindlicher Unschuld und Einsamkeit am Horizont – in der Zone zwischen Himmel und Erde –, wo sie sichtbar, aber nicht erreichbar sind.

Die Gemälde sind flächig ausgeführt, und die Leinwand saugt die Farbe geradezu auf, sodass die Materialität des Trägers betont wird. Es soll keine Illusion zustande kommen, die malerische Geste ist neutralisiert. In der Skulptur werden die Mädchen zu Gefässen für die Seele stilisiert. Gerade die Plastiken machen deutlich, dass das Thema vielschichtig und ambivalent und damit alles andere als harmlos ist. Etwa *Gelbe Figur mit drei Armen* (1996), deren Hände in die Augenhöhlen und den Mund gebohrt sind, suggeriert auch eine latente Erotik, die Lust an Gewalt und (Selbst-)Zerstörung.

Die Serie *Shadow Girl* von 1996 ist mit Aquarell nass in nass ausgeführt, sodass sich zwar die Silhouetten deutlich abzeichnen, die Figuren also Form annehmen, aber trotzdem «verschwommen» bleiben. Ähnlich wie bei den Urwesen ist hier die sichtbare Form ebenso wesentlich wie das Moment des Zustandekommens von Form. Das Werden der Mädchen als spirituelle Wesen ist wichtiger als ihre Körperlichkeit.

Den Blick abgewandt |
With Averted Look, 1995
Öl auf Leinwand | Oil
on canvas, 84,5 × 63 cm
[Kat. | cat. 71]

Den Blick abgewandt |
With Averted Look, 1995
Öl auf Leinwand | Oil
on canvas, 84,5 × 63 cm
[Kat. | cat. 71]

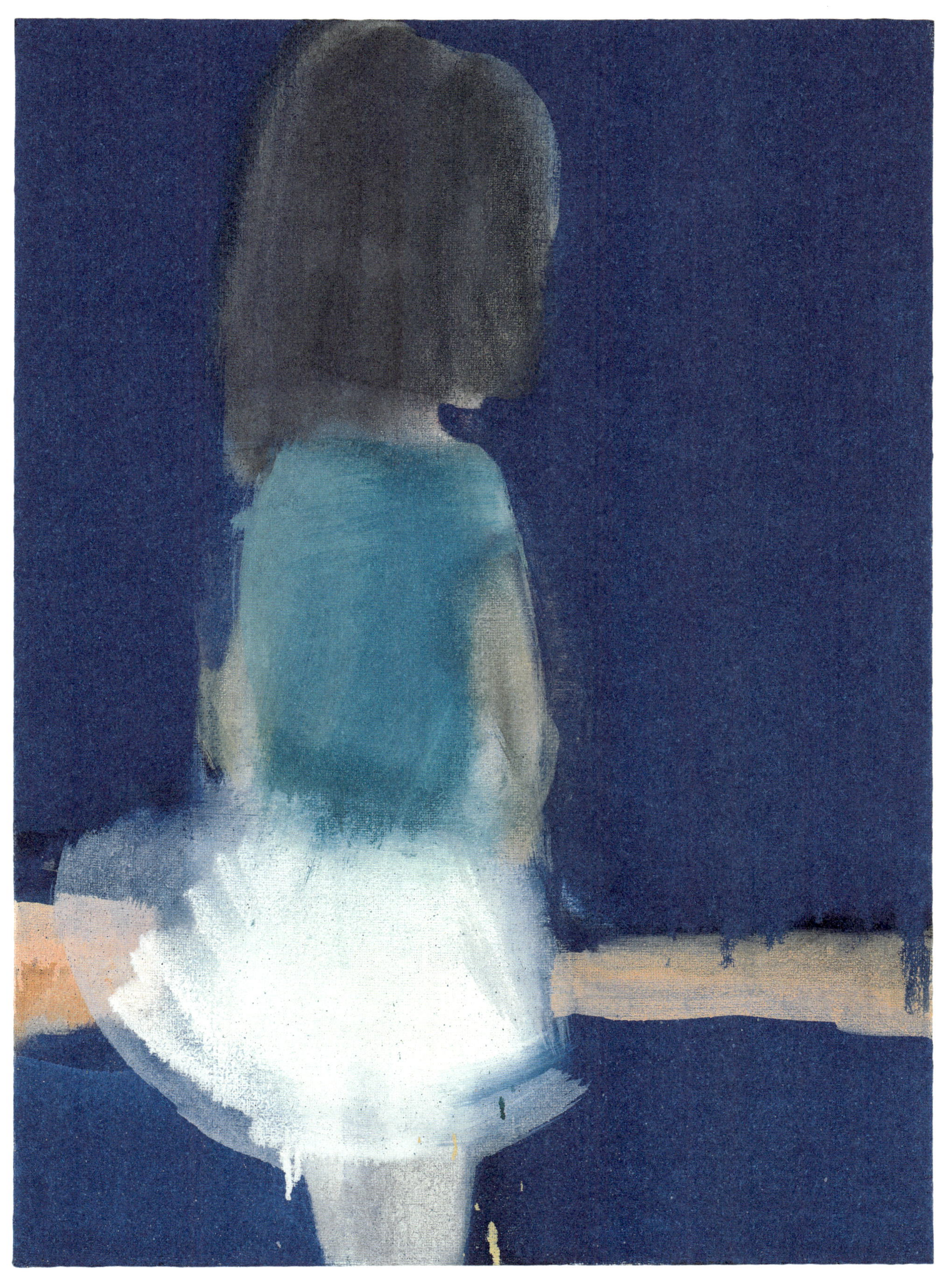

Schatten in Rosa |
Shadow in Pink, 1995/96
Öl auf Leinwand | Oil
on canvas, 95,5 × 73 cm
[Kat. | cat. 72]

Stehende mit Miko in
Gelb | Standing with Miko
in Yellow, 1995/96
Öl auf Leinwand | Oil
on canvas, 83,2 × 62,5 cm
[Kat. | cat. 73]

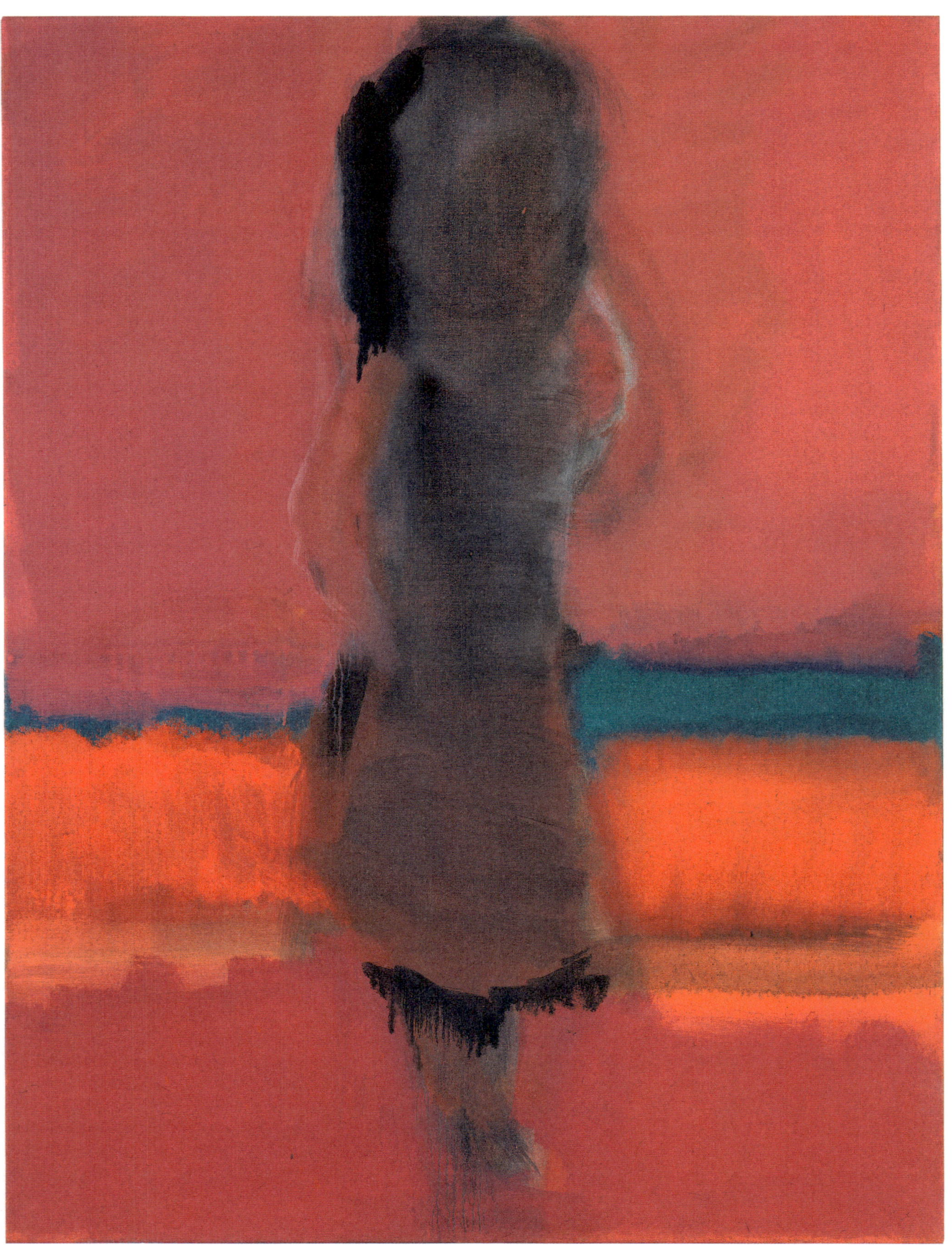

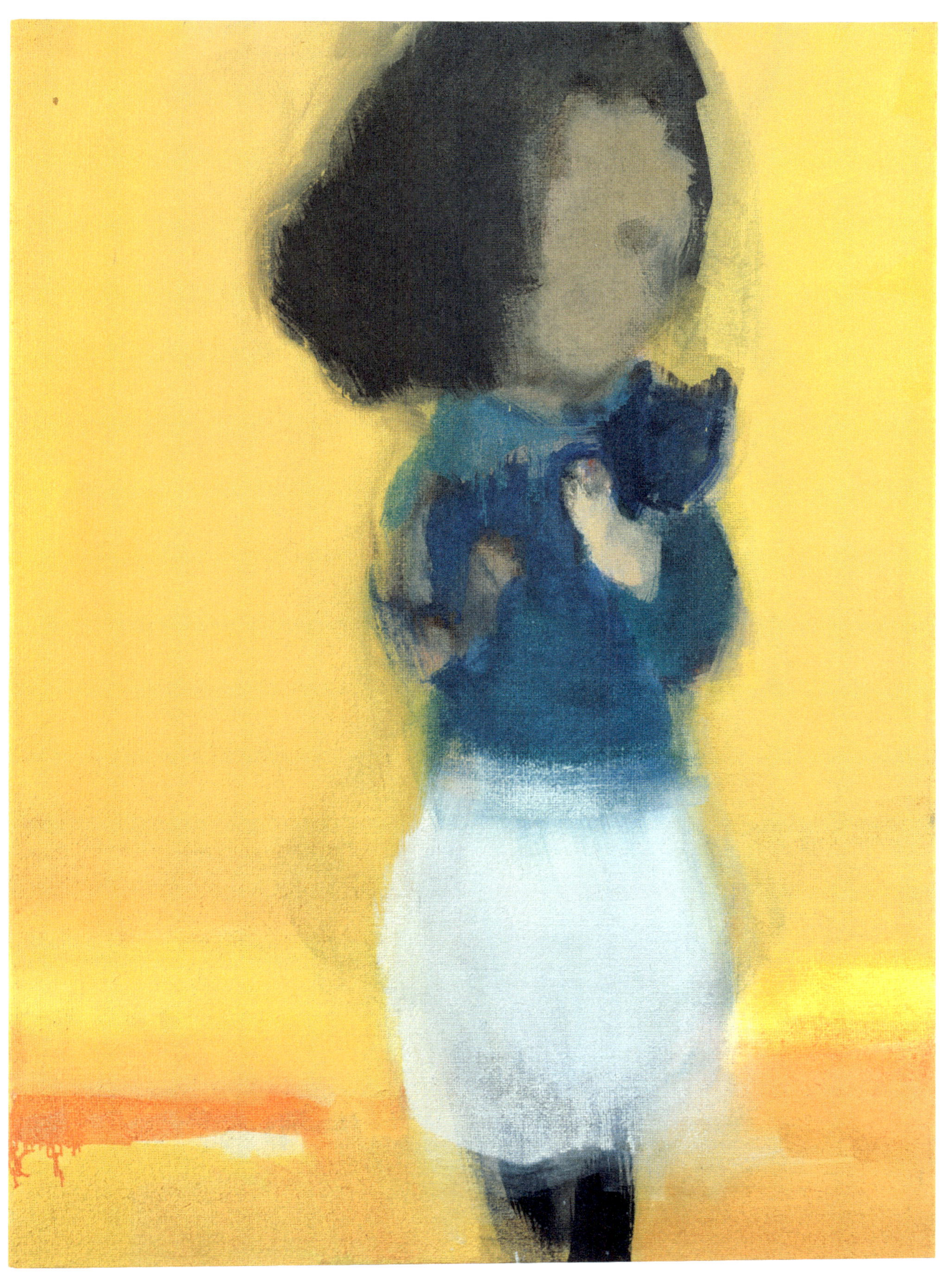

Shadow Girl
[Serie | series], 1996
Aquarell auf Papier |
Watercolor on paper,
je | each 42 × 30 cm
[Kat. | cat. 74–85]

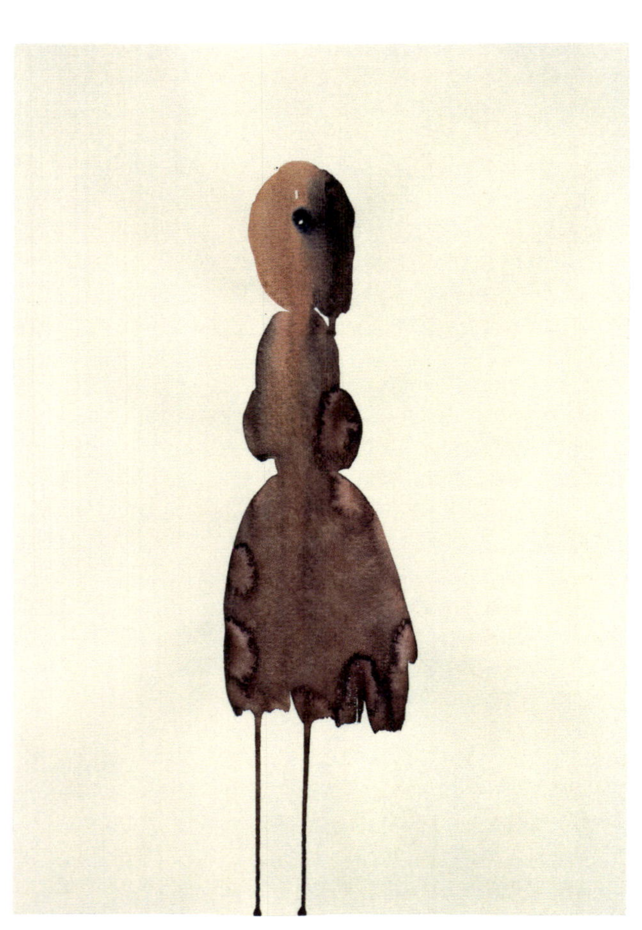
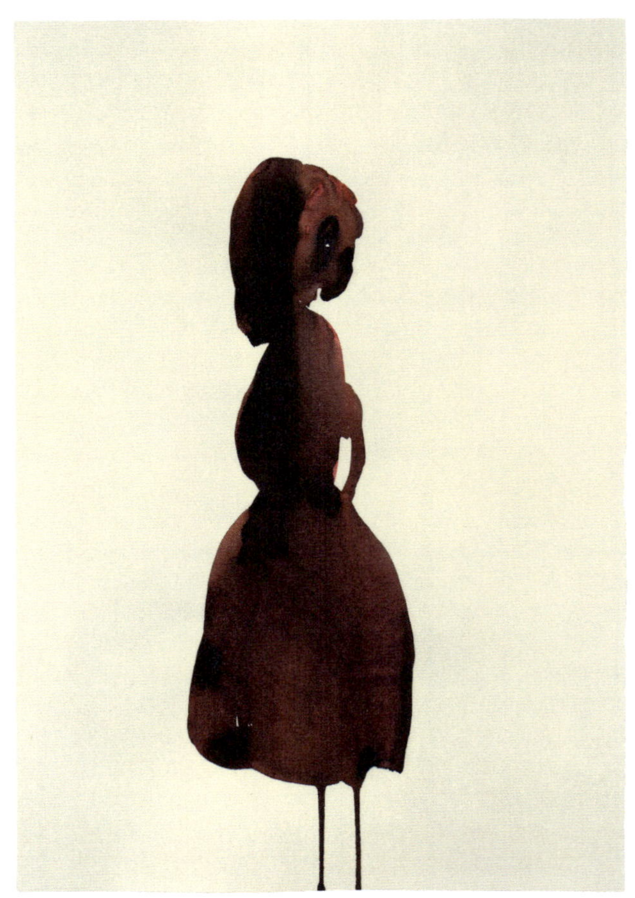

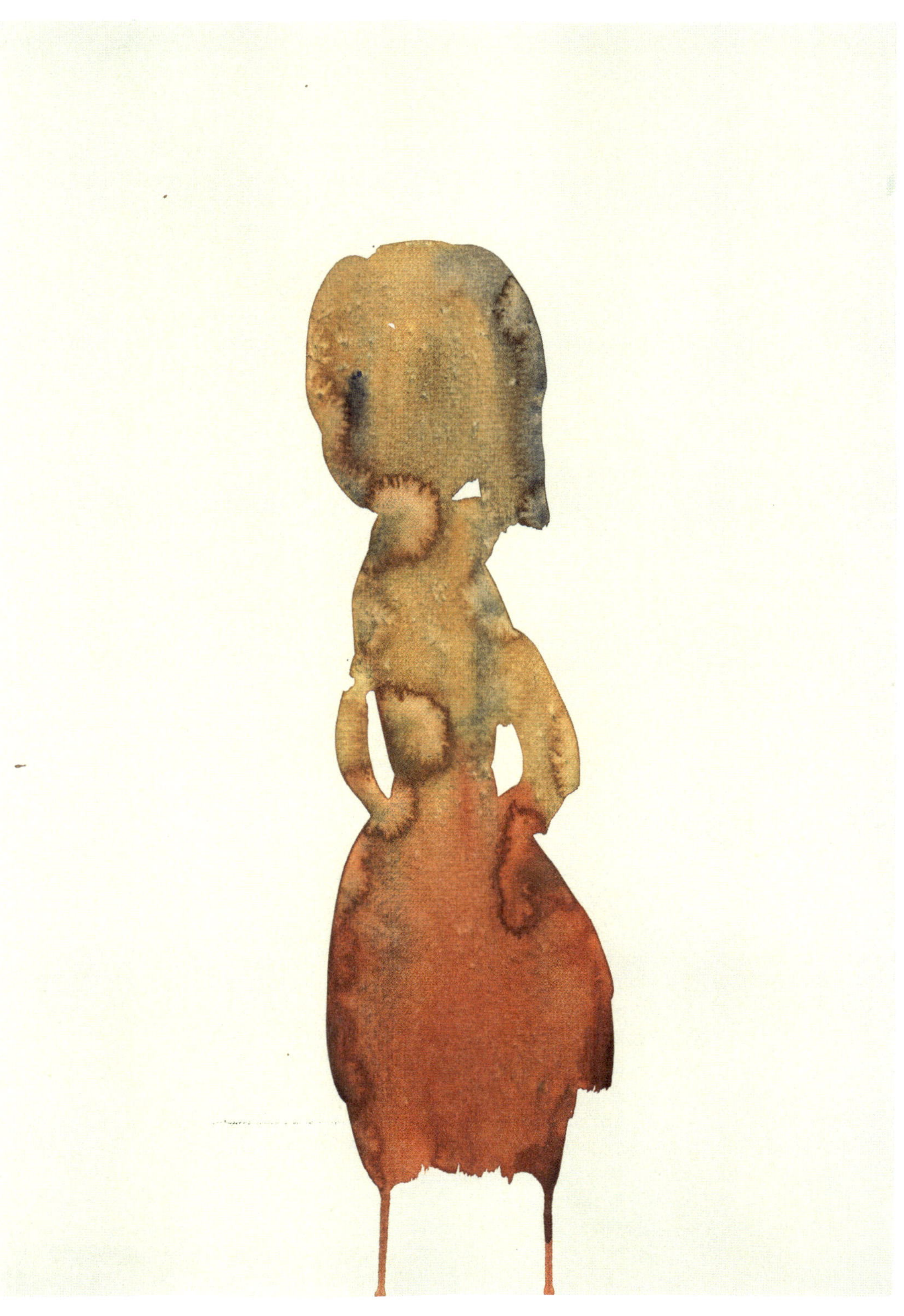

Shadow Girl
[Serie | series], 1996
Aquarell auf Papier |
Watercolor on paper,
je | each 42 × 30 cm
[Kat. | cat. 74–85]

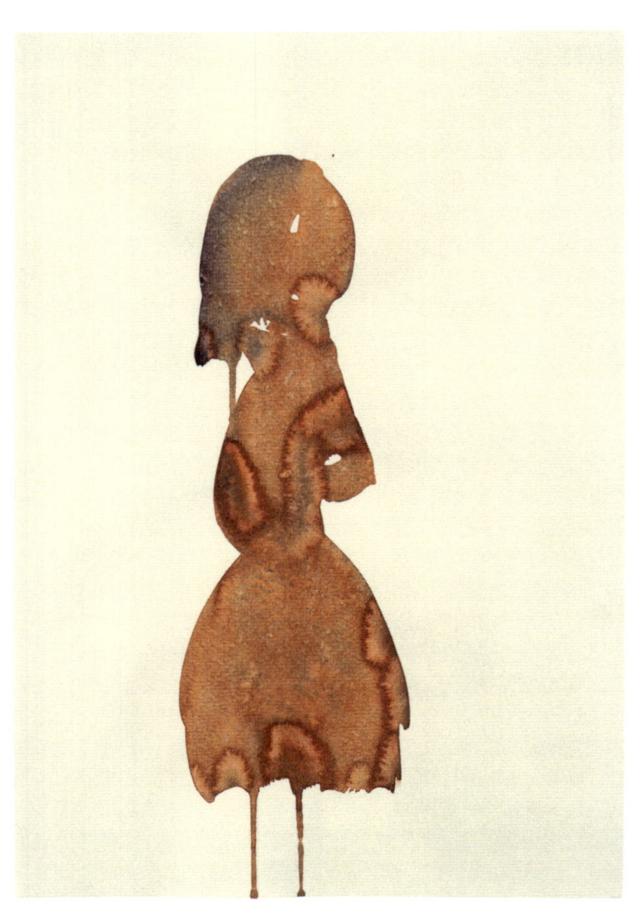
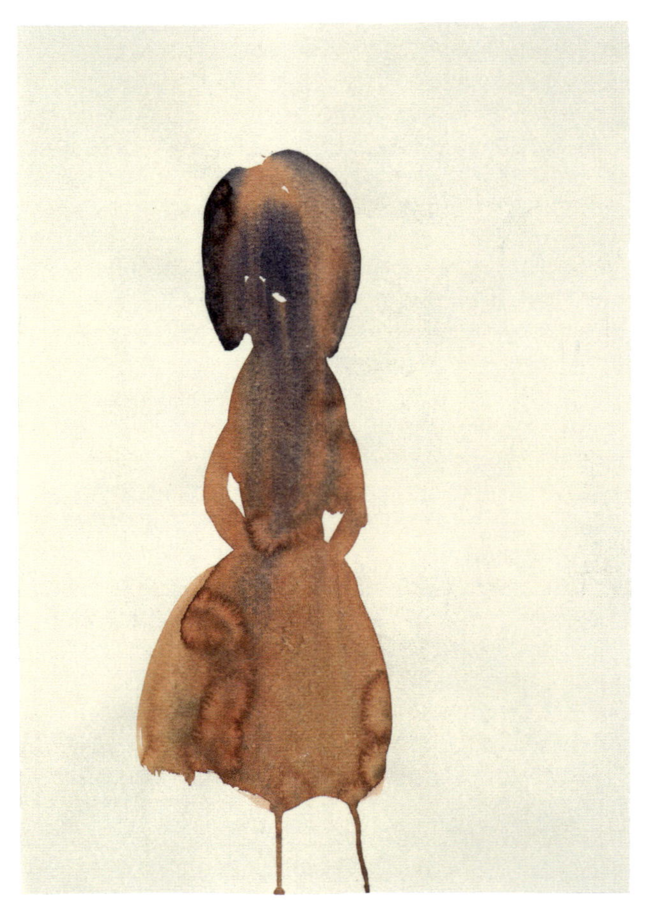
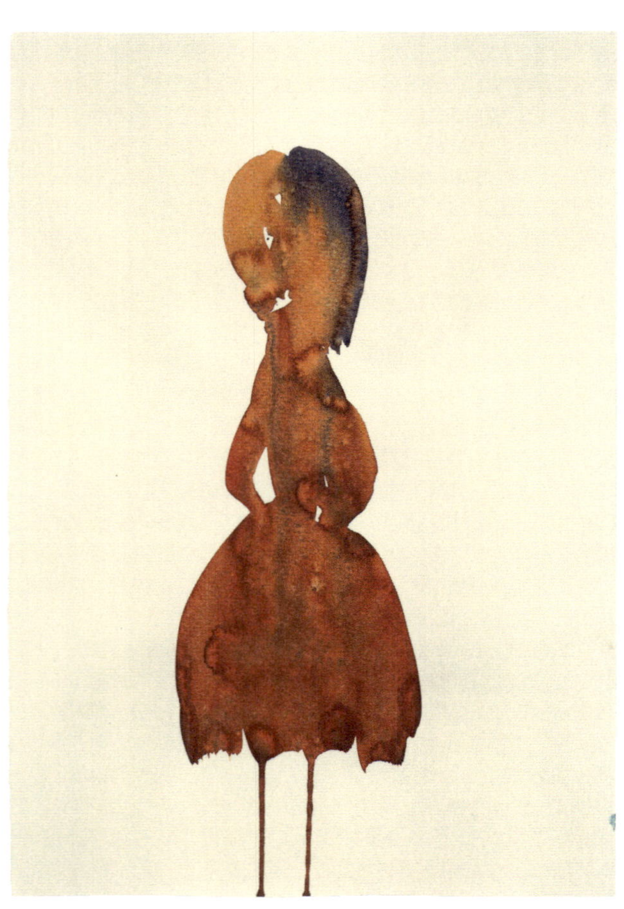
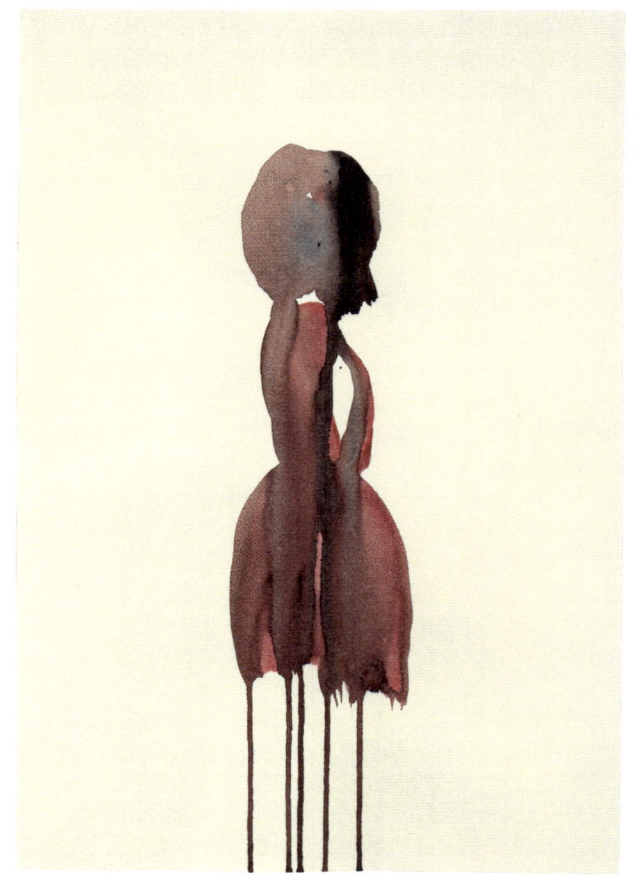

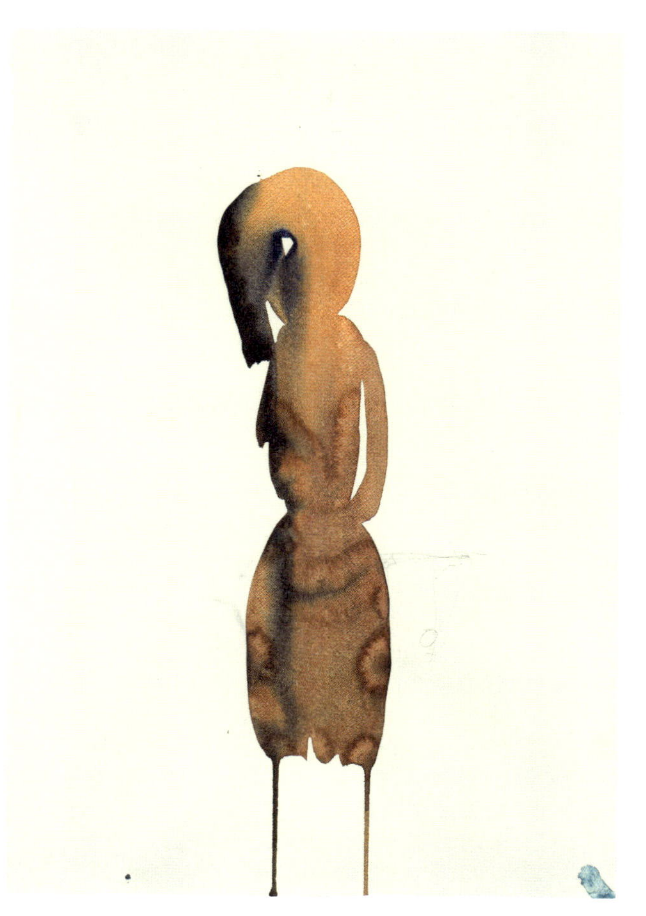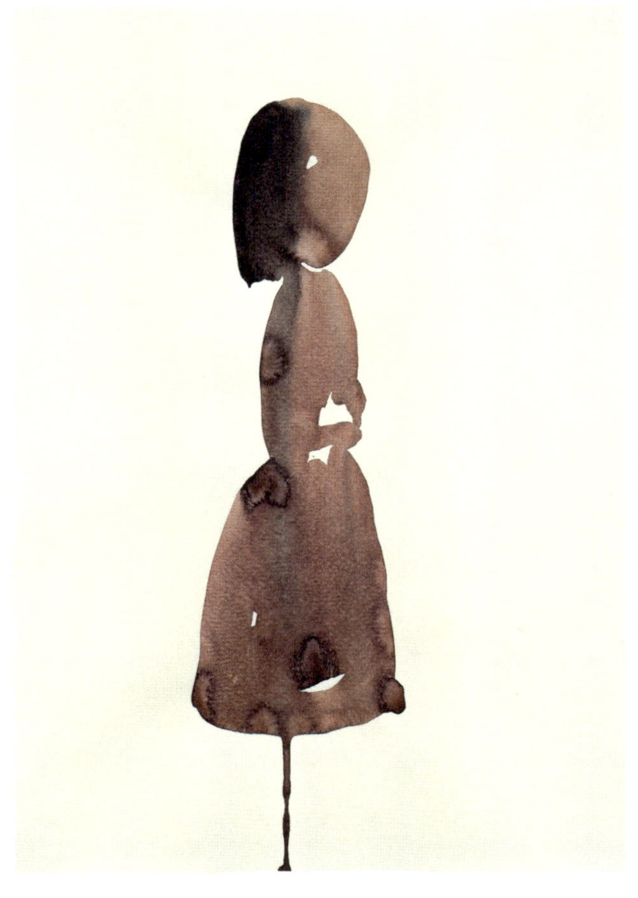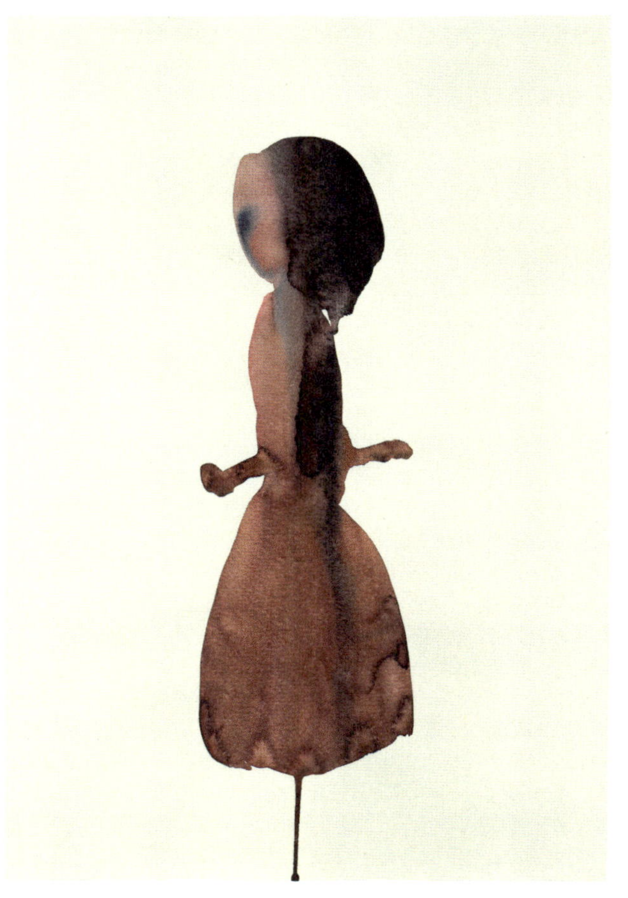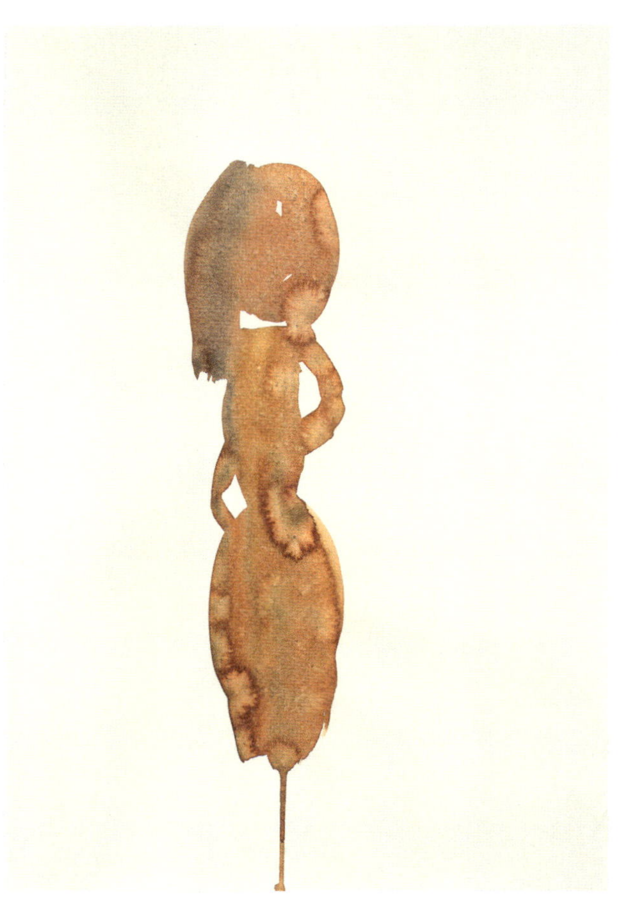

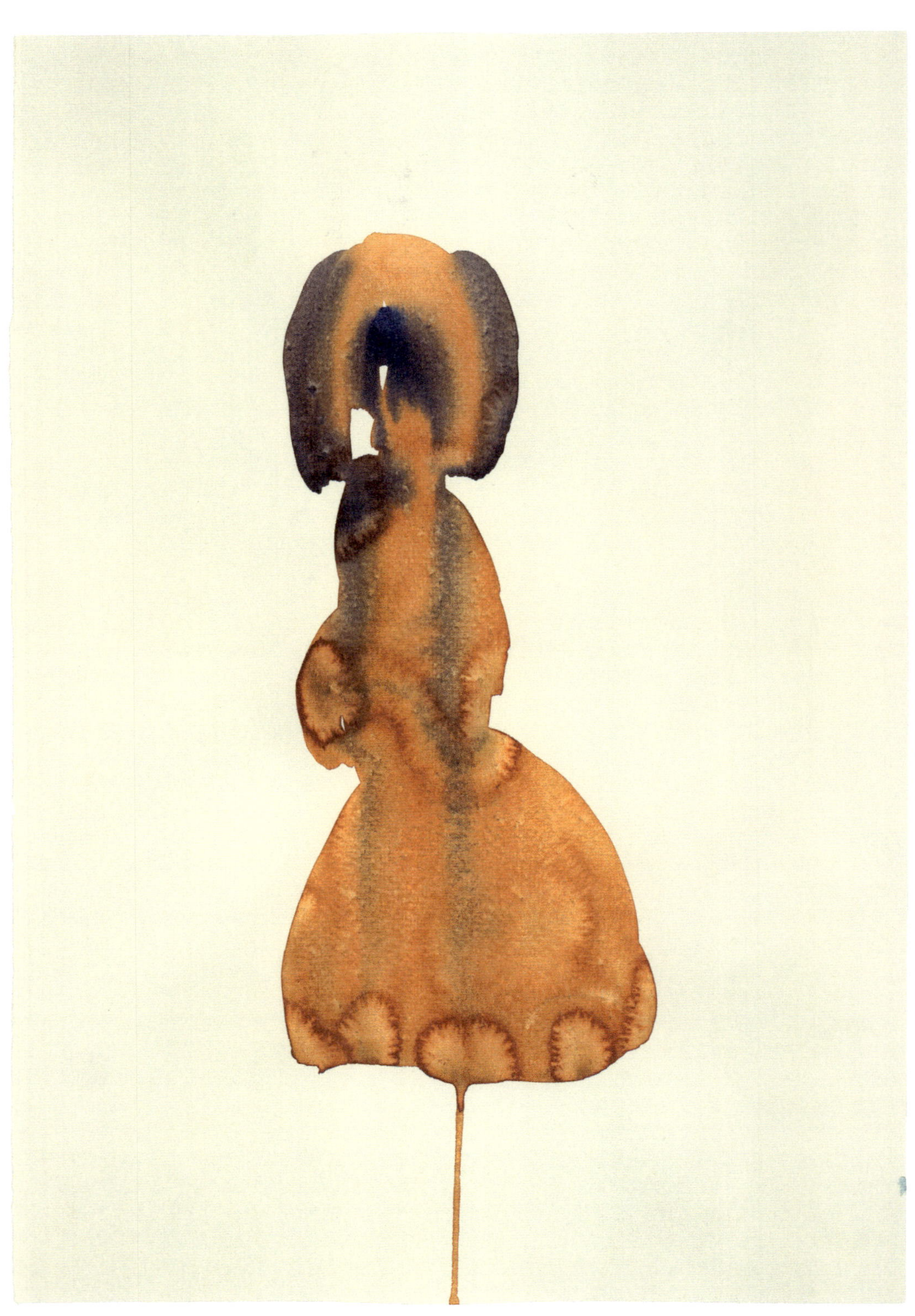

Shadow Girl
[Serie | series], 1996
Aquarell auf Papier |
Watercolor on paper,
je | each 42 × 30 cm
[Kat. | cat. 74–85]

*Gelbe Figur mit drei
Armen* | Yellow Figure
with Three Arms, 1996
Terrakotta, glasiert |
Terra-cotta, glazed,
31 × 31 × 65 cm
[Kat. | cat. 86]

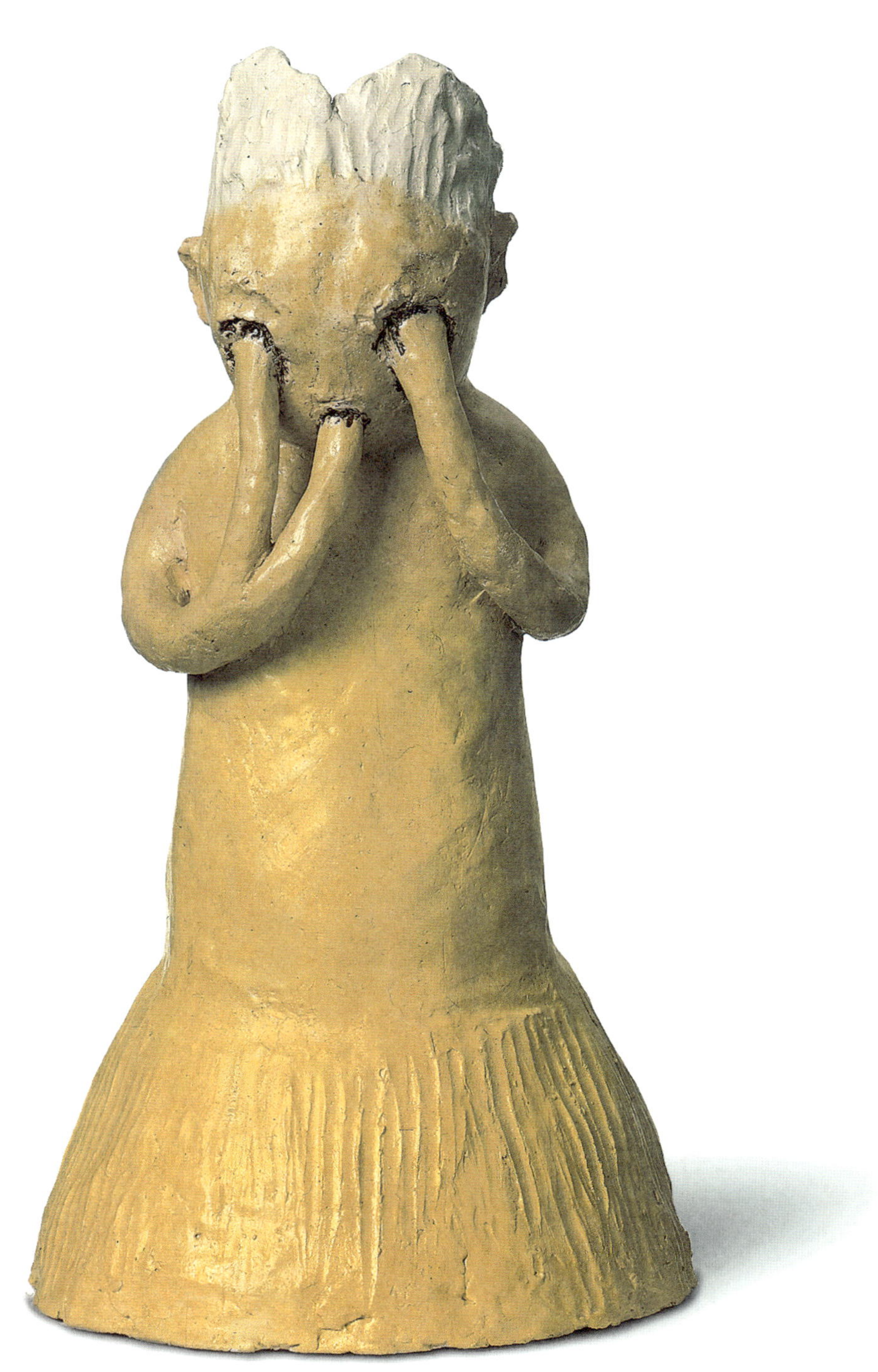

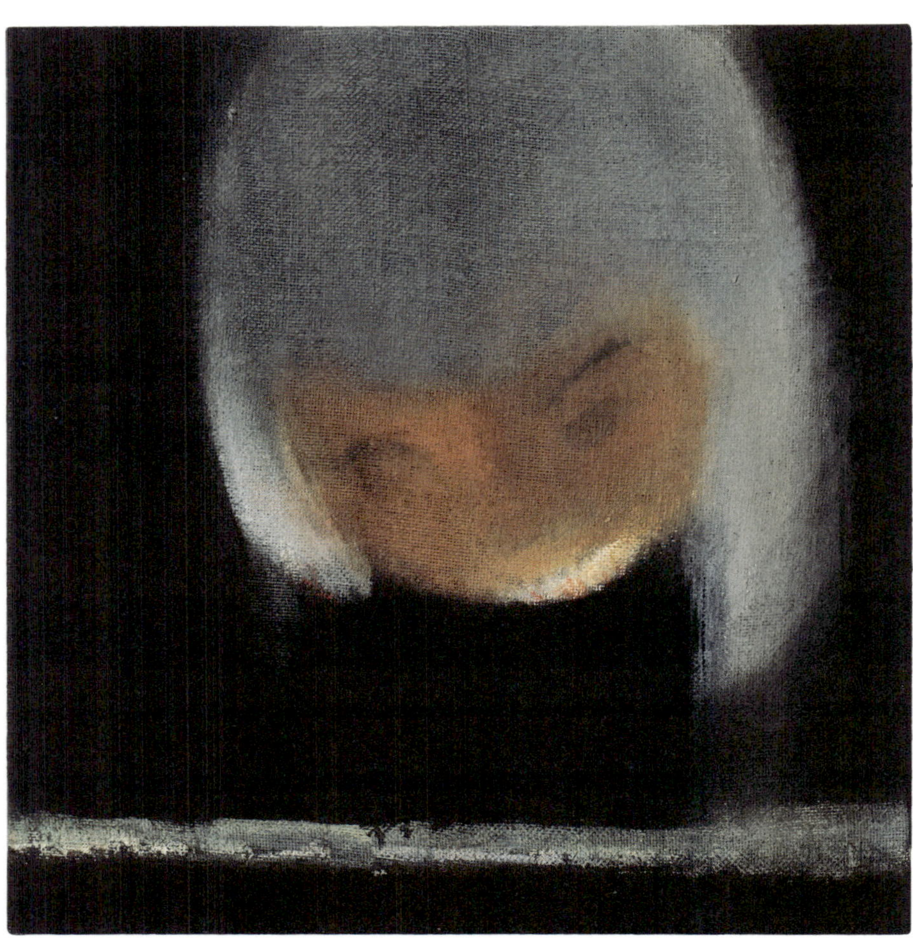

Gesicht in Schwarz |
Face in Black, 1998
Öl auf Jute | Oil on jute,
70 × 70 cm
[Kat. | cat. 88]

Eintauchen | Diving, 1999
Öl auf Jute | Oil on jute,
100 × 100,5 cm
[Kat. | cat. 91]

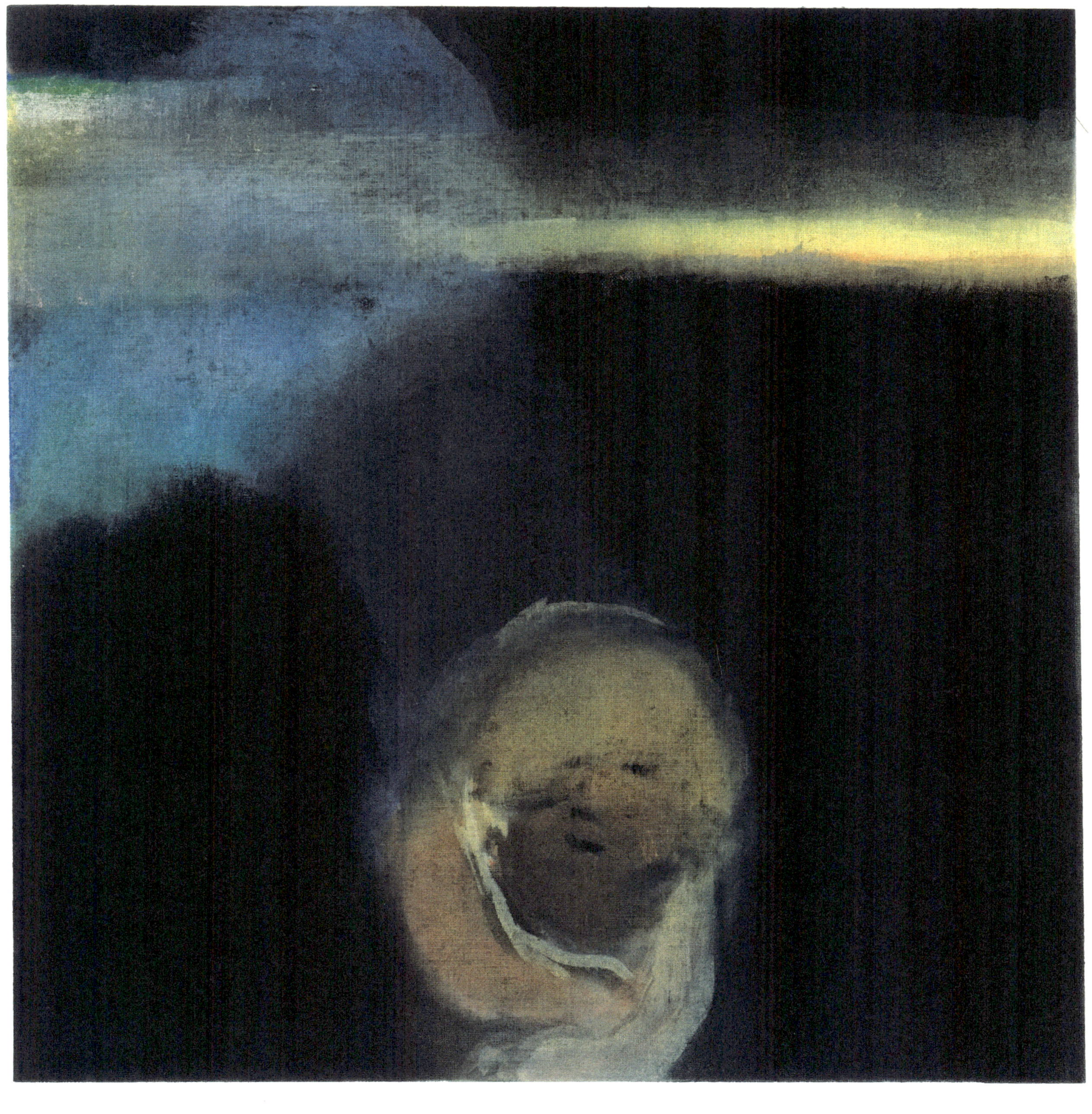

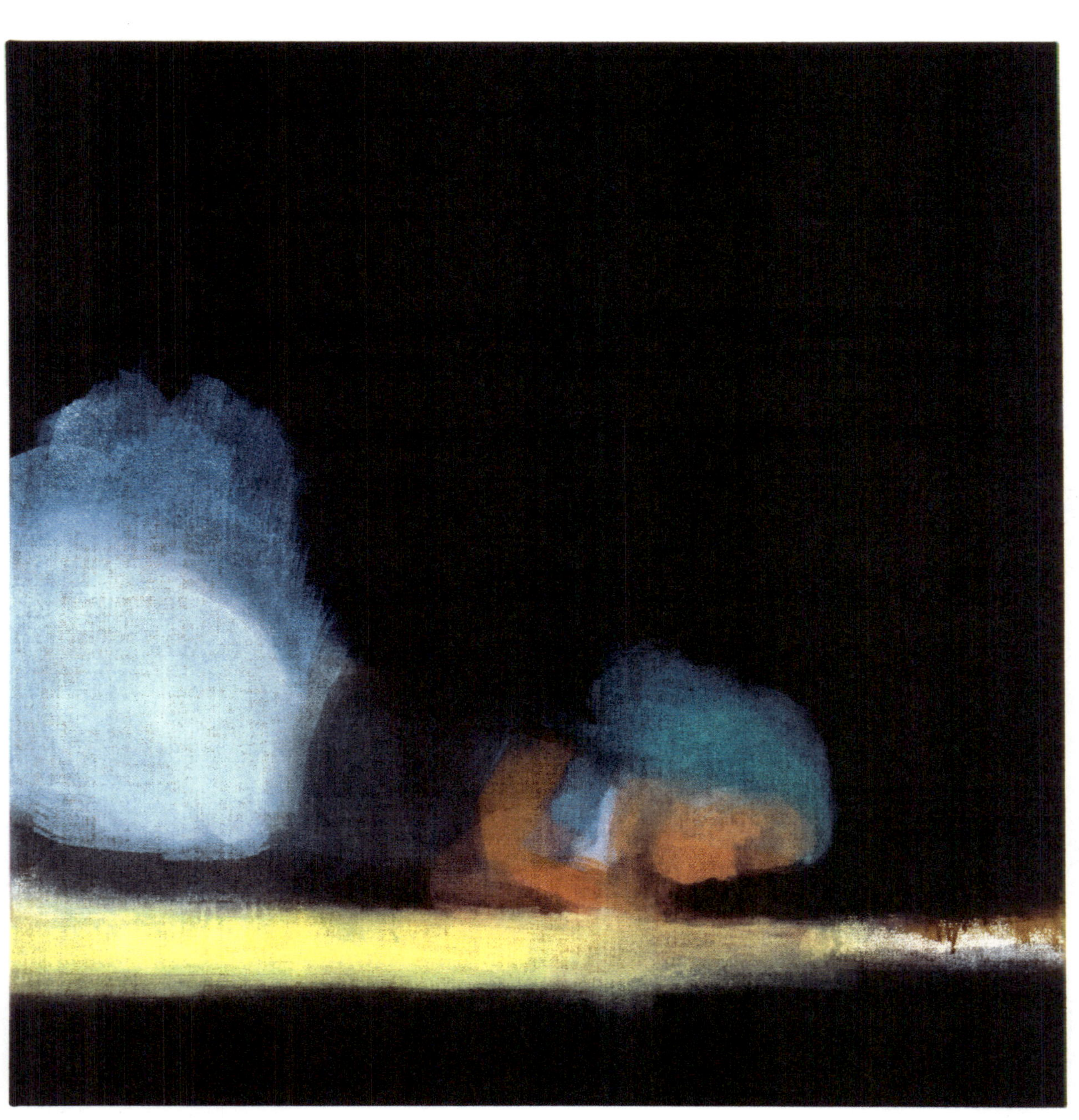

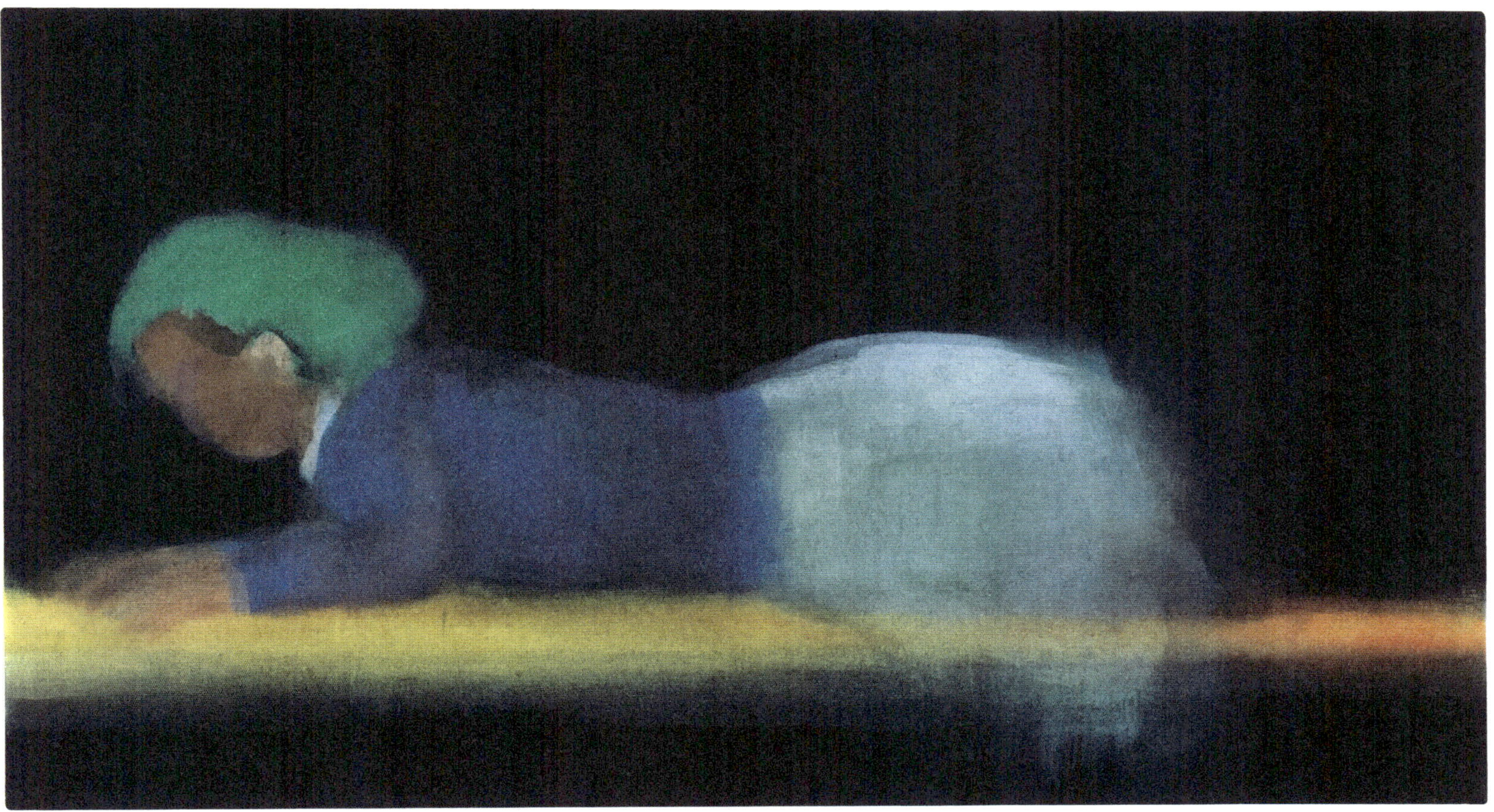

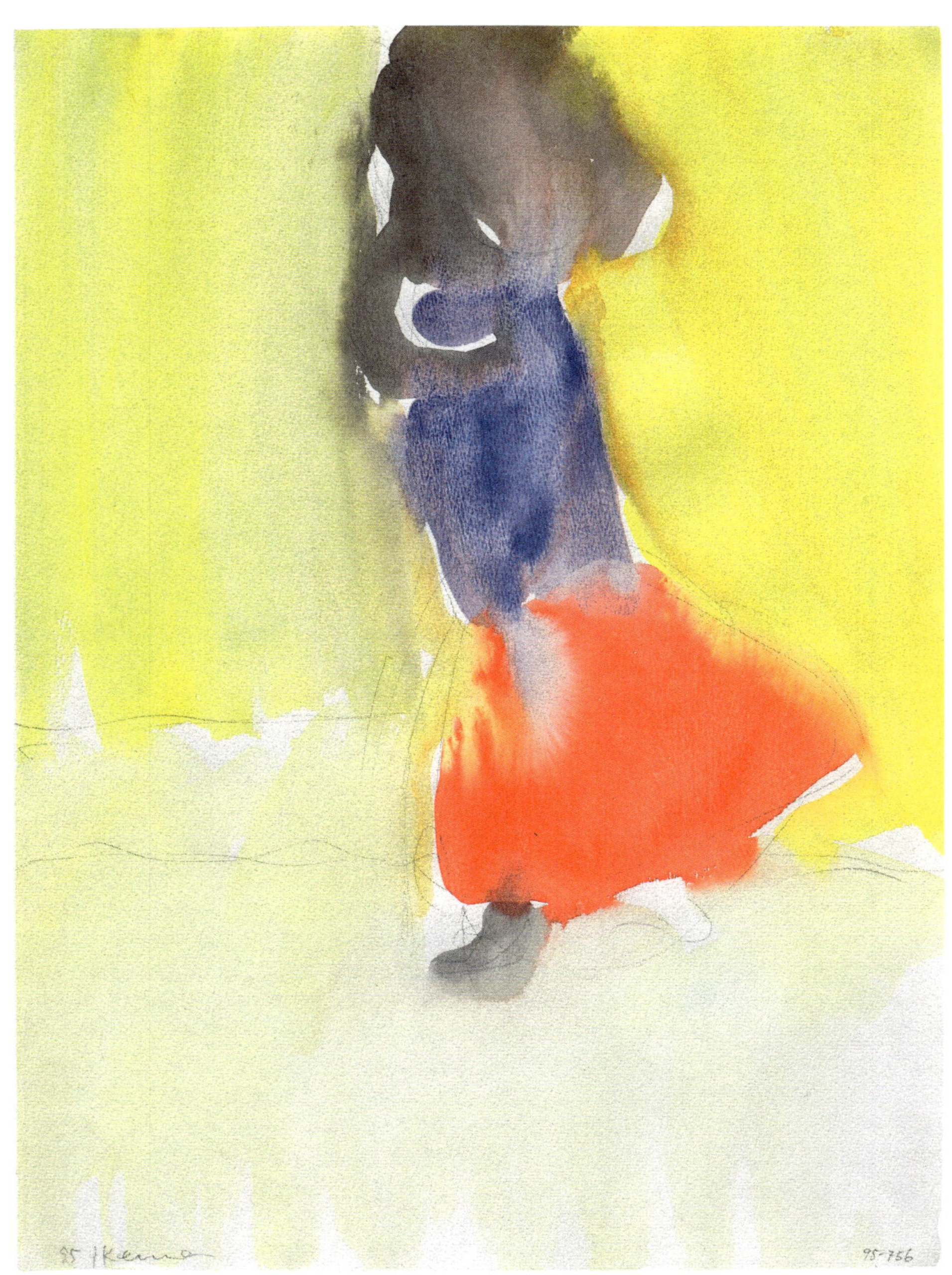

Girl in Yellow, 1995
Aquarell auf Papier |
Watercolor on paper,
48 × 36 cm
[Kat. | cat. 70]

*Hockende (Sich auf die
Augen stützend)* |
Squatting (Leaning on
Eyes), 1997
Terrakotta, glasiert |
Terra-cotta, glazed,
45 × 72 × 47 cm
[Kat. | cat. 87]

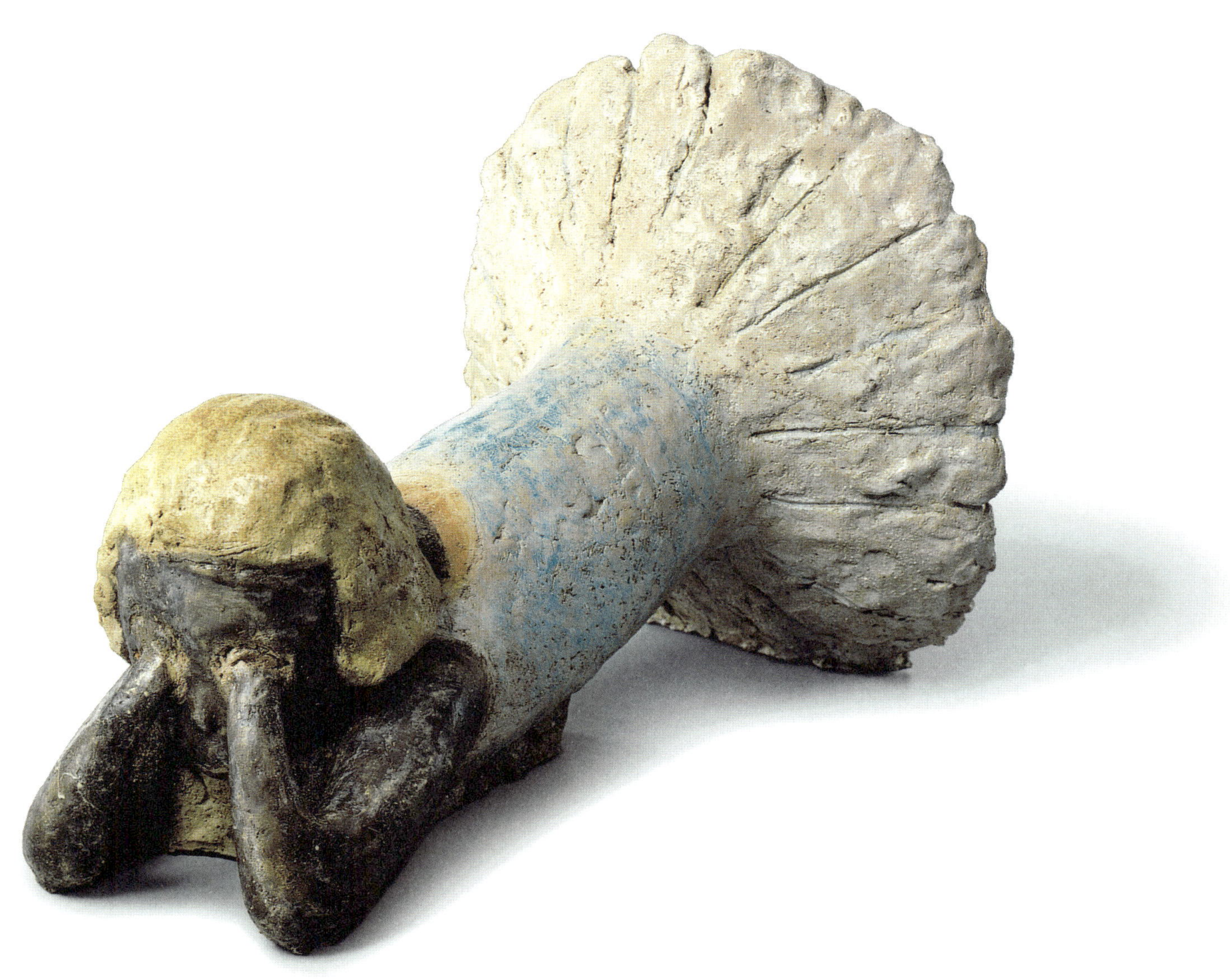

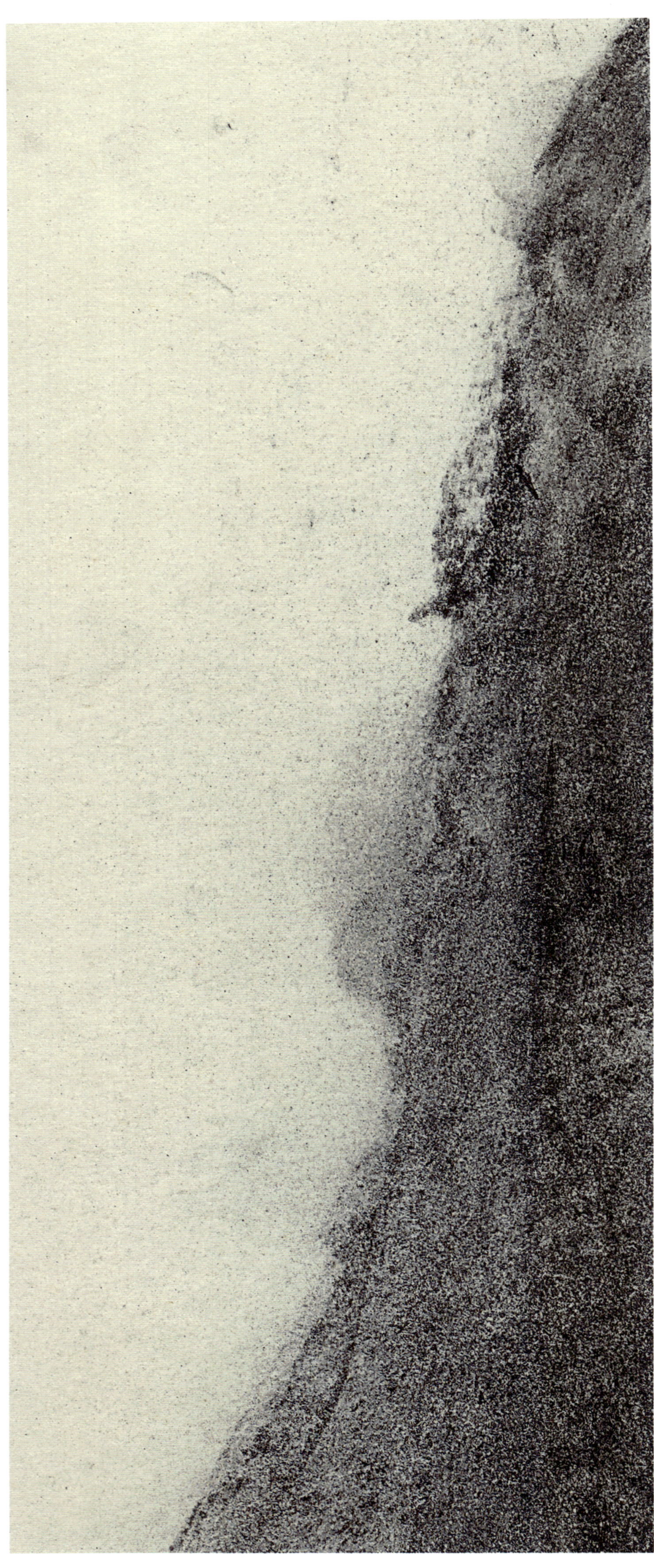

Landscapes of the Soul

The monumental drawing *Garten der Lüste* (Garden of Desire) is produced in 1983 during Ikemura's stay in Nuremberg. There, the confrontation with the legacy of the Second World War awakens memories of the postwar era of her parents' generation. Not just mutilated branches but entire trees reach upward like blazing tongues of flame. Their roots have detached themselves from the ground. The trees are also reminiscent of human creatures or spirits wandering homeless—or better, fleeing from something—in a dark and threatening landscape. The burning forest becomes a landscape of the soul.

An arc can be drawn from this work to the sculpture *Memento Mori* of 2013. This work embodies all the central aspects of Ikemura's art: the girl-like being is at once human and landscape, flower and mussel, radiating sensuality and vulnerability. The gouges on the upper body and the body cavities, as well as the deep eye sockets, evoke—as the title suggests—reflection on the transience of life. The form is situated in an interstitial realm, between earthly life and another world, and symbolizes the fragility of human existence. The sculpture, which radiates a deep sadness, is produced a year after the disaster at Fukushima.

Seelenlandschaften

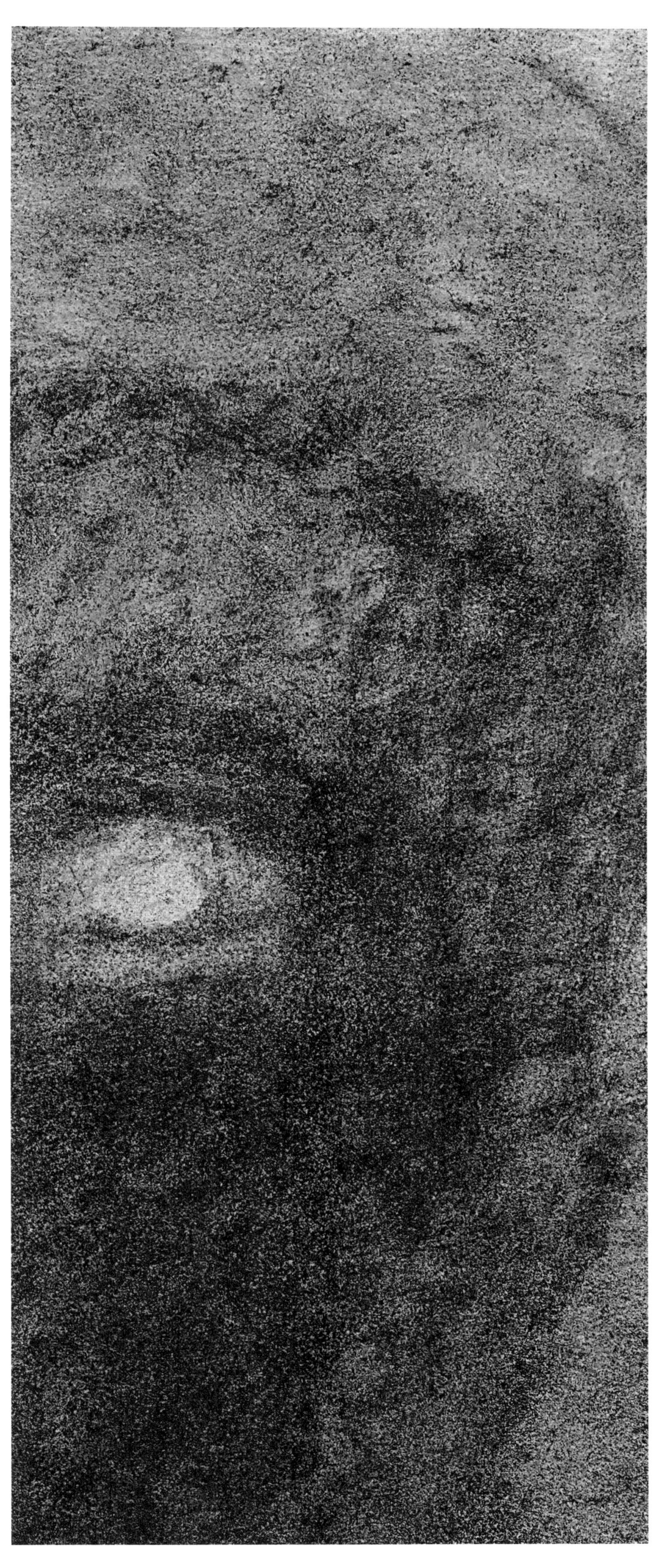

Die monumentale Zeichnung *Garten der Lüste* entstand 1983 während Ikemuras Aufenthalt in Nürnberg. Dort weckte die Konfrontation mit der Vergangenheit des Zweiten Weltkrieges die Erinnerung an die Kriegszeit, wie die Generation ihrer Eltern sie in Japan erlebt hatte. Wie züngelnde Flammen streben nicht nur verstümmelte Äste, sondern ganze Bäume in die Höhe. Ihre Wurzeln haben sich aus der Erde gelöst. Die Bäume erinnern auch an menschliche Wesen oder Geister, die heimatlos in einer düsteren und bedrohlichen Landschaft unterwegs, ja auf der Flucht sind. Der brennende Wald wird zur Seelenlandschaft.

Von diesem Werk lässt sich ein Bogen schlagen zur Skulptur *Memento mori* von 2013. Diese verkörpert alle zentralen Aspekte von Ikemuras Kunst: Das mädchenhafte Wesen ist zugleich Mensch und Landschaft, Blume und Muschel, strahlt Sinnlichkeit und Zerbrechlichkeit aus. Die Kerben am Oberkörper und die Körperöffnungen sowie die tiefen Augenhöhlen lassen – wie es der Titel suggeriert – an die Vergänglichkeit des Lebens denken. Die Gestalt befindet sich in eienem Bereich zwischen irdischem Leben und einer anderen Welt und versinnbildlicht so die Fragilität der menschlichen Existenz. Die Plastik, die tiefe Trauer ausstrahlt, entsteht ein Jahr nach dem Ereignis von Fukushima.

Garten der Lüste |
Garden of Desire, 1983
Kohle auf Papier |
Charcoal on paper,
267 × 270 cm
[Kat. | cat. 92]

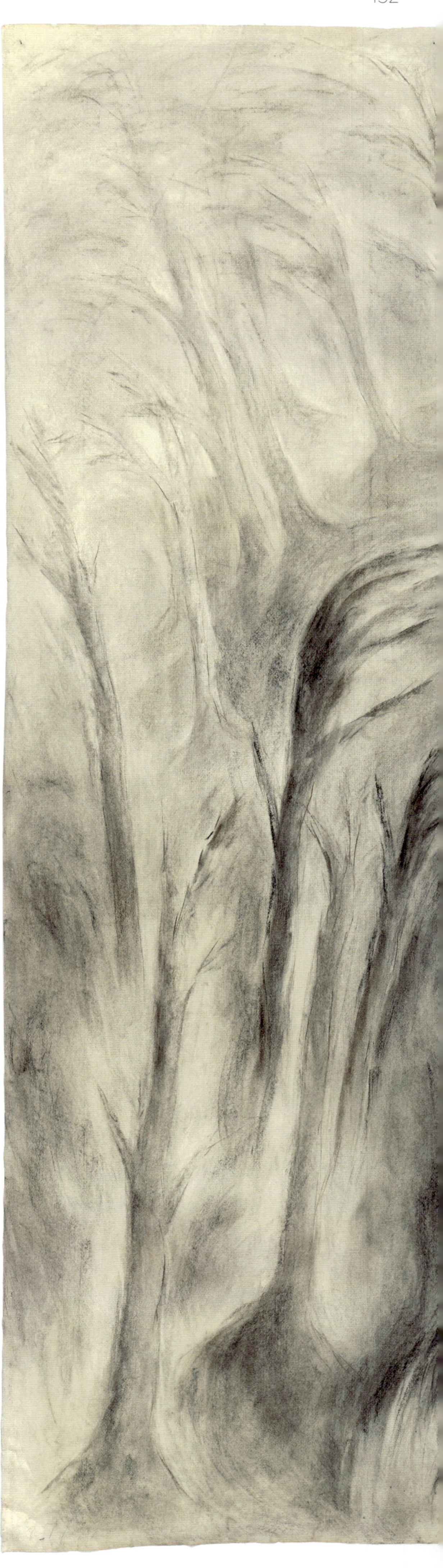

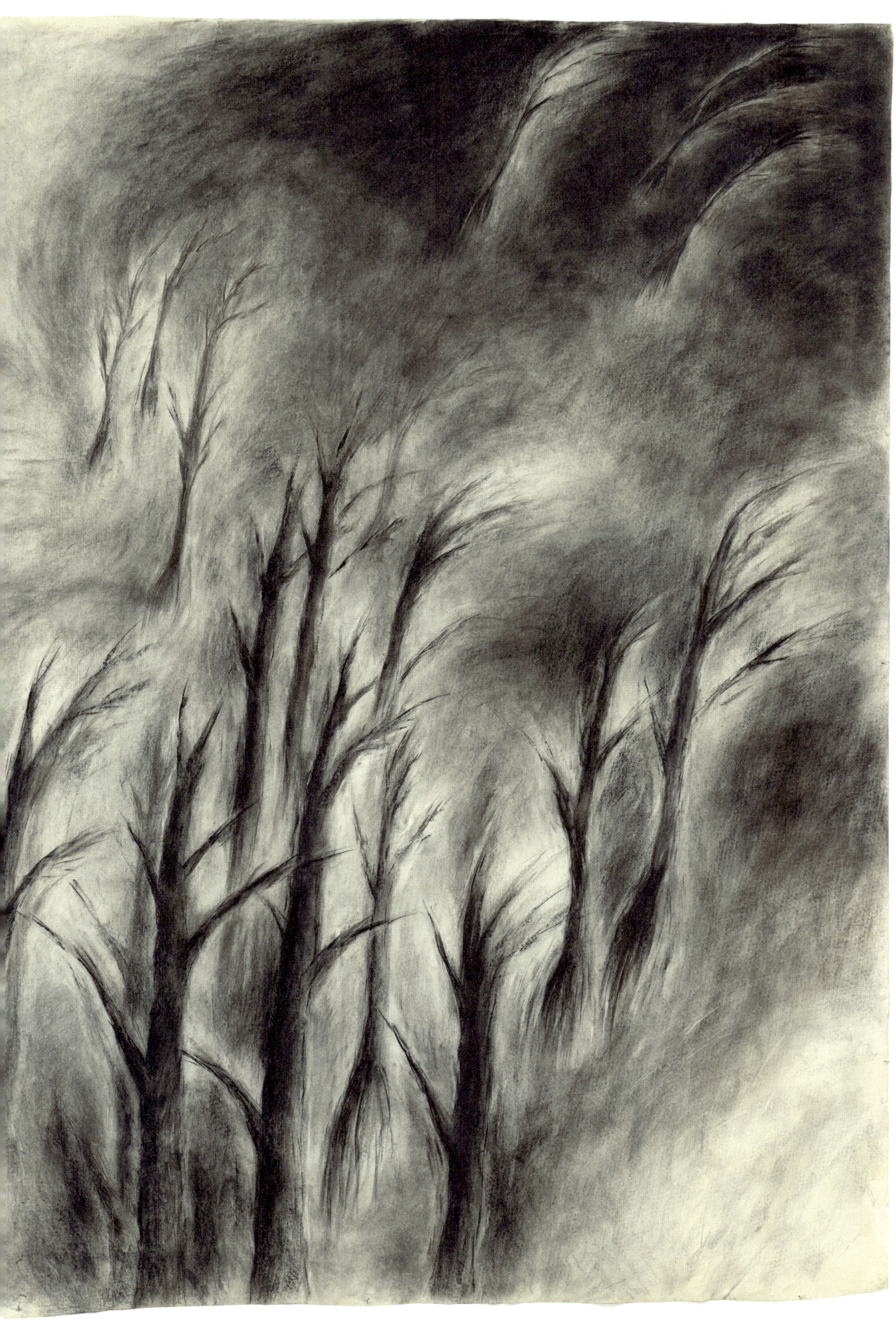

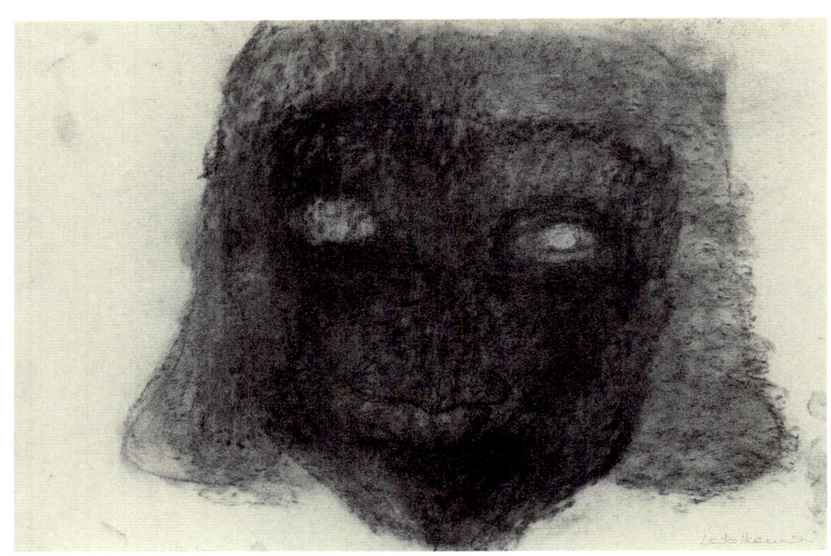

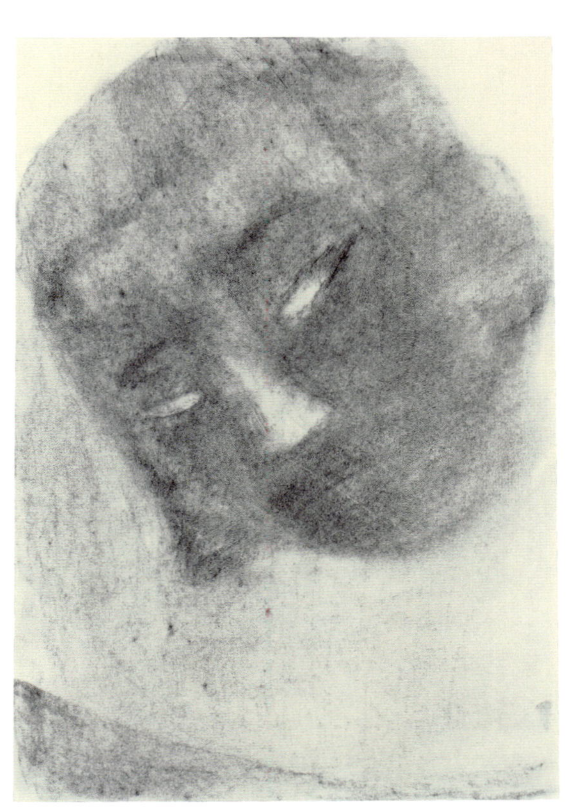

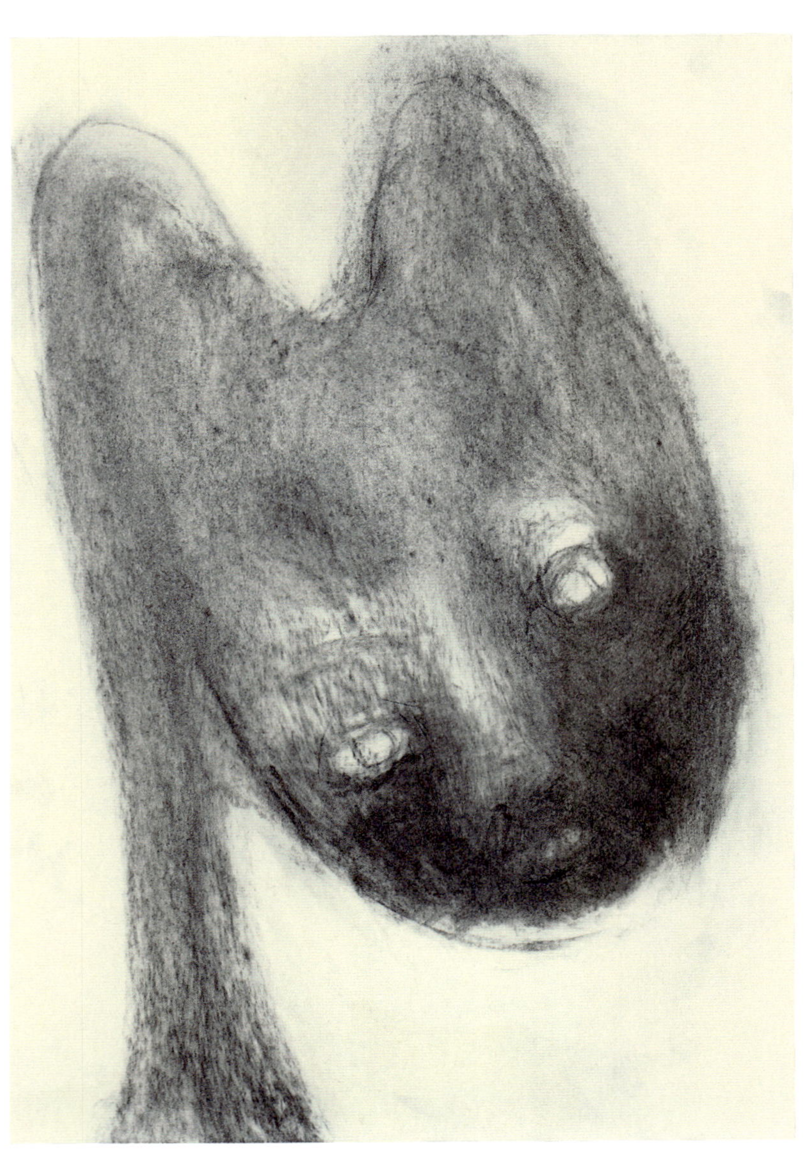

Black Head, 2008
Kohle auf Papier |
Charcoal on paper,
32 × 49 cm
[Kat. | cat. 100]

Black Head, 2008
Kohle auf Papier |
Charcoal on paper,
59 × 42 cm
[Kat. | cat. 104]

Black Head, 2008
Kohle auf Papier |
Charcoal on paper,
59 × 42 cm
[Kat. | cat. 103]

Black Face, 2008
Kohle auf Papier |
Charcoal on paper,
32 × 49 cm
[Kat. | cat. 96]

Black Face, 2008
Kohle auf Papier |
Charcoal on paper,
32 × 49 cm
[Kat. | cat. 98]

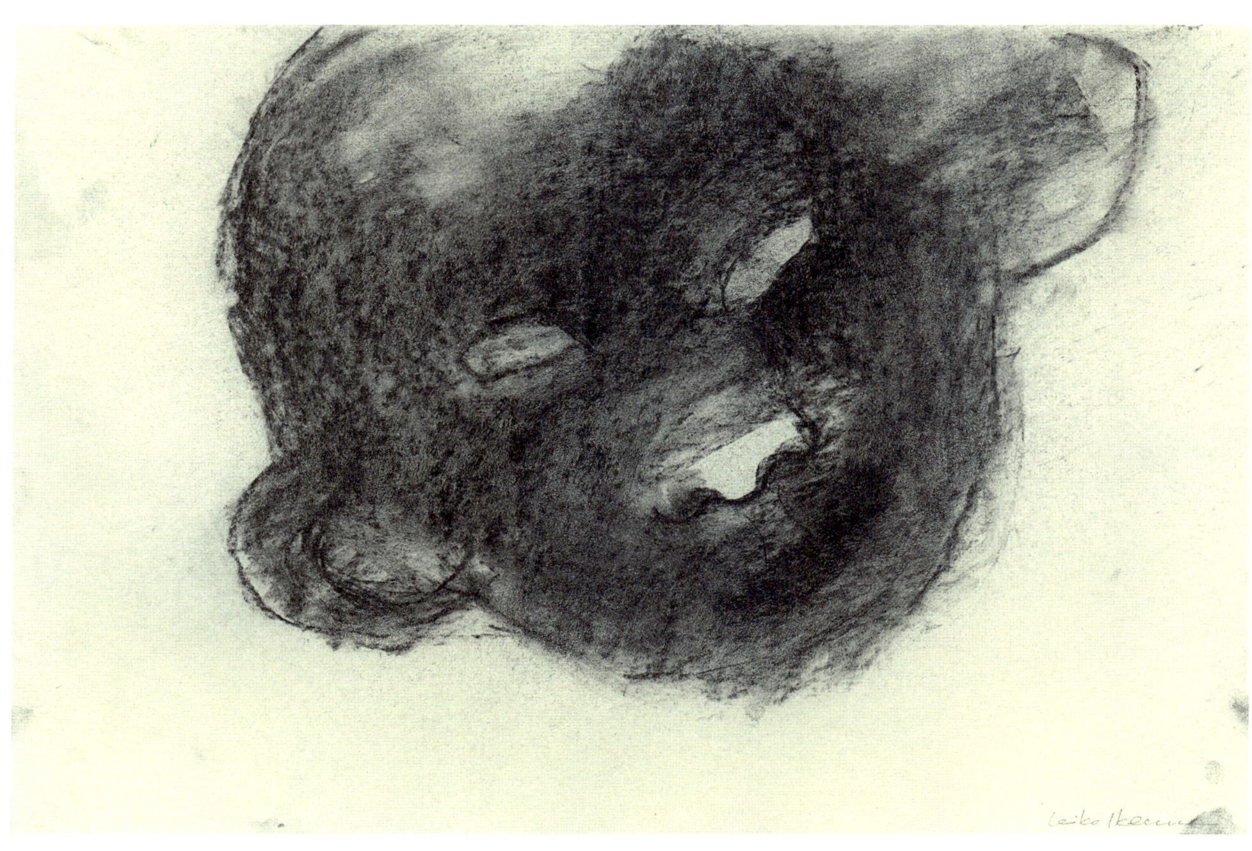

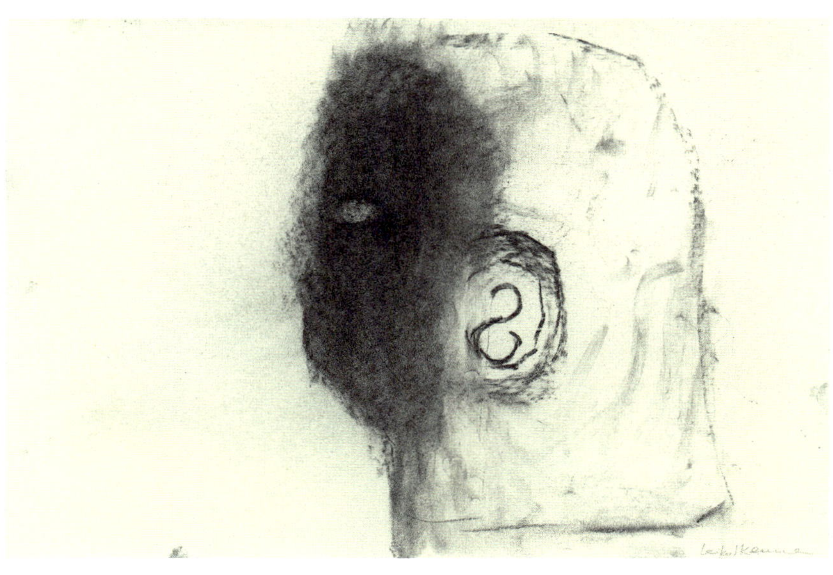

Black Face, 2008
Kohle auf Papier |
Charcoal on paper,
32 × 49 cm
[Kat. | cat. 99]

Black Face, 2008
Kohle auf Papier |
Charcoal on paper,
32 × 49 cm
[Kat. | cat. 95]

Black Face, 2008
Kohle auf Papier |
Charcoal on paper,
32 × 49 cm
[Kat. | cat. 107]

Black Head, 2008
Kohle auf Papier |
Charcoal on paper,
59 × 42 cm
[Kat. | cat. 102]

Black Face, 2008
Kohle auf Papier |
Charcoal on paper,
32 × 49 cm
[Kat. | cat. 97]

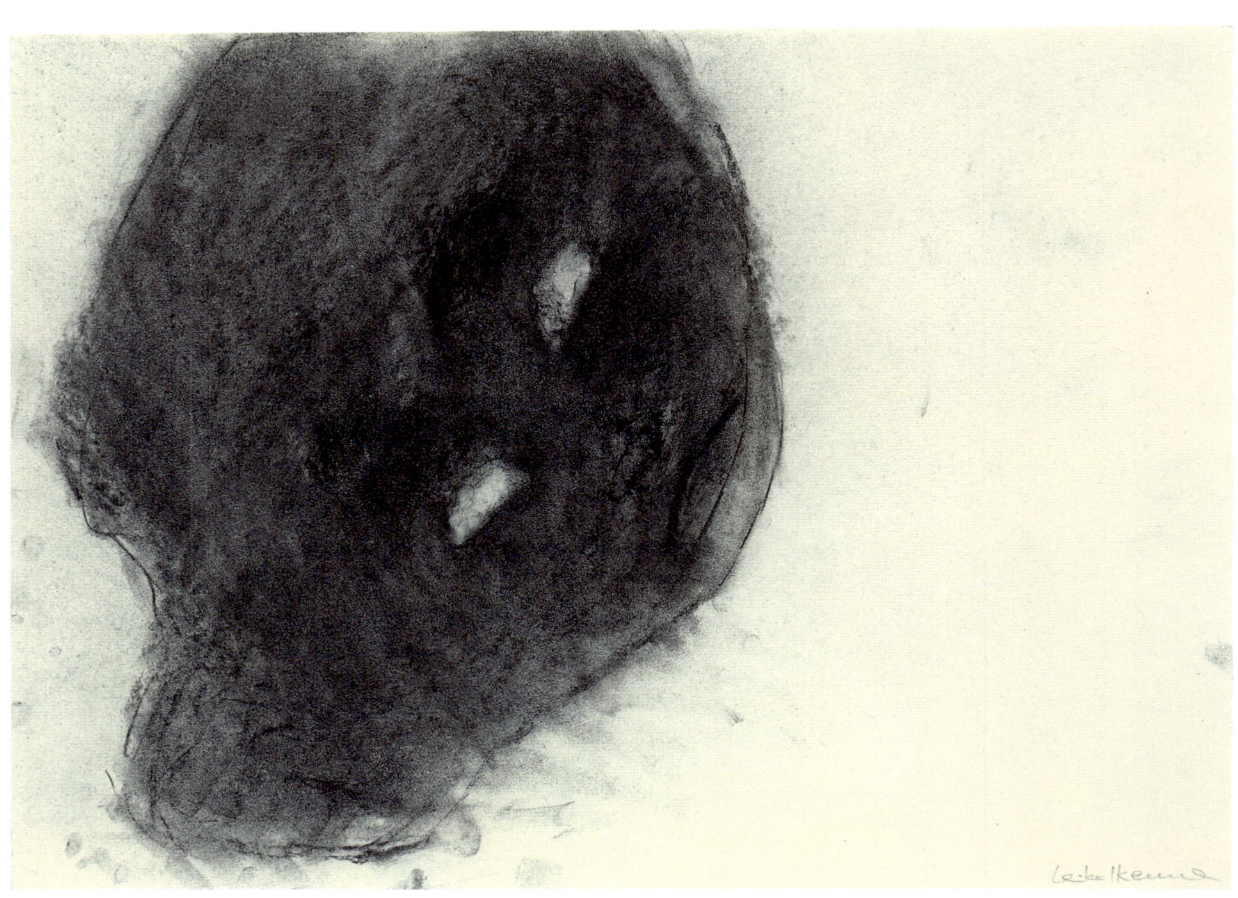

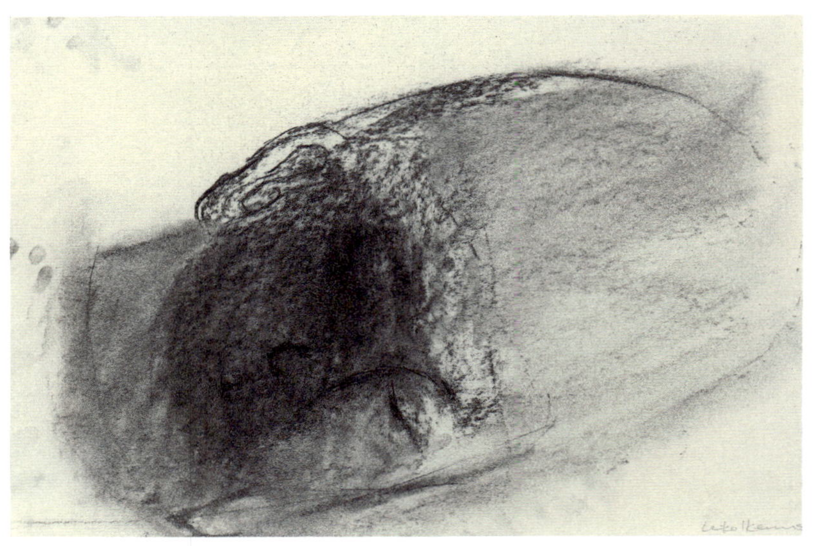

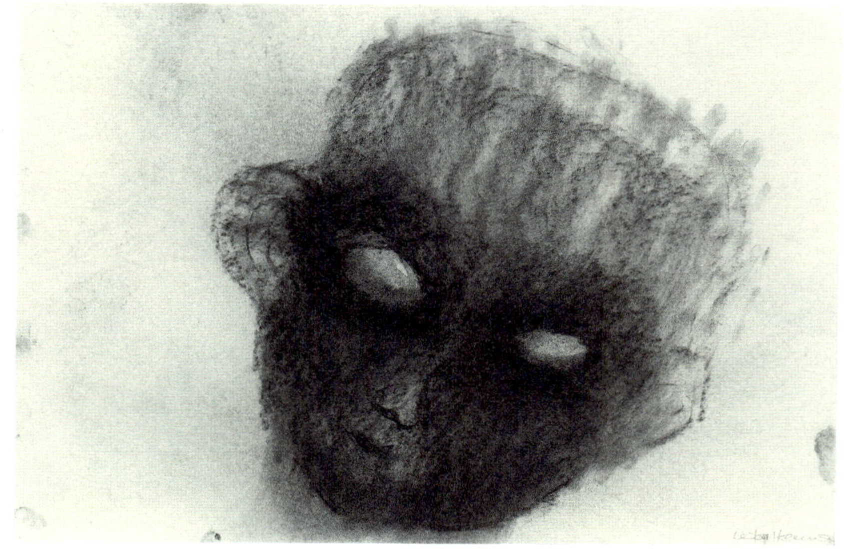

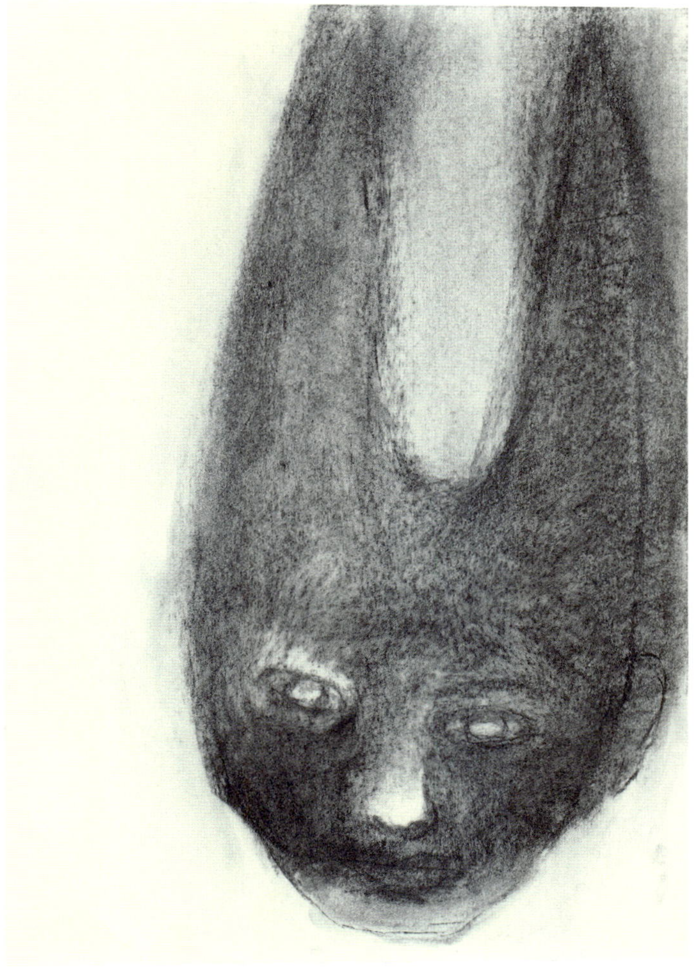

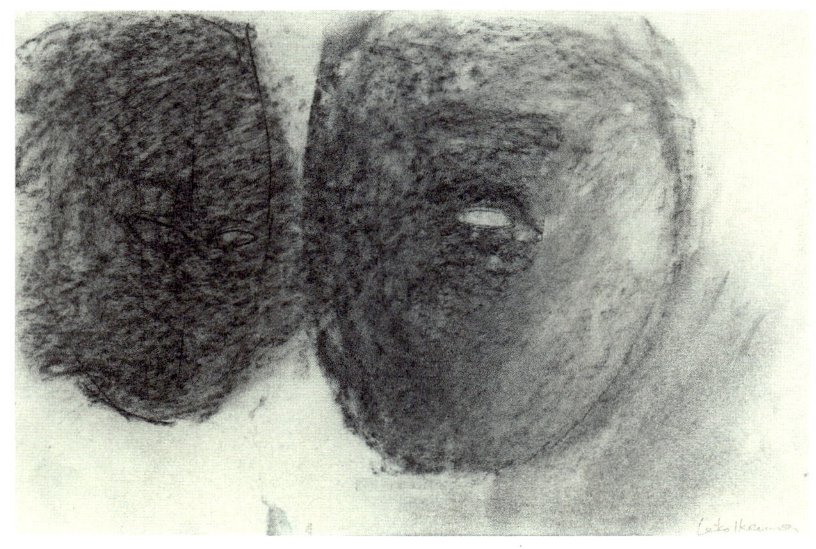

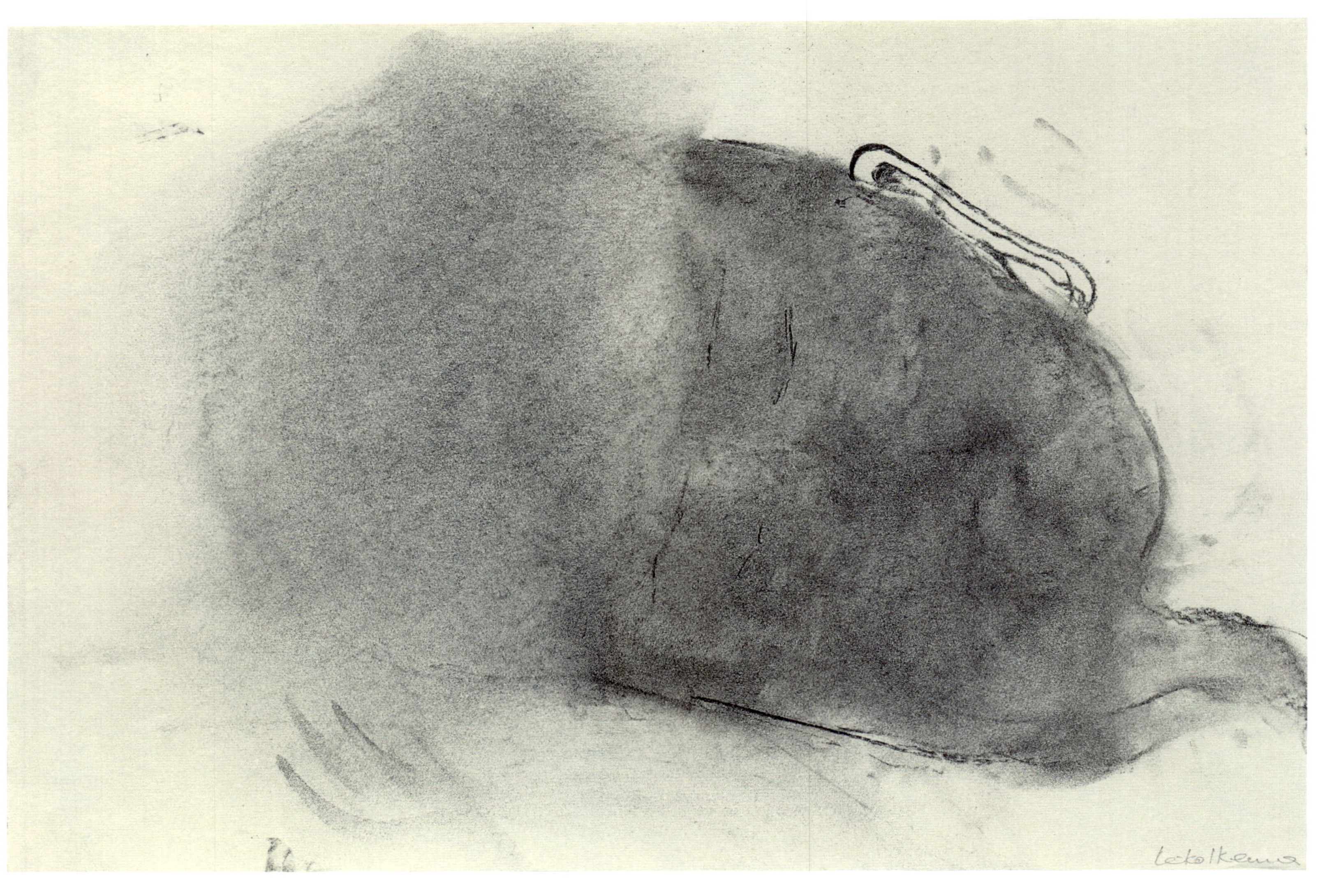

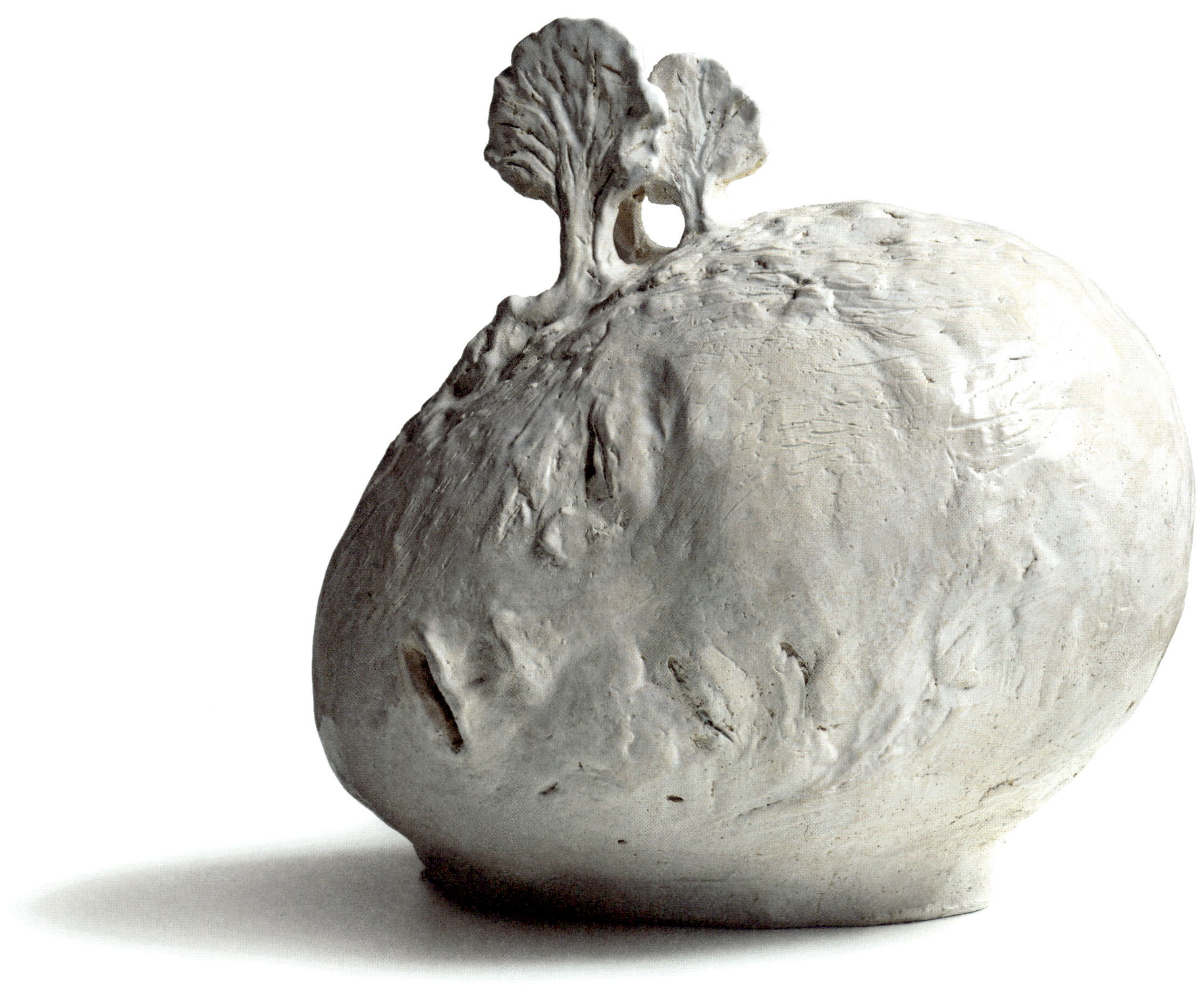

Memento mori |
Memento Mori, 2013/18
Bronze, patiniert |
Bronze, patinated,
38 × 135 × 38 cm
[Kat. | cat. 93]

Black Head, 2008
Kohle auf Papier |
Charcoal on paper,
59 × 42 cm
[Kat. | cat. 101]

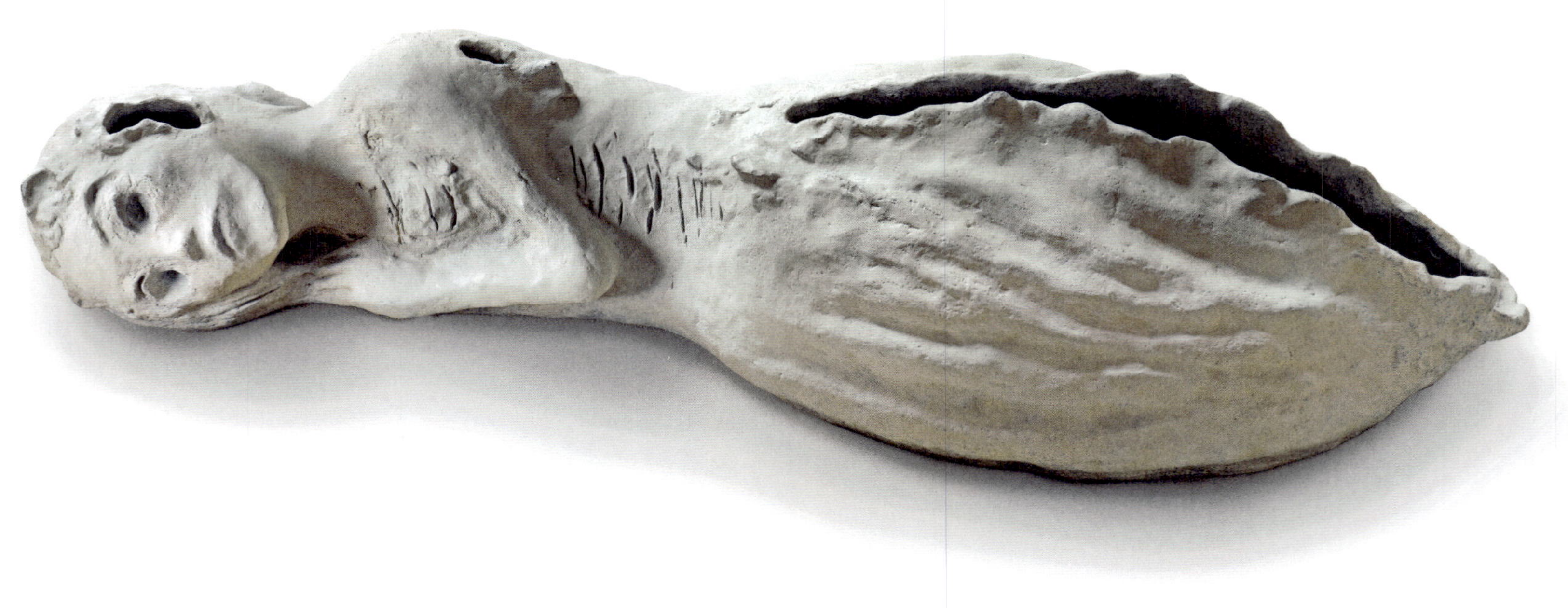

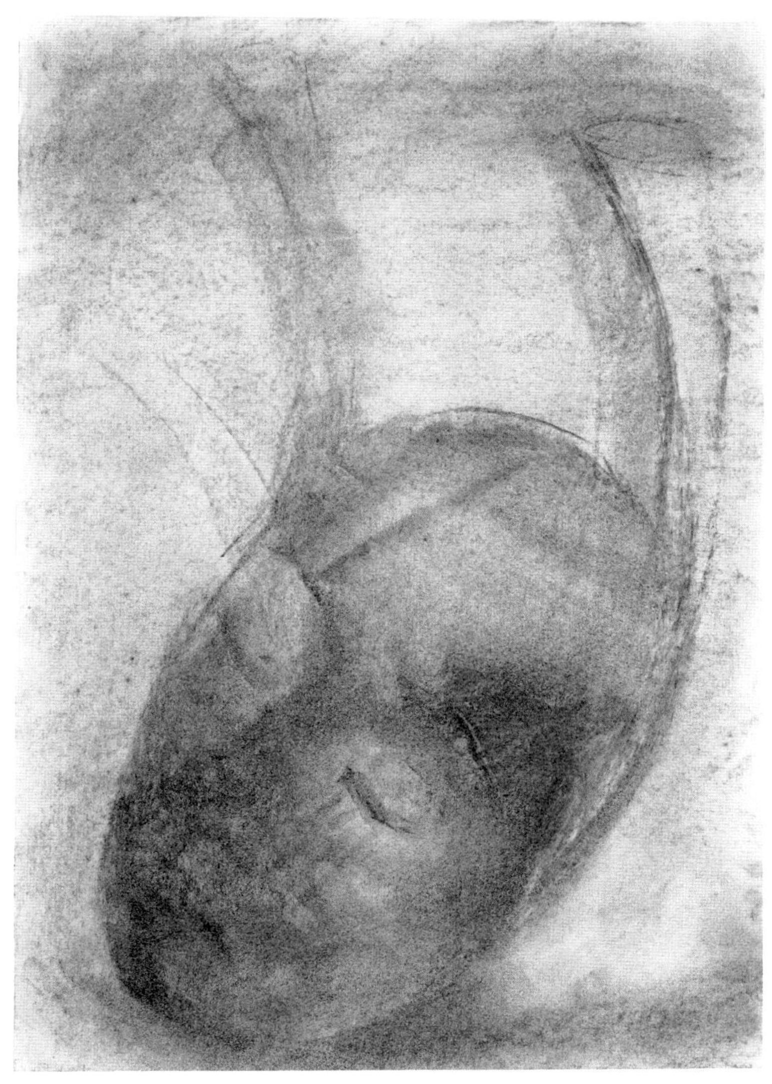

Our Planet

In a triptych of 2015, Ikemura brings cosmic landscapes forth out of amorphous shapes. The landscape is not understood as a concrete place but as the seat of the world soul and the metaphysical expression of an originary space of nature, in which human, animal, and plant build a unity. Here, the influence of Japanese Shintoism—which sees spirits and divine manifestations of nature in the forms of rocks and plants—is evident not only in the content of the work. In her present-day painting, Ikemura relies more heavily than ever on the East Asian tradition of ink painting. These works speak not least to the concern for the future of our planet in the face of the increasing threat to our living environment.

The nuclear catastrophe of Fukushima in 2011 and its consequences have reinforced the sociocritical aspects of her work and have shaped her most recent production. Although created in the wake of the impact of this catastrophe, the sculpture *Usagi Kannon* (2012) points beyond these concrete events: it represents woman and hare but is at the same time sculpture and temple. As a hare, it is the symbol of fertility and thus brings good luck. The protective temple is reminiscent, on the one hand, of the Bodhisattva, who can take on the suffering of others; and, on the other hand, of the Christian Madonna of Mercy. A connection can be made here with the Amazons, a series of sophisticated monotypes that transforms the impulsive war goddesses of Ikemura's early period into calm women with internal strength.

Unser Planet

In einem Triptychon von 2015 lässt Ikemura kosmische Landschaften aus amorphen Gebilden entstehen. Die Landschaft wird nicht als konkreter Ort verstanden, sondern als Sitz der Weltseele und metaphysischer Ausdruck eines ursprünglichen Naturraums, in dem Mensch, Tier und Pflanze eine Einheit bilden. Inhaltlich manifestiert sich in diesen Arbeiten der Shintoismus, der Geister und göttliche Naturerscheinungen in Form von Felsen und Pflanzen kennt, und auch technisch orientiert Ikemura sich an ihren japanischen Wurzeln, wenn sie in der Malweise heute stärker als je auf ostasiatische Tuschemalerei zurückgreift. Nicht zuletzt sprechen diese Werke von einer Sorge um die Zukunft unseres Planeten angesichts der zunehmenden Bedrohung unseres Lebensraumes.

Die Nuklearkatastrophe von Fukushima 2011 und ihre Folgen haben die gesellschaftskritische Seite ihrer Arbeit verstärkt und prägen ihr jüngstes Werk. Die Skulptur *Usagi Kannon* (2012) schuf Ikemura unter dem Eindruck dieser Katastrophe, sie weist aber über diese konkreten Ereignisse hinaus: Sie verkörpert Frau und Hase, ist aber zugleich Skulptur und Tempel. Als Hase ist sie Symbol der Fruchtbarkeit und damit Glück verheissend. Der schützende Tempel erinnert einerseits an Bodhisattva, der das Leid anderer auf sich nehmen kann, andererseits auch an die christliche Schutzmantelmadonna. Hier schliessen die Amazonen an, die Ikemura in einer Serie von raffinierten Monotypien aus dem Jahre 2015 darstellt. Aus den impulsiven Kriegsgöttinnen des Frühwerks sind innerlich starke und in sich ruhende Frauen geworden.

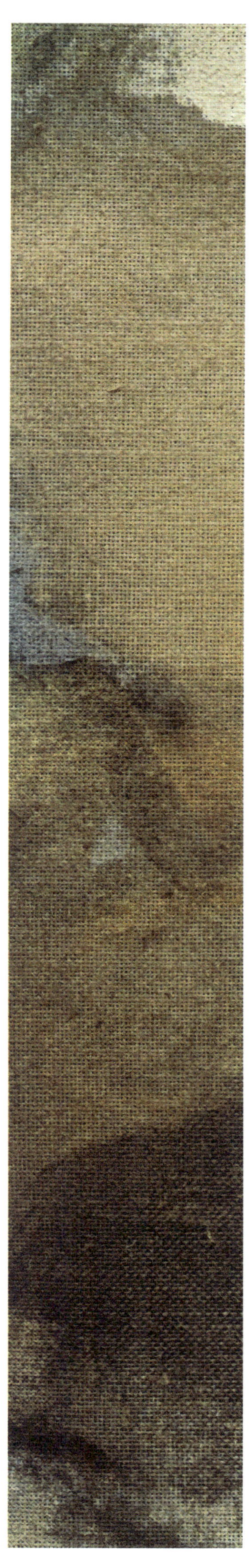

Tokaido, 2015
Tempera auf Jute |
Tempera on jute,
190 × 290 cm
[Kat. | cat. 110]

Genesis, 2015
Tempera auf Jute |
Tempera on jute,
190 × 290 cm
[Kat. | cat. 108]

Tokaido, 2015
Tempera cuf Jute |
Tempera cn jute,
190 × 290 cm
[Kat. | cat. 109]

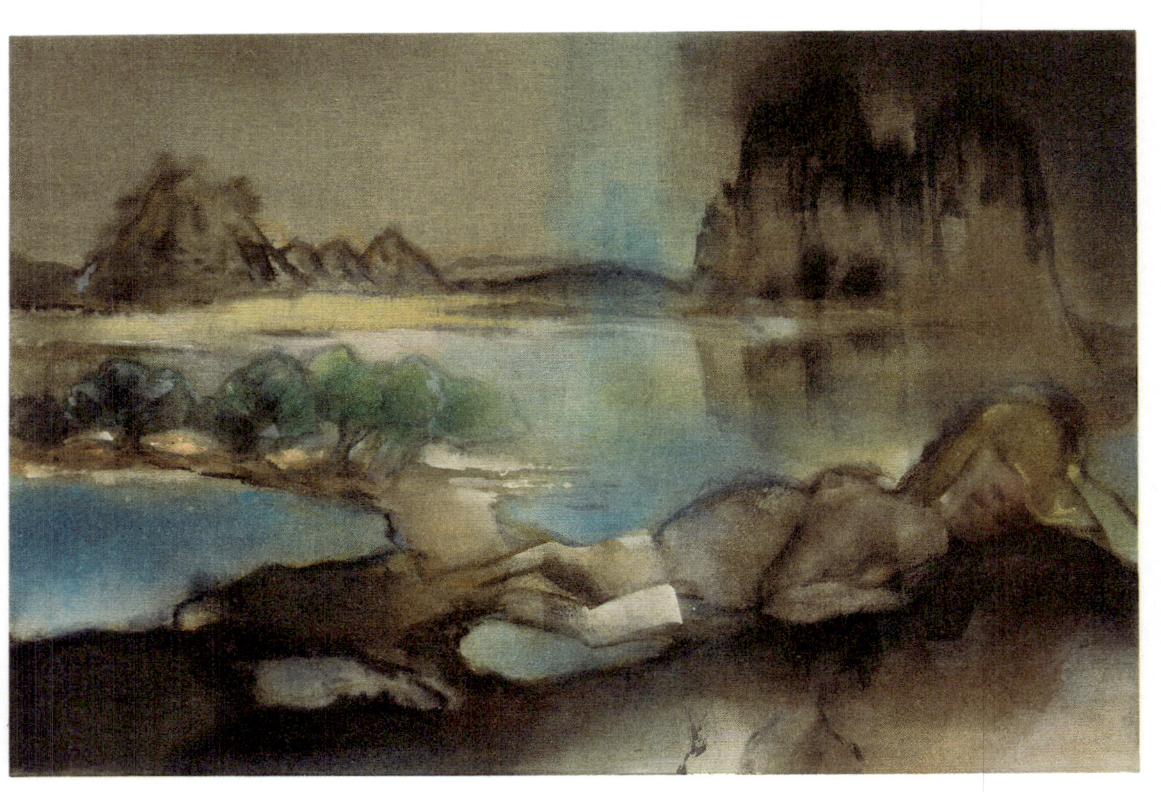

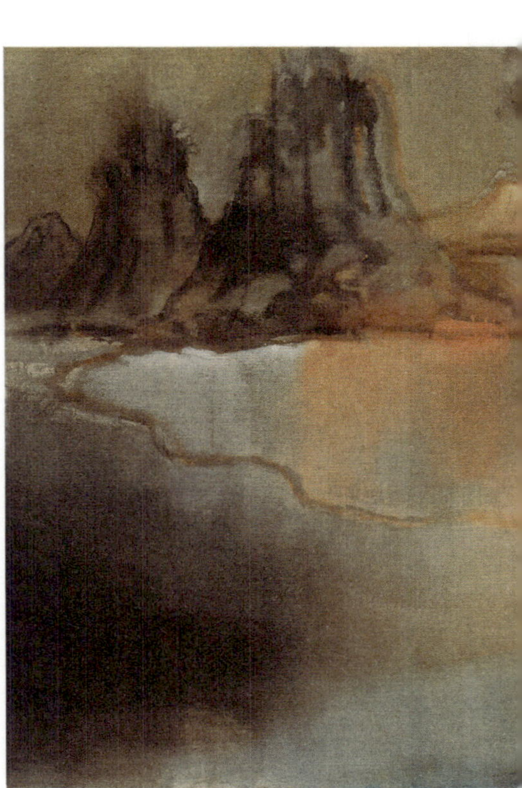

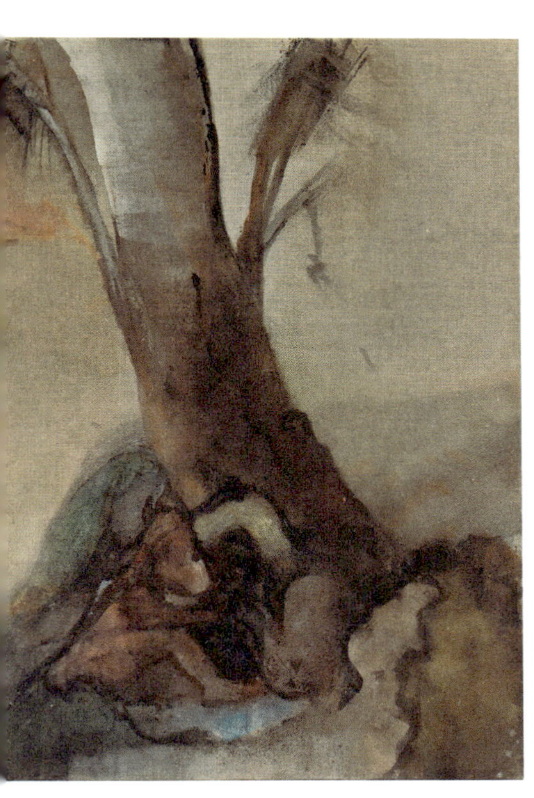

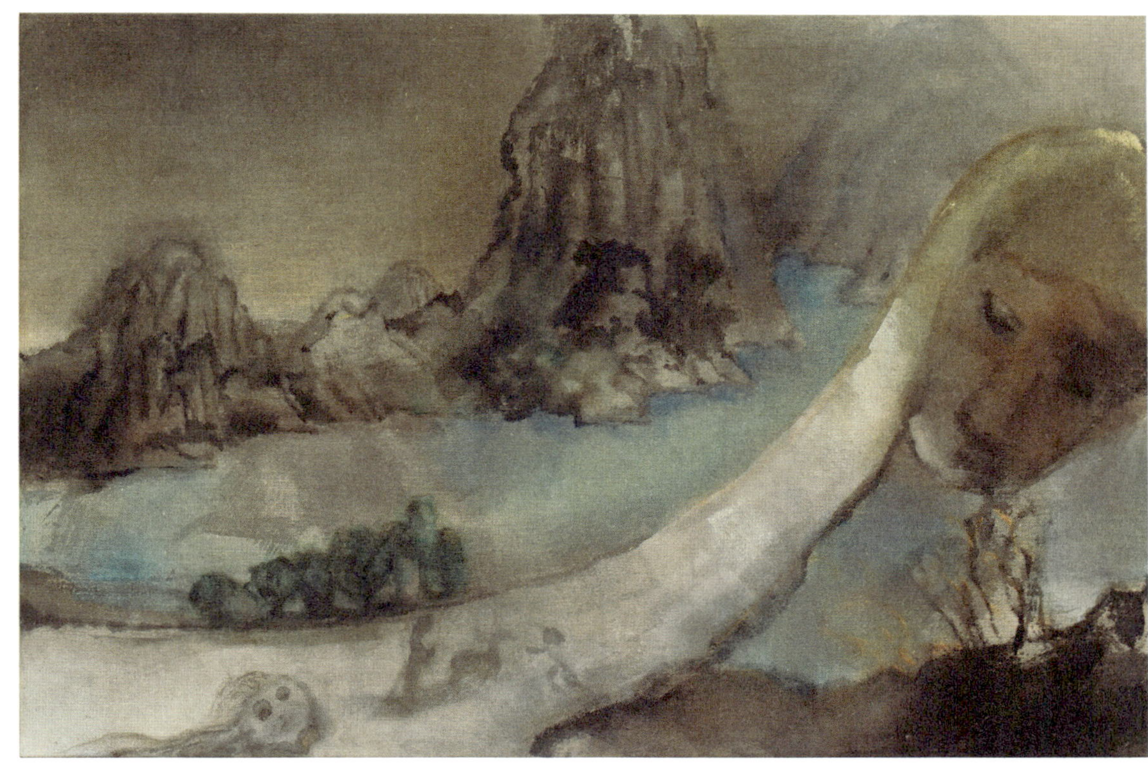

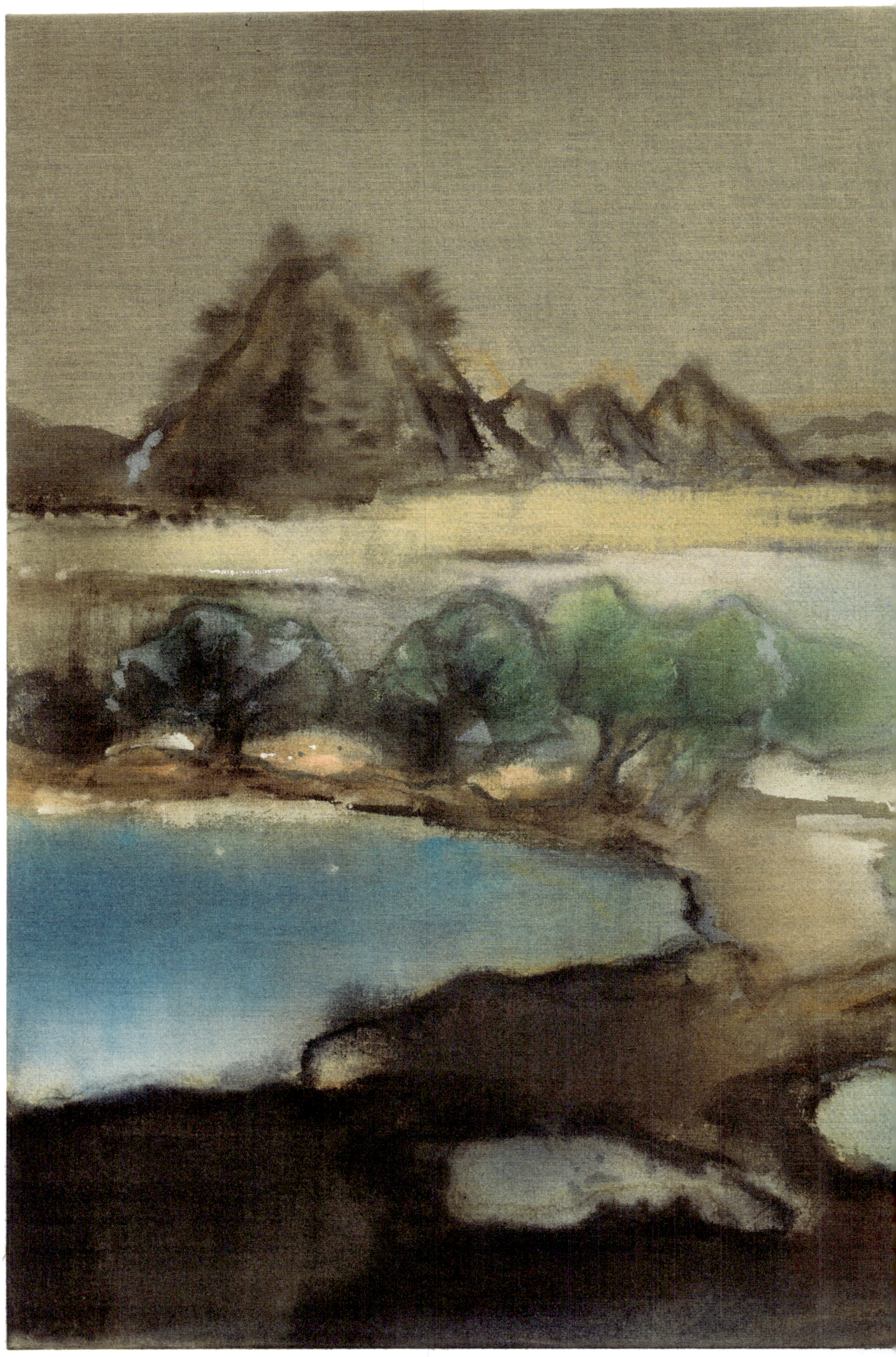

Tokaido, 2015
Tempera auf Jute |
Tempera on jute,
190×290 cm
[Kat. | cat. 110]

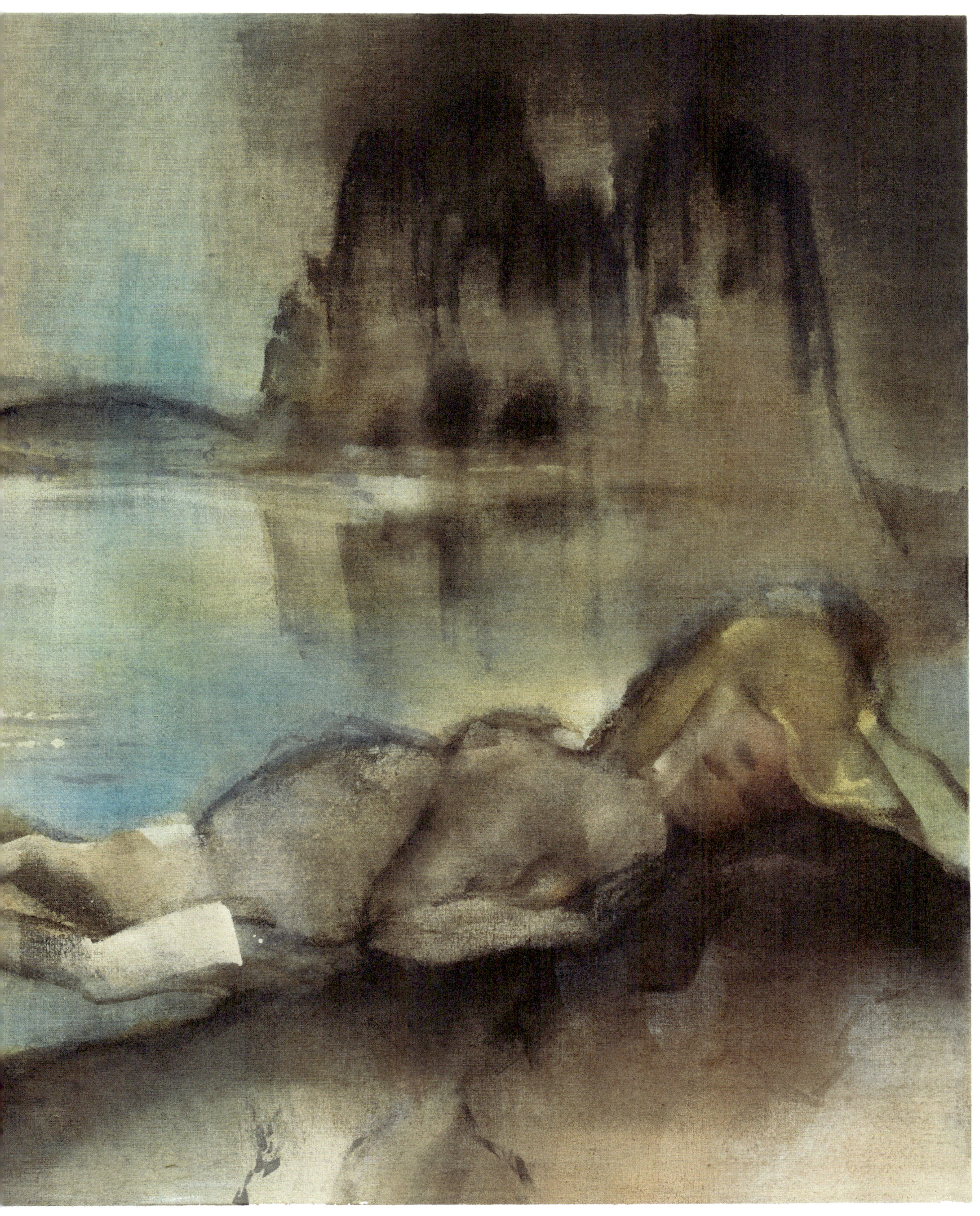

Genesis, 2015
Tempera auf Jute |
Tempera on jute,
190 × 290 cm
[Kat. | cat. 108]

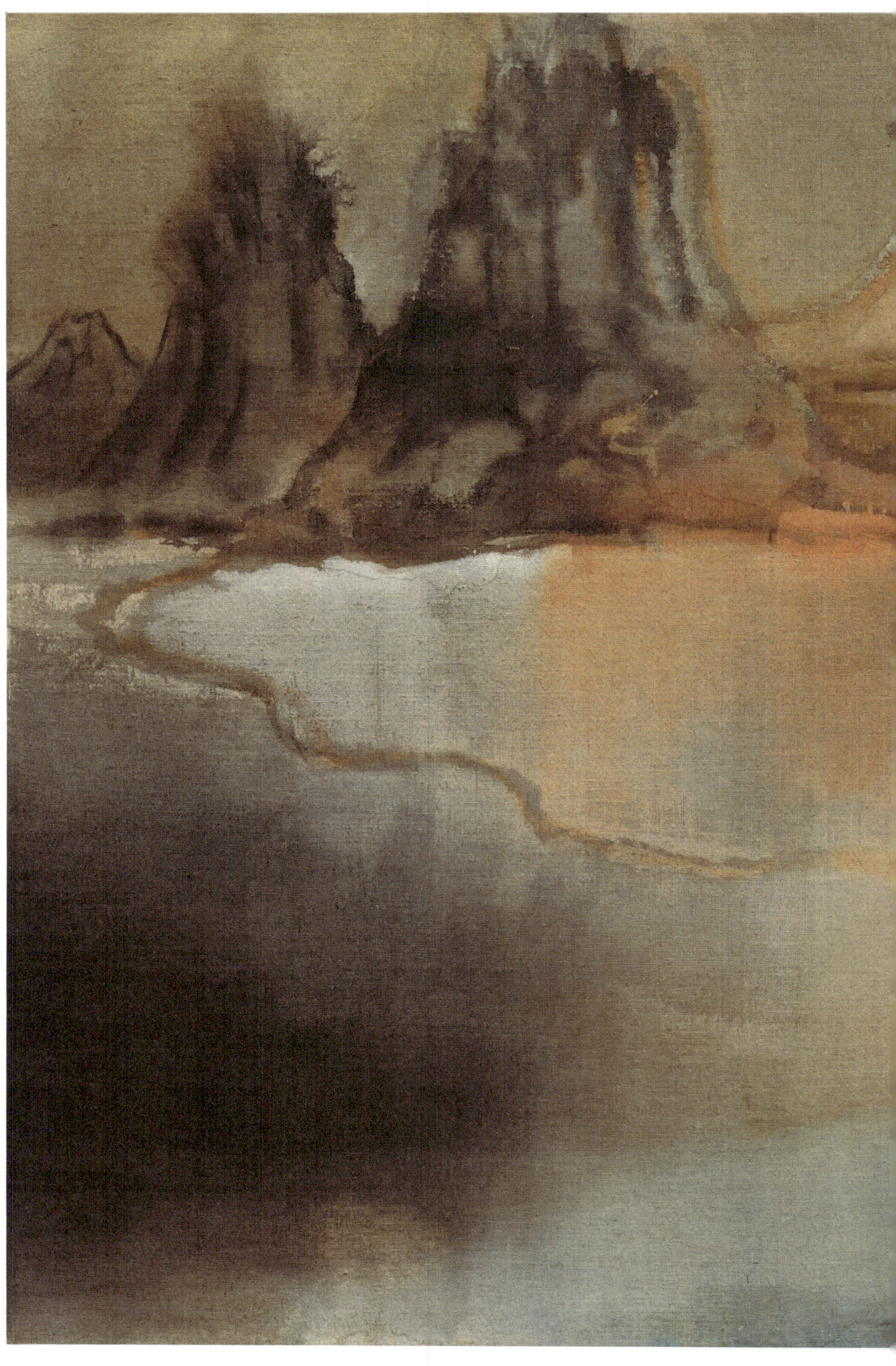

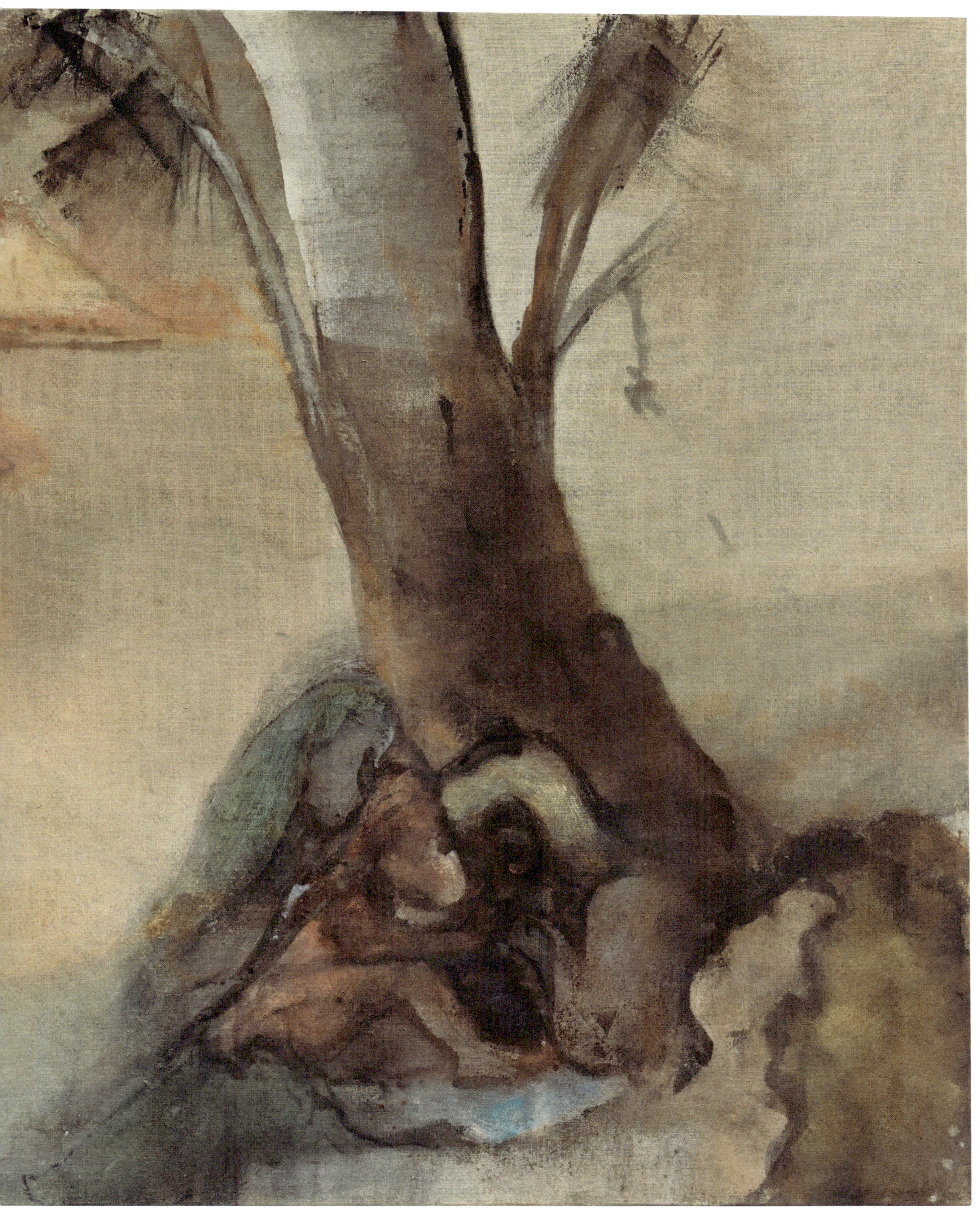

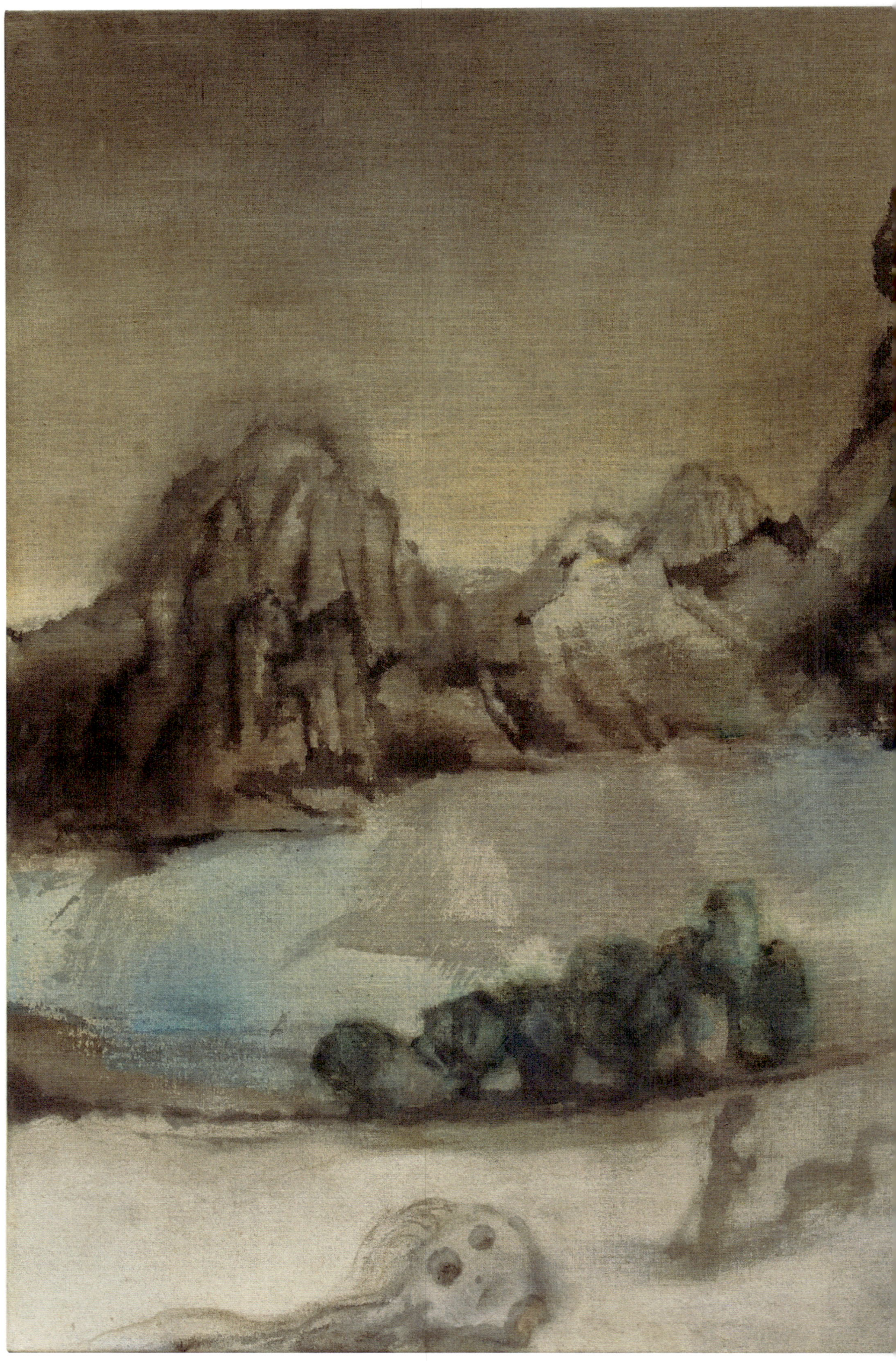

Tokcido, 2015
Tempera auf Jute |
Tempera on jute,
190 × 290 cm
[Kat. | cat. 109]

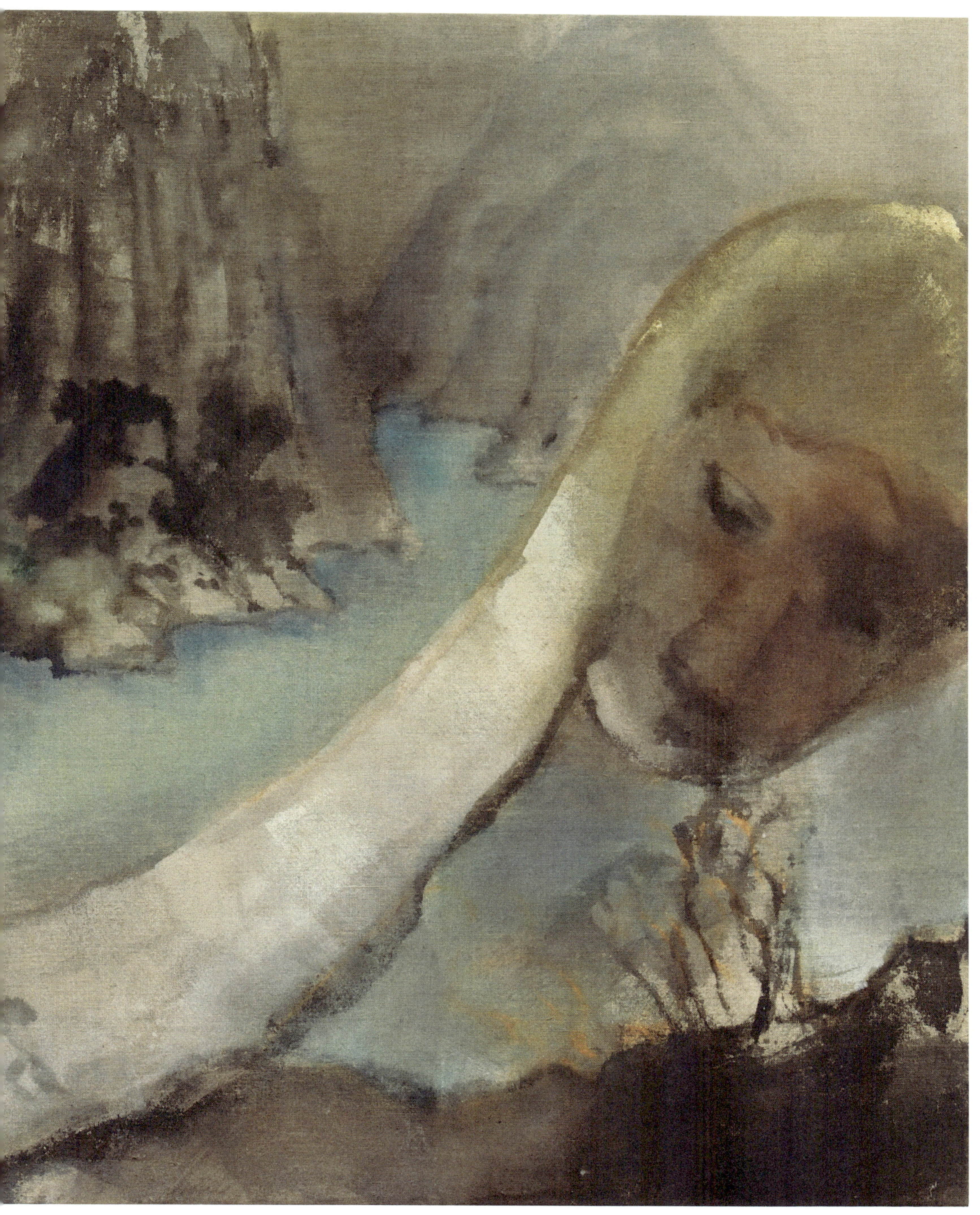

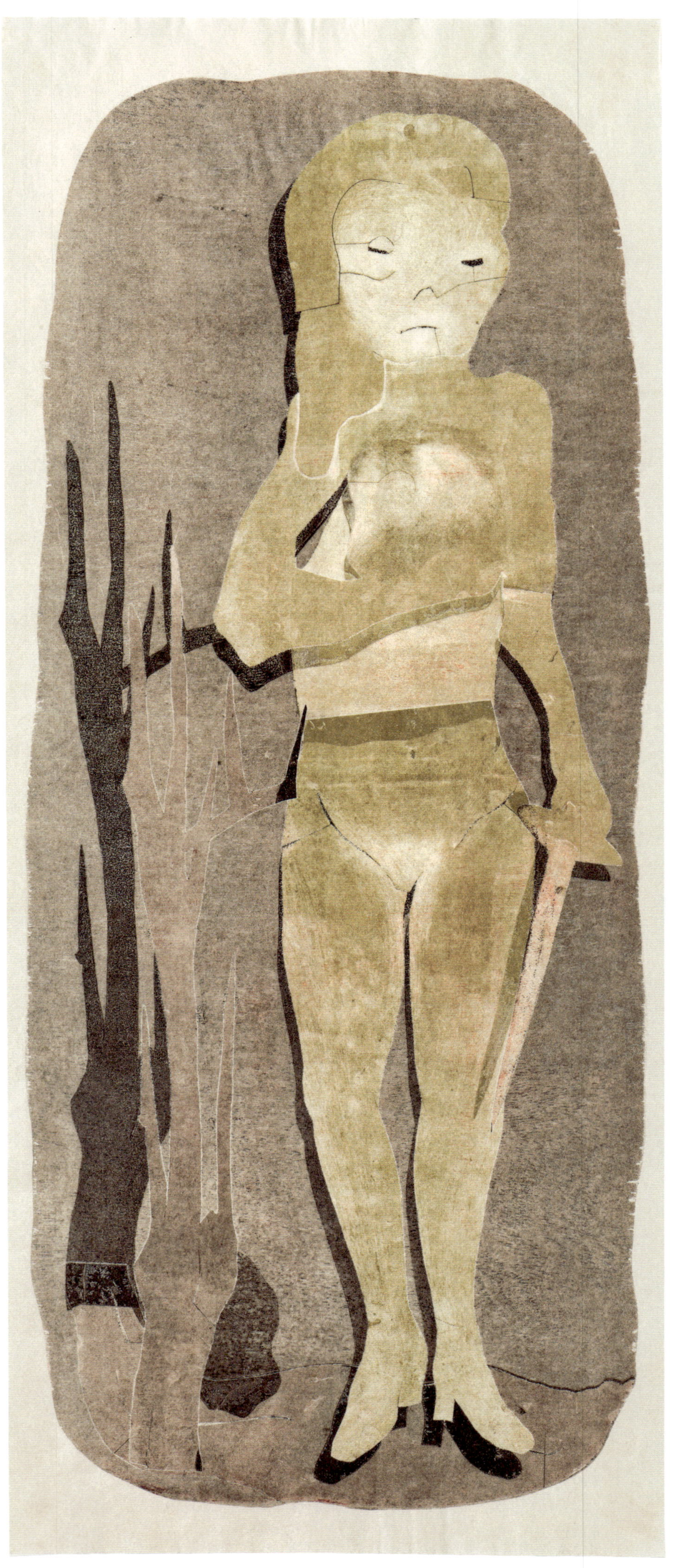

Amazona
[Serie | series], 2015
Monotypie auf Japan-
papier | Monotype
on Japan paper,
je | each 125 × 55 cm
[Kat. | cat. 111–115]

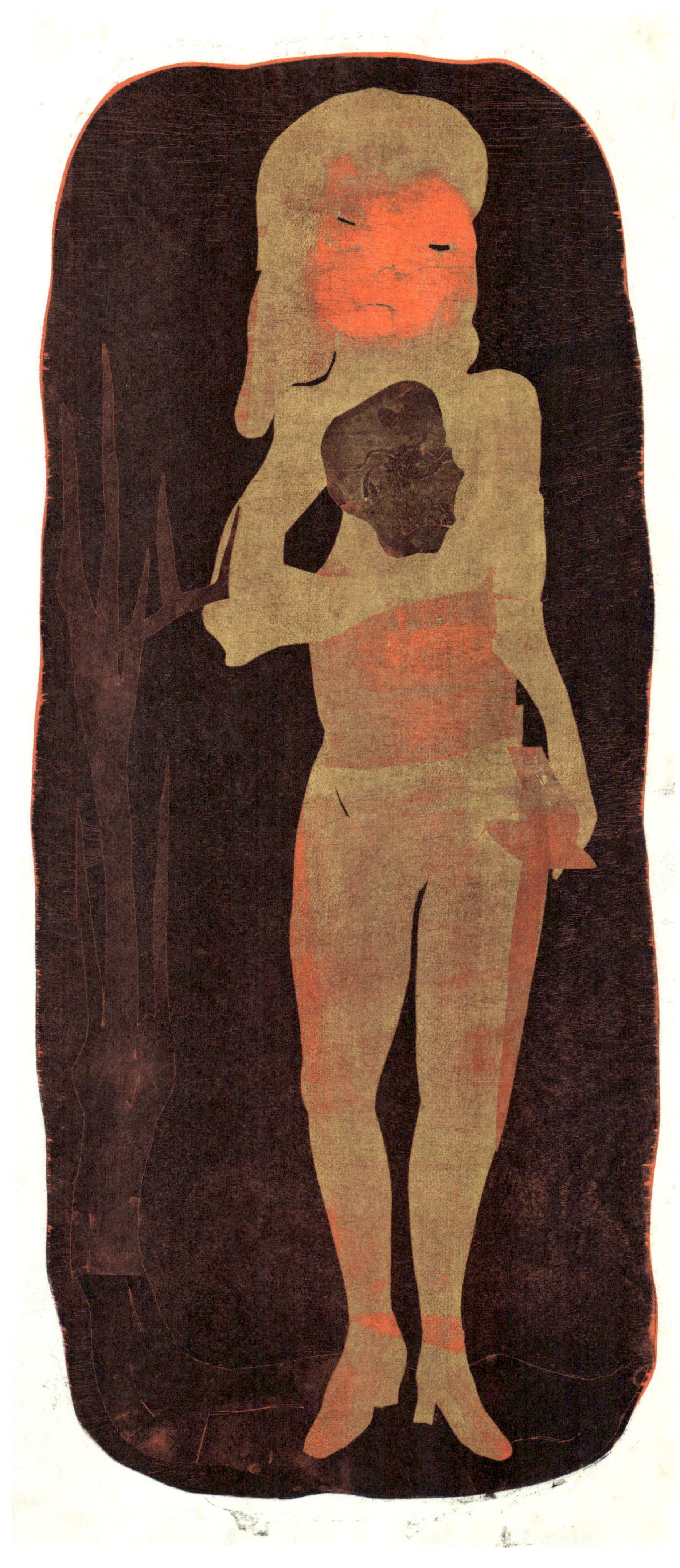

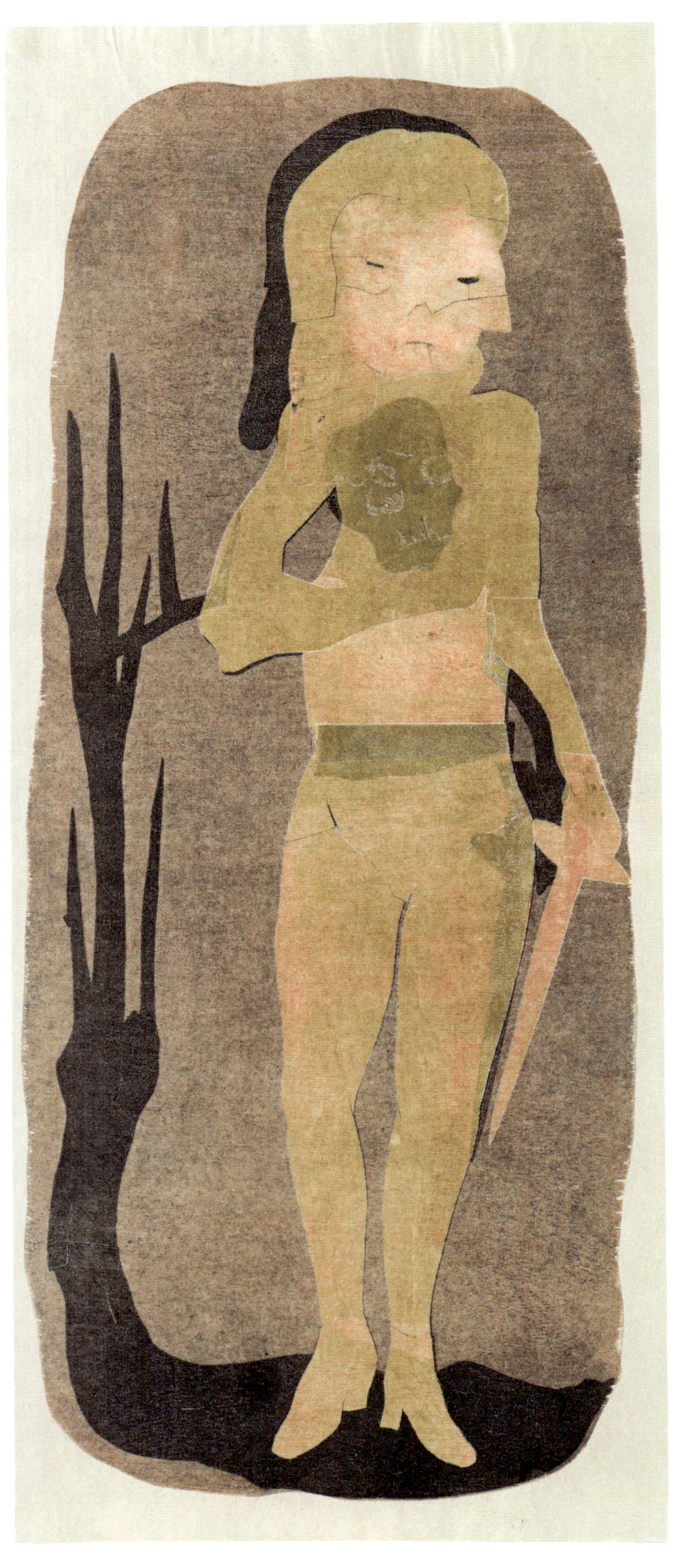
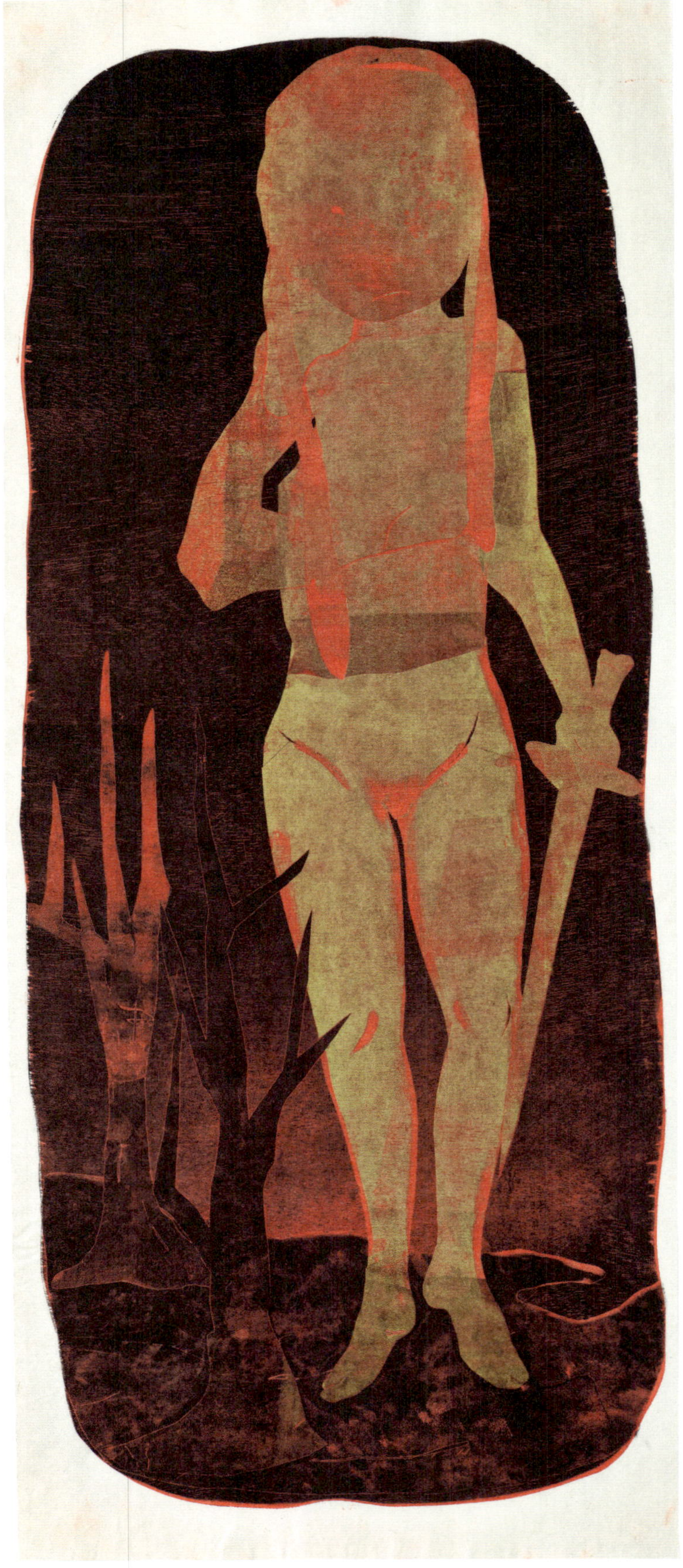

Amazona
[Serie | series], 2015
Monotypie auf Japan-
papier | Monotype
on Japan paper,
je | each 125 × 55 cm
[Kat. | cat. 111–115]

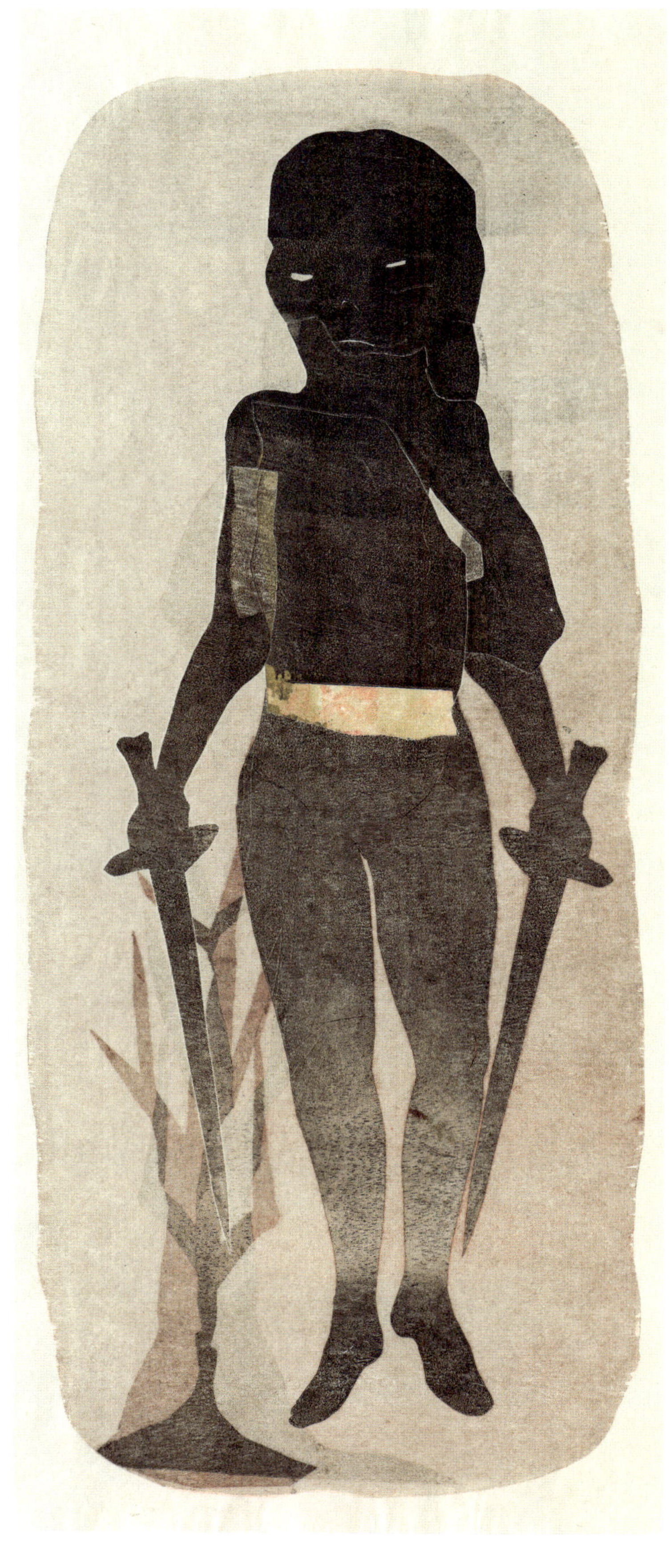

Usagi Kannon, 2012/19
Bronze, patiniert |
Bronze, patinated,
159 × 138 × 340 cm
[Kat. | cat. 116]

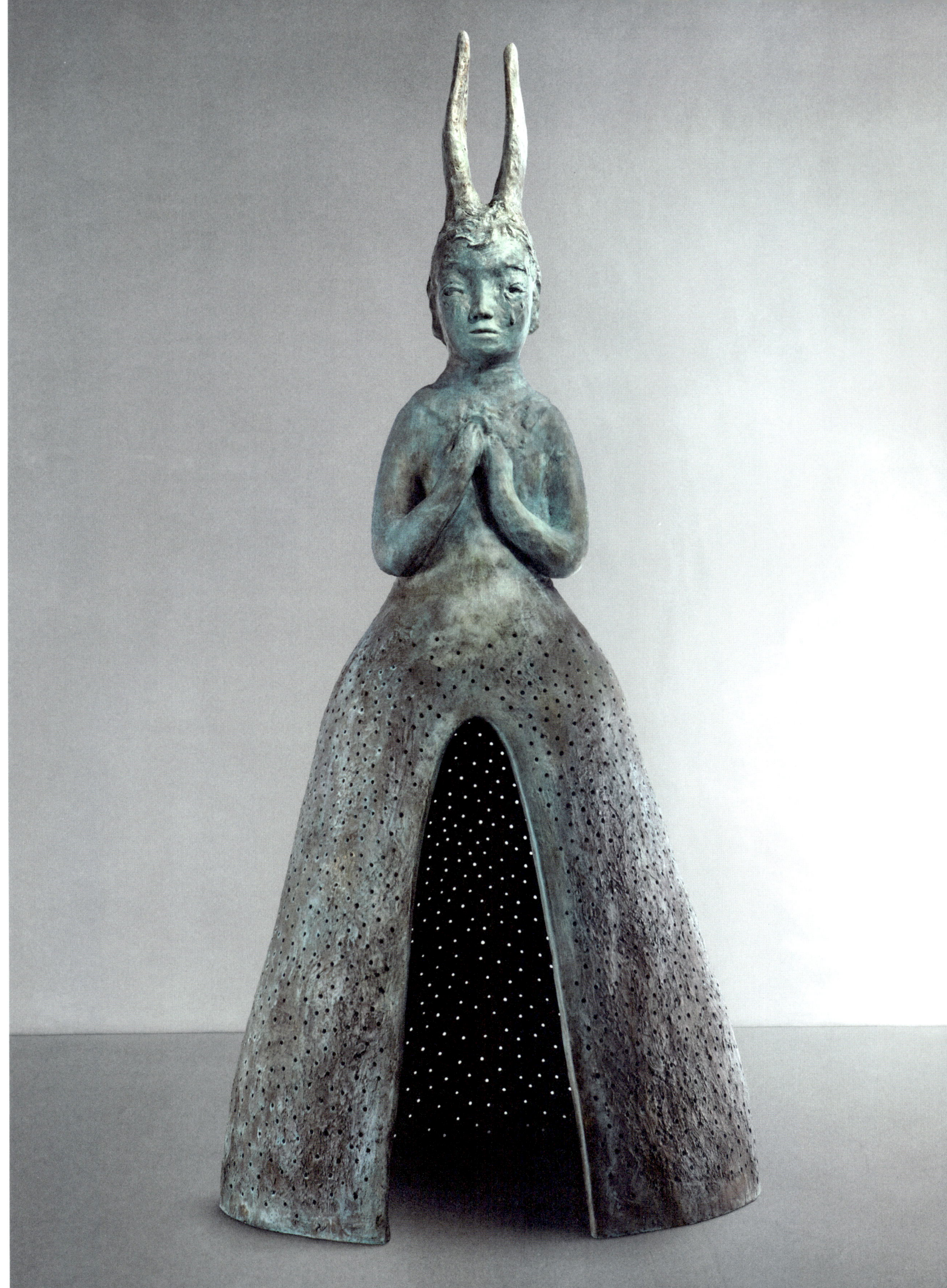

Leiko Ikemura Biography

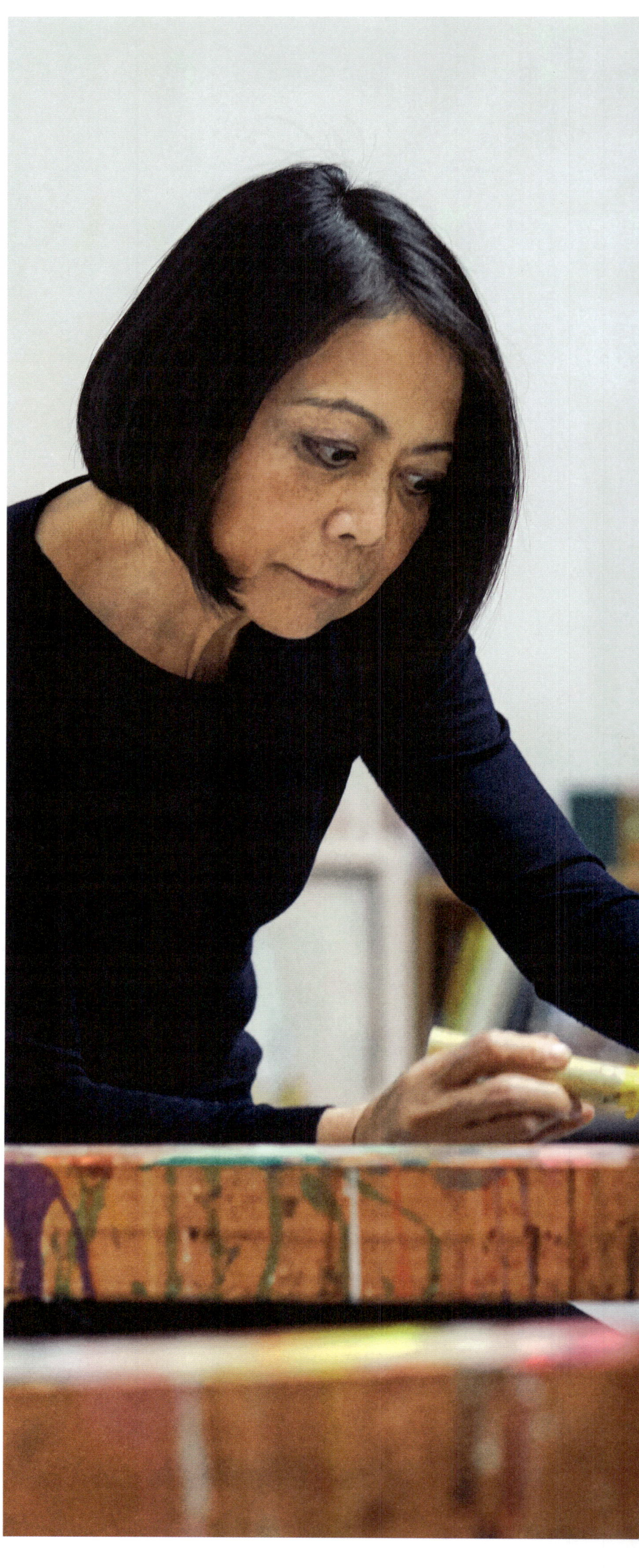

The Japanese artist Leiko Ikemra has lived since 1972 in Europe, where she has created a unique synthesis of Japanese and Western cultures. Her art developed out of engagement with the state of being foreign and the appropriation of new languages. She has repeatedly been drawn *Toward New Seas,* be it new countries and cultures or new artistic adventures. Ikemura's work encompasses painting and sculpture, drawings and prints, and even photography and poetry, and is exibited regularly around the world.

Her path led through Spain and Switzerland, where she became a sensation in the early 1980s with her expressive drawings and large-format paintings. This was followed by her move to Cologne and Berlin, where she became a professor at the Universität der Künste in 1991. While during the 1990s she became known primarily for her girl-like beings in paintings and sculptures, in the last decade she has produced monumental cosmic landscapes that increasingly draw on East Asian pictorial traditions and express concern for our planet.

Leiko Ikemura Biografie

Die Japanerin Leiko Ikemura lebt seit 1972 in Europa, wo sie als Künstlerin eine einzigartige Synthese zwischen der japanischen und der westlichen Kultur erschaffen hat. Ihre Kunst entwickelte sich in der Auseinandersetzung mit dem Fremdsein und der Aneignung neuer Sprachen. Immer wieder zog es sie *Nach neuen Meeren*, sei dies in neue Länder und Kulturen oder neue künstlerische Abenteuer. Ikemuras Werk, das Malerei und Skulptur, Zeichnungen und Druckgraphik sowie Fotografie und Poesie umfasst, wird regelmässig weltweit ausgestellt und rezipiert.

Ihr Weg führte über Spanien in die Schweiz, wo sie in den frühen 1980er-Jahren mit ihren ausdrucksstarken Zeichnungen und grossformatigen Gemälden Furore machte. Es folgte der Umzug nach Köln und Berlin, wo sie 1991 eine Professur an der Universität der Künste erhielt. Während sie in den 1990er-Jahren vor allem für ihre mädchenhaften Wesen in Gemälden und Skulpturen bekannt wurde, sind in den letzten zehn Jahren monumentale kosmische Landschaften entstanden, die sich noch stärker als das frühere Werk auf ostasiatische Bildwelten bezieht und die Sorge um unseren Planeten zum Ausdruck bringen.

Born 1951 in Tsu, Mie Prefecture, Japan

1970–1972
• Studies Spanish literature at Osaka University

1972
• Language immersion study in Salamanca and Granada

1973–1978
• Studies painting at the Escuela Superior de Bellas Artes de Santa Isabel de Hungría in Seville (later renamed Universidad de Sevilla, Facultad de Bellas Artes)
• Travels throughout Europe every summer

1979–1983
• Lives in Switzerland, first in Lucerne and then Zurich

1980/81
• First exhibitions: Galerie Pablo Stähli, Zurich; and Galerie Tony Gerber, Bern

1981
• Honored by the Stiftung für die Graphische Kunst der Schweiz (Foundation for the Graphic Arts in Switzerland), Zurich
• Award from the Kiefer Hablitzel Stiftung, Bern
• Fellowship from the City of Zurich

1982
• First purchases of the artist's drawings by the Karl August Burckhardt-Koechlin-Fonds, selected by Dieter Koepplin, director of the Kupferstichkabinett (Department of Prints and Drawings), for the Kunstmuseum Basel
• Prizewinner, 2nd Internationale Jugendtriennale der Zeichnung (International Youth Drawing Triennial), Nuremberg

1983
• First major institutional solo exhibition: *Leiko Ikemura*, Bonner Kunstverein, curated by Margarethe Jochimsen
• Fellowship: *Stadtzeichnerin* (graphic artist in residence) of Nuremberg
• Group exhibition: *aktuell '83: Kunst aus Mailand, München, Wien und Zürich* (current '83: Art from Milan, Munich, Vienna, and Zurich), Städtische Galerie at Lenbachhaus, Munich
• Purchases of the artist's work by the Stiftung KUNST HEUTE (now in Kunstmuseum Bern)

1984
• *Leiko Ikemura—Stadtzeichnerin von Nürnberg 1983* (Graphic Artist in Residence of Nuremberg 1983), Kunsthalle Nürnberg
• *Ancestors—Leiko Ikemura*, Kunstverein im St. Katharinen, St. Gallen

1985
• *Leiko Ikemura*, Kunsthalle Waaghaus, Winterthur
• Represented in the group exhibition: *Räume heutiger Zeichnung: Werke aus dem Basler Kupferstichkabinett* (Spaces of Contemporary Drawing: Works from the Basel Kupferstich-kabinett), curated by Dieter Koepplin, Staatliche Kunsthalle Baden-Baden and Tel Aviv Museum of Art (1986)
• Begins to visit Japan regularly again
• Moves to Cologne

Geboren 1951 in Tsu, Präfektur Mie, Japan

1970–1972
• Studium der spanischen Literatur an der Universität Osaka

1972
• Sprachaufenthalt in Salamanca und Granada

1973–1978
• Studium der Malerei an der Escuela Superior de Bellas Artes de Santa Isabel de Hungría in Sevilla, später Universidad de Sevilla, Facultad de Bellas Artes benannt
• Im Sommer Reisen in Europa

1979–1983
• Lebt in der Schweiz, zuerst in Luzern, dann in Zürich

1980/81
• Erste Ausstellungen in der Galerie Pablo Stähli, Zürich, und der Galerie Tony Gerber, Bern

1981
• Auszeichnung der Stiftung für die Graphische Kunst der Schweiz
• Preis der Kiefer Hablitzel Stiftung
• Stipendium der Stadt Zürich

1982
• Dieter Koepplin, Leiter des Kupferstichkabinetts im Kunst-museum Basel, beginnt mit Unterstützung des Karl August Burckhardt-Koechlin-Fonds eine Sammlung von Ikemuras Zeichnungen aufzubauen.
• Preis der 2. Internationalen Jugendtriennale der Zeichnung in Nürnberg

1983
• *Leiko Ikemura*, erste grössere institutionelle Einzelausstellung im Bonner Kunstverein, kuratiert von Margarethe Jochimsen
• Stadtzeichnerin von Nürnberg
• Teilnahme an der Ausstellung *aktuell '83. Kunst aus Mailand, München, Wien und Zürich* in der Städtischen Galerie im Lenbachhaus München
• Ankäufe durch die Stiftung KUNST HEUTE (heute als Schen-kung im Kunstmuseum Bern)

1984
• *Leiko Ikemura – Stadtzeichnerin von Nürnberg 1983*, Kunsthalle Nürnberg
• *Ancestors – Leiko Ikemura*, Kunstverein im St. Katharinen, St. Gallen

1985
• *Leiko Ikemura*, Ausstellung in der Kunsthalle Winterthur
• Vertreten in der von Dieter Koepplin kuratierten Ausstellung *Räume heutiger Zeichnung: Werke aus dem Basler Kupfer-stichkabinett*, Staatliche Kunsthalle Baden-Baden, und 1986 im Tel Aviv Museum of Art
• Ab diesem Jahr reist Ikemura regelmässig nach Japan.
• Umzug nach Köln

1987
• Die Ausstellung *Leiko Ikemura. Gemälde, Zeichnungen 1980–1987* im Kunstmuseum Basel, Museum für Gegenwarts-kunst, wird organisiert von Dieter Koepplin und wandert zu folgenden Stationen: Musée cantonal des Beaux-Arts, Lausanne; Neue Galerie der Stadt Linz, Wolfgang-Gurlitt-Museum; Museum Ulm; Stadtgalerie Saarbrücken.
• Beginn der Zusammenarbeit mit der Galerie Karsten Greve, Köln

1987
• *Leiko Ikemura: Gemälde, Zeichnungen 1980–1987* (Leiko Ikemura: Paintings, Drawings 1980–1987), Kunstmuseum Basel, Museum für Gegenwartskunst, organized by Dieter Koepplin; traveled to Musée cantonal des beaux-arts, Lausanne; Neue Galerie der Stadt Linz; Wolfang-Gurlitt-Museum, Ulm; and Stadtgalerie Saarbrücken
• Begins working with Galerie Karsten Greve, Cologne

1988
• Receives prize for original graphic work at the Internationale Triennale
• Group exhibition: *Contemporary Swiss Art,* Seibu Museum of Art, Funabashi, Tokyo, as part of Tokyo Biennale '88: The 17th International Art Exhibition, Tokyo Metropolitan Art Museum, Kyoto Municipal Museum of Art, Seibu Museum of Art, Funabashi, Tokyo

1989
• Six-month stay in Sarn; atelier in Fürstenau in Canton Grisons (near Thusis)
• Group exhibition: *Das Verhältnis der Geschlechter* (The Relation of the Sexes), Bonner Kunstverein
• Group exhibition: *A Perspective of Contemporary Art: Color and/or Monochrome*, National Museum of Modern Art, Tokyo, MOMAT; and National Museum of Art, Kyoto
• Group exhibition: *Drawing as Itself,* National Museum of Art, Osaka

1990
• Begins working with the ShugoArts Gallery, Tokyo

1991
• Professorship for painting at the Hochschule der Künste Berlin (now the Universität der Künste Berlin)
• Represented in the group exhibition *Zeichnungen des 20. Jahrhunderts: Karl August Burckhardt-Koechlin-Fonds* (Drawings from the 20th Century: Karl August Burckhardt-Koechlin Fund), Kunstmuseum Basel, Kupferstichkabinett
• First exhibition in the United States: *Double Take,* Soho Art House, New York, curated by Sueo Mizuma

1994
• Begins working with the Karsten Greve Gallery, Paris

1995
• Begins working with the Tony Wuethrich Gallery, Basel

1996–1998
• Artist residency, European Ceramic Workcentre, 's-Hertogenbosch, The Netherlands
• Group exhibition: *De Beuys à Trockel: Dessins contemporains du Kunstmuseum de Bâle* (From Beuys to Trockel: Contemporary Drawings from the Kunstmuseum Basel), Musée National d'Art Moderne, Centre Georges Pompidou, Paris
• Group exhibition: *Born of Clay: The Ceramic Figure since 1920*, Garth Clark Gallery, New York

1999
• Japanese Pavilion at the Melbourne International Biennial, curated by Itaru Hirano

1988
• Preis der Jury der Internationalen Triennale für Originalgrafik, Grenchen
• Teilnahme an der Ausstellung *Contemporary Swiss Art,* Seibu Museum of Art, Funabashi, Tokio im Rahmen der Tokyo Biennale '88. The 17th International Art Exhibition, Tokyo Metropolitan Art Museum, Kyoto Municipal Museum of Art, Seibu Museum of Art, Funabashi, Tokio

1989
• Sechsmonatiger Aufenthalt in Sarn, Atelier in Fürstenau im Kanton Graubünden (nahe Thusis)
• Teilnahme an der Ausstellung *Das Verhältnis der Geschlechter,* Bonner Kunstverein
• Beteiligung an Ausstellungen in Japan: *A Perspective of Contemporary Art: Color and/or Monochrome,* The National Museum of Modern Art, Tokyo, MOMAT, und The National Museum of Art, Kyoto, sowie *Drawing as Itself,* The National Museum of Art, Osaka

1990
• Beginn der Zusammenarbeit mit der Galerie ShugoArts, Tokio

1991
• Professur an der Hochschule der Künste Berlin (heute Universität der Künste)
• Vertreten in der Sammlungsausstellung *Zeichnungen des 20. Jahrhunderts: Karl August Burckhardt-Koechlin-Fonds* im Kunstmuseum Basel, Kupferstichkabinett
• Erste Ausstellung in den USA: *Double Take,* Soho Art House, New York, kuratiert von Sueo Mizuma

1994
• Beginn der Zusammenarbeit mit der Galerie Karsten Greve, Paris

1995
• Beginn der Zusammenarbeit mit der Galerie Tony Wuethrich, Basel

1996 – 1998
• European Ceramic Workcentre, Artist Residency, 's-Hertogenbosch, Niederlande
• Teilnahme an der Ausstellung *De Beuys à Trockel. Dessins contemporains du Kunstmuseum de Bâle,* Musée National d'Art Moderne, Centre Georges Pompidou, Paris
• Teilnahme an der Ausstellung *Born of Clay. The Ceramic Figure Since 1920,* Garth Clark Gallery, New York

1999
• Japanischer Pavillon der Melbourne International Biennial, kuratiert von Itaru Hirano

2000
• Ausstellung *Beyond the Horizon,* Toyota Municipal Museum of Art, Aichi, kuratiert von Tomoaki Kitagawa

2001
• Ausstellung *Leiko Ikemura. Les années lumières – Lichtjahre,* im Musée cantonal des Beaux-Arts, Lausanne, kuratiert von Caroline Nicod
• Deutscher Kritikerpreis für Bildende Kunst, Verband der deutschen Kritiker e. V.
• Beginn der Zusammenarbeit mit den Galerien Michael Haas und Michael Fuchs, Berlin

2000
• *Beyond the Horizon,* Toyota Municipal Museum of Art, Aichi, Japan, curated by Tomoaki Kitagawa

2001
• *Leiko Ikemura: Les années lumières—Lichtjahre* (Years of Light), Musée cantonal des Beaux-Arts, Lausanne, curated by Caroline Nicod
• Deutscher Kritikerpreis für Bildende Kunst (German Critics Prize for the Visual Arts), Verband der deutschen Kritiker (Association of German Critics)
• Begins working with the Michael Haas Galerie and the Michael Fuchs Galerie, Berlin

2002
• Artist residency, Josef & Anni Albers Foundation, New Haven, Connecticut

2004/05
• *Leiko Ikemura: Skulptur Malerei Zeichnung* (Sculpture Painting Drawing), Kunsthalle Recklinghausen, Pfalzgalerie Kaiserslautern, and Ulmer Museum, curated by Ferdinand Ullrich and Hans-Jürgen Schwalm
• *Leiko Ikemura: Sculptures, Paintings, Works on Paper,* Kolumba, Kunstmuseum des Erzbistums, Cologne
• Group exhibition: *The Subjective Figure,* Robert Miller Gallery, New York

2006
• *u mi no ko,* Vangi Sculpture Garden Museum, Shizuoka, Japan, curated by Koko Okano

2007
• Iserlohner Kunstpreis, Bürgerstiftung der Sparkasse Iserlohn/ Wessel-Verein, Germany

2008
• *Leiko Ikemura: Tag, Nacht, Halbmond* (Day, Night, Half-Moon), Museum zu Allerheiligen Schaffhausen, curated by Hortensia von Roda
• August Macke Prize of the Hochsauerlandkreis, Germany

2011
• *Leiko Ikemura: Transfiguration,* The National Museum for Modern Art, Tokyo, MOMAT, curated by Kenjiro Hosaka
• Organizer: *Breaking News: Fukushima and the Consequences,* KW Institute for Contemporary Art, Berlin; invites Shōmei Tōmatsu, Yutaka Takanashi, Daidō Moriyama, Rosemarie Trockel, and Wim Wenders, among others, to participate

2012
• *Leiko Ikemura: Mare e Monti* (Sea and Mountains), Kolumba, Kunstmuseum des Erzbistums, Cologne

2013
• Prize from the Stiftung zur Förderung japanisch-deutscher Wissenschafts- und Kulturbeziehungen (Foundation for the Promotion of Japanese-German Scientific and Cultural Exchange)
• *Leiko Ikemura: i-migration,* Staatliche Kunsthalle Karlsruhe, curated by Pia Müller-Tamm
• Begins working with Kewenig Galerie, Berlin

2002
• The Josef & Anni Albers Foundation, Artist Residency, New Haven, Connecticut

2004/05
• Ausstellung *Leiko Ikemura. Skulptur Malerei Zeichnung,* Kunsthalle Recklinghausen, Pfalzgalerie Kaiserslautern und Ulmer Museum, kuratiert von Ferdinand Ullrich und Hans-Jürgen Schwalm
• Ausstellung *Leiko Ikemura. Skulpturen, Gemälde, Arbeiten auf Papier,* Kolumba, Kunstmuseum des Erzbistums Köln
• Beteiligung an der Ausstellung *The Subjective Figure,* Robert Miller Gallery, New York

2006
• Ausstellung *u mi no ko,* The Vangi Sculpture Garden Museum, Shizuoka, kuratiert von Koko Okano

2007
• Iserlohner Kunstpreis, Bürgerstiftung der Sparkasse Iserlohn/ Wessel-Verein

2008
• Ausstellung *Leiko Ikemura. Tag, Nacht, Halbmond* im Museum zu Allerheiligen Schaffhausen, kuratiert von Hortensia von Roda
• August-Macke-Preis des Hochsauerlandkreises

2011
• Ausstellung *Leiko Ikemura. Transfiguration,* The National Museum of Modern Art, Tokyo, MOMAT, kuratiert von Kenjiro Hosaka
• Ikemura organisiert die Ausstellung *Breaking News. Fukushima and the Consequences* im KW Institute for Contemporary Art, Berlin, und lädt dazu u.a. Shōmei Tōmatsu, Yutaka Takanashi und Daido Moriyama sowie Rosemarie Trockel und Wim Wenders ein

2012
• *Leiko Ikemura. Mare e Monti,* Kabinettausstellung im Kolumba Kunstmuseum des Erzbistums Köln

2013
• Preis der Stiftung zur Förderung japanisch-deutscher Wissenschafts- und Kulturbeziehungen
• Ausstellung *Leiko Ikemura. i-migration,* Staatliche Kunsthalle Karlsruhe, kuratiert von Pia Müller-Tamm
• Beginn der Zusammenarbeit mit der Kewenig Galerie, Berlin

2014
• Berufung als Professorin an die Joshibi-Universität für Kunst und Design, Minami-ku, Präfektur Kanagawa
• Cologne Fine Art-Preis
• Ausstellung *Leiko Ikemura. Zwischenwelten – Zeichnungen, Gemälde, Skulpturen,* Museum Sinclair-Haus/Altana Kulturstiftung, Bad Homburg v.d.H., kuratiert von Johannes Janssen
• Ausstellung *Leiko Ikemura. PIOON,* Vangi Sculpture Garden Museum, Shizuoka
• Ausstellung *Leiko Ikemura. Last und Lust,* Neues Museum, Nürnberg, kuratiert von Thomas Heyden

2015
• Ausstellung *Leiko Ikemura. All About Girls and Tigers* im Museum für Ostasiatische Kunst, Köln, in der Ikemura ihre Werke mit Exponaten aus der Sammlung des Museums in Beziehung setzt, kuratiert von Adele Schlombs
• Verleihung des Sparda-Kunstpreises NRW

2014
• Appointment as professor at the Joshibi University of Art and Design, Minami-ku, Kanagawa Prefecture
• Cologne Fine Art Prize
• *Leiko Ikemura: Zwischenwelten—Zeichnungen, Gemälde, Skulpturen* (Interstitial Worlds—Drawing, Painting, Sculpture), Museum Sinclair Haus / Altana Kultur Stiftung, Bad Homburg vor der Höhe, Germany, curated by Johannes Janssen
• *Leiko Ikemura: PIOON,* Vangi Sculpture Garden Museum, Shizuoka, Japan
• *Leiko Ikemura: Last und Lust* (Weight and Want), Neues Museum, Nuremberg, curated by Thomas Heyden

2015
• *Leiko Ikemura: All about Girls and Tigers,* Museum für Ostasiatische Kunst, Cologne, in which Ikemura juxtaposes her own works with items from the museum's collection, curated by Adele Schlombs
• Sparda-Kunstpreis NRW

2016
• *Leiko Ikemura: Poetics of Form,* Nevada Museum of Art, Donald W. Reynolds Center for the Visual Arts, Reno, curated JoAnne Northrup
• *Leiko Ikemura…und plötzlich dreht der Wind / Leiko Ikemura… and all of sudden the wind is turning,* Haus am Waldsee, Berlin, curated by Katja Blomberg
• Begins working with Kenji Taki Gallery, Nagoya

2017
• *Ikemura und Nolde,* Kunstmuseum Ahrenshoop, curated by Katrin Arrieta
• *Leiko Ikemura—Märchenwald* (Leiko Ikemura—Fairy-Tale World), Hetjens—Deutsches Keramikmuseum Düsseldorf, curated by Daniela Antonin
• Group exhibition: *Leiko Ikemura: No No Noh,* Beck & Eggeling, Vienna

2018
• *Leiko Ikemura im Dialog mit Donata und Wim Wenders* (Leiko Ikemura in Dialogue with Donata and Wim Wenders), Stiftung Brandenburger Tor / Max Liebermann Haus, Berlin

2019
• Retrospective exhibition: *Leiko Ikemura: Our Planet—Earth & Stars,* National Art Center Tokyo, in collaboration with Kunstmuseum Basel, curated by Mitsue Nagaya
• Autobiography, published in Japan
• Group exhibition: *The Case of Hiroshima,* Museum on the Seam, Jerusalem
• First exhibition in Sweden: *Leiko Ikemura: Metamorphoses,* Nordiska Akvarellmuseet, Skärhamn, curated by Bera Nordal
• *Leiko Ikemura—Toward New Seas,* Kunstmuseum Basel, curated by Anita Haldemann

Leiko Ikemura lives and works in Berlin and Cologne.

2016
• Ausstellung *Leiko Ikemura. Poetics of Form* im Nevada Museum of Art, Donald W. Reynolds Center for the Visual Arts, Reno, Nevada, kuratiert von JoAnne Northrup
• Ausstellung *Leiko Ikemura. … und plötzlich dreht der Wind,* Haus am Waldsee, Berlin, kuratiert von Katja Blomberg
• Beginn der Zusammenarbeit mit der Galerie Kenji Taki, Nagoya

2017
• Ausstellung *Ikemura und Nolde,* Kunstmuseum Ahrenshoop, kuratiert von Katrin Arrieta
• Ausstellung *Leiko Ikemura – Märchenwald,* Hetjens – Deutsches Keramikmuseum, Düsseldorf, kuratiert von Daniela Antonin
• Beteiligung an der Ausstellung *Leiko Ikemura. No No Noh,* Beck & Eggeling, Wien

2018
• Ausstellung *Leiko Ikemura im Dialog mit Donata und Wim Wenders,* Stiftung Brandenburger Tor / Max Liebermann Haus, Berlin

2019
• Retrospektive *Leiko Ikemura. Our Planet – Earth & Stars* im National Art Center Tokyo in Zusammenarbeit mit dem Kunstmuseum Basel, kuratiert von Mitsue Nagaya
• Veröffentlichung der Autobiografie in Japan
• Beteiligung an der Ausstellung *The Case of Hiroshima,* Museum on the Seam, Jerusalem
• Erste Ausstellung in Schweden: *Leiko Ikemura. Metamorphoses,* Nordiska Akvarellmuseet, Skärhamn, kuratiert von Bera Nordal
• *Leiko Ikemura. Nach neuen Meeren,* Kunstmuseum Basel, kuratiert von Anita Haldemann

Leiko Ikemura lebt und arbeitet in Berlin und Köln.

Ausstellungsansichten | Installation views, *Leiko Ikemura.*
Our Planet – Earth & Stars, National Art Center Tokyo, 18.1.–1.4.2019

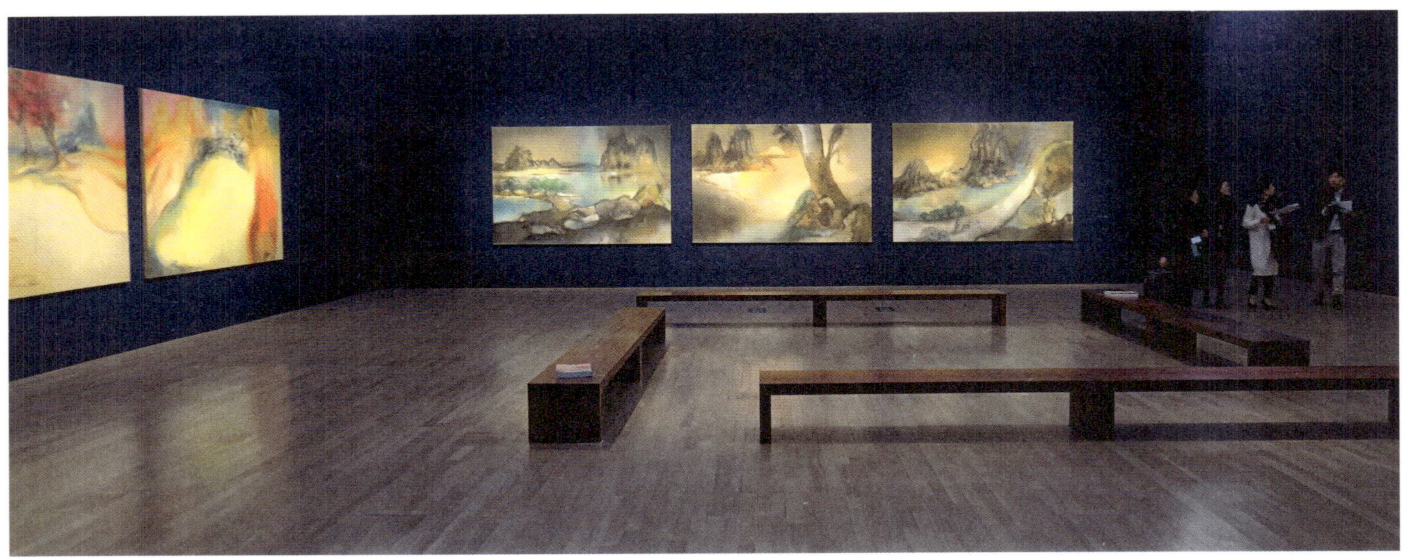

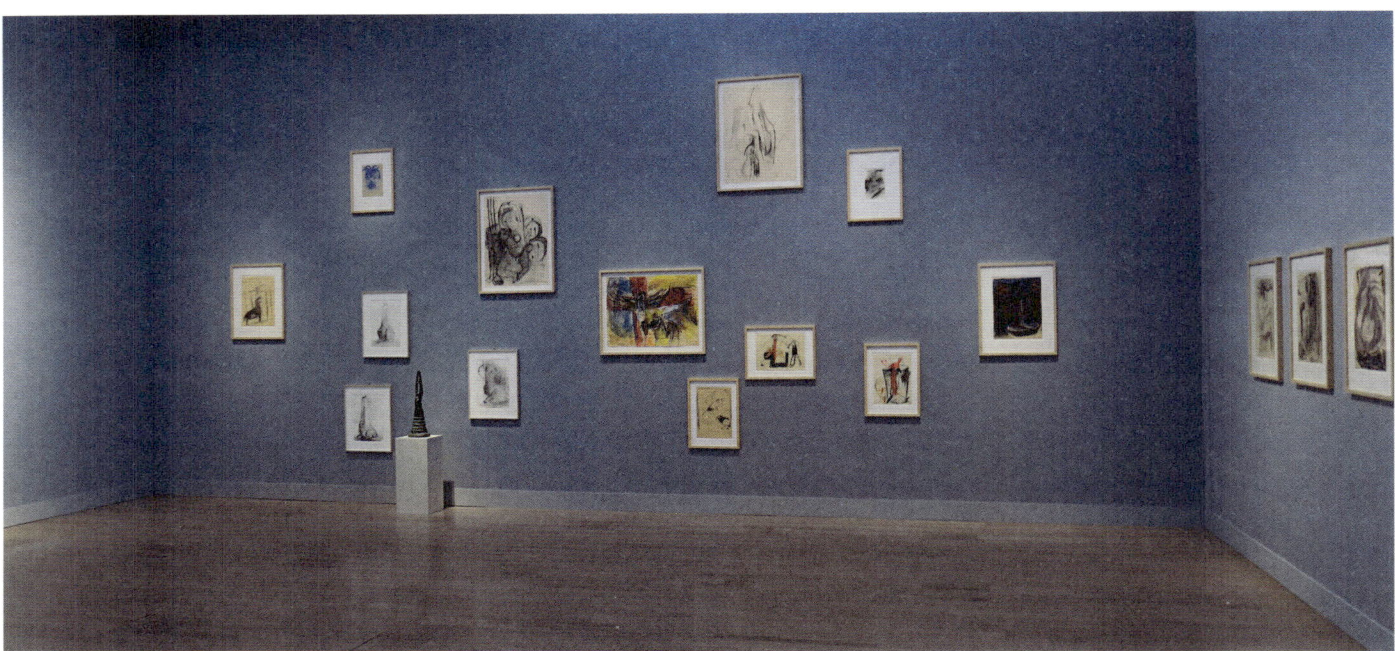

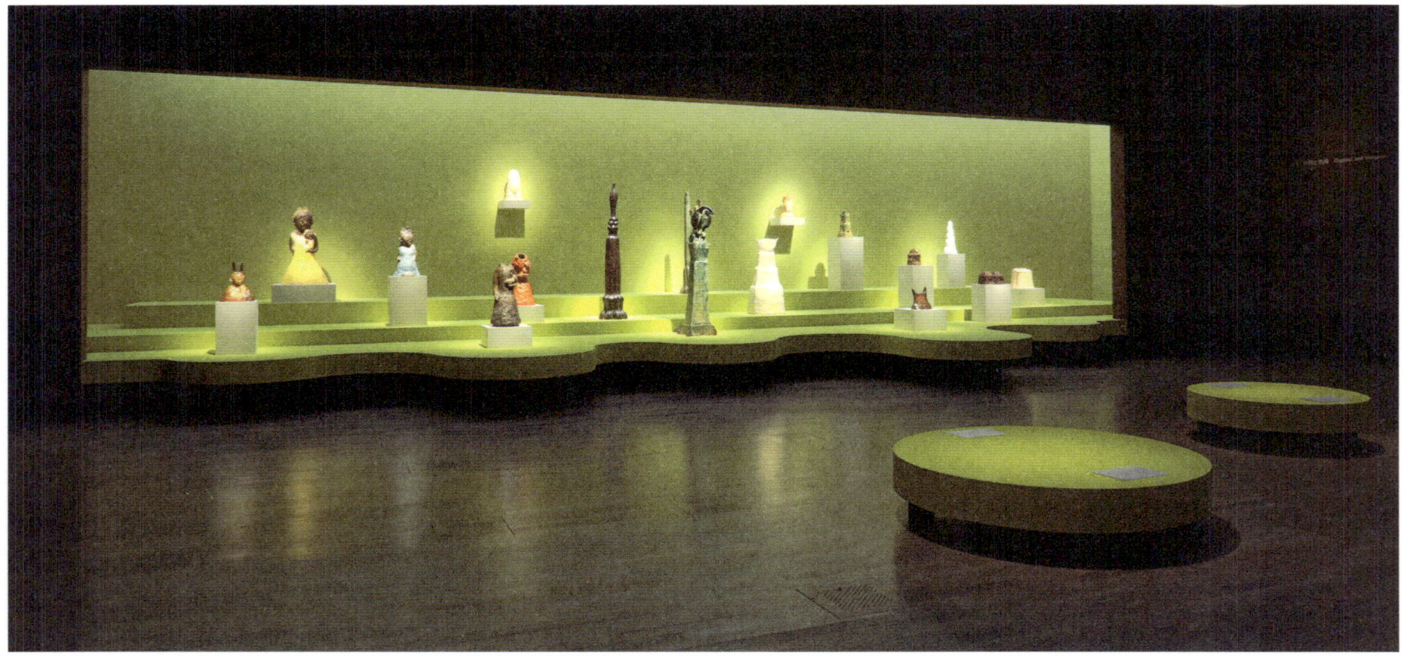

Ausgestellte Werke | Exhibited Works

1
Kamikaze
1980
Dispersionsfarbe auf Papier |
Dispersion paint on paper
120 × 90 cm
Christoph Schenker

2
Ohne Titel | Untitled
1980
Bleistift und Kohle auf Papier |
Pencil and charcoal on paper
21 × 14,7 cm
Kunstmuseum Basel, Kupferstich-
kabinett, Depositum der Freunde des
Kunstmuseums Basel, Schenkung
zum Dank an Dieter Koepplin
(Geschenk Dr. Franz Meyer, Zürich),
Inv. 1999.125

3
Ohne Titel | Untitled
1980
Tusche auf Papier | India ink on paper
14,7 × 20,9 cm
Kunstmuseum Basel, Kupferstichkabinett, Depositum der Freunde
des Kunstmuseums Basel, Schenkung
zum Dank an Dieter Koepplin
(Geschenk Dr. Franz Meyer, Zürich),
Inv. 1999.126

4
No me gustas tù!
1981
Kohle auf Papier | Charcoal on paper
21 × 29,6 cm
Kunstmuseum Basel, Kupferstichkabinett, Geschenk Dieter Koepplin,
Basel, Inv. 1983.413

5
In einem Hotel in Moskau | In a Hotel
in Moscow
1981
Kohle auf Papier | Charcoal on paper
21 × 14,7 cm
Kunstmuseum Basel, Kupferstichkabinett, Geschenk Hans Jakob
Oeri-Fonds, Inv. 1988.108

6
Ohne Titel | Untitled
1981
Kohle auf Papier | Charcoal on paper
21 × 14,7 cm
Kunstmuseum Basel, Kupferstichkabinett, Geschenk Hans Jakob
Oeri-Fonds, Inv. 1988.107

7
Ohne Titel | Untitled
1981
Kohle auf Papier | Charcoal on paper
21 × 14,7 cm
Kunstmuseum Basel, Kupferstichkabinett, Geschenk Hans Jakob
Oeri-Fonds, Inv. 1988.109

8
Ohne Titel | Untitled
1981
Kohle auf Papier | Charcoal on paper
14,7 × 21 cm
Kunstmuseum Basel, Kupferstichkabinett, Geschenk Hans Jakob
Oeri-Fonds, Inv. 1988.111

9
Ohne Titel | Untitled
1981
Kohle auf Papier | Charcoal on paper
21 × 29,7 cm
Kunstmuseum Basel, Kupferstichkabinett, Geschenk der Künstlerin,
Inv. 1987.344

10
Ohne Titel | Untitled
1981
Kohle auf Papier | Charcoal on paper
21 × 29,7 cm
Kunstmuseum Basel, Kupferstichkabinett, erworben 1987, Inv. 1987.111

11
Die Kastrierten | The Castrated
1982
Kohle auf Papier | Charcoal on paper
32 × 24 cm
Kunstmuseum Basel, Kupferstichkabinett, Geschenk Dieter Koepplin,
Basel, Inv. 1983.412

12
Ohne Titel | Untitled
1982
Kohle auf Papier | Charcoal on paper
21 × 29,6 cm
Kunstmuseum Basel, Kupferstichkabinett, Geschenk Dieter Koepplin,
Basel, Inv. 1983.414

13
Honigtasche | Honey Bag
1983
Kohle auf Papier | Charcoal on paper
14,8 × 21 cm
Kunstmuseum Basel, Kupferstichkabinett, Karl August Burckhardt-
Koechlin-Fonds, Inv. 1983.401

14
Ohne Titel | Untitled
1983
Kohle und schwarzer Kugelschreiber
auf Papier | Charcoal and black pen
on paper
14,8 × 21 cm
Kunstmuseum Basel, Kupferstichkabinett, Karl August Burckhardt-
Koechlin-Fonds, Inv. 1983.404

15
Ohne Titel | Untitled
1983
Kohle auf Papier | Charcoal on paper
14,8 × 21 cm
Kunstmuseum Basel, Kupferstichkabinett, Karl August Burckhardt-
Koechlin-Fonds, Inv. 1983.402

16
Ohne Titel | Untitled
1983
Kohle und schwarzer Kugelschreiber
auf Papier | Charcoal and black pen
on paper
24 × 16 cm
Kunstmuseum Basel, Kupferstichkabinett, Geschenk der Künstlerin,
Inv. 1986.431

17
Ohne Titel | Untitled
1983
Kohle und grüne Fettkreide auf
Papier | Charcoal and green oil chalk
on paper
29,6 × 41,9 cm
Kunstmuseum Basel, Kupferstichkabinett, Geschenk Dieter Koepplin,
Basel, Inv. 1984.91

18
Ohne Titel | Untitled
1983
Kohle auf Papier | Charcoal on paper
36 × 47,9 cm
Kunstmuseum Basel, Kupferstichkabinett, Geschenk Dieter Koepplin,
Basel, Inv. 1985.111

19
Ohne Titel | Untitled
1983
Kohle auf Papier | Charcoal on paper
29,7 × 41,9 cm
Kunstmuseum Basel, Kupferstichkabinett, Karl August Burckhardt-
Koechlin-Fonds, Inv. 1983.418

20
Ohne Titel | Untitled
1983
Kohle auf Papier | Charcoal on paper
29,7 × 41,9 cm
Kunstmuseum Basel, Kupferstichkabinett, Geschenk Dieter Koepplin,
Basel, Inv. 1983.415

21
Ohne Titel | Untitled
1984
Kohle auf Papier | Charcoal on paper
42,1 × 29,6 cm
Kunstmuseum Basel, Kupferstichkabinett, Geschenk Dieter Koepplin,
Basel, Inv. 1984.101

22
Ohne Titel | Untitled
1984
Kohle auf Papier | Charcoal on paper
29,8 × 42,1 cm
Kunstmuseum Basel, Kupferstichkabinett, Geschenk Dieter Koepplin,
Basel, Inv. 1984.97

23
Ohne Titel | Untitled
1984
Kohle auf Papier | Charcoal on paper
42,1×29,6 cm
Kunstmuseum Basel, Kupferstichkabinett, Karl August Burckhardt-
Koechlin-Fonds, Inv. 1984.94

24
Ohne Titel | Untitled
1984
Kohle auf Papier | Charcoal on paper
42,1×29,6 cm
Kunstmuseum Basel, Kupferstichkabinett, Geschenk Dieter Koepplin,
Basel, Inv. 1984.99

25
Ohne Titel | Untitled
1984
Kohle auf Papier | Charcoal on paper
42,1×29,6 cm
Kunstmuseum Basel, Kupferstichkabinett, Karl August Burckhardt-
Koechlin-Fonds, Inv. 1984.100

26
Vogelspinnen | Tarantulas
1983
Acryl auf Leinwand | Acrylic on canvas
179×199 cm
Kunstmuseum Basel, Geschenk
Dieter Koepplin, Basel, Inv. G 2018.7

27
Ohne Titel | Untitled
1985
Kohle auf Papier | Charcoal on paper
47,9×36 cm
Kunstmuseum Basel, Kupferstichkabinett, anonymes Geschenk,
Inv. 1985.116

28
Ohne Titel | Untitled
1985
Kohle auf Papier | Charcoal on paper
47,9×36 cm
Kunstmuseum Basel, Kupferstichkabinett, anonymes Geschenk,
Inv. 1985.118

29
Ohne Titel | Untitled
1985
Kohle auf Papier | Charcoal on paper
47,9×36 cm
Kunstmuseum Basel, Kupferstichkabinett, Geschenk Prof. Dr. Hanspeter
Landolt, Basel, Inv. 1985.103

30
Ohne Titel | Untitled
1985
Kohle auf Papier | Charcoal on paper
47,9×36 cm
Kunstmuseum Basel, Kupferstichkabinett, anonymes Geschenk,
Inv. 1985.119

31
Ohne Titel | Untitled
1985
Kohle auf Papier | Charcoal on paper
47,9×36 cm
Kunstmuseum Basel, Kupferstichkabinett, anonymes Geschenk,
Inv. 1985.106

32
Ohne Titel | Untitled
1985
Kohle und Bleistift auf Papier |
Charcoal and pencil on paper
42,1×29,7 cm
Kunstmuseum Basel, Kupferstichkabinett, Geschenk Dieter Koepplin,
Basel, Inv. 1985.35

33
Ohne Titel | Untitled
1985
Kohle auf Papier | Charcoal on paper
42,1×29,8 cm
Kunstmuseum Basel, Kupferstichkabinett, Geschenk Dieter Koepplin,
Basel, Inv. 1985.34

34
Studie zum Gemälde *Verkündigung* |
Study for the painting *Annunciation*
1985
Kohle auf Papier | Charcoal on paper
42×29,8 cm
Kunstmuseum Basel, Kupferstichkabinett, Geschenk Dieter Koepplin,
Basel, Inv. 1985.36

35
Verkündigung | Annunciation
1985
Acryl auf Leinwand | Acrylic on canvas
210×240 cm
Privatsammlung Schweiz

36
Ohne Titel | Untitled
1985
Kohle und farbige Kreide auf Papier |
Charcoal and color chalk on paper
47,9×36 cm
Kunstmuseum Basel, Kupferstichkabinett, anonymes Geschenk,
Inv. 1985.117

37
Blauer Kopf | Blue Head
1985
Blaue Kreide auf Papier | Blue chalk
on paper
29,8×21 cm
Kunstmuseum Basel, Kupferstichkabinett, erworben 1987, Inv. 1987.107

38
Trojanisches Pferd | Trojan Horse
1986
Kohle auf Papier | Charcoal on paper
48×36 cm
Kunstmuseum Basel, Kupferstichkabinett, erworben 1986,
Inv. 1986.437

39
Schlacht (Kriegsgöttin) | Battle
(Goddess of War)
1985
Kohle und Pastellkreide auf Papier |
Charcoal and pastel on paper
21×29,7 cm
Kunstmuseum Basel, Kupferstich-
kabinett, erworben 1986,
Inv. 1986.436

40
Ohne Titel | Untitled
1986
Kohle und Pastellkreide auf Papier |
Charcoal and pastel on paper
56,1×42 cm
Kunstmuseum Basel, Kupferstichkabinett, Geschenk Hans Jakob
Oeri-Fonds, Inv. 1987.343

41
Ohne Titel | Untitled
1986
Kohle, Bleistift und Farbstift auf
Papier | Charcoal, pencil, and crayon
on paper
29,9×39,9 cm
Kunstmuseum Basel, Kupferstichkabinett, Geschenk der Künstlerin,
Inv. 1987.92

42
Ohne Titel | Untitled
1987
Kohle, Aquarell, Kreide und Öl auf
Papier | Charcoal, watercolor, chalk,
and oil on paper
59,7×79,8 cm
Kunstmuseum Basel, Kupferstichkabinett, Geschenk Hans Jakob
Oeri-Fonds, Inv. 1987.84

43
Kriegsgöttin | Goddess of War
1986
Öl auf Leinwand | Oil on canvas
200×250 cm
Sammlung Tanner Teufen

44
Ohne Titel | Untitled
1987
Kohle und Ölkreide auf Papier |
Charcoal and oil chalk on paper
79,8×59,8 cm
Kunstmuseum Basel, Kupferstichkabinett, Geschenk Hans Jakob
Oeri-Fonds, Inv. 1987.347

45
Ohne Titel | Untitled
1987
Kohle, Wasserfarbe und Kreide auf
Papier, auf Leinwand aufgezogen |
Charcoal, watercolor, and chalk on
paper, mounted on canvas
80×59,6 cm
Kunstmuseum Basel, Kupferstichkabinett, Geschenk der Künstlerin,
Inv. 1987.346

46
Ohne Titel | Untitled
1987
Kohle auf Papier | Charcoal on paper
80×59,7 cm
Kunstmuseum Basel, Kupferstichkabinett, Geschenk Hans Jakob
Oeri-Fonds, Inv. 1987.82

47
Ohne Titel | Untitled
1987
Kohle und Bleistift auf Papier |
Charcoal and pencil on paper
79,9×59,9 cm
Kunstmuseum Basel, Kupferstichkabinett, Geschenk Hans Jakob
Oeri-Fonds, Inv. 1989.331

48
Wächter | Guard
1987
Ton, ungebrannt | Clay, unfired
29×16×28,5 cm
Kunstmuseum Basel, Kupferstichkabinett, Geschenk Dieter Koepplin,
Basel, Inv. G 2018.8

49
Ahnenhaus | Ancestral House
1989
Ton, ungebrannt | Clay, unfired
33×18×31 cm
Dieter Koepplin, Basel

50
Alpenindianer | Alps Indian
1989
Acryl auf Leinwand | Acrylic on canvas
127×88,5 cm
Musée cantonal des Beaux-Arts,
Lausanne, Ankauf 1991, Inv. 1991-003

51
Rot | Red
1989
Acryl auf Leinwand | Acrylic on canvas
103×124,5 cm
Museum zu Allerheiligen Schaffhausen, Dauerleihgabe der
Sturzenegger-Stiftung, Inv. A2257

52
Skifahrer auf dem Malojasee |
Skier on Maloja Lake
1990
Tempera auf Leinwand | Tempera
on canvas
120×94 cm
Toyota Municipal Museum of Art

53
Ur 8
1990
Kohle auf Papier | Charcoal on paper
42,0×29,7 cm

54
Ur 9
1990
Kohle auf Papier | Charcoal on paper
42,0×29,7 cm
Courtesy Leiko Ikemura/
Tony Wuethrich Galerie, Basel

55
Ur 11
1990
Kohle auf Papier | Charcoal on paper
42,0×29,7 cm
Courtesy Leiko Ikemura/
Tony Wuethrich Galerie, Basel

56
Ha
1991
Kohle auf Papier | Charcoal on paper
42,0×29,7 cm

57
Stehende Figur in Petrolblau |
Standing Figure in Petrol Blue
1990/91
Terrakotta, glasiert | Terra-cotta,
glazed
20×10×40 cm

58
Ur
1992
Bronze | Bronze
27,5 × 23 × 47 cm
Kunstmuseum Basel, Schenkung
Catherine und Bernard
Soguel-Dreyfus, Inv. G 2019.7

59
Türkises Baby | Turquoise Baby
1994
Terrakotta, glasiert | Terra-cotta,
glazed
17 × 13 × 43 cm

60
Hase-Frau | Hare-Woman
1990/91
Bronze, Edition: e.a. II | Bronze,
edition: a.p. II
19 × 19 × 58 cm
Courtesy Leiko Ikemura /
KEWENIG, Berlin

61
Grüne Ohren lang | Green Ears Long
1993
Terrakotta, glasiert | Terra-cotta,
glazed
19 × 16 × 41 cm

62
Stehende in einem rosa Rock |
Standing in a Pink Skirt
1994
Terrakotta, glasiert | Terra-cotta,
glazed
25 × 25 × 49,5 cm

63
Einäugiges Baby | Single-Eyed Baby
1994
Terrakotta, glasiert | Terra-cotta,
glazed
30 x 23 x 16 cm

64
Black Miko in Blue Dress
1995
Terrakotta, glasiert | Terra-cotta,
glazed
29 × 26 × 55,5 cm

65
Doppelfigur | Double Figure
1993
Öl auf Leinwand | Oil on canvas
50 × 36 cm
Kunstmuseum Basel, Schenkung
Catherine und Bernard
Soguel-Dreyfus, Inv. G. 2019.8

66
W-Boy
1993
Kohle und Pastell auf Papier |
Charcoal and pastel on paper
43 × 30,5 cm

67
Alone
1993
Kohle und Pastell auf Papier |
Charcoal and pastel on paper
42 × 29,5 cm

68
Alone
1994
Kohle und Pastell auf Papier |
Charcoal and pastel on paper
43,5 × 30,5 cm

69
Inclined
1994
Kohle und Pastell auf Papier |
Charcoal and pastel on paper
43,5 × 30,5 cm

70
Girl in Yellow
1995
Aquarell auf Papier | Watercolor
on paper
48 × 36 cm
Courtesy Leiko Ikemura /
Tony Wuethrich Galerie, Basel

71
Den Blick abgewandt | With Averted
Look
1995
Öl auf Leinwand | Oil on canvas
84,5 × 63 cm
Collection Segers-Plancke

72
Schatten in Rosa | Shadow in Pink
1995/96
Öl auf Leinwand | Oil on canvas
95,5 × 73 cm
Tony Wuethrich Galerie, Basel

73
Stehende mit Miko in Gelb |
Standing with Miko in Yellow
1995/96
Öl auf Leinwand | Oil on canvas
83,2 × 62,5 cm

74–85
Shadow Girl (Serie | series)
1996
Aquarell auf Papier | Watercolor
on paper
je | each 42 × 30 cm

86
Gelbe Figur mit drei Armen |
Yellow Figure with Three Arms
1996
Terrakotta, glasiert | Terra-cotta,
glazed
31 × 31 × 65 cm
Musée cantonal des Beaux-Arts,
Lausanne, Ankauf 2001,
Inv. 2001-018

87
Hockende (Sich auf die Augen
stützend) | Squatting (Leaning
on Eyes)
1997
Terrakotta, glasiert | Terra-cotta,
glazed
45 × 72 × 47 cm

88
Gesicht in Schwarz | Face in Black
1998
Öl auf Jute | Oil on jute
70 × 70 cm
Privatsammlung, Deutschland

89
Fliegende auf Schwarz | Flying in
Black
1998/99
Öl auf Leinwand | Oil on canvas
120 × 120 cm
Toyota Municipal Museum of Art

90
Liegende in Schwarz | Lying on Black
1998/99
Öl auf Leinwand | Oil on canvas
80 × 150 cm
Toyota Municipal Museum of Art

91
Eintauchen | Diving
1999
Öl auf Jute | Oil on jute
100 × 100,5 cm
Musée cantonal des Beaux-Arts,
Lausanne, Ankauf 2001, Inv. 2001-019

92
Garten der Lüste | Garden of Desire
1983
Kohle auf Papier | Charcoal on paper
267 × 270 cm

93
Memento mori | Memento Mori
2013/18
Bronze, patiniert, Edition: 4/5 |
Bronze, patinated, edition: 4/5
38 × 135 × 38 cm
Courtesy Leiko Ikemura /
KEWENIG, Berlin

94
White Head with Trees
2017
Terrakotta, glasiert | Terra-cotta,
glazed
40 × 38 × 26 cm
Privatsammlung, Deutschland

95
Black Face
2008
Kohle auf Papier | Charcoal on paper
32 × 49 cm

96
Black Face
2008
Kohle auf Papier | Charcoal on paper
32 × 49 cm

97
Black Face
2008
Kohle auf Papier | Charcoal on paper
32 × 49 cm

98
Black Face
2008
Kohle auf Papier | Charcoal on paper
32 × 49 cm

99
Black Face
2008
Kohle auf Papier | Charcoal on paper
32 × 49 cm

100
Black Head
2008
Kohle auf Papier | Charcoal on paper
32 × 49 cm

101
Black Head
2008
Kohle auf Papier | Charcoal on paper
59 × 42 cm

102
Black Head
2008
Kohle auf Papier | Charcoal on paper
59 × 42 cm

103
Black Head
2008
Kohle auf Papier | Charcoal on paper
59 × 42 cm

104
Black Head
2008
Kohle auf Papier | Charcoal on paper
59 × 42 cm

105
Black Head
2008
Kohle auf Papier | Charcoal on paper
59 × 42 cm
ohne Abbildung | not illustrated

106
Black Face
2008
Kohle auf Papier | Charcoal on paper
32 × 49 cm

107
Black Face
2008
Kohle auf Papier | Charcoal on paper
32 × 49 cm

108
Genesis
2015
Tempera auf Jute | Tempera on jute
190 × 290 cm
Courtesy Leiko Ikemura / Galerie
Karsten Greve, Köln / Paris / St. Moritz

109
Tokaido
2015
Tempera auf Jute | Tempera on jute
190 × 290 cm
Courtesy Leiko Ikemura / Galerie
Karsten Greve, Köln / Paris / St. Moritz

110
Tokaido
2015
Tempera auf Jute | Tempera on jute
190 × 290 cm
Courtesy Leiko Ikemura / Galerie
Karsten Greve, Köln / Paris / St. Moritz

111–115
Amazona (Serie | series)
2015
Monotypie auf Japanpapier |
Monotype on Japan paper
je | each 125 × 55 cm

116
Usagi Kannon
2012/19
Bronze, patiniert | Bronze, patinated
159 × 138 × 340 cm

Wenn nicht anders vermerkt,
befinden sich die Werke im Besitz
der Künstlerin. | If not stated
otherwise, the works are the property
of the artist.

Diese Publikation erscheint anlässlich
der Ausstellung
Leiko Ikemura. Nach neuen Meeren
Kunstmuseum Basel
11. Mai – 1. September 2019

This catalog is published in conjunction
with the exhibition
Leiko Ikemura—Toward New Seas
Kunstmuseum Basel
May 11—September 1, 2019

Eine Kooperation zwischen
The National Art Center Tokyo und dem
Kunstmuseum Basel

A collaboration between
The National Art Center Tokyo and the
Kunstmuseum Basel

Ausstellung Basel | Exhibition in Basel

Direktor | Director
Josef Helfenstein

Kaufmännischer Direktor | Administrative Director
Wolfgang Giese

Leiterin des Kupferstichkabinetts, Kuratorin der
Ausstellung | Head of Kupferstichkabinett (Department
of Prints and Drawings) and Exhibition Curator
Anita Haldemann

Assistenzkuratorin | Assistant Curator
Karoline Schliemann

Restauratorische Betreuung | Conservation
Werner Müller, Caroline Wyss Illgen, Kristin Bucher,
Sophie Eichner, Annette Fritsch, Amelie Jensen,
Chantal Schwendener, Annegret Seger, Lina Wyss

Fotograf | Photographer
Martin P. Bühler

Studienraum Kupferstichkabinett / Reprowesen |
Kupferstichkabinett (Department of Prints and
Drawings) Study Room / Rights and Reproductions
Annika Baer, Iris Müller

Head of Exhibitions and Collections
Charlotte Gutzwiller

Registrarinnen | Registrars
Svenja Held, Monika Mascus

Kurator Programme | Curator of Programmes
Daniel Kurjaković

Wissenschaftliche Assistenz Programme |
Research Assistant, Programmes
Tuula Rasmussen

Bildung und Vermittlung | Education
Hannah Horst, Christine Müller Stalder

Kommunikation und Marketing | Communication
and Marketing
Karen N. Gerig, Christian Selz, Vera Reinhard

Ausstellungsaufbau | Exhibit Installation
Claude Bosch, Felix Böttiger, Dominique Gfeller,
Stefano Schaller, Philipp Gueniat, Bruno Liechti

Die Ausstellung ist eine Kollaboration mit |
The exhibition is a collaboration with
Atelier Philipp von Matt Arch. BDA
(Philipp von Matt, Stefano Tiracchia)
Ikemura Foundation
Studio Leiko Ikemura (Andrea Grljusic,
Magdalena Heinrich)

Ausstellung Tokio | Exhibition in Tokyo

Leiko Ikemura. Our Planet – Earth & Stars
The National Art Center Tokyo
18. Januar – 1. April 2019 | January 18—April 1, 2019

Direktor | Director
Tamotsu Aoki

Chefkuratorin | Head Curator
Mitsue Nagaya

Assistenzkuratorinnen | Assistant Curators
Mina Hisamatsu, Shiori Takano

Ausstellungsarchitektur | Exhibition Architects
Philipp von Matt, Stefano Tiracchia

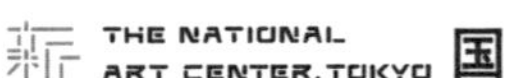

Bildnachweis | Photo Credits

Jörg von Bruchhausen: Kat.|cat. 57, 60-62, 70, 92,
94–100, 106–115; S.|p. 20, Abb.|figs. 3-4; S.|p. 37,
Abb.|fig. 8; S. | pp. 112/113; S. | pp. 130/131; S. | pp. 142/143

Kioku Keizo: Kat.|cat. 101–105

Studio Lange: Kat.|cat. 116

Jochen Littkemann: Kat.|cat. 59, 64, 71, 72, 74–88;
S.|p. 39, Abb.|fig. 10

Shinji Minegishi: S.|pp. 158/159

Lothar Schnepf: Kat.|cat. 43, 50-52, 66-69, 73, 89–91;
S.|p. 30, Abb.|fig. 1; S.|p. 34, Abb.|figs. 3–5; S.|pp. 84/85

The National Museum of Modern Art, Tokyo:
Kat. 53–56; S.|pp. 98/99

TNM Image Archives: S.|p. 31, Abb.|fig. 2

Philipp von Matt: S.|p. 164 (oben, Mitte und unten |
top, center, and bottom)

Kunstmuseum Basel, Marin P. Bühler: alle anderen |
all others

Umschlag-Vorderseite | Front cover: Leiko Ikemura,
Eintauchen | Diving (Ausschnitt | detail, Kat.|cat. 91)

Umschlag-Rückseite | Back cover:
Friedrich Nietzsche, *Die fröhliche Wissenschaft,*
Anhang: *Lieder des Prinzen Vogelfrei,* in: ders., *Werke,*
hrsg. von Ivo Frenzel, Frankfurt a. M. 1999, S.|p. 542.
Ins Englische übersetzt von Sharon Krebs (lieder.net)
und bearbeitet von Christopher Davey. | Translated
into English by Sharon Krebs (lieder.net) and edited
by Christopher Davey.

Katalog Basel | Basel Catalog

Herausgeber | Editor
Kunstmuseum Basel, Anita Haldemann

Redaktion | Managing Editor
Karoline Schliemann

Gestaltung | Layout
Sibylle Ryser, Basel

Projektleitung Prestel | Project Manager
Anja Besserer

Lektorat Deutsch | German Copy Editor
Barbara Delius, Berlin

Lektorat Englisch | English Copy Editor
Christopher Davey

Übersetzung Deutsch – Englisch |
German–English Translation
Anna Brailovsky
Nicolas Grindell (Essay Stefan Kraus)

Übersetzung Japanisch – Deutsch |
Japanese–German Translation
Sabine Mangold (Essay Mitsue Nagaya)

Übersetzung Japanisch – Englisch
Japanese – English Translation
Christopher Stephens (Essay Mitsue Nagaya)

Gesamtherstellung | Production
Cilly Klotz

Lithografie | Lithography
Helio Repro GmbH, Munich

Druck und Bindung | Printing and Binding
Kösel GmbH & Co. KG, Krugzell

Schriften | Typefaces
Scala, Brown

Papier | Paper
Munken Lynx Rough 150 g/m²
Peylin 130 g/m² (Cover)

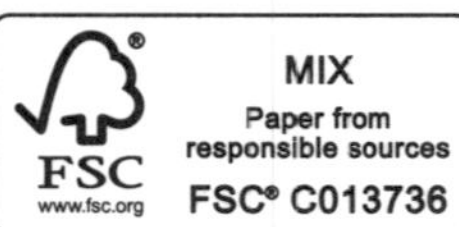

Verlagsgruppe Random House FSC® N001967

Printed in Germany

© 2019 Leiko Ikemura, Kunstmuseum Basel, the authors
and Prestel Verlag, Munich · London · New York

Prestel Verlag, Munich
A member of Verlagsgruppe Random House GmbH
Neumarkter Strasse 28, 81673 Munich

Prestel Publishing Ltd.
14-17 Wells Street, London W1T 3PD

Prestel Publishing
900 Broadway, Suite 603, New York, NY 10003

In respect to links in the book, the Publisher expressly
notes that no illegal content was discernible on the linked
sites at the time the links were created. The Publisher
has no influence at all over the current and future design,
content, or authorship of the linked sites. For this reason
the Publisher expressly disassociates itself from all content
on linked sites that has been altered since the link was
created and assumes no liability for such content.

A CIP catalogue record for this book is available from the
British Library.

ISBN 978-3-7913-5890-1 (Handelsausgabe | trade edition)
ISBN 978-3-7913-6939-6 (Museumsausgabe | museum
edition)

www.prestel.de
www.prestel.com